ALFRED A. KNOPF

1915 · 100 YEARS · 2015

AMERICAN WARLORD

American Warlord

A TRUE STORY

JOHNNY DWYER

ALFRED A. KNOPF   NEW YORK   2015

THIS IS A BORZOI BOOK
PUBLISHED BY ALFRED A. KNOPF

Published in the United States by Alfred A. Knopf,
a division of Random House LLC, New York, and distributed
in Canada by Random House of Canada Limited, Toronto,
Penguin Random House companies.

www.aaknopf.com

Some of the material in this work is derived from the author's article
"American Warlord" (*Rolling Stone* magazine, September 15, 2008).

Library of Congress Cataloging-in-Publication Data
Dwyer, Johnny.
American warlord : a true story / Johnny Dwyer.
pages cm
ISBN 978-0-307-27348-2 (hardcover)   ISBN 978-0-385-35303-8 (eBook)
1. Taylor, Chucky, 1977– 2. Taylor, Charles Ghankay. 3. Political violence—
Liberia. 4. Soldiers—Liberia. 5. Liberia—History—Civil War, 1989–1996—
Atrocities. 6. Liberia—History—Civil War, 1999–2003—Atrocities. 7. Liberia—
Politics and government—1980– I. Title.
DT636.53.T395D87 2015   966.62033—dc23   2014025451

Front-of-jacket photograph: Liberian warlord Charles Taylor
by Pascal Guyot (detail), AFP/Getty Images
Jacket design by Oliver Munday
Cartography by Mapping Specialists

Manufactured in the United States of America
First Edition

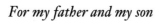
For my father and my son

It's nothing to be proud of to be a Congo man.

—Roy Belfast Jr. (aka Chucky Taylor)
July 28, 2011

CONTENTS

TIMELINE OF EVENTS

FEBRUARY 6, 1820—Settlers depart from New York Harbor to resettle along the coast of West Africa.

JULY 26, 1847—The settlers adopt a constitution and form the Republic of Liberia.

DECEMBER 1871—Jefferson Bracewell, an ancestor of Charles Taylor, from Valdosta, Georgia, arrives in Arthington, Liberia.

JANUARY 28, 1948—Charles McArthur Taylor is born in Arthington, Liberia.

APRIL 14, 1979—In Monrovia, a protest over the increased cost of rice, a staple food, turns violent, and government troops fire on protesters.

APRIL 12, 1980—Soldiers from the Armed Forces of Liberia storm into the president's bedroom at the Executive Mansion, killing him. Master Sgt. Samuel Kanyon Doe assumes control of the country, giving Taylor a role in the government.

1983—Taylor flees Liberia for the United States with $990,000 in government funds. He is arrested and incarcerated at Plymouth County House of Corrections.

SEPTEMBER 15, 1985—Taylor breaks out of jail at Plymouth and escapes the United States.

DECEMBER 24, 1989—Taylor launches the civil war under the mantle of the National Patriotic Front of Liberia (NPFL) in Gbutuo, Liberia.

JULY 1990—American diplomats broker an agreement with Taylor to avoid an assault on Monrovia. West African peacekeepers land; weeks later President Doe is killed by a rival warlord.

MARCH 23, 1991—The Revolutionary United Front (RUF), backed by Taylor's forces, attempts to take over the government of Sierra Leone.

SUMMER 1992—Charles Emmanuel (aka "Chucky Taylor") arrives in Liberia to be reunited with his father.

OCTOBER 1992—Taylor launches Operation Octopus in an attempt to seize control of Monrovia, but it is beaten back by West African forces.

APRIL 6, 1996—Fighting engulfs Monrovia, forcing the evacuation of the U.S. embassy.

JULY 19, 1997—Charles Taylor is elected president of Liberia.

1998—Taylor forms the Anti-Terrorist Unit; Chucky assumes leadership.

APRIL 21, 1999—An assault on Voinjama, in northeastern Liberia, marks the opening of the final phase of the Liberian civil war.

JULY 7, 1999—The RUF and the government of Sierra Leone sign a peace agreement.

2002—Investigators with the Special Court for Sierra Leone pursue Charles Taylor's connection to the civil war in that country.

MARCH 10, 2003—Taylor is indicted under seal by the Special Court for Sierra Leone.

JUNE 4, 2003—While Taylor is attending peace talks in Accra, his indictment is unsealed in Freetown.

JULY 2003—Rebels lay siege to Monrovia as President George W. Bush tells Taylor to step down. Chucky flees Monrovia for exile in Port of Spain, Trinidad and Tobago.

AUGUST 11, 2003—Taylor steps down and enters into exile in Calabar, Nigeria.

JANUARY 2004—In the United States, Immigration and Customs Enforcement (ICE) opens a weapons-trafficking investigation into Liberia.

MARCH 21, 2006—Liberia's president Ellen Johnson Sirleaf arrives in Washington for a state visit and addresses a joint congressional session.

MARCH 29–30, 2006—Charles Taylor is arrested near the border with Cameroon; Chucky Taylor is taken into custody at Miami International Airport by ICE.

DECEMBER 6, 2006—Chucky Taylor is indicted under U.S.C. § 2340A, the federal antitorture statute, becoming the first person charged under that law.

JUNE 4, 2007—Charles Taylor's trial for crimes against humanity begins at the Special Court for Sierra Leone, located at The Hague.

JANUARY 9, 2009—After a two-month trial, Chucky Taylor is convicted on eight counts of torture and related charges and is sentenced to ninety-seven years.

FEBRUARY 18, 2011—After the Eleventh Circuit upholds Chucky Taylor's conviction, the Supreme Court declines to consider further appeals from him.

MAY 30, 2012—Following his conviction and appeals, Charles Taylor is sentenced to fifty years for crimes related to the civil war in Sierra Leone.

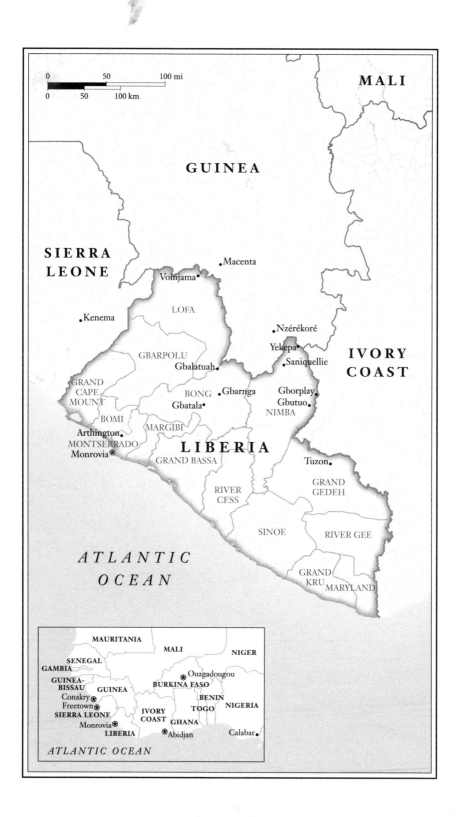

MALI

GUINEA

SIERRA
LEONE

0   50   100 mi
0   50   100 km

•Macenta
Voinjama•
•Kenema
LOFA
Nzérékoré•
Yekepa•
GBARPOLU   •Saniquellie
Gbalatuah•
GRAND
CAPE
MOUNT   BONG   •Gbarnga   Gborplay•
Gbatala•   Gbutuo•
BOMI   NIMBA
MARGIBI
Arthington•
MONTSERRADO   LIBERIA
Monrovia⊛   GRAND BASSA   Tuzon•
GRAND
GEDEH
RIVER
CESS
SINOE   RIVER GEE

IVORY
COAST

ATLANTIC
OCEAN
GRAND
KRU   MARYLAND

MAURITANIA
MALI
NIGER
SENEGAL
GAMBIA
GUINEA-   Ouagadougou⊛
BISSAU   GUINEA   BURKINA FASO
Conakry⊛   BENIN   NIGERIA
Freetown⊛   TOGO
SIERRA LEONE   IVORY
COAST   GHANA   Calabar•
Monrovia⊛   LIBERIA   Abidjan⊛
ATLANTIC OCEAN

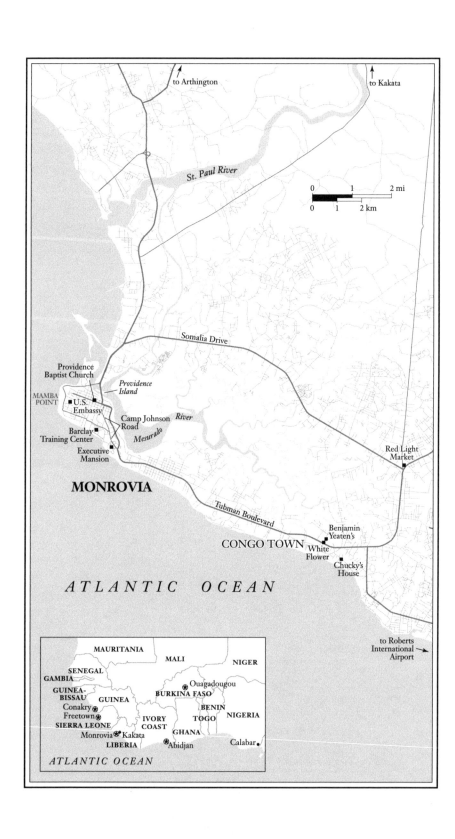

to Arthington

to Kakata

St. Paul River

0   1   2 mi

0   1   2 km

Somalia Drive

Providence
Baptist Church

*Providence
Island*

MAMBA
POINT

■ U.S.
Embassy

Camp Johnson
Road   *River*

Barclay ■
Training Center

Mesurado

Executive
Mansion

MONROVIA

Red Light
Market

Tubman Boulevard

Benjamin
Yeaten's

CONGO TOWN White
Flower

Chucky's
House

ATLANTIC   OCEAN

to Roberts
International
Airport

MAURITANIA

MALI

NIGER

SENEGAL
GAMBIA

**GUINEA-
BISSAU**   **GUINEA**

⊗ Ouagadougou
BURKINA FASO

Conakry ⊗

Freetown ⊗

SIERRA LEONE

**IVORY
COAST**

BENIN
TOGO   **NIGERIA**

GHANA

Monrovia ⊗◉ Kakata

LIBERIA

⊗ Abidjan

Calabar ●

ATLANTIC OCEAN

AMERICAN WARLORD

Prologue

MAY 10, 2007

NATIONAL POLICE HEADQUARTERS

STOCKHOLM, SWEDEN

At just before four p.m., the American revealed the photo lineup.[1] Sulaiman Jusu considered the set of photographs, which were projected on a screen in the conference room: six men, all dark-skinned, frowning, and clad in khaki prison garb.[2]

Let me know if there is anybody in any of the photos that you recognize, the American said.

Jusu understood. He had grown up in an English-speaking country in West Africa: Sierra Leone.[3] Nine years earlier he, his wife, Isaatu, and his three brothers had set off on foot from Kenema, a small city in eastern Sierra Leone, to escape fighting between rebels and government militias that had torn through the nation's small diamond-producing region. They had drifted from town to town along the frontier—Mano Junction, Sagbema, Daru, Bomaru. As they moved, their options dwindled. Rebels, tribal militias, and foreign fighters had made life a gamble for civilians throughout much of the region. Isaatu was six months pregnant, and they could not remain on the move forever, so Jusu, his wife, and her twin sister crossed into Liberia, choosing to become refugees. Their journey eventually took them to Sweden, but only after a detour that nearly cost Jusu his life.

The American sitting across the table from Jusu was a special agent from Immigration and Customs Enforcement named Matthew Baechtle.[4] From the outset, his investigation had been a long shot, a vague directive to look into a civil war halfway across the globe to see whether any U.S. citizens had violated any international sanctions or laws. For years the case had meandered and stagnated, searching for a focus, until suddenly, a year earlier, Baechtle had found a target and a crime. But he needed more evidence. Weeks earlier he had learned of Jusu's identity (and of his potential as a witness), and he'd flown to Stockholm to see what, if anything, this man knew.

Jusu was tall and slender with a drawn face; at thirty-six, he had five children and had steadily built a new life in Sweden. He'd attended university and settled in Stockholm. For the most part, his horrific experiences had been relegated to memories.

He scanned the photo spread. Did he recognize anyone? None of the faces on the bottom row of the lineup registered. The top row depicted another set of three faces. One stood out: that of a man wearing a bushy beard over a moon-shaped face. The man's dark eyes sat under a furrowed brow. Jusu's mind held the image of a man, younger and without a beard. He looked at the photograph and his memories returned.

It has been a long time since I've seen Chucky, he told Special Agent Baechtle.

Nearly a decade earlier the convoy Jusu was traveling in had stopped at a makeshift checkpoint in Gbalatuah, a village in northeastern Liberia on the St. Paul River.[5] The checkpoint was spare, but it blocked the dirt roadway toward Monrovia. The date was April 22, 1999; one day earlier mysterious rebels had attacked Voinjama, a city on Liberia's border with Guinea, forcing hundreds of refugees, Jusu among them, to flee.[6] It was the first significant challenge to Charles Taylor's territory since he had taken office as president of Liberia in 1997.

Taylor had emerged as the victor in a seemingly intractable civil war, his power legitimated through an election. Liberia was traditionally the United States' closest ally in Africa, and Taylor was positioned to emerge as the strongest leader that that nation had ever seen. He simply needed to follow the pattern of his predecessors and abide the interests of the United States in Liberia.

But to American officials, it was unclear whether President Charles Taylor was a "good guy" or "bad guy." He was unique. Handsome and eloquent, he was a product of both Liberia and the United States. Born in Arthington, a tiny encampment outside the capital, Monrovia, he could trace his bloodlines both to the indigenous people who had populated Liberia long before the nation existed and to the freed American slaves who had resettled there and eventually created West Africa's first democracy.[7] Taylor was an American-educated economist and bureaucrat who had learned the tradecraft of political violence from one of Africa's most powerful men: Muammar Qaddafi.[8] Above all these things, he was a revolutionary intent on seizing power over Liberia.

When news of the attack on Voinjama reached Monrovia, details were scant. It was clearly blowback from Taylor's long-running proxy war in Sierra Leone, where he had backed the Revolutionary United Front, a rebel faction that had shocked the world by using amputation as a weapon of terror.[9] The president ordered his newest paramilitary group—the Anti-Terrorist Unit, known to many as the "Demon Forces"—to join the fight and to retake Voinjama.

Gbalatuah was little more than a stopover for travelers crossing the bridge over the St. Paul River, a barely navigable strand that snakes for 280 miles through the nation before spilling into the Atlantic.[10] On one side of the road sat a squat cement building with a red tin roof. Across the road, a veranda stood above the scene on a low overlook. Plainclothes and uniformed men who had been posted to the checkpoint by the government milled about the roadway: some wore dun desert camouflage, while others were dressed head to toe in black, and still others in green American-style fatigues.

The vehicles carrying Jusu, his wife, Isaatu, her sister, Mariana, and his brother-in-law Albert came to a stop at the checkpoint at Gbalatuah, and immigration officers ordered the civilians down from the truck. Harassment was a fact of life for refugees in this part of the world; officials preyed upon the displaced for bribes or looted valued possessions in exchange for passage.

For the past forty-eight hours, the two couples had tried to stay close to one another, but as they jumped down to the roadway, the security forces separated the men from the women, pushing them to opposite sides of the road. As Mariana watched, the soldiers struck her husband and Jusu with the butts of their rifles, forcing them out of sight. The soldiers ordered the men to produce identification, then demanded they hand over their money and remove their clothes.

Jusu and Albert emptied their pockets and stripped to their underwear. They took a seat with a group of other men under a mango tree next to the building. The men were afraid to move. They didn't yet understand why they had been pulled aside. Across the road, the women grew anxious and impatient. Some women bribed the officers for permission to cross the road to speak with their men. Albert sat and waited. Mariana did not appear.

Suddenly the women who had been pleading and arguing with the security officers stopped. Several guards, who'd been resting under the veranda, rushed to the roadway. A truck and two jeeps appeared in the distance. At the front of the convoy was a white Land Cruiser.

A murmur moved through the crowd. *The chief was coming.*

A convoy of a Land Rover and several jeeps pulled to a stop at the checkpoint. A man appeared from the lead vehicle, a bandanna wrapped around his head, clutching a long silver pistol. He screamed at the officers to remove the women from the roadway.

The security officers began pushing the crowd away. The man holding the pistol was livid that women were milling about the area surrounding the checkpoint. He stalked through the crowd screaming orders. He noticed the group of men sitting by the side of the road near the MP's office and walked directly toward them. A handful of men in camouflage and red berets, carrying Kalashnikovs, followed him.

Mariana sensed the commotion across the road but could see nothing. She was anxious for Albert's release and intent on continuing toward Monrovia before nightfall, when much of the countryside would fall into a darkness punctuated only by firelight and the occasional building illuminated by the power of a running generator. The women waited, but no word came from the other side of the road.

The naked men continued to sit silently at the roadside. Most of those who had been separated out were military-age males who hailed from Sierra Leone. The line between a refugee and a combatant was often blurred in West Africa. One could easily become the other simply by taking up a weapon.

The man with the bandanna drew his pistol and approached the group. He told the men that he'd heard that Kamajors, tribal fighters from Sierra Leone, had slipped among the refugees. Kamajors were a militia comprised of traditional hunters from the Mende tribe who fought against the rebel force backed by Charles Taylor. The Kamajors were enemies of Charles Taylor. The man ordered any members of the tribe to stand up and step aside from the group.

None of the men moved. They weren't sure what to make of the accusation. Whoever had attacked Voinjama had fled almost immediately back across the border to Guinea. It didn't follow that the rebels would discard their weapons and attempt to mix in with refugees after an attack. But ever since moving back into Liberia, the Sierra Leoneans had grown accustomed to being abused by the Liberian security forces. They knew better than to respond.

The man with the pistol began selecting individuals from the crowd and ordering them to kneel away from the other men. Albert looked up and realized that he had been selected.

The man giving orders approached, holding his pistol at his side. Across the road, Mariana could still not see Albert. As soon as the convoy arrived, the few conversations allowed between the women and captive men had stopped. Mariana's heart shook in her chest.[11] "Oh, why did they take our men away?" she asked her sister. "[What] has happened to them?" She wanted only to catch a glimpse of Albert. Then she heard the gunshots.

As Jusu watched, Albert slumped to the ground. Without a word, he witnessed the man wearing the bandanna fire shots—in quick succession—into the back of each man's head. *This is a demonstration,* Jusu told himself. *He wants to show us how serious he is.*

When the man finished the executions, he still visibly seethed with anger. He turned to his men and ordered that the bodies be taken away. The fighters tied the bodies to the back of a jeep and dragged them out of sight. Jusu tried to steady himself against his terror. He was certain he'd be killed next.

Jusu had seen this man before, just a month or so earlier in Voinjama—though they had never met, as he would tell to a federal court in Miami six months after the meeting in Stockholm.[12] He'd endured harassment from Liberian security personnel along the way at any number of the checkpoints he'd passed. He'd even been arrested once. But he'd always been allowed to move on.

Jusu had learned to differentiate among the myriad Liberian security forces by their uniforms. The newest among these units, the Anti-Terrorist Unit (ATU), wore American-style green, brown, and black tiger-stripe camouflage with a patch depicting a cobra and scorpion. The men at the bridge were ATU.

Jusu waited, paralyzed with fear. A short time later the soldiers who had removed Albert's and the others' bodies returned. They were holding the men's severed heads, including Albert's. They mounted two of the heads on poles at the checkpoint. One head was placed on one of the trucks.

Jusu knew the name of the man with the gun, though he knew little else about him. This was the president's son, an American known as Chucky Taylor.

PART I

1

Been-To

From the North, but I ride with Floridian tacts, South you it's gritty, where I perfected my jack, stone heart cause my trauma, dawg nevers statin the acts.[1]

—*United States vs. Belfast*, EXHIBIT CE-4

The labor carried on through the night of February 12, 1977. It wasn't until the next morning that Bernice Emmanuel finally saw her son. She had been admitted to St. Margaret's, a century-old free hospital for women a few blocks from the apartment where she lived in Boston's Dorchester neighborhood. A girlfriend had rushed her there as she went into contractions, which continued through the night until Emmanuel passed out. When Bernice, who was twenty-two at the time, awoke the next morning, she found the doctors in conference around her. They had decided to perform an emergency C-section. Emmanuel resisted; she wanted to deliver the child on her own. Her girlfriend coached her through each excruciating contraction until, at last, she heard the child's first cries. He weighed twelve pounds, fourteen ounces. When the nurse handed him to her, she saw that he was a boy with gray eyes and a strikingly pale, almost Caucasian complexion.

On the morning of her son's birth, she recalled, the child's father appeared in the doorway. He had arrived at the hospital the evening before, but she had told him to return after the child arrived.

When the father showed up at the hospital on the morning of the birth, he stared in disbelief at the child.

"He didn't believe that the boy was his kid," Bernice said. "He didn't look like he was a black baby."

The father, nevertheless, embraced the newborn and gave him his own name: Charles.

The boy was the product of Bernice's relationship with Charles Taylor, a charming twenty-nine-year-old graduate student and Liberian expatriate with a passion for politics. The two had met more than a year earlier, a chance encounter on a day when Taylor had gone to visit a cousin in Dorchester, a short drive from his apartment in South Boston. As he stepped into the lobby of his cousin's apartment building, he passed a striking woman just a year or two out of high school. He stopped and asked for her number.

Her name was Bernice, although she also went by Yolanda. She was a Trinidadian-American with a wide smile and fair skin, inherited from her white grandfather. She had been born in New York City to immigrants from Trinidad but had grown up in the West Indian community in Boston.

"I don't give my number," she later recalled telling him. But she didn't immediately dismiss him. She had noticed the dapper young African man even before he approached her.

Taylor had arrived in Boston nearly five years earlier, a junior government accountant looking to set himself apart with a degree from an American university. He had worked in Monrovia under the Liberian minister of finance Stephen Tolbert, the brother of President William R. Tolbert. Previously an understated and studious vice president, William Tolbert had been thrust into power in 1971 when President William Tubman died in office after twenty-seven years in power. Stephen had the reputation of being an effective technocrat and, like many family members of government officials, had established himself as a private businessman, even as he worked in government.

Taylor had been an ambitious young man long before joining the government. As a young man, he taught junior high school in an iron-ore-mining town. The work suited him, he recalled, and even though many of his students were older men working for the mining company, Bethlehem Steel, he always felt he was the master of his classroom. Once in the capital, he continued his education with correspondence courses affiliated with La Salle University in Chicago, and he worked the small network of connections of his father Neilson, a judge in Monrovia. He eventually applied for a position at the Ministry of Finance, performing well enough on an examination to be hired on as an accountant. Another young economist serving in the ministry at that time was Ellen Johnson Sirleaf. Both would later become president of Liberia, but the two would meet only in passing.

Taylor's position at the ministry guaranteed him a salary and conferred a measure of respect on him within Liberian society, but he wanted more. Following the path of a civil servant would ensure only that he remained a bystander to true political power. By looking to his boss, Stephen Tolbert, he could see the blunt realities of Liberia's meritocracy: education might be rewarded with greater roles and responsibilities, but power still was strongly derived from family and tribe. The strongest tribe within the nation wasn't, in fact, a tribe at all; it was those few who could trace their ancestral line to the United States. Taylor was among them—at least on his father's side—yet his family was far from the elite.

Taylor decided that he had to go to America to take his next step in life. He later attributed the decision to a superficial event—his girlfriend at the time dropped him for someone with a master's degree who had just returned from the United States. The degree reflected not just attainment but also heightened status in Liberian society as a "been-to"—someone who had traveled to and received education outside the country.

Each month Taylor quietly saved his accountant's salary, eventually mailing an application to Chamberlayne Junior College, outside Boston. He did not have the means to travel abroad but wasn't dissuaded from pursuing the opportunity. Soon afterward he received an acceptance from Chamberlayne and stitched together enough support from a mentor at the ministry to raise funds for airfare. He would become a been-to.

By the time Taylor arrived at Chamberlayne's leafy campus in Newton, Massachusetts, in the fall of 1972, he had burned through his meager savings. When he showed up at orientation with empty pockets, the administration gave him a job washing dishes and mopping floors. That alone would not cover his tuition and board; Chamberlayne applied his earnings to cover his coursework but asked Taylor to move off campus. Forced to find a place to live, he turned to the loose network of Liberians along the East Coast. A cousin, Edwin Holder, found him a Liberian roommate, Edwin Lewis.

Taylor soon grew restless with school. Accounting guaranteed a solid, vocational career path, but he had a thirst for politics and wanted to participate in the changes occurring in Africa and Liberia specifically. Liberia was no longer just an exodus point for freed African-American slaves; it was a country with a diverse native population. During this era Ellen Johnson Sirleaf attended a graduation ceremony at the University of Liberia, she later recalled, and witnessed "a moving moment when the university choir had sung one of its songs in a local language. Everyone in the audience had applauded with great warmth and pride. But lost on no one, at least not upon me, was the fact that it was French that was stressed in the university curriculum, not [native languages] Kpelle, Vai, or Bassa."[2]

In 1959, when Taylor was eleven years old, Kwame Nkrumah, the hero of Ghana's independence movement and its first president, had traveled to Liberia to meet with President William Tubman and Guinea's Sékou Touré. The three African leaders met in the decidedly humble but symbolic setting of a thatched-hut village of Saniquellie, in northern Liberia. What became known as the Saniquellie Summit was a portrait of statesmanship that reflected the times in Africa; as seventeen nations stood poised to claim independence in the coming months, these three countries were standard-bearers of sovereignty.

Nkrumah stood out from his revolutionary peers: not content to define himself solely in opposition to colonialism, he held a larger vision for a unified Africa that he hoped could elevate the continent's geopolitical strength. But even as a young man, Taylor could see that Nkrumah's Pan-African ideology was not attractive to the political establishment in Liberia, which drew its strength from the United States.[3]

If Nkrumah—a fierce, independent African thinker—represented to Taylor the new face of Africa in a postcolonial world, he also represented something unique to Liberians grappling with their nation's identity crisis. Indeed, Liberia faced unique obstacles to "independence." For one, the country was not a colony—at least officially—of any other country. Unlike neighboring Guinea, Ivory Coast, and Sierra Leone, no Western ruling power stood in the way of complete enfranchisement for its citizens.[4] (In fact, Liberia had a sort of reverse apartheid that did not permit Caucasians to become citizens.) It had no colonial military or police force on which to focus rage against the injustices of society. Instead it had something more amorphous but equally pernicious: the division between the descendants of settlers and indigenous Liberians. The corrupt political culture that had taken hold in the society served only to reinforce this division. The weak, poor, and powerless were not only the majority; they were also those who worked the rubber plantations in Harbel and mined the iron ore in Yekepa. The powerful families in Monrovia passed position and privilege from one generation to the next. In the harsh dawn of postcolonial Africa, the greatest obstacle to progress for Liberia was clearly the type of "independent" nation it had become.

There was little chance that Taylor could participate in the sort of continental change that Nkrumah advocated simply by moving numbers across the page within a government ministry. He wanted a hand in making policy. He was influenced, he later recalled, by the views of the development economist Walt Rostow, a Kennedy and Johnson administration official and advocate of the Vietnam War, as well as by Stephen Tolbert's efforts to develop the Liberian economy.[5] His ability to study economics was limited in Liberia. Despite having little money, Taylor chose to enroll in Chamberlayne.

To raise the $3,025 tuition, Taylor needed to work full-time while studying. He found a job in nearby Somerville at Sweetheart Plastics, owned by a Jewish man named Max Greenbaum, who did not let the prejudices and racial anxieties of the moment color his relationship with the young African student. "He was a very generous man," Taylor would say. "He permitted me to do my university and put in time to fill in the lost hours."

Politics, though, quickly supplanted Taylor's academic interests.[6] Within the increasingly active diaspora of Liberians living along the East Coast, he found a forum. He began making the circuit of parties held by local groups in Boston, Rhode Island, New York, and Philadelphia. Taylor met several other eagerly political Liberians, Tom Woewiyu, a Cornell graduate based in New Jersey, and Blamoh Nelson, whom Taylor soon came to respect for his skill and dedication as a paper pusher.[7] As active as the local groups were, they very much resembled society back home: inherently defined by divisions of tribe and background. The activist politics embraced by this group provided an opportunity for an ambitious young man like Taylor.

In 1974 the Union of Liberian Associations in the Americas (ULAA) was founded to bring together diaspora groups along the East Coast and provide a single voice for these Liberians in their nation's domestic politics.[8] But it also established a hierarchy in the expat community. (Taylor would claim to be among the group's founders, but he would not serve on the board until 1979.) For Taylor, the ULAA was a starting point—the first of several pivotal organizations with which he would be associated.

Although this group was far removed from the domestic politics of Liberia, it had real leverage with President Tolbert. His predecessor, Tubman, the son of a freed slave from Atlanta, was credited with opening Liberia to foreign investment and modern development, but he represented the interests of the Americo-Liberian establishment. President Tolbert entered office determined to open Liberian politics and culture, declaring "war on disease, ignorance and poverty."[9]

Some of the efforts that followed were true reforms: Tolbert ordered bureaucrats to be at their desks on time every morning, and he eliminated the requirement that government workers pay a month's salary to Liberia's only political party, the True Whig Party.[10] Other efforts were more symbolic. Tolbert took his oath of office in an open-necked safari suit, rather than the top hat and coattails traditional to the elite, and he addressed the audience in Kpelle, one of the indigenous tongues. He even reached out to Monrovia's poorest, promising that his administration would work to improve their standard of living.

Many Liberians thus viewed Tolbert as a leader in tune with the currents of history, but in fact he held fast to many of the fundamentals of elitism. He was a thirty-third-degree Freemason; membership in the group remained a prerequisite of political power. (When Tolbert met with President Gerald Ford, the Liberian president learned that his counterpart also held this distinction.[11]) His personal life left little to admire. One U.S. official, Edward Perkins, took a very harsh view of the president: When Perkins met the Liberian president and first lady, he said, "She was recovering from the effects of a beating he had given her."[12] Tolbert was a Baptist minister who, aside from viewing himself as a reformer, had passed a law lowering the age of consent to twelve. He was "nothing short of a psychopath," Perkins said.

In the late 1970s, as Tolbert settled into power, the future of the nation could be seen in the diaspora. This supraclass of Liberians included both the offspring of the traditional elite and a new generation of indigenous students and professionals, drawn to universities and institutions in the United States. Western education, along with the cultural literacy and connections that came with living abroad, was nearly as beneficial as familial connections and ethnic background. The diaspora organized and spoke with an—at times—unified voice that demanded the attention of leaders in Monrovia. It was easy to ignore the complaints of university students and marginalized activists in Liberia but less so among this new class of Liberians, who had a broader reach in the political and business communities outside of West Africa. For young, educated indigenous Liberians, the barriers to leadership positions in business and government, while still very real, appeared to be weakening. That was how the future looked for Liberia in the mid-1970s.

Charles Taylor was just one face in the crowd of young Liberians coming up in the diaspora. He belonged to both worlds, the traditional Americos (who inherited privilege and position) and the indigenous (who clamored for mobility in the new Liberia). His familial connections and experience all but guaranteed him a comfortable ministerial position if he chose to return to Liberia with an MBA.

As he became increasingly engaged in Liberian politics, Taylor also encountered political tensions in Boston. He moved into a flat in Roxbury, a predominantly African-American neighborhood that abutted the largely white Irish-American South Boston.[13] After a 1974 Massachusetts federal court ruling, communities around the country were navigating the school desegregation issue. It took a particularly ugly face in these two neighborhoods in South Boston, where both white and black students were shuttled into their respective communities for high school. Riots and violent clashes between blacks and whites were common. In August 1975 black youths shut down Roxbury for four days, blocking street traffic to anyone other than black motorists. The crisis appeared entirely separate from the divisions Taylor was familiar with within his own society, but it gave him a glimpse of what political change looked like when taken to the street.

.   .   .

Soon after their encounter in the lobby, Bernice and Charles began dating. His pedigree set him apart from other young men in her heavily Caribbean neighborhood: he was an African, the son of a prominent family, and on a career path in government. When the two began to spend time together, she discovered that Taylor could also be shy and intelligent. Bernice had little interest in the diaspora activism that preoccupied her boyfriend outside work and school. His political life wasn't a problem in their burgeoning relationship.

Indeed, despite their different backgrounds, the two had much in common. Both had children from previous relationships: Taylor's child and her mother lived in Liberia, and Emmanuel's daughter, Maisha, lived with her. Both were driven: Taylor's interest in playing a larger role in the politics in his homeland was matched by Emmanuel's desire to leave the ranks of the immigrant working class and provide a life of relative comfort for Maisha.

The couple soon moved into a Queen Anne shingled apartment building on Monadnock Street in the Upham's Corner section of Dorchester. Taylor saw the arrangement as "French co-habitation," but for Emmanuel, who was the sole breadwinner while her boyfriend remained in school, the relationship took on all the features of a common-law marriage including—nearly a year after they met—a child.[14]

On that February morning in 1977, Chucky Taylor was born between several worlds. Boston was almost incidental to the family history; it was simply where his parents' lives collided. Chucky's mother's family had migrated to Boston decades earlier to find work, while his father had sought his education there. Underlying the family history were other, more significant migrations. On Taylor's side, there were the journeys back and forth across the Atlantic, into bondage and back to freedom in Liberia. On Emmanuel's side, there was the voyage from Trinidad, a polyglot island in the Caribbean—once believed to be the mystical El Dorado—that had been settled, in part, by African slaves brought in to work on the sugar plantations.

These two worlds shared cultural and spiritual links. Christianity, particularly the Baptist Church, was the dominant faith in both cultures, but traditional beliefs also held significant sway. In Liberia, the secret belief-systems of the bush—Poro and Sande, where the natural world of the forest was imbued with spiritual powers—were still part of Christian men and women's initiation into adulthood.[15] Trinidad, for its part, had the spiritual practice of Obeah, a type of folk magic believed to have migrated from Africa's Gold Coast, or what is now Ghana, in the seventeenth century.[16] In Liberia, the outward face of Poro is the "bush devil," a stilted figure wearing a mask of shells. A similar figure can be seen in Trinidad: the Mocko Jumbie, a figure who walks on stilts, wears a mask, and represents a link to Obeah. The Jumbie, whose name means "ghost," is associated with the spirit of a child who died before baptism and is cursed to eternally roam the earth.

Chucky was the firstborn son to both Taylor and Emmanuel. In Liberia, that role came with the inherent privileges and responsibilities of tribal societies; even among Christian Americo-Liberians, it carried symbolic importance within a family. In Trinidad, meanwhile, if the father of a child committed any wrongs during his life, his first son would be born with "a light on him," meaning he would bear a curse for his lifetime.[17]

Juggling these diverse influences, the family settled into life in Dorchester. Taylor worked jobs at Sears and Mutual of Omaha, but Emmanuel was the more consistent breadwinner. She recalled Chucky as "the happiest baby" while the family lived together under the same roof.[18] But the truth was that Taylor did not have the time to be a father. Around the child's first birthday, he returned home one day to see his son drinking from a baby bottle. As Emmanuel would recall, Taylor plucked the bottle from his son's hand and tossed it out the window, declaring, "You're too grown for bottles."

More important, the politics of his homeland were changing rapidly—he longed to be involved.

On the morning of April 14, 1979, a crowd gathered on Broad Street in downtown Monrovia. Many were students from the nearby university, but soon people from all walks of life began to join what was a rare protest. A student group, the Progressive Alliance of Liberia, had called the march over an issue felt keenly by all Liberians: the cost of rice. The staple of the national diet, its price had leaped in cost due to a disastrous government intervention. A policy aimed at boosting local rice agriculture—Liberia had once been a significant rice-producing nation—had pushed the cost of rice to more than a third of an average family's income. This increase was meant to stimulate farming, but the primary rice producers included large plantations owned by President Tolbert's siblings; the president appeared to be profiting from his own people's hunger. The opposition had organized a peaceful protest, but as the crowd in Monrovia swelled to nearly ten thousand, protesters burned cars and looted businesses, unleashing tensions that had been building up for more than a century.

President Tolbert, sitting a little more than a mile away at the Executive Mansion, had underestimated the degree of popular anger. The change that he had promised had moved too slowly or failed to materialize at all. His government had little experience or facility to deal with unrest, particularly in the capital. His impulse was to seek counsel, not from his military leaders but from the chief of the military mission at the U.S. embassy, Col. Robert Gosney.[19]

Gosney, a former offensive guard for Texas A&M University with a brawny, no-nonsense attitude, had earned the Distinguished Flying Cross while serving as a U.S. Army helicopter pilot in Vietnam.[20] He'd been in the country just a few months, working with the Armed Forces of Liberia (AFL), but had already made his presence known as a capable trainer. He'd learned that the military leadership was "crooked as snakes." The generals used military resources as their own, divvying out pay, housing, and rank along tribal lines. When he sat down with the president and his chiefs of staff that day, it became apparent that "the thrust of that meeting was that they wanted me to take control of the army."

Gosney mobilized two battalions at Barclay Training Center, a military installation on the edge of downtown Monrovia. The plan was simple: move through the capital in a show of force. Before the soldiers departed the camp, Gosney later said in an interview, he ordered them stripped of ammunition and outfitted with batons and tear gas. The rioters were unruly and violent, but they were not armed. Gosney didn't want a massacre.

The rioting crowds had gutted much of downtown Monrovia, emptying out storefronts and shops, many owned by Lebanese merchants who were now pleading for help from the president and the embassy. When the crowd approached the Executive Mansion, a contingent of security forces armed with live ammunition fired into the crowd. As protesters scattered, nearly forty were killed by the gunfire. The military forcibly dispersed those remaining, leaving several hundred injured in the process and setting off another rampage among the retreating protesters.

The city's thriving business district was scarred by fire and looting. Eventually, the Liberian government requested help from neighboring Guinea to enforce calm. Gosney later said he didn't recall any of the shooting deaths from the riots, but he understood the implications of the rioting and violence that followed—the rising hostility was palpable not only among the Liberian people but also within the military, where inequalities angered many.

"If you don't get ahold of generals who were robbing their soldiers of their pay, there was going to be a coup," Gosney recalled saying.

The violence in Monrovia—known as the Rice Riots—was felt almost immediately in Liberian communities throughout the East Coast; the uneasy inertia of Liberian politics had been forever altered. Taylor and his friends in the United States were appalled by Tolbert's reaction and his decision to call in troops, especially the contingent from Guinea.

The crisis provided Taylor with an unprecedented opportunity: a path to power separate from the political establishment in Liberia. At a ULAA board meeting soon after the Rice Riots, members of the group proposed purchasing weapons to send to the opposition back in Liberia.[21] One member met with a contact in Washington, D.C., to arrange the purchase of several handguns. The plan dramatically underestimated the firepower that would be required of a successful armed insurrection: the conventional force that had just used automatic rifles on a crowd of unarmed protesters was American-trained and -supplied. The ignorance, however, didn't matter as the contact was, in fact, an FBI informer.

At a meeting in Washington months after the Rice Riots, FBI agents arrested the Liberian weapons buyer. In the next days that followed, arrests continued through the ULAA's ranks, including Taylor, who was apprehended a short time later in Boston. He would be brought before a grand jury in Washington, D.C., but avoided prosecution.

For Taylor, the episode offered an abbreviated lesson. "Bad thinking," he recalled later, "but that was the time."[22]

Even after the FBI sting, members of ULAA continued a campaign of agitation against Tolbert. Taylor led a small group of ULAA activists, mostly students and young professionals, to the Liberian consulate in New York. The group took over the consulate's suite of fourth-floor offices at 820 Second Avenue and demanded that Tolbert resign. Taylor knew better than to think the president would be pressured by a disorganized sit-in across the Atlantic, but the group hoped to have their voices heard in Monrovia.

Winston Tubman, a nephew of former president William Tubman and head of the consulate, showed up to remove the protesters. Without hostility, he addressed Taylor, who appeared to be leading the group. "Gentlemen," he said, "the events at home have shocked us all. I hear that there were many deaths."[23] Trying to connect with the protesters, Tubman mentioned that he was uncertain whether a friend of his had been injured in the violence.

"Screw your friend!" Taylor screamed. "Our country is being destroyed by killers, and here you are, talking about your friend!"

Tubman was stunned. If the men refused to leave, he warned them, they would be arrested. Taylor challenged him to do so. Tubman didn't want to see the men arrested, but there was little he could do. Exasperated, he left the room to confer with Monrovia. Soon afterward officers from the NYPD walked into the consulate and arrested Taylor and five of his followers.

Even after two arrests, Taylor and the ULAA continued to press their case against Tolbert. In September 1979 the president, who was then chairperson of the Organization of African Unity (OAU), traveled to the United Nations to address the General Assembly. Taylor again drove down to New York, having organized a group to protest on First Avenue outside the UN building while several members of the ULAA entered the assembly hall.

As Tolbert stepped up to the podium to speak, the young Liberians began shouting down their president. Rather than ignore the protesters, he engaged them. He arranged to meet Taylor and several other ULAA leaders at the Liberian embassy in Washington.

President Tolbert did not have to meet with members of the ULAA. They represented a peripheral, dislocated component of his growing political opposition. The fact that many had received education and work experience in the United States set them apart within Liberian society, but their influence on domestic politics remained questionable.

At the meeting, Taylor aired the group's grievances: the government's lack of reform and its failure to punish the minister of justice and police director for the killings of civilians during the Rice Riots.

"I am doing the best that I can to bring about change," Tolbert said. "It is slow, but I want change."[24]

Then he chose to hold out a laurel to them.

"Look," he said, "some of you have been in America very long and may not have all of the details of what's going on in Liberia, so I now extend an invitation to you, Mr. Chairman, and a delegation to come and visit Liberia and tour the country, where we think you would be better informed as to what is happening on the ground."

Taylor had not been home since he'd arrived in the United States seven years earlier. An invitation from the president conferred upon him and the other ULAA leaders what he considered "almost rock star status." But it also came with some risk. "It did cross our minds that we could, even if not get killed, . . . have gotten locked up like the other guys that were already in jail," he later recalled.

But Taylor also read an implicit challenge in the president's offer, which he found impossible to resist. "It is good and well to sit in the United States and demonstrate on the streets where at most the police will arrest you, take you in, book you, and let you go," he said. "But now when it comes to the time to—what we say literally in Liberia—to show your juice and you run away, I mean, we just couldn't do that."

He and the others immediately accepted.

Taylor's political ambitions did not include a role for his American family. As he plied the East Coast, immersing himself in expatriate politics, he became involved with another woman, Enid Tupee Songbie, a younger Liberian who was also the niece of a popular army officer, Thomas Quiwonkpa. As Tupee later told a journalist, Taylor courted her over eight months after they met at a party years earlier in 1975, when Taylor was twenty-seven and she was just sixteen.[25] By 1979, the relationship had developed into more than a liaison. There was nothing remarkable about Taylor's infidelity to Bernice—they were not married. An ambitious Liberian man had no clear political advantage in being tied to a Trinidadian-American woman.

Taylor, according to Bernice, did offer to take the family back to Liberia with him.[26] But she didn't even entertain the idea; her view of Africa was gleaned from television documentaries: a world of thatched-hut villages and women in straw skirts. "We weren't educated enough to know that Africa wasn't backward," she said. She had an altogether different idea of how she wanted to raise Chucky, educating him at a private school, living near his cousins and grandparents. "Why would I leave here?" she asked.

Soon afterward Charles Taylor disappeared from her and her child's life. He married Tupee, a fortuitous alliance for Taylor because of her familial connections. Bernice, when asked about the marriage two decades later, refused to acknowledge it. She recounted their separation in March 1980 as her own decision—one that had left her a single mother caring for two children. (The split may not have been as stark as Bernice describes: other family members have snapshots that appear to show Chucky with his stepmother and stepsister in Liberia in 1982.)

Chucky entered Berea Seventh Day Adventist Academy in Mattapan, two miles from the apartment she used to share with his father and his half sister Maisha, who was four years older than he. Bernice kept life simple for the children, she says, but she refused hand-me-downs, insisting on brand-name clothes. The children's lives revolved around school and church; their grandparents, aunts, uncles, and cousins; and weekly dinners at York Steak House. She tried to instill in her children manners and a sense of propriety. Eventually she found for Chucky the one thing in life he didn't have: a father.

Roy Belfast was a Trinidadian man from Bernice's old neighborhood.[27] A welder who had trained at Chaguaramas Naval Training School in Trinidad, he had made his way to Baltimore and then to Dorchester in the 1970s. She had met him around the same time she'd met Charles Taylor, but Roy was nearly ten years older than she, and he was married. So she became deeply involved with the young Liberian student, while Belfast faded from view.

In 1982, when Bernice reconnected with Roy, the two were sharing a mutual experience in heartbreak. She had been without Taylor for two years; Roy was still married, but after thirteen years his marriage was little more than a formality. He and Bernice began seeing each other. When he proposed to her, his divorce had not been finalized. The following spring, after Chucky's sixth birthday, the couple married at a ceremony in Exeter, New Hampshire. Bernice now had a new life and a new family—without Taylor.

Yet Charles Taylor was never far from her view. News of a brutal coup in Liberia in April 1980 shocked the international community, which had long seen Liberia as a beacon of stability in the upheaval of post-colonial Africa. In the coup, William Tolbert, the last of a line of Americo-Liberian presidents, was murdered in his bedclothes by a handful of noncommissioned officers from the Armed Forces of Liberia.

The events surrounding Tolbert's murder are mysterious. What is known is that on the night of April 12, the president opted to sleep at the Executive Mansion, on the shores of the Atlantic in central Monrovia, rather than at his personal residence outside the city. At some point in the middle of the night, soldiers burst into the room, surprising him and his wife, Victoria.

The first lady later described the scene in her memoir *Lifted Up*: "Then . . . six virtually naked and horrifyingly masked men rushed by me. Their bodies were painted for war, in tribal fashion—like the warriors of Cape Palmas during Liberia's tribal wars. Only jagged and weathered scraps of fabric hung securely about their loins. I could see that their gruesome masks, designed to terrify, disguise and intimidate, were painted on. . . . I didn't recognize any of those men. . . . Suddenly, a deafening explosion blasted our ears. One of them had shot [President Tolbert]. He sank to the chair, his walking stick dropped to the floor, and I knew he was dead."[28]

The men spared the president's wife, who belonged to the indigenous Vai tribe.

According to the lone surviving American embassy official present in Monrovia, the killing of the president was no cathartic purgation of tribal hatred.[29] It was little more than a drunken lark, undertaken by a handful of underpaid and aggrieved soldiers. Within hours of the president's murder, Col. Robert Gosney appeared on scene at the Executive Mansion. There he found the members of the junta, not celebrating their victory, but disoriented and terrified, sulking in a pagoda outside of the mansion. It was a dangerous situation: the capital threatened to spin out of control without a clear line of authority.

"Is there anyone there that could run the government?" his boss, the chargé d'affaires, radioed him.

"I reckon there is," the colonel responded. Gosney was familiar with some of the men from training they had received from U.S. Special Forces weeks before the coup. By his own account, Gosney lined up the men and appointed them roles in the junta according to their rank. His account can't be independently verified (the others present are deceased), but it is known that two men within this group, Master Sgt. Samuel Kanyon Doe and Sgt. Thomas Quiwonkpa, emerged as the most powerful figures in Liberia. Each would shape Taylor's development as a political force.

Both leaders came from tribal backgrounds—Doe was a Krahn tribesman from Grand Gedeh County in Liberia's southeast, and Quiwonkpa was a Gio from Nimba County along the eastern border. Both men had little schooling but were professional soldiers. Doe became the president and Quiwonkpa the head of the armed forces for a new government, the People's Redemption Council. Together they represented a new idea for Liberia: indigenous rule.

The coup dismantled the power structure that had ruled over Liberia for more than a century and simultaneously awakened tribalism as a political force. For ordinary Liberians, the world was turned on its head: the elite became the hunted, the disenfranchised became powerful. The tension in Liberian society had been building toward such a reversal for generations, but when it finally came, the change was spontaneous, not the result of an organized coup plot. The violence that followed in the days after Tolbert's murder was shocking: thirteen cabinet members and government ministers were gunned down at a military camp before a firing squad. The one thing that remained consistent was support from the United States. The Reagan administration, once it was convinced of the Doe regime's anti-Soviet leanings, began plying the new government with military and economic support.

For Bernice in America, the news likely confirmed that the political change that Charles and his friends had agitated for was being realized. It wasn't clear where Taylor would fit within this violent new order, but he couldn't have been too far from the action. Even as she moved on with her life, rumors about Taylor surfaced perennially: that he'd returned to the United States, that he'd been arrested and then broken from prison. She was left to wonder whether he was somehow connected to the crisis back in his country.

But Bernice ultimately decided that what happened in Liberia was not relevant to the family she was trying to hold together. The father to her child had disappeared, and apparently it would be better if he remained in the void. By 1987 she and her new husband had decided to leave Boston—leaving her daughter Maisha behind with her grandparents—to raise Chucky in Florida, far from his birthplace and far from wherever his father would think to look for him.[30]

Pine Hills was a stretch of suburban Orlando crafted from an idealized vision of America. Developed in the 1950s as tracts of tidy, affordable single-family homes on open farmland west of downtown, the neighborhoods and cul-de-sacs were built around fixtures of middle-class Floridian life: the community golf course, the swimming pool, and the shopping mall.[31] In the 1950s a typical Pine Hills resident held a job at nearby Lockheed Martin and could comfortably afford a $4,000 starter home. In nearly all cases, a Pine Hills resident was white.

As the civil rights movement developed and desegregation became law during the 1960s and 1970s, the racial tensions of the era were keenly felt in Pine Hills. The neighborhood, although part of relatively metropolitan Orlando, was a segregated southern community. The local Ku Klux Klan remained entrenched in the Orange County government and sheriff's office until the 1950s, and until the 1960s many home titles in the neighborhood contained the provision that the property could not be sold to a black owner. In 1973 Pine Hills residents openly protested school busing aimed to desegregate their school systems. But just seven years later, in 1980, the *Orlando Sentinel* would describe Pine Hills as "the leading edge of racial change in the Orlando area." Over the course of the 1980s, white residents would flee the neighborhood in droves, dropping from 91 percent of the residents in 1981 to just 28 percent in 2000.

In April 1987 Bernice purchased a two-story home on a quiet street off a county road in Pine Hills.[32] (Though she was married to Roy, the deed listed her as "unmarried.") The Belfasts' appearance on the block was part of a larger migration of West Indian families from the North-east to Orlando. When Chucky entered school, however, he found that his background carried some stigma. The children drew cultural lines not just between island kids and locals but also between "northerners" and Floridians.[33]

A rise in crime rates contributed to the tensions in the area.[34] In the late 1980s Orlando, like other U.S. cities, suffered a lethal combination of children and guns. By the early 1990s Pine Hills became a front line in this crisis. Local teens formed gangs like the Hiawassee Posse, the Pork n' Beans gang, and the Pine Hill Boys. These crews resembled groups of neighborhood friends more than organized street gangs like those in Los Angeles and Chicago. Local cops attributed the trend to popular movies like *Colors*, which depicted—and glamorized—gang culture and violence. But as these groups acquired guns—and began using them—the distinction mattered little to local law enforcement. The Orange County sheriff's department created a task force called the Alpha Team to deal with the emerging problem.[35]

In 1990 the local police began officially counting drive-by shootings—a phenomenon that had been a novelty just two years ear-lier. By 1991 the office tracked twenty-six drive-bys among the more than two thousand shootings countywide. At times, the law enforce-ment response drew controversy. In 1991 Orange County sheriff's deputies shot three Pine Hills teens—the youngest, fifteen years old—during a robbery sting. The incident drew public recriminations and prompted Florida's governor to call for an investigation into the use of police force.

This violence was not abstract for Chucky, whose neighborhood became known as "Crime Hills." Children were forced to adopt the sort of self-preservation tactics that were more familiar in inner cities. As a young teen, he had to stake out his name among the neighborhood kids. Having grown from a lanky adolescent into a huskier teen, he soon developed the reputation as a tough kid in a tough crowd—as one former girlfriend said, "an alpha among alphas." Schoolyard legends surrounded him: according to one, Chucky took on a crowd of Florid-ians who had singled him out as a northerner, holding them off alone with a brick. All this translated into problems at school, which eventu-ally landed Chucky in a high school for discipline cases.

Meanwhile, shortly after their arrival in Orlando, Chucky's parents' relationship began to deteriorate.[36] From the day of their wedding in 1983, their marriage had had baggage: Roy's unresolved divorce from his prior marriage, Bernice's marriage to a hairdresser in 1989 (while she remained married to Roy), and eventually Bernice's suspicions that Roy was unfaithful and spending all the family's money on other women. Eventually Roy moved out of the family home to a smaller house several miles away. But the issue that pushed the marriage over the edge was neither infidelity nor money problems: it was Charles Taylor.

In late 1989 Chucky's father reappeared halfway across the world. He was no longer an angry student activist but a smooth-talking and charismatic face of an inscrutable war in the jungles of Africa. Bernice and Roy's instincts told them to distance their son even further from him. In the weeks after Taylor launched his first assault into Liberian territory, the couple brought the child before a family court judge and asked to change his name. He took the name of the man who had raised him, Roy Belfast. The name didn't take, however; few called the boy by any other name than "Chucky."[37]

Taylor, meanwhile, had not forgotten his American son. A year or two later, as Bernice recounts the story, she returned home one day, and Chucky told her, "My dad called."[38]

Something in his voice told her that he wasn't referring to the man who had raised him. But she could only ask her son, "Who's your dad?"

2

Reunion

Doctrine stitched to my mind, while the wisdom from the wars stay stuck to my spine, taught to fight in conditions be it day or night.

—*United States vs. Belfast,* EXHIBIT CE-4

More than a century earlier, on a mid-December afternoon in 1871, the *Edith Rose* moored in Monrovia.[1] It was a black-hulled trading barque out of New York, with sixteen sails drawn from its three towering masts. It carried 243 Americans on a journey to start a new life in Liberia. The nation's half-century-old capital sat hard on a peninsula of bone-white-sand beaches and belled palm trees, which formed a natural barrier between the Atlantic and the wetlands of the Mesurado River. The ship arrived at the height of the region's dry season. An equatorial sun hovered brightly in the sky, obscured only by swiftly moving packs of low silver clouds. The landing of the *Edith Rose* was like the many others that had preceded it since the settlers first arrived in 1822, but it remained distinct in that those aboard were fleeing not slavery but the violent prospect of living as free blacks in the American South.

Liberia's creation story had begun centuries earlier, when it existed only as a vast territory situated just above the equator, between four and eight degrees north latitude along the Atlantic coast. This territory stretched outward from the swampy Atlantic coastal plain into rolling green hills ringed by mist, toward an interior of more than twelve million acres of dense rain forest, eventually rising up into a range of gray, cool mountains and highlands near the western border. The interior held riches that would increase in value over the centuries: diamonds, timber, iron ore, and rubber. Eventually two colonies would draw boundaries around it: Sierra Leone, an English possession, to the north, and Ivory Coast, belonging to the French, to the south. The territory was the ancestral home to nearly sixteen indigenous tribes, speaking as many languages; some had hunted and fished along the shores for millennia, while others had migrated across the Sahel through Mali and Guinea. But until the first Europeans arrived in the late fifteenth century, this mysterious, verdant inland expanse was to them little more than undiscovered, uncharted, and dangerous territory.

The first European contact on the Liberian coast occurred when a Portuguese explorer named Pedro de Cintra came ashore in approximately 1461.[2] De Cintra immediately discovered a valuable commodity: an abundance of melegueta pepper, which the locals used to season food. He also encountered an insurmountable language barrier with the indigenous tribes who lived along the coast. As a way to document his discovery, the explorer kidnapped a tribesman and brought him back to Lisbon, hoping this man would elaborate on this strange and unknown land to geographers there. The journey north did little to make the two men more comprehensible to each other, and after the ship arrived in Lisbon, the geographers fared no better in understanding the tribesman. After some time—and with the help of a slave woman—their interrogations were finally able to reveal one fact of this unexplored land: it was home to unicorns.

But the market was for slaves rather than unicorns, and a slave trade soon flourished along what became known as the Grain Coast, after the grains of the melegueta pepper. Over the next two centuries, the coastal tribes became not only fluent and experienced providers of slaves to Portuguese and Spanish traders but also seasoned combatants in the internecine wars that came with competition in the trade.

Slavery would also connect this territory to the people of the United States. The American Society for Colonizing the Free People of Color of the United States, or simply the American Colonization Society, saw in this uncolonized region a solution to the legacy of American slavery.

The society, which fashioned itself a progressive philanthropic group, came into being on December 21, 1816, at the Davis Hotel in Washington, D.C., where a handful of white American clergy, judges, and congressional leaders gathered to plot out a solution to what many viewed as a developing domestic crisis: the growing numbers of free blacks.[3] The group provided a nexus for all manner of contemporary beliefs and prejudices about blacks, slavery, and the prospect of the emancipation of American slaves. Abolitionist members of the group viewed slavery as a taboo, a sinful remnant of the prior generation. Others simply rejected the idea that freed slaves could live alongside white Americans, enjoying the same rights of citizenship. For them, deportation was the best solution. And some members saw in the emerging crisis of emancipation an opportunity to spread the word of God, or as one of the society's founders put it: "We should send to Africa a population partially civilized and Christianized for its benefits; our blacks themselves would be in a better situation."[4]

Despite their disparate ideologies and beliefs, the group converged on the same idea: that the best solution to the "problem" of emancipation was a program of African emigration. The idea also found support in black communities in free states but was not universally embraced. When the society's first ship sailed from New York Harbor in 1820, members envisioned the occasion as the departure of an African *Mayflower*. But within the manumitted communities, it stirred debate as to whether the path toward true freedom was in Africa or in the United States.

A half-century later, several years into emancipation and well into the Liberian experiment, when the *Edith Rose* arrived, the notion of a sovereign black nation on a black continent still had appeal for many African-Americans. The settlers aboard the *Edith* had set sail from Hampton Roads, Virginia, more than a month earlier, carrying with them little more than blankets, shoes, tools, and farming implements. The ship followed the Gulf Stream for several weeks, braving winter gales until it crossed the equator. Conditions were cramped but livable. Below deck, children attended to their studies in a makeshift classroom, while all the passengers congregated each night to pray and—when the weather allowed—to celebrate the Sabbath.

The settlers belonged to two companies: the Clay Hill Company from South Carolina and the smaller Georgia Company from Valdosta, the seat of Lowndes County, Georgia. The Valdosta émigrés were led by Jefferson Bracewell, the head of his sixteen-person family, who had left at a moment of extreme tension between blacks and whites,

Republicans and defeated Confederates, the civilians and military. Despite—or perhaps because of—the presence of a garrison of the 103rd Infantry Regiment of the U.S. Colored Troops in Valdosta, the area saw violence—including bombings, looting, and murders—long after the Confederacy capitulated. Political violence was an experience that had been shared by the South Carolinians.[5] Reverend Elias Hill, who led them, had testified before Congress on the abuse he had suffered after the war at the hands of the Ku Klux Klan, which had pushed him to seek a new home in Liberia.[6]

Over the weekend of their arrival in Monrovia, the passengers were carried to shore along with their belongings. The women and children of the *Edith Rose* remained in the capital, while the men boarded eight small boats and made their way up the St. Paul River into the bush toward a settlement called Arthington.

Arthington was just the type of place the society's founders had envisioned as a starting point for this program. The settlement lay several dozen miles inland from Monrovia along the St. Paul River; it had been established only two years before the arrival of the *Edith Rose*. A party from North Carolina had pioneered it on a forested and hilly bank offset from the river.[7] The town took its name from its sponsor, Robert Arthington, the hermetic heir to a British industrialist family who had donated one thousand pounds sterling to start the encampment.[8] With his gift, the North Carolina company, led by a deacon named Alonzo Haggard, cut a town from the forest, constructing a school, a handful of homes, and, most important, a church.

The surrounding territory had already been "pacified" over five decades by settlers in a series of armed contests with the local tribes. The first emigrants in 1822 had established settlements on land where the indigenous tribes had lived for generations; within a few years, two of the dominant indigenous tribes, the Dei and Gola, set aside their traditional enmity to form an alliance against the newly arrived Americans.[9] The tribes had a shared economic interest that was threatened by the new arrivals: the slave trade, carried on with French and Spanish traders like Theodore Canot and Pedro Blanco. Attacks and kidnappings soon became a hazard of life in the bush for the settlers. Eventually they decided the assaults required a response, and marching into the bush, they overtook a tribal fortress manned by fighters from the alliance. The victory stunned the tribesmen, and their alliance soon broke apart. While the Dei would lose strength over time, the Gola would remain antagonists of the settlers for decades.

In the 1830s and 1840s the government in Monrovia eventually came to support the settlers along the St. Paul River, sending a militia force to suppress the Golas' slave trade. The conflict had further entrenched the hostility between settlers and the indigenous population, which would persist for generations. Two classes of Liberians emerged: the indigenous tribal Liberians and the settlers, called Americo-Liberians or, more pejoratively, Congo people. With each wave of settlers, the division became more entrenched.

By the time the *Edith Rose* landed in 1871, that split was fundamental to Liberian society. Émigrés like Jefferson Bracewell, the elder of the group, first faced the challenge of survival, before confronting the local politics. Bracewell, forty-seven, and his wife, Rhoda, forty, had a family of fourteen children and grandchildren, the youngest a six-month-old girl, Phillis. He was a carpenter by trade and immediately began working just under forty acres of land with his sons, cultivating coffee, cotton, sugarcane, potatoes, and rice. Some of the crop was for their subsistence; the remainder—in particular, the sugar and coffee—was for sale. The Bracewell women tanned leather and assembled clothing, spinning and weaving their own fabric.

One visitor to Arthington in 1877 traveled through the bush to the settlement.[10] After five days, he came upon a two-story wood-frame home, built in an American style, neatly bounded by a fence—a jarring contrast to the thatched native dwellings he had passed on his journey through the interior. The village, now populated with four hundred settlers, sat on a plateau overlooking the forested banks of the St. Paul River. A vast coffee orchard surrounded the town, the hue of the leaves changing from green to yellow. "The view was delightful," the visitor wrote, "not a blade of grass or slightest appearance of weeds among the trees." The town had grown to house two schools and three churches, a Baptist, a Methodist Episcopal, and an African Methodist Episcopal congregation, and in that year, twelve new houses had been built. By 1888 the settlers were farming produce for local markets and as much as 100,000 pounds of coffee for export. One uncomfortable fact, not highlighted in the society's publications, was the settlers' reliance on coerced tribal labor to maintain their existence.

Indeed, by the late nineteenth century, Americo-Liberian society had become a grotesque mirror of the one the settlers had left behind in the American South. This was particularly apparent in Monrovia, where plantation dress and lifestyles had become the norm among the nation's elite. "Nowhere else have I seen so large a number, proportionally, of dress-suits, frock-coats, and stovepipe hats as in Monrovia on Sundays or days of celebration. . . . Town, houses, dress, life—were all reproductions of what was considered elegant in the days before removal," wrote Frederick Starr, a University of Chicago anthropologist, in 1913.[11]

> It is and always has been the custom for Liberians to speak of themselves as "white men," while they have considered the natives "bush niggers." The Liberian has never indulged to any extent in manual labor; he has done but little even in agricultural work. The native has always been considered the natural laborer of the country; socially an inferior, he has been despised and neglected.

As early as 1858, the new Liberian government was accused of selling tribesmen into bondage to the French as "apprentices." Even the topography of early-twentieth-century Monrovia reflected this stark distinction between the classes: the Americo-Liberians lived on a peak—literally looking down on the rest of the city's inhabitants.

The elite held fast to the vestiges of the American establishment and, in particular, to secret societies, which took root and flourished more quickly than political institutions: the Freemasons, the Grand United Order of Odd Fellows, the United Brothers of Friendship, and the Sisters of the Mysterious Ten all had active local chapters.[12] In fact, the first request to start a Grand Lodge of Masons in Liberia was sent in 1824, nearly twenty-three years before the government was founded. (The nation would become a constitutional republic only in 1847, after the American Colonization Society severed financial ties with the territory.)

The indigenous culture had its own secret rites. The traditional belief systems of Poro (for men) and Sande (for women) had long relied on secret initiation rites. In the case of Poro, a "bush devil"—a masked figure serving in the role of a priest—presided over rituals, almost completely undocumented, that were said to include cannibalism and human sacrifice. Similar reports of ritual violence would follow the Freemasons in Liberia, who erected a temple atop Monrovia's Mamba Point. Both societies preserved their secrecy but eventually opened to one another. "It's a pity you are not a Mason," one Liberian told a Western researcher investigating Poro. "For then I could tell you more. The Poro is just like Freemasonry."[13] As the notion of political power and influence developed in the young republic, these societies would be instrumental in the lives of the nation's leaders.

Liberia's political culture also inherited unique contradictions from the United States. In *Bitter Canaan*, the definitive history of the creation of Liberia, Charles S. Johnson points out that Liberia's "constitution was a quickly drawn instrument," embodying the ACS's idealistic intentions rather than the realities the settlers faced.[14] It was crafted to echo the U.S. Constitution, lauding democratic notions that "governments derive their just powers from the consent of the governed." The author of the constitution was Simon Greenleaf, a Harvard professor who had never set foot on the African continent. He lacked any direct knowledge of the indigenous people who would be "governed" by the constitution, let alone the complex political systems they had developed. Moreover, there was little precedent in Africa for the establishment of a democracy by a foreign power: the typical structures imposed on indigenous peoples were colonial governments that "made no pretense of democratic principles."

At its founding, the government in Liberia professed to be a representative democracy, while it was in fact a one-party semifeudal state. It would take a century before indigenous Liberians would be granted suffrage. Even then the political elite remained entirely Americo-Liberian for 132 years, a ruling minority of 2 percent that was attached to the mainline Christian churches and Masonic societies, unwilling to yield their political power.

Yet the exchange between cultures wasn't entirely one-sided. Tribal societies, traditionally governed by powerful chiefs who distributed power and wealth within the community, provided an example for the settlers. Monrovia's top-down style of governance was more reflective of the society of the indigenous people.

The society's division manifested within the settlers' households, even just a generation removed from the Valdosta settlers. Serena Anne

Bracewell and Philip Andrew Taylor, both first-generation Americo-Liberians, married in March 1918.[15] As had become customary among settler families, the couple took in a teenage indigenous girl as a house servant, a practice that hearkened back to white slave masters who brought young black women into the home to perform domestic duties (and also to field sexual advances). Her name was Yassa Zoe, from the Gola tribe. Family members recalled her as a strikingly gorgeous young girl; yet as was common for her tribal background, she spoke limited English and had received only a third-grade education.

Serena Taylor ran a strict Baptist home, but her son, Neilson, in his early twenties, became romantic with Yassa Zoe, who became pregnant. Faced with the impending birth of a child, the family's religious leanings ran headlong into the prejudice against indigenous Liberians. One side of the family saw intermarriage between the two communities as a greater taboo than allowing the child to be born outside marriage; the other disagreed. Ultimately, Neilson Taylor married Yassa Zoe, who took on the Anglo name Louise.

In the early twentieth century, the marriage of Neilson and Louise, if ahead of its own time, reflected the inevitable intermingling of cultures. With each generation the settlers became less American and more Americo-Liberian, a unique culture synonymous with power. In 1948, nearly seventy-five years after the Bracewells departed Valdosta, Neilson Taylor and Louise brought their third child into the world. They did not choose for him a Gola name like Jahmale. They chose Charles, a name descended from his father's American line. The child's place of birth, Arthington, made clear that he was a son of this new nation, Liberia, but his name—Charles Taylor—left no doubt as to which tribe he belonged.

When Chucky first heard from his father in late 1991, the call was not entirely unexpected.[16] Many Americans caught their first glimpse of Charles Taylor on ABC's *Nightline* in June 1990. He presented himself not as the military leader of a revolution but as a clearheaded civilian leader, dressed in a blue-and-white tracksuit with a single gold chain around his neck, speaking forcefully but persuasively into the camera about his ambitions to remove the peacekeepers from his country. His accent was not American, but the manner in which he spoke was.

"We want . . . for the American people to understand that this is not a bunch of headhunters out here in West Africa trying to shoot up a country for power. I'm not interested in that," Taylor said.[17] The statement was typical: a bit of truth balanced by a lie. Taylor's army—really a coalition of ethnic militias—served little purpose other than to seize control of Liberia. For American audiences, it was a faraway conflict with little connection to U.S. national security. The interest for the U.S. government was to try to minimize the damage done to the intelligence and communications facilities it operated in Liberia.

When Bernice changed Chucky's name in the weeks following Taylor's December 1989 invasion, she sought to make him more difficult to find, should Taylor seek him out.[18] For Roy, the name simply reflected the reality of the situation: he was the little boy's father. He supported the family with his welding business and organized a steel drum band to connect his stepson and other neighborhood children to their Trinidadian heritage. In Pine Hills there was nothing unusual about the family or how they were raising their son. But as the war in Liberia dragged on, Bernice's view of Charles Taylor began to shift.

In another report, nearly two years later, he portrayed a cool charm in an interview.[19] The camera panned the scene, a portrait of the provisional and, to outsiders, exotic nature of his power: fighters milled around him, holding automatic rifles, clad in mismatched military and civilian gear. Some men wore corsets, top hats, welding goggles, and large crucifixes.

He did not mince words. "We will fight to the last man. I will get weapons from wherever I have to get it. If the Pentagon got some," he said, turning to look into the camera, "please give me some. I'll use it."

The man Taylor had become was all but unrecognizable from the man Bernice had lived with and loved for years. To be sure, he was still charming, intelligent, and well spoken, but he was no longer an overeducated, underemployed student rich only in ambition. He was a leader of men now, the face of a revolution. He was a man who had—if only for a moment—the attention of the world.

It's unclear whether Chucky had any recollection of his father, but after the call, his life suddenly expanded to include an alternate reality: Liberia. In Bernice's retelling, she was stunned, but her protective instinct had disappeared. She would not comment on this inexplicable change of heart. While Charles Taylor did represent lawlessness and violence as the face of his revolution, he also represented power, ambition, and a sense of larger purpose. When he offered her and their son a chance to come to Africa, she accepted. In the summer of 1992 she prepared Chucky to reunite with his father.[20]

Chucky could see, upon their arrival, that he was not in Florida anymore. The landscape outside the car window resembled nothing that either he or his mother had ever known. There was no planned sprawl of county roads lined with fast-food restaurants, billboards, stoplights, and barren sidewalks. Instead, he passed villages of thatched huts along crumbling red dirt roads, shoeless children in gleaming white shirts walking to school without a backpack or a book.

It was the summer of 1992 and he and his mother had traveled to West Africa to see his father, despite the considerable danger the trip presented. Their destination was Gbarnga, a tiny city in central Liberia, home to Taylor's political movement and the capital of his rebel territory. Their journey provided an unedited version of sub-Saharan Africa, and their arrival inducted the American mother and son into the civil war. The city teemed with fighters and weaponry, but the soldiers didn't appear to belong to any army; they were clad in pieced-together uniforms, T-shirts, and shorts, carrying hand-me-down rifles and machetes. Liberia was entirely foreign to everything Chucky had known in life.

His father was the most powerful man in the country.[21] Controlling the most men and the most territory, he had a firm grip on the nation's fate. Chucky had little basis to understand what this meant. Liberia was a nation of two million people, roughly ten times the number in Orlando at the time, but it had little significance for Americans. Few understood the historical connections between the two nations, and even fewer knew about the U.S. role in supporting the Doe regime and engendering the hatred that had fueled Charles Taylor's rise.

Despite Taylor's power, the war had made it difficult to access his territory. Gbarnga, the bush capital he had carved out for himself, lay in the nation's lush heartland, 120 miles from the capital. The city and the territory surrounding it were called Taylorland. Living there, he bided his time and plotted to retake Monrovia and, with it, the nation. Monrovia, for its part, was fortified by an African peacekeeping force that protected the weak interim government from Taylor's army (and from another competing band of rebels comprised of the National Patriotic Front of Liberia's [NPFL] ethnic rivals).

There were two types of teenage boys in Taylorland: those who carried weapons and those who did not. Many of the teenagers Chucky initially met—distant cousins and the children of members of Taylor's National Patriotic Reconstruction Assembly Government—fit into the latter category. Their familial connections protected them from the demand to participate in Taylor's revolution. They attended private schools or, like Chucky, lived in the United States during the school year.[22] If Taylor's revolution succeeded, they would be the beneficiaries of their parents' alliance with the rebel leader.

The other type of boys were poor and often had been violently taken from their families; they had fewer choices or prospects. In some cases, these children had been forced to commit an atrocity within their community—such as killing their own parents or raping a neighbor—that would effectively exile them into Taylor's revolution. Once within the NPFL, they typically fell under a commander—the closest thing to a parent—who introduced them to the means of survival within Taylorland: the gun.

For a teenage boy from Orlando, the arsenal available to these boys seemed to come straight from action films: G-3 and AK-47 automatic rifles, rocket-propelled grenade launchers, mortars, and truck-mounted missile systems.[23] When an American diplomat asked one of Taylor's deputies why they used child soldiers, he said, "Because you can control them." Children followed through on orders regardless of the moral implications of their actions. These children represented a troubling paradox of power: they were powerless to control their own lives, but they were empowered to take the lives of others.

In many senses, Liberia's civil war was an amplified version of the environment Chucky's mother had sought to spare him from in Orlando: armed gangs, territorial feuds fueled by the imperatives of violence. Moreover, the environment orbited around Charles Taylor, the man she had once felt it necessary to keep her child distanced from.

Bernice had known for some time that Charles Taylor was looking for his son.[24] Even before the two spoke a year earlier, friends and family had been receiving calls from him. He had also asked for her, but according to Roy Belfast, Bernice did not want Taylor to know where she was or how to contact her. Nearly a dozen years had passed since she had spoken with him. She had assumed the relatively quiet life of a suburban homemaker and had immersed herself in the West Indian community in Orlando. Nothing should have been farther from her concerns than the war in Liberia.

Even the source of the initial contact between Taylor and her is unclear. She insists that Taylor sought out his child and her, but those close to Taylor understood that it was Bernice who initiated contact. "She was trying, in her own motherly way, trying to get what's his for her son," said a businessman close to Taylor's inner circle, likening her to an "overbearing, beauty pageant mom."[25]

In either case, Bernice reunited Chucky with his father, undertaking a difficult trip to one of the most dangerous places on earth. In 1992 flights were still available to Liberia, into Robertsfield, the airport outside Monrovia, but that area lay behind enemy lines. To get from there to Taylor's stronghold would have required crossing territory that was contested by Taylor's army and its enemies. Not even Taylor himself would have been able to guarantee their safety. The most common route to reach him, which visiting journalists and diplomats often took, was to fly into Abidjan, Ivory Coast, and travel by road to the border with Nimba County, where Taylor had launched his war a few years earlier.[26] There an escort would meet them and bring them to Gbarnga.

Throughout that journey, the fighters made an impression on Chucky. Weapons were ubiquitous, carried in broad daylight by strange figures clad in civilian garb, many adorned with fetishes, occasionally complemented by a camouflage or olive drab garment. Checkpoints manned by these men dotted the roads leading to Gbarnga.

Taylor's residence sat atop the town's highest point. It was a single-story concrete open-air structure with rooms fanning off a long interior corridor. From the hilltop, Bong County's low, green hills radiated out toward the horizon. Gbarnga's few roads and clusters of homes on neighboring hillsides could be seen, but otherwise the location was rural. The seat of Taylor's government sat far removed from Monrovia—where the majority of Liberia's population lived, and where the nation's economy was centered. Taylor needed to control the capital before he could claim true political legitimacy.

In the absence of constitutional authority over the country, Chucky's father's had created its appearance in Taylorland. The territory had its own newspaper, radio, and television station, which broadcast the message of the revolution. Taylor outlawed Liberian money and issued his own currency, backed by a newly opened bank in Gbarnga. His representatives soon began seeking out the lifeblood of Liberia's economy, foreign investment, negotiating with Firestone Rubber to restart production on the plantations within their control.[27] Above all, Taylorland seemed to function. The authority of the government in Monrovia had been fractured, and Taylor presented an alternative state, one that seemed to suggest what Liberia could be under his ultimate authority.

It was there that mother and son arrived to see a man whom neither had ever known. Taylor had left when Chucky was too young to develop anything more than distant childhood memories of his parents' time together. The man Chucky knew as his father was the man who had raised him: the soft-spoken, Trinidadian welder who was more interested in preserving his culture through music than in attaining political power through armed insurrection.

Charles Taylor, too, was struck by their first encounter. His followers knew that their leader had several wives and daughters, but the appearance of a son marked something new. "I remember the first time Taylor [saw] him [saying], 'Oh my God, he looks just like me,'" Taylor's brother-in-law—and Chucky's uncle—Cindor Reeves said.[28] In the years that had passed, Chucky had grown from a child to a teenage boy on the cusp of manhood. "It was kind of astonishing to see that he had such a big son," Reeves recalled.

The emotion of the moment caught Bernice off guard. "I thought time had passed and everybody had moved on with their life [sic]," she said.[29] Just as Bernice had moved on, so had Taylor: he had married and remarried and had fathered daughters both with Tupee and with his new wife, Agnes. Bernice now saw in stark terms the consequences of the decision she'd made a decade earlier to not follow Taylor to Liberia. "It destroyed our family," she said. She also recalled being surprised at "how much it hurt [Taylor]."

In the few public statements Taylor has made about the couple's relationship, his feelings are unclear. In any case, he told Bernice that he'd prepared separate accommodations for her; his son would be staying with him.

Chucky spent that first night in Liberia with his father. It was a departure from the narrow horizons of Orlando and grim streets of Pine Hills, where his mother had raised him. Liberia presented to Chucky the possibility that he was heir to something larger.

3

Jailbreak

Man was born in pain, Alpha hold the frame, maintain like a
monk, forever shifting the pain.

— *United States vs. Belfast*, EXHIBIT CE 9

Seven years earlier, in 1985, long before Charles Taylor became a warlord, he had been a prisoner at the Plymouth County House of Cor-
rections in Massachusetts.[1] One September evening he found himself
trying to squeeze out of a laundry room window on the third tier of the
aging jail. His plan was to clamber down to the rooftop below, drop
another level into the courtyard, and scale a tiny span of fence that was
not strung with razor wire. If he got that far, he'd have to jog to the
waiting getaway car—all without attracting the attention of the guard
patrolling the jail's perimeter.

His incarceration in Plymouth resulted from the April 1980 coup
that overthrew President Tolbert, when Taylor had risen from a student activist to a senior government administrator nearly overnight. As
someone born of mixed Americo and tribal blood, he could have been
arrested or killed in the days following the uprising, which represented
a rupture between the indigenous and settler communities. Indeed,
during the coup, Taylor was staying at the Holiday Inn near the Executive Mansion in downtown Monrovia as a guest of the deposed president. (Taylor had been part of a delegation of diasporan activists whom
Tolbert had flown in in January 1980.[2]) But, rather than being targeted
for his settler background, Taylor had been summoned by members

of the junta within hours of the president's murder for help in kick-starting the revolutionary government.

This first meeting on the morning following the coup made clear the reversal of the power structure in Liberia—and Taylor learned where he fit in. He recounted how soldiers had arrived at his hotel and loaded him into a jeep, making clear he was not a prisoner but a potential collaborator with the junta. When he arrived at the spare military office at the Barclay Training Center, Taylor noticed several men lying on the floor, their arms bound behind them—including several senior government ministers and the speaker of Liberia's legislature. Behind the desk sat Thomas Quiwonkpa, a twenty-two-year-old army officer. Even though he was a relative of Tupee's, the men had never met, according to Taylor.

"Oh, Taylor," Quiwonkpa said.

Taylor responded, "Yes, general."

"Sit down, let's work." Quiwonkpa looked over at him. "Do you remember us?"

Taylor did not.

Quiwonkpa recounted an incident from a trip to Nimba County that Taylor had taken with President Tolbert several days before the coup. When Taylor had returned to Liberia at the president's invitation in March 1980, he had pressed Tolbert to visit imprisoned activists. The president demurred, instead asking the young activist to accompany the presidential delegation on a tour to the interior, to a village called Gbutuo in Nimba County, near the border with the Ivory Coast. By coincidence or design, Taylor would launch his revolution from there nearly a decade later.

Taylor had followed along on the junket, playing the critic to the president. Tolbert understood that Liberian society demanded reform. What he failed to identify was the source of the most potent discontent: it wasn't progressive leaders like Taylor but rather Tolbert's own military. The president wasn't alone in this miscalculation—Taylor too had failed to anticipate that the military would play the pivotal role in restructuring Liberia's society. While it may not have been clear from within Liberia's political culture, it was hardly surprising. West Africa had experienced a series of military coups, beginning in 1963 with the killing of Togo's president Sylvanus Olympio, outside the U.S. embassy

in Lomé, and leading up to the military takeover of Ghana in 1979.[3]
Moreover, the Armed Forces of Liberia had all the elements of fer-
ment: they were staffed in large part by semiliterate soldiers of a tribal
background, who were well trained and reasonably well equipped but
poor, hungry, and not incentivized to remain loyal to the existing power.

Even under the president's wing, during the weeks before the
coup, Taylor held to his activist instincts. In one incident on the tour
of Nimba County, he witnessed a government minister insulting a local
legislator. Rather than let the incident pass as a fact of life in Liberia's
provincial society, he called the minister to task, castigating him for
patronizing the legislator within his own community. It was a minor
incident that Taylor had forgotten. But it provided the basis for the
working relationship between a junior bureaucrat and the military officer. The soldiers providing security for the delegation had looked on
quietly, taking note of this young activist.

Now as Taylor settled into Quiwonkpa's office at Barclay Training
Center, the soldiers reminded him of a press conference Taylor had
later held criticizing the president's party. "We know that you have
come and you want to be fair, this is why we have called you down to
work," a soldier told him.

The junta government, known as the People's Redemption Council
(PRC), became the center of power in the new Liberia, making decisions out of public view and ruling by decree.[4] The PRC did not exist
prior to the April coup. When it came together, it consisted of twenty
members of the "revolution" and functioned similarly to a cabinet,
with Samuel Doe as the de facto head. Ideology was a tertiary concern
within the PRC, particularly since there were so few civilians in leadership positions. Some members had Marxist-socialist leanings, while
others, like Taylor, were market-oriented. But predominantly the cabinet members were military officers—sergeants and captains from the
Armed Forces of Liberia who saw their rank within the service trans-
posed to ministerial positions within the government—roles in which
the men had no expertise. "By all rights, this government should trip
over its own feet and fall under its own weight," the U.S. ambassador at
the time wrote.[5] "But the fact is that Liberians have grown accustomed
over the years to government which provides little of the substantive
support that Western standards assume."

Taylor's admission to this group was remarkable in that he was the only member with Americo-Liberian lineage among a group dominated by members of the Krahn, Gio, and other tribes. He was put in charge of the General Services Agency (GSA), which became his fiefdom. GSA was the procurement arm of the Liberian government; his position as its head made even government ministers beholden to him. The GSA job "was a very, very powerful position," Taylor recalled.[6] He brought in Blamoh Nelson as a deputy, an old friend from his student days in the United States whom Taylor recalled as a natural-born bureaucrat, "a man who really loves paper." Taylor quickly moved to centralize all government purchasing decisions within the GSA rather than within each individual ministry—a system he borrowed from the American bureaucratic model. The policy change came with an inherent benefit, he said: "I then had the authority to make certain decisions regarding supplies that ministries received."

With his new authority came a legion of enemies. Taylor found government vehicles to be a particularly controversial issue. He took a hard line regarding cabinet ministers' use of these vehicles for personal purposes. The decision, while sound, was politically risky, particularly within the ethnic context of the coup. "Here is this Congo man, who is the head of the GSA, who does not want us to gain some status," he recalled ministers griping.

The leader of the coup, Samuel Kanyon Doe, could not have been a starker deviation from Liberia's traditional government leaders.[7] He was young—just thirty—educated only through eleventh grade, and coming from the Krahn tribe. He hailed from Tuzon, a village in Liberia's Grand Gedeh County, along the southeastern border with Ivory Coast. Though he was from a relatively remote corner of the country, American influences reached him from an early age. His village benefited from a stream of Peace Corps volunteers from the early 1970s, and by the time Doe joined the Armed Forces of Liberia in 1969, the military was an American-style force, supplied, trained, and in part funded by American taxpayers.

As president, Doe morphed from a suggestible and illiterate soldier into a paranoid, superstitious, and insular despot. He relied on two sources of power, in arguably equal parts: the Reagan administration and tribal magic (juju).[8] Among his earliest orders of business, as the first indigenous Liberian head of state, was the public execution of thirteen largely Americo-Liberian government ministers charged with treason (only four of whom received even perfunctory trials). In April 1980, before a crowd of international press and other observers who had been invited hours earlier at a government press conference, the men died facing a firing squad of drunken soldiers. In the first fusillade, many of the gunmen missed their mark, and the survivors had to be executed at close range. The soldiers then implored the media to photograph the corpses. One State Department official described it as "one of the most grisly and horrifying things ever seen."[9]

For Taylor, it was an object lesson in the political stakes in the new Liberia; the dark side of tribal ascendency in Liberia had shown its ugly face. This tribal anger was directed not only outward to the settlers but also inward at other tribes competing for position in the new government. The Krahn junta leadership's response to threats—or perceived threats—took on tribal and religious aspects. In one instance, Doe's men singled out a community that they believed to be sympathetic to the former regime. They chose to punish the leader of the tribal secret society, a Zoe, by forcing him to eat his own ear—akin to brutalizing a cardinal as an insult to the Catholic Church.[10] The insult radiated throughout the country's secret societies, disrupting the perennial cycle of "bush schools" that the societies ran to initiate youth into adulthood within tribal communities. For young boys and girls, these schools constituted a crucial hinge point between childhood and adult life: the children were spirited away to locations in the forest for a month to a year, where they underwent a secret education into their roles as men and women within their culture. While the Americo governments had subjugated indigenous peoples, the Doe regime's targeting of traditional practices of rival tribes marked a new rift in the society.

A State Department report divined the real danger: "[Though] the various tribes now feel the animosities toward their neighbors which have been suppressed for the past 158 years, there is no evidence of any group or grouping organizing to overthrow the present Krahn-Kru coalition. However, the alienation is there. It may not mean anything but it could be a straw in the wind for the future."[11]

Indeed, divisions within the junta emerged quickly. Just eight months after the coup, a mysterious group, "The Committee for a Free and

United Liberia," circulated a six-page letter around the capital.[12] In almost Swiftian rhetoric, it accused the government of graft, corruption, and even drug trafficking, specifically calling out Doe's greed for the construction of a mansion in his home county.

"Fellow citizens," the letter read, "you can plainly see this has now become a revolution of personal enrichment and Krahn tribal dominance, with everybody in the PRC together with certain members of government doing everything possible to get more and more." The letter concluded, "The real enemies of the revolution are those PRC rogues."

While the author of the letter was never identified, Doe's government—whether justified or not—saw Taylor's hand in it. The two had had a fractious relationship up to that point, with Taylor unafraid to confront Doe's appointees. The minister of justice ordered Taylor's arrest on March 11, 1981; soon afterward soldiers arrived at his office, stripped him to his underwear, and loaded him into a jeep.[13] Like the ministers who had been detained in the hours after the coup, he was driven to Barclay Training Center and jailed, not far from where he had first been asked to join the coup government a year earlier. After several harrowing hours, Taylor's patron, Thomas Quiwonkpa, demanded his friend's release.

This incident marked the first time the U.S. embassy reported on Charles Taylor to Washington, noting:

> Regarding the problems of political prisoners and due legal process in Liberia, Quiwonkpa called for "fair treatment" for anyone who had committed a crime against the state and said anyone arrested without due process of law must be released. (Comment: Quiwonkpa followed his words with actions that same night. Justice Minister [Chea] Cheapoo summarily ordered the arrest of General Services Agency Director Charles Taylor for "sedition," based on Taylor's possession of three mimeographed letters from "The Committee for a Free and United Liberia." Quiwonkpa maintained he personally saw to Taylor's release.)[14]

While Taylor and Quiwonkpa had forged an alliance, they could not have been more different: Quiwonkpa remained something of a

national hero for his role in the coup. He was a jocular military officer and proud son of Nimba County, deep in Liberia's forest frontier.
Furthermore, he had the support of the U.S. government; one diplomat noted shortly after the coup that "his brigadier's star shines the
brightest of all in the current AFL galaxy."[15] As an army officer who
enjoyed popularity among both his own soldiers and American officials,
Quiwonkpa was on an obvious collision course with the increasingly
paranoid Doe.

It was also clear that Taylor's mixed heritage was viewed as a liability within the insular government, as was his willingness to use his relatively small government office to exert power. While Taylor was able
to return to service in the government, Doe had effectively demoted
him. After several public clashes with the president, both Quiwonkpa
and the young bureaucrat fled to the United States in the spring of
1983, going their separate ways. Quiwonkpa moved quickly to galvanize fighters to stage a raid on Liberian territory.[16]

Taylor was keenly aware of his tenuous position when he arrived
back in the United States: he was the guest of a nation that actively supported a leader who sought his arrest. It was a matter of whether the
United States would take the initiative to do something about it.

Knowing that Doe would likely track him to the United States,
Taylor hired a lawyer to help him: Ramsey Clark. Clark, a plainspoken
Texan whose father had sat on the U.S. Supreme Court for eighteen
years, served as attorney general in the Johnson administration, from
1967 to 1969; his career afterward was characterized by the clients he
took on, including Slobodan Milošević, Saddam Hussein, Leonard Pel-
tier, and David Koresh.

Clark recalled Taylor's arrival at his office at 113 University Place in
New York's Greenwich Village. He appeared dressed in a business suit
and looking like any number of African students and immigrants whom
Clark had represented in the past. When the two sat down, Taylor
explained his situation, his role in the government, and why he sought
counsel. "He thought he was going to have a problem with the government of Liberia," Clark said. "He had come to oppose Samuel K. Doe
and was concerned about reprisals."

Taylor hadn't been charged with any crime at that time, but after
he fled, Liberian officials discovered nearly $1 million missing from
GSA coffers. Before leaving Liberia, Taylor had wired funds to several

accounts in New York, in what appeared to be legitimate purchases of spare parts from a New Jersey–based company, International Earth-moving Equipment.[17] The parts were never delivered, and government auditors grew suspicious that Taylor had orchestrated the scheme to embezzle funds. Before leaving Clark's office, Taylor left a retainer. Clark didn't recall the exact amount but said it "couldn't be more than $5,000."

The charges eventually caught up to Taylor on May 24, 1984.[18] He had been staying at the apartment of one of his former roommates in Somerville, Massachusetts, not far from the apartment he had once shared with Bernice and Chucky. Federal marshals bearing an order to extradite him to Liberia surprised him there, placed him into custody, and brought him to Plymouth to be jailed. The Liberian government wanted to prosecute him for the bogus transaction involving the equipment. The assistant U.S. attorney who was handed the case, Richard G. Stearns, couldn't muster FBI resources to look into it, so he traveled down to New York himself to pore over the bank statements. Taylor had made little effort to hide the fraud. When Stearns spoke to his Liberian counterparts, the extradition request did not appear to be political. (In fact, Doe's fear was that Taylor was using the pilfered money to bankroll the opposition.)

Taylor could do little to prevent his extradition, other than claim that he would be harmed upon returning to Liberia. When he asked Clark to represent him, he warned that Doe wanted to throw him "into a crocodile stream." At a succession of hearings, Taylor and the U.S. government made their respective cases. The government had received assurances from the Liberians that Taylor would receive a fair trial following his extradition, Assistant U.S. Attorney Stearns recalled, though he acknowledged that "there was concern at the time [that] the Doe regime didn't have the most savory of reputations." Taylor had real reason to fear for his life should he lose the extradition battle. Doe had ordered the execution of colleagues who had been much closer to him than Taylor ever was—though those men had been accused of plotting to overthrow him. Clark put documents into evidence and presented witnesses to build the case against extradition, but Stearns said only that some of the testimony was "pretty weird."

The gravity of the decision before the court can easily be perceived in hindsight, but there was little indication of what was on the line during the proceedings. "For a very young guy," Stearns recalled, "Taylor was in a position of prominence. And he obviously embezzled huge amounts of money, which he wasn't spending freely, so he was obviously banking something. He was reasonably educated and polished in his own way. But I did not honestly see him at that time as what he became, which was bloodthirsty."

Even in his growing paranoia, Doe may have had a lucid sense of the potential threat Taylor posed. His push to extradite Taylor came at a moment when the specter of a coup was becoming more real. The ranks of disaffected government officials were growing, and with them came rumors of hostile governments that were willing to provide sanctuary to members of the Liberian opposition, including Libya, Cuba, Ethiopia, and the USSR.[19] The most tangible threat was in the United States, where Thomas Quiwonkpa had found haven before launching the first significant raid into Liberian territory during Doe's regime in November 1983. Doe may have known well that Taylor and Quiwonkpa were in contact in the United States and that both were plotting a return to Liberia with the shared goal of achieving a Liberia without Samuel Doe.

To return to Liberia a free man, Taylor needed first to break jail in Massachusetts and avoid extradition. Throughout his later political career, he would offer differing accounts of his escape, varying in detail and attribution but always serving the same purpose: to cultivate his own mystery and lend himself an intangible legitimacy.

In 1992 he explained vaguely to the American novelist Denis Johnson, who had been sent by *The New Yorker* to profile the young warlord: "I wouldn't even be in this country today if not for the CIA. My escape from the American jail in Boston—I think they must have arranged that. One night I was told that the gate to my cell wouldn't be locked. That I could walk anywhere. I walked out of jail, down the steps, out into America. Nobody stopped me."[20]

In another version, Taylor recounted that a guard simply escorted him to the room where two other inmates had already completed sawing through the bars. "I don't know who cut it," he said, "but I think the guards had made these arrangements."

But according to one of the men who broke Taylor from jail, the truth was less fantastic. There was no official involvement, either from the government or prison officials. Instead, Taylor had arranged with another inmate, twenty-two-year-old Thomas Devoll, to engineer the escape.

The jail, which was overcrowded and nearly a century old, had suffered multiple escapes in the decade prior.[21] Devoll worked as the "runner," the inmate responsible for doling out ice-cream sandwiches and microwaveable cheeseburgers from the prison canteen; as such, he had access to the span of the prison.[22] The job gave him the opportunity to learn "every inch" of the place, as he recalled. Most important, he could map the daily rituals that made the jail function.

Nearly fifteen years Devoll's senior, Taylor was fatherly to him rather than patronizing, unlike a lot of Plymouth's old-timers. The two men spent hours together boxing and playing gin. Devoll developed something personal for his friend. "I also felt sympathy for Charlie," he later said. "The man had children."

"Getting out of here is no different than planning a score," he told Taylor.

The escape was planned for September 15. Devoll had arranged for several high-tempered hacksaw blades to be smuggled in through inmates working on the jail's farm. Early on the day of the escape, Taylor's wife Tupee visited, delivering cash and mail to him.[23] (Tupee, who knew that her family connections to both Taylor and Quiwonkpa could make her a target in Doe's Liberia, had moved to Rhode Island, not far from the jail.) The two men, with a teenage prisoner Anthony Rodrigues, planned to break out from a second-floor laundry room, which had been converted to a cell.

After dinner the three drifted back to the third tier, detouring to the laundry room. Devoll removed the bars, and the men clambered out the window, dropping onto a roof below. From there they hopped down into the courtyard. Devoll had timed the patrol of the guard on his walk around the prison's perimeter and had figured out how much time they had to get to the fence. As they were about to climb it, Taylor stopped. He'd had second thoughts.

That moment of hesitation had huge implications for his future. Taylor would later argue he was breaking jail for a greater good: to return to Liberia to oust Doe and help the nation return to an electoral democracy. He would slip out of the United States, he later claimed, via Mexico and eventually land back in West Africa.[24] (Others maintain he flew from New York on a false passport.) In a few short weeks, on November 12, 1985, Quiwonkpa would attempt to overthrow the regime, only to be slaughtered, his body paraded through Monrovia. Taylor would assume the life of a peripatetic revolutionary, doing prison stints in both Ghana and Sierra Leone before coming under the wing of Qaddafi.[25] Taylor would build his revolutionary army from the men and boys who were displaced from Nimba County by the regime.[26] He would transit them secretly from Ivory Coast, through Burkina Faso to their training base in the Libyan desert, preparing them for the moment to take up his cause and return to Liberia to overthrow Doe.

But on that night in September, an uncertain future lay in front of him. "The guy showed fear," Devoll remembered.

It was too late, he told Taylor. "I ain't pushing your fat ass through those bars again."

Nearly a decade later, when Chucky first met his father at the villa in Gbarnga, the civil war was in its third year. The jailbreak at Plymouth had long been enshrined as part of his father's legend, just one of many struggles his father had endured en route to power. Gbarnga teemed with activity in the summer of 1992, but Taylor's revolution was in purgatory, having ground to a halt a year and a half earlier, when a West African peacekeeping force, comprised largely of Nigerians, moved in around Monrovia to provide a buffer between the rebels and government troops.[27]

The war had started with a lone assault two years earlier. In the darkness before dawn on December 24, 1989, several dozen rebels threaded their way through the bush deep in the rain forests of Nimba County. Their destination was Gbutuo, along the Ivorian border. The town held little strategic significance but was an important symbol in the tribal struggle taking place. Soldiers belonging to the president's tribe, the Krahn, were garrisoned among the villagers, who were mostly of the Gio tribe—a group that had been persecuted and dispossessed by a U.S.-backed junta government.[28] The insurgents anticipated assaulting a battalion of trained soldiers loyal to the Monrovia-based regime; instead they found a small detachment of sleeping men unprepared to defend the village. Armed with little more than a few hunting rifles, the rebels moved quickly, killing the commander, seizing a large weapons cache, and hunting down the remaining soldiers. When the assault ended, the rebels announced themselves to the encampment over a loudspeaker. The villagers sang and rejoiced, as if they had been liberated.

Liberia had long simmered with tensions. Doe's repressive government had split the society even more starkly between those it sheltered and those it viewed as threats. With the assault on Gbutuo, the regime's fears came to life. It wasn't simply an isolated attack on a lonely outpost; it marked the opening of the longest-running and most brutal conflict in West Africa's modern history. What started with a few dozen men armed with hunting rifles would end with an entire generation robbed of their youth, opportunities, and future in a region awash in AK-47s and RPGs. Behind this violence—which over the course of the next decade would subsume Sierra Leone and parts of Ivory Coast and Guinea—was a single man: Charles McArthur Taylor.

The U.S. government gave Taylor a platform to pursue power at any cost. This was not by design but rather through indifference, negligence, and a failure to grasp who Taylor was. In the early 1990s—as genocide in the Balkans and Rwanda were confounding the international community—Taylor introduced the world to a new type of violence. Indelible images began appearing in the media: fetish-clad fighters and child soldiers fighting African peacekeepers on the outskirts of Monrovia; survivors of rebel attacks in the diamond fields of Sierra Leone, appearing in Freetown with their hands severed, lips cut off, and the initials RUF—for Taylor's proxy army, the Revolutionary United Front—carved into their chests. The violence was unspeakable and unstoppable.

After the assault on Gbutuo on Christmas Day 1989, Taylor's revolution spread from Liberia's interior toward the capital on the coast. His army, the National Patriotic Front of Liberia (NPFL), found a forceful accelerant in the tribal hatred stirred by Doe's campaign against rival ethnic groups.[29] This hatred was particularly potent in Nimba County, which served as the launching point for Taylor's revolution. The NPFL's ranks swelled with men, women, and children largely from tribes aggrieved by government purges following Thomas Quiwonkpa's coup attempts—the Gio, the Mano, and the Kpelle. Even Armed Forces of Liberia troops sent to quash the revolt joined the ranks willingly. Taylor portrayed it as a popular rebellion, but many of the fighters, particularly the women and children, had little choice but to join.

The notion of giving consent, in the context of the newly divided Liberia, was often reduced to choosing the most survivable option. Civilians often found themselves caught between government and rebel forces but also, equally significant, within an upended economy. While some commanders turned to brutalities—such as killing off family members—to force conscripts to join, Taylor found that protecting civilians in major towns, as well as their commerce, incentivized their support.[30] (This system often broke down outside major population centers.)

From the earliest days of the conflict, the United States refused to take clear sides. In 1988 the Liberian government had defaulted on a $7 million military loan from the United States, with the result that Doe effectively destroyed the relationship with his largest financial supporter.[31] (In a last-bid effort to avoid default, Doe exhorted the Liberian people to contribute their pocket change in "Operation Pay the United States," even as he stashed cash in footlockers at the Executive Mansion.) The distrust became mutual.

When Doe heard the news of Taylor's opening attack on Gbutuo, he came to suspect American involvement with the rebels, especially after several U.S. embassy vehicles were seen proximate to the assault.[32] (The ambassador and other American personnel were traveling along the roadway over the Christmas holiday.) As Doe's army rushed to the bush to confront Taylor's rebels, U.S. Army Rangers followed with them—not to offer military guidance but to ensure, with little success, that the Liberian soldiers' discipline didn't break down.[33] After a few months, Doe realized that Taylor's insurgency posed an existential threat to his government. He pleaded for tangible U.S. support, providing *The Washington Post* with a letter written to President George H. W. Bush imploring him to "help your stepchildren," but it was too late.[34]

As the fighting stretched into the early summer of 1990, the NPFL revealed itself as only marginally less brutal than Doe's forces. Nearly as soon as the invasion started, NPFL commanders began terrorizing civilians and forcibly conscripting children. An NPFL general named Noriega was accused of executing dozens of men, women, and children from the Sapo tribe in Sinoe County; one elder later recounted to the Truth and Reconciliation Commission (the investigative body formed by the postwar government to document crimes committed during the 1990s civil war) that this commander had ordered civilians marched to a creek, where they were "beaten, butchered or shot to death. The bodies were then pushed into the water. Over 500 persons were killed and 100 children abducted and taken to Nimba County."[35]

For foreign observers, the situation in Liberia had gone from fluid to confounding. A new faction, the Independent National Patriotic Front for Liberia (INPFL), had split from Taylor, led by one of Taylor's best—and most unpredictable—fighters, Prince Yormie Johnson, an effective military commander. Johnson's smaller yet better-trained faction quickly advanced to the edge of the capital.

The State Department searched for a viable path to peace. Separately, the Bush administration's National Security Council (NSC) debated what role—if any—the United States should play in mediating the conflict. The State Department saw Doe as a lost cause, and while Taylor left much to be desired, it recognized his power, both militarily and politically. Lawrence Eagleburger, then deputy secretary of state, wrote a cable to James Baker on June 8, 1990, about whether Herman Cohen, assistant secretary of state for African affairs, should visit the region to press for a resolution.[36] State's key objective was to prevent the war from moving into the capital. But officials within the NSC, including Deputy National Security Adviser Robert Gates, began to reassess American involvement. Beyond the several million dollars' worth of surveillance and communications equipment housed in the country, Gates argued, the United States had no compelling interest in Liberia.

President Bush, ultimately, made the final decision about the U.S. role in the rapidly deteriorating situation. Initially, he supported sending Cohen to enable Doe's departure, but then he began to waver. "After learning that the President might be having second thoughts about not sending Hank Cohen to Liberia, I spoke to [National Security Adviser] Brent [Scowcroft] and outlined the reasons why you and we thought it would be useful," Baker wrote, outlining the need for Doe to "stand down peacefully" and the eagerness to avoid any sort of American military intervention.[37] "While we cannot know whether

Taylor will be better or worse than Doe in the long run, we can be sure that in the short run a bloody siege of Monrovia will not play well for Liberians or Americans."

Meanwhile in Washington, D.C., Liberian opposition leaders in the diaspora gathered to take a position on the growing rebellion.[38] Taylor did not belong to the opposition establishment—insofar as one existed—and as the distinct possibility of the government's collapse loomed, expats in the United States organized to have a separate voice. The group, calling itself the Association for Constitutional Democracy in Liberia (ACDL), included Ellen Johnson Sirleaf. Then living in Alexandria, Virginia, Johnson Sirleaf had met Taylor in Paris, months earlier, in a meeting brokered by a mutual friend who was active in diaspora politics, Tom Woewiyu.

Several differing accounts of this meeting have emerged, but none of the parties denies it occurred, in a hotel restaurant near Charles de Gaulle Airport.[39] Taylor and Johnson Sirleaf had not seen each other since their first encounter nearly a decade earlier, at the Ministry of Finance. While she had not had time for him then, she was willing, on the prodding of Woewiyu, to meet with the man who was now poised to launch a revolution. Taylor testified that Johnson Sirleaf was an "old revolutionary" who'd had a direct hand in Quiwonkpa's failed 1985 coup—a fact that she denied—and their meeting served to secure funding for Taylor's trainees from the Liberian exiles. Taylor brought with him photographs of the recruits, as proof that he wasn't simply a hustler. Johnson Sirleaf offered to raise money, according to Taylor, and to have Woewiyu act as a courier, bringing the funds from the United States to West Africa.

Johnson Sirleaf's recollection differs. She wrote in her memoir that while she did meet with Taylor, he did not make a positive impression. As she tells it, when she was ordering breakfast, Taylor admonished her, "The money you spend to pay for breakfast you could just give to us." She handed Taylor the money she had with her. "It was clear to me that whatever their plans, they were not going well at the moment," she wrote. But Woewiyu prevailed upon her to reserve judgment. "I trusted him and felt I owed his passionate belief in Taylor at least the benefit of the doubt."

While Johnson Sirleaf made no mention of it in her memoir, she eventually acknowledged to the Truth and Reconciliation Commission that her support had been more substantial. She admitted to providing

$10,000 to Taylor through the ACDL, but that figure too has been called into question. The third party at the meeting, Woewiyu, would eventually break his silence about Johnson Sirleaf's early support for the NPFL and offer a "conservative estimate" of $500,000 raised through the ACDL.

Following the Christmas 1989 invasion, Johnson Sirleaf explained that the U.S. State Department had asked for her and the ACDL to contact Taylor and urge restraint. The group decided they would provide the rebels with a small sum of money to purchase food and relief supplies. (Taylor insists that Johnson Sirleaf's role was not as limited as she has described, saying in testimony before the Special Court, "Ellen is lying, and she knows that she is lying, okay. Ellen was in America raising money. . . . Do you take a government by relief supplies? Nonsense.")

In May 1990 Johnson Sirleaf crossed rebel lines to visit Taylor's fighters in Gborplay, a town where the NPFL had set up its headquarters.[40] She was one of the first opposition leaders to return to Liberia following the invasion. By her account, she was distressed by what she saw: hundreds of male and female soldiers "all with blank, bloodshot eyes," "huge and frightening guns," and a "heavily guarded Taylor."[41]

"Charles Taylor knew that he was going to win," she recalled. "And implicit in his confident, boasting rhetoric was the fact that he would do whatever it took to make his belief a reality."

Not long afterward, in early July 1990, the war arrived in Monrovia, tearing at the very fabric of Liberian society.[42] Thousands of refugees streamed out of the city to avoid the fighting. The civilians who remained found themselves caught between the two factions, Prince Johnson's INPFL approaching the city from the north, Taylor's NPFL from the south, and Doe's ragged and hunted government force caught in between. Effectively under siege, the city became host to a humanitarian crisis. There was little food or protection from the fighting; Doe's control over the capital—and country—shrank to a few blocks surrounding the Executive Mansion.

That month several hundred civilians sought refuge in St. Peter's Lutheran Church, a large chapel along Monrovia's main thoroughfare. The church, a short drive from the Executive Mansion, is located directly across the street from a popular hotel. According to witnesses, soldiers loyal to Doe entered the church's compound and set upon the refugees with knives and machetes, then eventually opened fire into the crowd.[43] While exact numbers of the dead are unverifiable, the U.S. embassy reported immediately afterward that "the 186 persons killed in the massacre at the Lutheran Church remain where they fell. After six days, the bodies can no longer be moved, and MSF [Médecins sans Frontières, Doctors Without Borders] Belgian doctors hope to find means to blanket the place with a caustic solution or to burn the bodies which would probably entail burning the church itself."[44]

U.S. policy had shifted to reflect the violence on the ground: the priority of the Bush administration was to now minimize bloodshed and damage to the nation's infrastructure. The most direct path to this objective was not to throw more support behind Samuel Doe—who had demonstrated little regard for civilians—but to work with Charles Taylor. In the background, the administration negotiated a transfer of power to the rebel leader.

That summer, as rebels closed in on Doe, the United States took on the role of mediating the transfer of power. Herman Cohen had negotiated an exile agreement for Doe to receive political asylum in Togo, should he step down, but ensuring that Doe made it to Togo alive was not a priority for the Bush administration.[45]

One of the primary American negotiators, a political officer in the U.S. embassy to Ivory Coast, outlined in chilling terms Taylor's seizure of power in Monrovia.[46] In a transcript of the July 3, 1990, radio conversation between Taylor and an unidentified U.S. embassy official from Abidjan, which the Bush administration's National Security Council declassified, the American made clear to Taylor that Doe's personal safety did not have to be guaranteed should the rebels move on Monrovia: "We want to clarify a message we sent this morning. Doe's spokesmen have asked for protection for Doe's followers, not for Doe himself, as a condition for his resignation. Are you clear on that distinction?"[47]

Taylor responded, "That sounds reasonable."

"If Doe resigns, would you be in a position to cease hostilities?" the official asked.

"Almost immediately," Taylor replied. "If Doe resigns and names his speaker of the House of Representatives now to hold over for the next few hours, we will cease hostilities and set up an interim government. I even intend to have a surprise announcement for the world that we intend to stick to the process of free elections at the soonest possible time."

None of this came to pass. The Bush administration scuttled it, believing that greater involvement would lead to greater responsibility. Deputy National Security Adviser Robert Gates saw little existing responsibility of the United States toward the Liberian people and "was adamantly against us doing anything in Liberia," according to Cohen.

Taylor's path to the presidency in Liberia was also obstructed by the army of his former commander Prince Yormie Johnson. Johnson hardly presented the image of a disciplined military leader: he entertained journalists and onlookers with renditions of the reggae spiritual "By the Rivers of Babylon," complete with his own backing band; he also executed looters and fired into civilian vehicles with little warning.[48] At an impromptu meeting with the commander of a newly arrived Nigerian peacekeeping force, he ambushed Doe's security detail, capturing the president after his men had been gunned down. In one of the most macabre moments of the war, the gruesome torture of President Doe, in the hours leading up to his death, was chronicled on video.[49] Johnson oversaw the episode, sitting by nonchalantly drinking a Budweiser and trying to raise the U.S. embassy on a radio, as a shirtless and bloodied Doe begged for his life.

Doe's murder threw the U.S. negotiation into disarray. Taylor believed the Americans—in particular Cohen—had misled him. As a Nigerian-backed peacekeeping force established control over the capital, Taylor found all his momentum squandered. Following Doe's death, a joint offensive between Johnson's forces and the African peacekeepers pushed Taylor's army back into the interior. The war ground to a stalemate as his comparably ragtag force now faced off against conventional forces from Nigeria, Ghana, and Senegal, including devastating airpower launched from an airfield in Freetown, Sierra Leone.[50]

Taylor had been reduced from the heir to executive power in Liberia to a warlord sidelined by history. He was forced to negotiate a peace between himself and Johnson, while the larger, better-equipped peacekeeping force chipped away at his ranks and territorial control. Taylor could not acknowledge to his remaining loyal fighters that he'd capitulated to their rivals.[51] In the summer of 1992, when his son visited, he was preparing his defining offensive: Operation Octopus, an attack that would encircle Monrovia and drive out the international peacekeepers in hopes of finally seizing power over the country.[52]

Though Chucky was likely too young to realize it, he had arrived at a decisive moment in his father's career. Taylor was powerful, yet he didn't have the influence to force compliance among his own fighters. For one thing, his half-Americo identity remained a political liability. Furthermore, the commanders who had helped him win vast swaths of Liberian territory had their own economic interests and had used the lull in fighting to build their own small empires, trading in timber, diamonds, and coffee. This business model worked well in sustaining Taylor's war machine, but it allowed him little flexibility to negotiate for anything other than total control of the country, since any compromise would likely threaten his loyalists' economic interests. One commenter at the time called Taylor a "prisoner of his own dream."[53]

As tenuous as Taylor's hold on power was, he remained in control of Taylorland when his son arrived for the first time. Pine Hills was hardly Mayberry, but Chucky was clearly not accustomed to life in this new environment, where electricity and running water were luxuries rather than essentials. A cousin from Arthington who met Chucky for the first time that summer, Koisee Garmo, marveled at the bizarre contrast of this American boy staying with his father in this environment.[54] Despite his surroundings, Chucky at first behaved very much like an American child. "The war was going," Garmo said, but Chucky "was at home watching TV. Eating cornflakes."

Eventually, Chucky began venturing beyond his father's compound without his mother's knowledge. One of Taylor's confidants was given responsibility for the American child, and the two would drive into the bush outside Gbarnga. Later that summer Chucky ventured even farther from the interim capital, following his half sister Zoe and her boyfriend, a fighter named Bill Horace, to Bong Mines, an iron-ore-mining town halfway between Gbarnga and Monrovia, on the front lines where fighting flared in the spring and summer of 1992.[55]

Horace had a reputation for brutality that stood out even among Taylor's rebels. He served as a commander of a contingent of Taylor fighters called the "Marine Division," overseeing a sprawling area of operations in Grand Bassa and Maryland County surrounding the port city of Buchanan. In a civil war characterized by atrocities, the Marine

Division carried a singular reputation for depredations. As one of Taylor's generals would explain more than a decade later to the Truth and Reconciliation Commission: "If the Marine pass somewhere you will know . . . because of the flies. . . . the whole NPFL was afraid of them, even the Charles Taylor was afraid of them. . . . The Marine was the ones that brought the wickedness to the people."[56]

Another member of the unit told the commission, "We don't take prisoners for they instructed us not to do so."[57] The unit's rules of engagement were less rules than a license "to kill anybody and destroy anything," he testified. In the middle of all this violence, Horace became known for a signature act. "He was in the habit of killing the crucifix way," one former fighter said, describing how Horace would mount victims on makeshift crosses.[58]

News filtered back to his father's inner circle that Chucky had been venturing toward the edge of Taylor's territory. As one frontline fighter recounted, these trips went beyond a teenage boy exploring the lurid world of violence on the fringe of his father's area of control; he used the trips as an opportunity to join in on the action. "Chucky would get access to the front lines and use guns," he said.

While Chucky will not acknowledge his experiences with Horace that summer, his appearance drew attention among Taylor's fighters. A Marine Division fighter, Morris Padmore, who would later implicate himself in a series of massacres of civilians, testified to the Truth and Reconciliation Commission about the American boy. Chucky was naïve but fascinated. At one point he asked for the chance to kill a prisoner, Padmore said, and had his wish granted.

"That was his first-time killing," he testified.

Cindor Reeves said the rumors that Chucky killed prisoners for sport enraged his father. And when Bernice learned of her son's forays to the battlefront, she also grew livid, Reeves recalled. "She was so angry, but Chucky apparently enjoyed it."

The details of what Chucky saw and did in the summer of 1992 are secrets he is determined to keep. What is clear is that the father-son reunion had introduced him to a world with fundamentally different notions of right and wrong, law and order, power and powerlessness. He returned home to Orlando forever changed by the experience.

4

Pine Hills

You be sleepin if you think it's all Disney and dreads, Impalas
and Marauder, known to fuck up some Duke boys, load'n' lock,
before they gone on da block, little nigga done things that I can't
even speak.

— *United States vs. Belfast*, EXHIBIT CE-4

One fall afternoon in 1992, a pretty thirteen-year-old named Lynn
Henderson walked home from school with a friend.[1] Lynn was still in
junior high, a petite Korean-American girl with large, round brown
eyes, a shy smile, and a soft voice that trailed off as she spoke. Their
route took them along Kensington High Boulevard in Pine Hills, a
quiet street of drab single-family homes set back by parched lawns and
lined with looming yellow pines. The block was the portrait of the
stultifying boredom of the suburbs just outside Orlando's city center,
silent except for the hum of traffic in the distance, the residents largely
remaining behind closed doors or on screened-in back porches. Lynn
had grown up not far from there in a three-bedroom ranch house with
a swimming pool tucked in a cul-de-sac near a pond called Horseshoe
Lake. Her parents—a Korean mother and an American father—had
raised four children in their Pine Hills home after moving to the area
in the 1980s. Lynn was the youngest of three sisters.

As they walked by, a voice called out to the girls. Lynn looked to
see a boy sitting alone on the front steps of one of the larger houses on
the block. She didn't know him, but something about him immediately
struck her. *He's obnoxious*, she thought. Nonetheless, the girls stopped.

Lynn's friend knew him: she played Pan—the traditional Trinidadian music—with him in his stepfather's steel drum orchestra.

Chucky was lean but broad-shouldered, with strong arms and a knowing smirk. He'd arrived home from Liberia weeks earlier, and his return to school had not gone well. That afternoon he was at home for a specific reason: he was under house arrest, with an electronic monitoring device strapped to his ankle to ensure that he didn't stray into the streets of Orlando. The anklet he was wearing, Lynn would soon learn, was the take-home prize for a brush with the law after returning from Liberia. It kept him confined to his home, but didn't prevent him from asking for Lynn's number as she walked by.

The racial barriers that had once existed in Pine Hills and that might have separated the two teens had collapsed by that time. In Lynn's house, race was never an issue. Her father, as an American serviceman, had met her mother, a South Korean citizen, while serving in U.S. Army Intelligence in South Korea. The family had moved to Orlando, like many others, from the Northeast. Lynn was bused to a school where her first friends were largely African-American—many of them from West Indian families. She was neither intimidated nor impressed with the older boy who was asking for her number; she just saw him as a juvenile delinquent.

Chucky offered little to counter that impression. Two years older than Lynn, he should have been enrolled at nearby Evans High School. But by the time he was fourteen, he'd simply stopped attending school altogether. Despite her initial repulsion, something about Chucky convinced Lynn to begin seeing him.

Chucky ran with a tough crew of Pine Hills kids—a group who called themselves the Blunt Headz.[2] Most of the boys had family roots in Haiti, Jamaica, or Trinidad, and all had had more than a few encounters with the law. One story about an arrest was something of a local legend. Chucky and several friends drove to the mall in upscale Winter Park and, once inside a department store, grabbed clothing and bolted, stopping only to smash the front window as they tried to make their escape. Their caper was hardly a success, but it had earned Chucky the pedigree of being something of a criminal.

Over the next few months, Lynn began sneaking over to Chucky's house in the afternoons, telling her parents, who both worked, that she was at her friend's house. Chucky remained confined under house arrest at the time, though she didn't know the details of his legal situation—and didn't care to ask. For all his reputation and tough-guy swagger, he showed kindness and tenderness to her. She saw another side of him: a teenage boy who came off more like a grown man, who had presence despite saying very little, who commanded fear and respect within the neighborhood. She was, by her own admission, naïve. They spent hours in his room, listening to music and talking. "He was a bad boy," Lynn said. "But he was always nice to me."

Initially, Chucky's family life didn't come up in conversation. But as Lynn spent more time at his house, she came to know his parents. Bernice was kind to her, but Lynn also saw her "very verbal, very aggressive" side, a contrast to the quiet, hardworking demeanor of Roy, to whom she remained married. Lynn noticed that though Chucky had taken his stepfather's name, he never used it. He went by Charles or Chuck, and to his parents, he was Charlie. Even though he was known to most as Chucky, he took offense when people he was not familiar with used it. Eventually she learned that Charles was his father's name and that Chucky had taken a trip the prior summer to Africa to visit him, an experience Chucky had little to say about at the time. Like many Americans, Lynn knew little about Liberia back then. The name Charles Taylor meant even less to her.

As their relationship developed, however, she began to see a darker, more volatile side to Chucky. He remained extremely close to his mother, though the two fought often. This volatility carried over to other relationships. Lynn noticed Chucky's "wishy-washy" relations with others—one moment he would be close with a person, the next they would be on the outs. Lynn wasn't scared away by any of it, though. In fact, the more time she spent with Chucky, the closer she felt to him. What began as a teenage crush, over the course of the school year, turned into something completely different.

"I was totally, totally in love with him," she recalled.

An average Saturday night for Lynn included a stop at the nearby roller-skating rink, the Funtastic Skating and Entertainment Center. The rink drew hundreds of kids every weekend, some as young as four, from the surrounding neighborhoods, for what one local preacher described to the *Orlando Sentinel* as a "powder-keg situation": horny, unattended, and often armed minors from different gangs converged on one location.[3] From Lynn's perspective, it was relatively harmless teen fun, but the *Sentinel's* reporter was aghast at the scene surrounding the dance floor, where "the littlest ones watch, eyes wide, index fingers curved to mouths, while kids as young as eight crouch, bump and grind as if to simulate sex. Floor-level speakers that tower over their heads pound out songs about sex and violence from groups such as 2 Live Crew." Often a night at the Funtastic would be punctuated with violence. In most cases, these were minor scuffles, but in at least one incident the rink was the site of a shooting. "All the fights were about nothing," a member of the sheriff's gang unit told the *Sentinel*. "This is where they try to impress other kids by fighting."

Orlando had set up a dedicated program to cope with children like Chucky called Treatment Alternatives to Street Crime, or TASC. Chucky stood out among the crowd of hoodlums he ran with because of his experience in Liberia. The events of that African summer remain a closely held secret—one that Chucky was reluctant to share with the few people close to him, including Lynn. His stepfather saw Chucky as a "tough" but "normal" kid. For Bernice, the problem was simple: Chucky moved with the wrong crowd.[4] But in September 1993, following a scrape with the local police, court officials ordered a mental health assessment of the boy.

The case officer knew little about Chucky other than that his juvenile court records showed "an extensive history of aggressive criminal charges."[5] When the two sat down, Chucky came across as extremely guarded. But as they spoke, a picture began to emerge. The counselor suspected that drugs and alcohol fueled some of Chucky's criminal impulses, but there was something deeper at work as well: he had difficulty controlling his anger, and as Chucky acknowledged, he'd even considered killing himself.

In fact, Chucky had already tried to take his own life. The suicide attempt was a family secret—he never brought it up to Lynn. Instead it was Chucky's mother who eventually confided to her the details of what had happened. One afternoon, shortly after mother and son had returned from Liberia, Bernice discovered Chucky lying in the bathtub bleeding heavily from his wrist. He had cut vertically, slicing through flesh and tendons. Bernice pulled him from the bathroom, brought him downstairs to their car, and rushed him to a nearby emergency clinic.

No clear event had precipitated Chucky's attempt on his life: no fight, outburst, or insult appeared to have pushed him over the edge. The family's response to the suicide attempt was unusual according to Lynn: Chucky was not hospitalized and received no medical or psychiatric care beyond physical therapy. Between Lynn and Chucky, the incident wasn't open for discussion. It represented a vulnerability that she otherwise didn't see in her boyfriend, who even as an adolescent sought to portray himself as manly and deserving of respect. For Chucky's stepfather, the suicide attempt blindsided him. "For any parent, when a child does something like that, it's terrifying," Belfast recalled.

According to Lynn, however, Bernice ascribed the suicide attempt to something beyond her control.[6] During Chucky's summer visit to Liberia, one of Charles Taylor's former wives had given him a gold ring. The ring, Bernice explained, was cursed. "She thought it was black magic," Lynn said. *The ring* had pushed Chucky to attempt to take his own life, Bernice told her. It was a telling statement. In some Trinidadian traditions, where Baptist Christian churches often melded European and African mysticism, mental illness is attributed to curses and demonic possession. This superstition, as one study noted, served to provide "escape from unpleasant reality, and diminution of guilt by projecting blame onto an intruding agent."[7]

In Trinidad, the cure for a curse like this was a "bush bath," a mixture of roots and herbs concocted as part of a prayer-filled ritual.[8] Chucky, however, faced a different kind of healing process. He bore deep scars on his wrist from the suicide attempt and had to work with a physical therapist to regain the full use of his hand.

It was a missed opportunity for Chucky's family to pursue the psychological causes of his pain. His mental health assessment only touched on his behaviors: the frequent run-ins with the police, the suspected drug and alcohol abuse, the violence and aggression. A psychologist would have likely tried to understand whether these behaviors reflected deeper problems: whether he was narcissistic, callous, or manipulative; whether environmental factors were at work, like an unstable environment at home or the rejection of a parent; in short, whether he was demonstrating age-appropriate antisocial behavior or was developing into a psychopath. Even if those signs had been discovered, however, Chucky would have likely gone undiagnosed. In 1993 the American Psychiatric Association did not permit the diagnosis of patients under the age of eighteen with any type of antisocial personality disorder.[9] The mental health community was split on the point; some viewed adolescence as a transitional period where socially deviant behavior may be isolated, while others saw it as the moment when lifelong disorders first emerge and when prevention of future behaviors can be pursued.

In any case, Chucky continued on his own trajectory, his parents unable to rein him in and blind to the risk that his antisocial behavior would become more dangerous. Ample evidence pointed to this possibility. Like other cities around the country, Orlando was experiencing the lethal combination of children and guns, and in the late 1980s and early 1990s, Pine Hills became a front line in this crisis.[10] In one incident, two ten-year-old children and a twelve-year-old were arrested for breaking into a home and attempting to steal shotguns. In another, a Pine Hills homeowner was surprised when a barbecue was hurled through his front window; moments later teens in ski masks stormed the house. Before the homeowner could stop them, a teen opened fire, shooting him in the thigh. One of Chucky's neighbors, a seventeen-year-old boy, was shot twice in the back as he left a local fair by two teens who peppered his car with 9mm and .45-caliber pistols.

On the night of February 25, 1994, nearly a year and half after he first met Lynn, Chucky got his hands on a .38 automatic pistol.[11] He walked along North Pine Hills Road with two friends, seventeen-year-old Daniel Dasque and Philip Jackson, a twenty-one-year-old who had been arrested two years earlier after leading Orange County sheriff's deputies on a high-speed chase through Pine Hills. The young men made their way past the one-story Eglise Baptiste Philadelphie Church, toward the Indialantic Drive intersection. Chucky wore a red sweatshirt and black baseball cap. Tucked into his pants was the pistol. He was not the only one armed, according to a police report; either Jackson or Dasque held a concealed stock barrel .410-gauge shotgun.

At around eight-thirty p.m., the trio spotted a lone teenager walking toward them. Steven Klimkowski had grown up nearby but did not know Chucky or his friends. He had only just stepped out of his house. Within moments, Dasque confronted him and demanded money. Klimkowski replied that he didn't have any.

"Yes, you do," Dasque responded.

Klimkowski tried to brush past the group, but Chucky and his friends set upon him. He broke free and bolted to his house, just eight doors down the street. The trio chased the teenager to his lawn, where he yelled out for help to his father.

When Robert Klimkowski stepped onto his lawn, a terrifying scene came into view: three young men were accosting his son, one of them armed. At the sight of the boy's father, Chucky and his friends bolted down the street. Father and son immediately gave chase. Chucky stopped in his tracks and turned on the Klimkowskis. He flashed his .38 and leveled it at Robert Klimkowski's head.

Klimkowski, who is white, referred to the incident as the time "the black guy pulled a gun out on me."[12] Years later he recalled Chucky saying to him, "What're you going to do about it?"

Chucky then turned the weapon toward Steven Klimkowski's head.

Chucky's accomplice Philip Jackson had stopped to egg him on, according to the police report, crying, "Shoot him! Shoot him!"

Steven backed away, saying, "I ain't doin' nothin."

Chucky didn't pull the trigger. Instead he let his pistol arm drop to his side, then turned to run off into the night with his friends. They didn't get far. The trio attempted to hide out at a friend's house, a few doors from the scene of the crime, but the police easily tracked them. When they placed Chucky under arrest, he still had the .38 in his possession.

The state's attorney charged him with four felonies: two counts of aggravated assault with a firearm, one count of attempted robbery, and possession of a firearm in commission of a felony. Bernice had to post bail to secure her son's release pending a trial, which was scheduled for August. For the first time in his juvenile criminal career, Chucky was looking at real jail time.

The house arrest, the suicide attempt, and now a potential jail term—Chucky's latest arrest marked a turning point for Bernice. She had grown resigned to the fact that she could no longer control her son. But now his behavior had become more than just a threat to himself and his future—it had become a threat to other people. All she had to do was turn on the nightly news or look in the *Sentinel* to see where her son's path could lead. She no longer wanted the responsibility of handling the boy.

Soon afterward she called Liberia to speak with her son's father.[13]

Taylor had little sway with his son and even less influence in the United States to try to ensure that Chucky would not be imprisoned. But Bernice wasn't looking for Taylor to intercede on their child's behalf.

"I've had him until he's seventeen," she told him. "Now it's your turn."

PART II

5

Revolution

Ain't Kevlar, but a lion when I stand, know to the last strand born
to fight, genetic from pops and his clan, to long to hate me.

— *United States vs. Belfast*, EXHIBIT CE-4

By the time the police were at the door, Chucky had no time to hide
his stuff. He wasn't in any position to fight or flee—he could only hope
they didn't find everything.

He had been in Accra, Ghana, for only several weeks, and somehow
he'd already drawn the attention of the local cops.[1] Jaded as he was for
an American teenager, he was uninitiated in Africa. He had been relocated there by his mother and Charles Taylor, to remove him from the
reach of the Florida prosecutors, making him a fugitive from justice
and dropping him into the complex and conflicted political situation in
West Africa. Taylor's revolution had progressed little in the two years
since Chucky's first visit to Liberia. A handful of factions had ground to
a bloody stalemate, but none was strong enough to claim control over
either the capital or the country. It left Liberia a dangerous and chaotic
place—hardly the environment to educate a boy who was desperately in
need of positive influence.

Taylor chose to enroll Chucky at Accra Academy, a six-hundred-
student boys' boarding school located in Bubiashie, a suburb on the
capital's western side. It was modeled after British-style public schools
and intended to educate the children of the country's elite. In its sixty
years, the school had survived Ghana's struggle against British colonial
rule, as well as the series of coups that followed independence. Its crest

bore a sun, a cocoa and palm tree, and three connected chain links with the motto *Esse Quam Videri*, which translates as "To be, rather than to seem."

Chucky did not want to be there, but he had little choice. He moved into a nearby hotel, rather than bunk in a dormitory on campus with his classmates. Few of his fellow students registered his presence on campus, and even fewer had any sense of who his father was.[2] He was noticed for his absence from the typical activities: classes, meals, and sports. He hadn't attended high school for more than a year before arriving in Accra, and he appeared to have little interest in resuming his education in an African country. His stints in African schools would turn out to be short-lived.

Accra had been a stopping-off point for Charles Taylor as well. Nearly a decade earlier, shortly after escaping from Plymouth, he had appeared in the Ghanaian capital, one of many Liberian dissidents who chose the city as a base. In 1985 Accra had become the nexus for all fragments of the Liberian opposition.[3] Dissidents gathered there to collect themselves and plot their next move, eyeing one another warily. Most were resigned to exile on the margins of political action. The scene was reminiscent of Monrovia in the 1960s, when foreign anticolonial fighters had sought shelter in one of Africa's few black republics.[4] Now, in the months following the death of Quiwonkpa, a man whom even Doe appeared to fear, the opposition remained traumatized. If a man with his training, experience, and support within the military—and apparent support from foreign powers—couldn't unseat Doe, who could?

An air of mystery surrounded Charles Taylor when he first arrived in Accra in the mid-1980s. Liberians who did know him recalled him from his student days in the ULAA or his brief tenure with Doe's government from the GSA. He had always been outspoken and intelligent but nonetheless content to second an ordained leader like Quiwonkpa. With new status as a fugitive from American justice, he began positioning himself as a potential heir to Quiwonkpa's mantle.

Accra was the obvious destination for Taylor. He boasted to friends that he was "good friends" with the senior officials in the government of Jerry John Rawlings, an air force officer who had staged a military coup in 1979 and become Ghana's president in 1981.[5] He represented a return to the Pan-African ideals of Kwame Nkrumah, the Ghanaian leader to whom Taylor and many other young Africans had been drawn.

The story of his jailbreak, Taylor quickly learned, was both a liability and an asset in Accra's suspicious environment. Some read into it as a measure of Taylor's ingenuity and the tacit stamp of approval from the United States. Others doubted the story and assumed that Taylor's sudden and improbable reappearance could be explained more cynically— that he had cut a deal with the Americans and was under their thumb. Ghanaian authorities briefly placed him under arrest. "You cannot tell us that you got out of . . . a maximum security prison in the United States and come here if the CIA didn't help you to come, so you are a spy," Taylor recalled the authorities saying.[6] They held Taylor for seven months, but after his supporters interceded with Ghanaian officials, they released him.[7]

Ghana was a decidedly leftist environment. Rawlings had come to power under a party with strongly socialist leanings, views shared by many of the Liberians who had fled to Ghana. In the mid-1980s, ideology did not drive Liberian dissident politics. Tribal affiliation and patronage networks drew supporters more readily than any particular vision for Liberia's political future. The primary preoccupation shared by these groups concerned how to dismantle the Doe regime, which had evolved over the course of the decade into a vast patronage scheme for members of his tribe rather than a functioning government. A similar relationship bound Doe and the United States; he understood that aid dollars would flow to him as long as Liberia remained a non-Communist state.

Liberian dissidents, such as Amos Sawyer, remained in Accra under the wing of the Rawlings government, where they were safely kept from pursuing any revolutionary plans back home. These arrangements were mutually beneficial: activists could remain safe and comfortable there, provided they made no moves to stir up trouble in Liberia and, by extension, the region. Rawlings had little incentive to push for Doe's ouster, even if their political views differed. Rawlings and Doe both belonged to a generation of West African military leaders who had recently taken power—including Thomas Sankara in Burkina Faso, Lansana Conté in Guinea, and Ibrahim Babangida in Nigeria—yet the Liberian and the Ghanaian had little in common. Rawlings, a liberal committed to democracy, ushered in an era of development and economic growth.

Doe, whose politics were tribal, paid little attention to the development of the Liberian state. The men were neither rivals nor allies. Rawlings had little reason to come down hard on foreign dissidents arriving in Ghana on behalf of Doe or, for that matter, to actively encourage them.

But Charles Taylor was intent on unseating Samuel Doe. In Accra, he set about building an alternate network of political support, connecting with operatives from Maktub Tasdir al-Thawra, Muammar Qaddafi's "bureau for the export of revolution," thereby linking himself with like-minded insurgents—including Burkina Faso's Blaise Compaoré—and gaining the opportunity to train in revolutionary warfare and politics in Libya.[8] The Mathaba, as the group was called, operated throughout Africa proselytizing Qaddafi's theory of perpetual revolution and Pan-African ideology, dangling the potential for material and political support for ambitious insurrectionists.

Most men who aligned with Qaddafi played along with his politics, which envisioned African nations uniting to become a global power, in exchange for receiving training at Tajura, a former U.S. Air Force base outside Tripoli. But the goals of Compaoré and Taylor were more self-serving: to forcibly seize power in their home countries for their own political purposes. In 1987 in Burkina Faso, Compaoré achieved this. Thomas Sankara, the popular revolutionary president who pursued women's rights, the abolition of tribal authority, and the nationalization of industries, was assassinated along with his cabinet. Compaoré, who once fought alongside his president, reportedly engineered his death. The Liberian rebel commander Prince Yormie Johnson testified two decades later that both he and Taylor had played a role.[9] As Taylor began training rebels in Libya under Qaddafi's authority, the partnership he forged with Compaoré would prove integral to his own revolution.

By 1988, as his fighters trained at Tajura in the Libyan desert, Taylor approached regional leaders about his plans to depose Doe. In November 1985 Thomas Quiwonkpa had staged his assault on Doe from Sierra Leone; now three years later Taylor approached Joseph Momoh, the Sierra Leonean president. He did not find a receptive audience—Momoh instead threw Taylor in jail. The sudden disappearance of the face of the revolution nearly led to a mutiny in the ranks of the Liberians training in Libya and almost cost Taylor his opportunity to unseat Doe. It was a betrayal he would not forget, long after he successfully launched his invasion—and one that many believed would motivate his incitement of Sierra Leone's civil war.

Two years later, in February 1991, Taylor took his revenge on Momoh. While training in Libya, he had met several Sierra Leoneans bent on overthrowing their government, including Foday Sankoh and his deputy, Augustine Gbao. Sankoh, the son of a farmer who had served in the Sierra Leone military, then was imprisoned for nearly seven years for his role in an attempted mutiny, was a decade older than Taylor. He had spent many years as an itinerant photographer, shooting weddings and portraits; his time on the road connected him to political activists and ultimately led him to Libya. There he made a connection with the burgeoning NPFL. An NPFL officer named Gen. John Tarnue began to train fighters from Sierra Leone, though he later testified that their purpose was not clear to him at the time.

In 1991 Taylor convened a meeting in Gbarnga that would change the course of his country and Sierra Leone, according to prosecutors and witnesses with the Special Court.[10] Around then the Sierra Leonean Army had deployed soldiers to Liberia to support the West African peacekeeping mission, which also included forces from Gambia, Guinea, Nigeria, and Ghana. Taylor had invited Gbao and Sankoh for war planning. Their objective: bring civil war to Sierra Leone.

Taylor called the meeting to order, according to several witnesses, addressing the NPFL leadership and the small cadre of fighters from Sierra Leone. He laid out his intentions to back a group of Sierra Leonean insurgents with weapons and personnel. The initial assault would be part of a broader joint venture. The elements required for success would be: the forced conscription of fighters, men, women, and children; the elimination of those who resisted; and the extraction of resources to support the war effort. Nimba County's plentiful iron ore was a cumbersome resource, but Sierra Leone had diamonds and gold, which could be easily—and clandestinely—transported across the border into Liberia. Taylor instructed the Sierra Leoneans that any minerals mined from the territory they won would be shipped to Burkina Faso and Libya and returned in the form of ammunition, money, and food to support the revolution against Momoh's government. When Taylor invaded Liberia in 1989, revolutionaries from Sierra Leone had

aided his incursion; he offered to reciprocate with weapons and Liberian fighters to participate in their initial assault on targets in Sierra
Leone.

The meeting was by necessity secret, for more than military
purposes—it shielded Taylor from the severe political fallout that would
follow from launching an incursion into another nation. The NPFL
had developed a reputation as a barbaric, undisciplined, and unstable
fighting force, but it was intent on replacing the government of Liberia. Any public recognition that Taylor had ambitions beyond Liberia
would threaten not only his internal popularity but also the clandestine
support he was receiving from Burkina Faso and Libya.

In November 1990, in an interview with the BBC, Taylor issued
a warning of his intentions.[11] He told African correspondent Robin
White, "I have had enough of the Sierra Leonean government permitting Nigerian aircraft to come out and kill my people. I'm saying that
planes are taking off from bases at the international airport in Freetown
at the end of the runway, that leave and they come and blow Liberian
babies, women, and old people away, and my patience has run out in
Momoh permitting this to happen from his territory."

"But how exactly do you propose to stop [it]?" White asked.

"It's anybody's guess," Taylor responded. "Maybe Momoh doesn't
know, but he'll soon find out."

"Are you suggesting that you will go and attack Sierra Leone yourself?" White asked.

"That's not what I'm saying," Taylor said. "But it's for Momoh to
determine."

The fighting had been going in Sierra Leone for nearly three years
when Chucky arrived in Ghana in 1994. He was the definition of a
misfit: an American, a fugitive, son to a father he barely knew. He also
inherited some of the aura surrounding his father's reputation as a
political fire starter. His mother had accompanied him to Ghana and
stayed, but Orlando was now firmly in his past.

His arrival in Ghana came at a crucial moment between his father
and President Jerry Rawlings. Taylor and Rawlings's relationship had
grown complicated since Ghana intervened in the Liberian civil war
as part of the peacekeeping force in 1991. Despite their personal rela-

tionship, Taylor's forces had attacked peacekeepers that Rawlings had sent to Liberia. The Ghanaian president was nevertheless determined to work with Taylor, recognizing that peace in Liberia would require the warlord's cooperation. Indeed, in meetings with U.S. officials, Rawlings privately insisted to them that Taylor was not Liberia's central problem.[12] U.S. policy makers had adopted a hands-off approach to the conflict, leaving it to West African leaders to broker a peace, but Rawlings feared that the United States would pursue its interests covertly. He warned Deputy Secretary of State Strobe Talbott in late 1994 that any efforts to "take Taylor out" would only lead to more violence.

The larger politics surrounding his father had little impact on Chucky's behavior. In his short time in Ghana, he'd been able to acquire a gun and access to drugs—which likely led to the tip-off to Ghanaian authorities. The officers arriving at his apartment quickly located the contraband among his belongings. Bernice had been through all this before with him. But he was in Africa now, and the stakes were different. This time Bernice couldn't simply post bail and move him elsewhere. The officers placed him under arrest and continued sifting through the apartment, finding items that didn't fit with his past life: a military uniform and radio handset.[13]

The incident forced Charles Taylor to bring his son to Liberia despite the dangers. There was no functioning government in place, only an interim group of leaders cobbled together by the regional powers. By June 1994, peace talks among the three major rebels groups had broken down, devolving into skirmishes around the countryside as the factions regrouped and rearmed.[14] The humanitarian situation grew bleaker as more than one million residents crowded into Monrovia, which had been a city of 300,000 just four years earlier. The U.S. government had given more than $326 million in relief, attempting to stave off disaster, while West African nations, including Nigeria, Guinea, and Sierra Leone, poured in military support, from ground troops to fighter-bombers, to prevent the conflict from breaching the borders and destabilizing surrounding countries.[15]

The armed intervention did little to stem Taylor's ambitions. The rebel leader often found himself outgunned and politically isolated, but he defended the territory he had gained in Liberia's hinterland by striking alliances and sponsoring rebel groups in his neighbors' countries.[16] Taylor was developing a strategy that acknowledged the limitations of his military strength. The ill-disciplined and perpetual attenuation of his forces meant he could not muster a reliable border defense force. Instead he found that if he could bedevil his regional rivals with shadowy guerrilla attacks and campaigns of terror, they would be less capable of putting pressure on him.

Chucky was receiving an on-the-ground education in West African politics simply by watching his father. He appeared at events and conferences alongside Taylor, looking sheepish and uncomfortable in a suit and tie. He opened a window into this world to Lynn, in a letter drafted on four sheets ripped from a legal pad.[17] He had disappeared from Orlando without telling anyone, including her. It had been a silent, jarring conclusion to her first real romance. Her parents saw Chucky's departure as a positive development, but Lynn couldn't help but feel a small measure of heartbreak. As quickly as he had appeared, he was gone, and she had no way to reach him.

"Surprise," Chucky's letter began, "it's me the one you forgot about Chucky." He offered no apology for disappearing, only a convoluted explanation:

> if somebody could stand all the bullshit i dished out, then i think i will try my hardest to stay with that person.

Lynn, you have to realize it will be a long time before we see each other, he wrote.

> I'm in a place called Gbarnga, Bong County Liberia on the West African side of the continent. It's hard to explain the situation over here.

Chucky embellished on his experience in Accra, placing himself at the center of the political situation:

> I was in Ghana, not no more yea muthafuckers for no reason arrested me a locked my ass up for 5 days not knowing it was a plot to kill me for political reasons. When they set me free I bounced by the time I got to my father it was all over the world, B.B.C. . . . V.O.A. . . . I guess they thought I wanted to over through [sic] the country.

The letter can be read as the swagger typical of a teenage boy trying to impress a girl. But it also reflects Chucky's new view of himself as a central figure in the events around him. The letter went on to describe the civil war, the convoluted set of factions, and where he fit within all of it: "N.P.F.L. is our organization they brought the revolution 1989 December 25th . . . it's a complex issue that needs a lot of research. . . . Look up L.I.B.E.R.I.A., and N.P.F.L leader Charles Ghankay Taylor my father," Chucky continued. "It will shed light on what the fuck I'm going through."

"Everybody is scared of my father," Chucky wrote. "They say he wants to de-stabilize the whole of West Africa."

West Africa was already destabilized. The region had evolved from early-twentieth-century colonialism to authoritarianism in the 1960s and 1970s and then to the revolutions of the 1980s. The groundwork had been laid for the 1990s, as Ghanaian political scientist Eboe Hutchful put it, to become "a decade of subaltern revolt."[18] It was the politically dispossessed—in particular, the youth—in nations like Liberia and Sierra Leone who gave force to revolutionary politics that found little traction in other African nations like Ghana.

The violence was also unique to the era. Though regional conflicts had raged throughout the decade, there was a glaring paradox to the fighting in West Africa: the near complete absence of international war coupled with the fundamental lack of domestic peace.[19] Arie M. Kacowicz, an international relations scholar, referred to this condition as "negative peace." Cross-border conflict did occur, but it was not easily distinguished from indigenous conflicts. What dominated was a brand of civil war and "subaltern revolt" that did not take hold throughout the region and had limited geopolitical relevance. As horrifying as the fighting driven by leaders like Charles Taylor and Sierra Leone's Foday Sankoh was, it was spurred only by domestic ambitions.

While the war in Liberia had placed his father on the political map of West Africa, Chucky began to receive attention of his own. Soon after his arrest in Accra, the U.S. embassy began reporting on him, but with few details. "Taylor has a son, 'Chucky, Junior,' who is 19–20 years old we believe by an American citizen who is now resident in Florida," a June 1995 cable from the U.S. embassy in Monrovia to Ouagadougou explained.[20] This was the first mention of Chucky by the State Department, a single reference tucked at the end of a three-page cable entitled "Taylor's Domestic Affairs," which detailed the status and background of the NPFL leader's wives, children, and grandchildren.

On Chucky, the U.S. embassy had little to report other than the Accra incident, elaborating slightly on the political backdrop: "The story here is that he was subsequently released after the intervention of Rawling's associate. . . . Chuckie [*sic*] Junior then apparently saw the attraction of a month's sojourn in Gbarnga."

That "sojourn" lasted much longer than the month the embassy reported. Once Chucky arrived in West Africa, his father struggled to not only control his son's behavior but also to mitigate the embarrassment he could cause. In the fraught political environment, Chucky's behavior threatened to complicate Charles's already tenuous relationships between leaders—in Ghana, his activities had drawn the attention not only of local authorities but also of the country's leadership. Taylor had dealt with disobedient soldiers, traitorous commanders, and double-crossing foreign governments, but the insouciance of his teenage son was a new challenge for him.

Despite the chaos in Liberia, Chucky's father was intent on his completing high school. Taylor placed his son in Cuttington University, an Episcopal college founded in 1889 that was not far from the NPFL headquarters.[21] The school had educated members of the political class for more than a century, but the campus became a battlefield that year. A joint attack in September 1994 conducted by ECOMOG, the peacekeeping force, and two rival factions flushed Taylor and his forces from his stronghold, temporarily pushing the NPFL into disarray; rebels took over the school's campus.[22] Charles Taylor's militias eventually retook Gbarnga, and while fighting persisted throughout Liberia, Taylor maintained reliable control over the center of the country.

But that control was fiercely contested, and it wasn't long before Chucky was again caught in the crossfire. On November 6, 1995, forces from Alhaji Kromah's largely Mandingo and Krahn militia attacked Gbarnga while Chucky was staying with his father. The assault came in three waves, the last hitting Taylor's stronghold at two a.m.[23] If the compound was overrun and Chucky was captured, he could expect no mercy from his father's enemies. As the fighting raged, Chucky snapped a photograph of one of his guards crouching in olive fatigues and a ballistic vest, clutching an AK-47, a cigarette dangling from his lips, wearing a sly smile.

The attack illustrated the paradox of Bernice's choice. She had traded the dangers of life on the streets of Orlando—and potentially in prison—for those of Liberia's civil war. Chucky, for his part, had not completely abandoned his Americanness. When he wasn't appearing publicly with his father, he dressed like a gangsta, twisting his hair into cornrows, carrying a red bandanna, and wearing sparkling Nikes. Before long he found access to guns, sporting body armor and a pistol. He nonetheless made some effort to fit in by learning to affect Liberian English, the distinct English creole spoken in the country, often in addition to one or more tribal languages. Like Trinidadian English, which Chucky grew up hearing, the Liberian vernacular shared much vocabulary with American English, but the grammar, syntax, and pronunciation were fundamentally different: syllables dropped off of the end of words; the phrase *a little bit* became *small-small*, and *bribe* or *payment* became *white heart* or *cold water*. There were also highly formal remnants of late-nineteenth-century American English: things were not *weird* or *strange*, they were *peculiar*; people were not *beaten* or *assaulted*—they were *flogged* or *abused*. Mastering the language was important, not just to blend in but also to be intelligible to Liberians who had little exposure to the dialect of American English that Chucky spoke.

But Chucky also began to adopt another, more select vernacular: his father's distinct brand of warlordese. Charles Taylor had a gift for oration that few warlords in Liberia shared. His chief adversaries, Alhaji Kromah and George Boley, rivaled his intellect and education but not his charm or self-awareness. Kromah was a former journalist and professor with a power base in the predominantly Muslim Mandingo community; Boley, a member of the Krahn tribe, like Taylor had been educated in the United States and returned to Liberia as a bureaucrat. Each man had emerged as the leader of a faction that competed against Taylor for power: Kromah with United Liberation Movement of Liberia for Democracy, and Boley with the Liberia Peace Council. Taylor could harangue these enemies over radio broadcasts throughout his territory, then shift to the coded language of peace and stability at negotiations with emissaries and diplomats.[24] He considered himself a revolutionary, but publicly he held himself accountable to the law—

reminding interlocutors when necessary that his struggle was for elections and the sanctity of the Liberian constitution. He promised that if
the people voted against him in an election, "we will surrender to their
will."[25] It was an unbelievable statement from a man who had overtaken
much of the nation by force. Taylor had grown enormously wealthy and
powerful in the absence of elections. Like the man he had launched his
revolution to depose, he wanted only an election he would win.

Eight years into the war, in 1997, Taylor finally achieved the nominal
purpose of his revolution: to conduct a democratic election. The goal
had seemed laudable in 1985, when General Quiwonkpa stormed over
the border a month after Samuel Doe rigged the polls and stole the
presidency, or even four years later, when Charles Taylor appeared in
the bush as the new standard-bearer of Quiwonkpa's revolution. But
the path to the polls had been costly for Liberians. Conservative estimates placed the loss of life at 80,000, while the United Nations offered
a broader estimate of 150,000 to 250,000 dead.[26] Few survived without
suffering. Of Liberia's 2.3 million people, nearly one-third had fled the
country for refuge, while 1.8 million had been displaced. The conflict
had metastasized to nearly a half-dozen factions and subfactions fighting for dominance, while Liberia's interim governments failed to secure
anything approaching a monopoly on the use of force within its borders.
Corruption, looting, and war profiteering among the Nigerian-backed
peacekeeping forces only served to aggravate the conflict. Between
1990 and 1995, the combatants entered into ten separate peace agreements. The latest peace accord, the Abuja Agreement signed in August
1995, laid out a timetable for a cease-fire and demobilization program
that would lead into elections. During that interim period, a five-
member Council of State, a temporary ruling body meant to act as an
executive branch representing all parties to the conflict, would govern
the nation. The council had little mandate beyond holding the country
together through the cease-fire and disarmament process leading into
elections. Liberians danced in the streets to celebrate the inauguration
of the council as a harbinger of the official end of the civil war, but the
animus among warlords remained.

By October 1996, Chucky had moved with his father to the capital
in preparation for the election. Charles Taylor had finally reached the

Executive Mansion, but not on the terms he would have liked. Total control of the country still eluded him. He and five others—including politicians and his warlord rivals—had been chosen as members of the Council of State. The council was, effectively, a political Band-Aid, which the African powers prayed would not come off prior to the election scheduled for the summer of 1997. Taylor was assigned an office on the building's sixth floor.[27]

Despite the cease-fire instituted at Abuja, the capital remained tense in October. Months earlier the city had erupted in a spasm of violence between Taylor's forces and rival factions, referred to as the "April 6" war. The battle had left its mark throughout the capital and prompted the evacuation of the U.S. embassy. While Charles Taylor referred to the event as only a "fracas," it had in fact been a humanitarian disaster that stunned the international community.[28] More than half of the city's 850,000 residents fled during the fighting, 3,000 people were killed over the course of one month, and thousands evacuated the country.

After the fighting wound down, the African peacekeeping force fanned out into the countryside to begin the delicate process of disarming the factions. It had little success, as the factions opted to hide their weapons rather than turn them over.[29] Liberia's experiment in power sharing had failed to stop the violence completely, but two of the most powerful faction leaders, Taylor and Alhaji Kromah, remained willing to stake their political futures on elections and hoped that they could persuade their militias to stand down.

Once Chucky moved to the capital with his father, he could no longer attend school at Cuttington. Taylor enrolled him at the College of West Africa, Monrovia's top private high school.[30] CWA, as students called it, was not a college but the nation's oldest and most prestigious high school. It had been founded in 1839, eight years before Liberia declared its nationhood. The building stood on Ashmun Street, at the edge of a bluff overlooking Providence Island, where Liberia's American settlers first encamped, and the green estuaries threaded into the Mesurado River. The school had educated presidents, chief justices, and leaders of industry. It was a fitting choice for the son of the political leader widely viewed as the most powerful man in Liberia. Whether it could educate a child with a past as troubled as Chucky's was a separate question. At first glance Chucky was indistinguishable from many of the boy students arriving at school in pressed white short-sleeve oxfords and navy pants. Many who met him saw a natural intellect and curiosity. His father hoped he would focus and finally complete his education in Monrovia.

Up until that point, Chucky had never lived in Monrovia. The capital was significantly smaller than Orlando, or Accra for that matter, but compared to Gbarnga, it was a metropolis. At that time the city was a battle zone gone quiet. "In town," as Liberians refer to the city's central business district, bullet holes and blast burns decorated government buildings, many of which remained windowless and without power. Though the streets were paved, mounds of trash piled up along the gutters, rotting in the sun. Throughout the capital, residents were required to pass through barbed-wire and sandbagged checkpoints manned by peacekeeping soldiers who peered through makeshift fortifications, machine guns trained on the horizon. The family moved into a large home near the U.S. embassy in the Mamba Point neighborhood.[31] It was the city's most cloistered community, set out on a peninsula and divided from downtown by Monrovia's highest hilltop.

Even as he arrived in the nation's capital with his father, Chucky's thoughts drifted back home to Orlando. He would disappear into his father's office and use his satellite phone to dial the United States, often calling Lynn.[32] Though they hadn't seen each other for nearly two years, she still considered it a long-distance relationship. Her life had changed significantly since Chucky fled Orlando: her relationship with her parents had become strained, and she had left home to finish high school, attending the public Clarkstown South High School in West Nyack, New York. Their opinion of Chucky had not changed—Lynn later recalled that her mother would make a "Korean sound of disgust" at the mention of his name—and they didn't support her continued interest in a boy whom it seemed unlikely she'd ever see again.

The secret phone calls continued for months. As complex as the circumstances surrounding their relationship were, for Lynn it was simple: they were high school sweethearts. Like any other teens, the hours they spent on the phone together disappeared. "I don't know what we would talk about," she said.

There was one topic they would always return to: when they could finally see each other again. Returning to the States was not an option for Chucky. The charges in Orlando continued to hang over his head.

Lynn was focused on finishing high school—a trip to Africa seemed beyond the realm of possibility. And Monrovia, as much of an improvement as it was on Gbarnga, was far from the ideal backdrop for daydreams of their reunion.

Chucky faced his own challenge of fitting into a decidedly foreign environment. When he first arrived at CWA, the other students couldn't help but notice him. It wasn't simply his uncanny resemblance to his father or the fact that at nearly twenty, he was only entering the eleventh grade: unlike any of the other students, he arrived on campus with an armed security detail in tow.[33]

Since his son had been in Liberia, Taylor had posted one of his personal security guards to him. In many cases, these minders weren't fighters but rather old-timers whom Chucky was less likely to order around, such as a jaundiced man in his forties named Ceasley Roberts or simply CR.[34] He was a civilian, but he was always armed with a pistol. The guard and his weapon were not welcome at CWA, though the school administration could do little to forbid it. Taylor's concerns for his son's safety were inarguable, yet even in Monrovia, the presence of an armed figure in the classroom was disruptive.

One day at school a classmate pointed this out. "Why do you have to bring your security on campus?" the student asked.

This may have been an innocent question, but Chucky didn't interpret it that way. He was the new kid at a new school—this might be a challenge to test him. Long before arriving in Liberia, he had had experience in tough neighborhoods where backing down from confrontations wasn't an option. But politics also shaped his actions: his father was among the most feared men in the nation, and this high school student was taking a warlord's son to task in public. Chucky's response would reflect on his father, whether he shrank from the challenge or confronted it.

"None of your business," he shot back, slapping the student across the face.

The administration immediately suspended Chucky. Typically students faced expulsion for fighting, but the school hesitated to go that far with Chucky. There was an inherent risk in confronting Taylor about the behavior of his child. Instead, the administration sent him a form letter detailing the incident, explaining that his son would be allowed to return to school after his suspension. Chucky's father did not take issue with the suspension. In fact, the principal recalled, "he welcomed it." The administrators were relieved that they hadn't provoked Taylor. As for Chucky, the principal said, "he never came back."

Indeed, Chucky would never go to school again. He was restless to return to Orlando, though the possibility of doing so remained remote. He eventually called Lynn with an offer: he would fly her to visit him in Liberia.[35] She was only seventeen and had never traveled farther than the Caribbean, but there was nothing stopping her. Monrovia was a world unknown to her, while Chucky was only beginning to find his place there.

On the morning of Halloween 1996, Charles Taylor stepped out of his residence in Mamba Point to his waiting motorcade.[36] The Council of State was set to meet later that morning, and he intended to arrive at his office in time to put in a few hours of work. As he prepared to depart, he noticed within the assembled convoy an armored Peugeot that he'd been given as a gift. The vehicle was designed for the charge to ride in the front, while the bodyguards sat in the rear, positioned to return fire in the event of an attack.

"Listen," he told his driver, "I want to ride the Peugeot today because we haven't been using it."

Taylor's aide-de-camp, Gen. Jackson Mani, a Gambian dressed in full military uniform, climbed into the rear, and the convoy set off toward the Executive Mansion, a secured area controlled by African peacekeepers. Any outside security forces entering the compound were required to surrender their weapons. After Doe's capture and murder, which had taken place directly under the nose of the Nigerian peacekeepers, the members of the council had reason to be wary of this protocol but complied nonetheless.

That morning Taylor's convoy was tracked from the moment it pulled onto the mansion's grounds. Assassins perched on the sixth floor watched his Peugeot drive up to the building's entrance as they prepared their assault. Taylor and several members of his entourage, including General Mani, entered the building and rode the elevator to Taylor's office.

The moment the elevator's doors opened, the group was met with an explosion. Gunfire rattled through the hallways as Mani shoved Taylor into a nearby doorway. Unarmed, the rest of the entourage fled in panic. Several were cut down by the gunfire. Others leaped the six stories to the pavement below, the impact snapping their legs. Taylor found himself in a bathroom, hiding inside a bathtub. He watched through the doorway as the gunmen descended on the general and opened fire, killing him.

By the time Taylor's security forces fought their way into the mansion to rescue him, five members of the entourage had been killed. The assassins had disappeared. The security forces found Taylor, holding a rifle, escorting a wounded Nigerian peacekeeper off the floor.

While there had been several attempts on Taylor's life, none had come so close to achieving its aim. Taylor believed he had survived only because the assassins had mistaken General Mani, who had departed the backseat of the Peugeot, for their target. Rattled but otherwise unharmed, Taylor drove directly to a nearby radio station to assure his followers that he was alive.

The incident effectively put an end to the Council of State experiment. The group would never again convene at the mansion. Taylor suspected that George Boley, the leader of one the rival Krahn faction, was responsible. (Nearly fifteen years later American officials seeking to deport him from the United States would accuse Boley of General Mani's killing in an American immigration court.[37] At the time, however, the U.S. embassy suspected Alhaji Kromah.) The identity mattered little. Taylor could never feel safe with any power achieved through compromise.

The attack also had implications for Chucky. If his father were killed and his security forces crumbled or defected, he too could be targeted. He drew his own lesson from the attack: the old-guard NPFL security forces were not up to the task of protecting his father. After eight years of fighting, more than a dozen peace accords, and the mantle of legitimacy that the Council of State provided, his father's security detail appeared to have gone soft.

"A lot of those guys I see around my father they smile too much," he observed to his uncle Cindor Reeves.[38] "I've been thinking that I want to organize a group that would be really mean."

Facing an indefinite future in Liberia, he looked to place himself within the closest ring of his father's power. The stakes were different from anything he had previously known. The United States, and even

Ghana, had rule of law; for the juvenile delinquent Chucky, that meant a navigable world of bail, court dates, and maybe jail time. Liberia had nothing resembling that. The only law was power, and the terms were simple: life and death. The only fact working in Chucky's favor was that Charles Taylor remained the most powerful man in the country.

"I will speak to my father," Chucky told his uncle.

In 1997 Monrovia was not the expected backdrop for a teenage romance. When Lynn arrived there, at the beginning of the rainy season in early summer, she'd graduated from high school only weeks earlier.[39] Unlike her friends, she wasn't searching out a summer job or preparing for college. She was acting on her feelings, which led her to a country that had little to offer her other than the boy with whom she'd fallen in love. Chucky's mother and his half sister Maisha flew with her, acting as escorts on the array of connecting flights that linked Orlando and Robertsfield. Knowing that Chucky would be meeting her when she landed, Lynn was more excited than afraid. She had spent hours on the phone with him planning for this moment. Finally, with her parents' reluctant blessing, it was happening.

"I should've started college," she later recalled, shaking her head. "But I didn't because I wanted to go to Africa."

When she finally arrived, Chucky seemed much as she remembered him, though more a man than the boy from Orlando. Then as he addressed someone in passing, she noticed him speaking with a strange accent. This was Liberian English.

As happy as she was, she was unprepared for the harsh reality of Monrovia. By American standards, the capital was a city only in name. "There was no running water, no electricity," she recalled. "They had just gotten out of war."

Chucky had moved into his own place, a modest home set down a hillside behind White Flower, the mansion his father had settled in, along one of Monrovia's main thoroughfares. When Lynn arrived at the house, she learned that she would be bathing out of a bucket, as much of the country did. There was no functioning municipal plumbing system; the hydroelectric plant outside Monrovia had been sacked and disabled; basic utilities that much of the world took for granted had to be created ad hoc. Fresh water had to be trucked in. Even Charles

Taylor relied on a generator to provide power to his home. Despite all this, Chucky was, by any comparison, privileged.

The prospect of meeting Chucky's father made Lynn nervous. She wasn't concerned about Charles Taylor, the warlord-turned-president; she worried about how the African father of her boyfriend would view a girl of Asian descent. She also knew that Chucky and his father had clashed at times. "It was always a strange relationship," she said. "He knew his dad loved him, and he knew he loved his dad. But his dad was really unemotional." She also knew that many people feared Charles Taylor.

She finally met Taylor at White Flower, the sprawling residence he'd taken up in Congo Town, an oceanfront neighborhood several miles south of the city center. White Flower was an apt image of power in a country like Liberia. On Tubman Boulevard, one of the city's main arteries, in a neighborhood several miles from downtown Monrovia, the building could be mistaken for a warehouse by passersby. The windowless concrete two-story facade hid the luxurious home inside. The building beveled down the hillside in a series of levels that terminated with an outdoor tennis court where Taylor liked to challenge visitors to matches. The interior reflected Taylor's love for the garish. "*House* is not the right word, for with its opulent furnishings—expensive carpets, oil paintings, sculptures, and other objets d'art—*palace* is a more apt term," wrote an American diplomat who visited shortly after the election.[40]

Taylor met his son's girlfriend with his famous charm: he was warm and articulate, immediately putting her at ease. "He welcomed me to his country. He was very good to me," Lynn said. As to her ethnicity, she said, "he wasn't embarrassed."

Monrovia had entered in the final stages of the presidential campaign when she arrived. The war had dragged on for so long, it was easy to forget that elections were what all the fighting had been about in the first place. Whatever hope Liberians carried with them into the 1997 elections had been tempered by the fear that Liberia could not exist in anything other than a permanent state of war.

But for a society weary of broken peace accords, the path to the polls was laid out clearly. The August 1995 agreement negotiated in Abuja had called for a series of milestones: disarmament in January 1997, voter registration throughout the dry season, and finally an election in May.[41] When Lynn arrived, the timetable had been pushed toward a July poll date, but Chucky's father's campaign was fully operational. Among the twelve candidates—including his warlord rivals, George Boley and Alhaji Kromah, and exiled opposition figures like Ellen Johnson Sirleaf—Taylor remained the favorite.[42]

Taylor's popularity as a candidate perplexed Western observers. Much journalistic hash has been made of a popular chant among Taylor's followers: "He killed my ma, he killed my pa, I will vote for him." This was interpreted to mean that the electorate was fearful he would reignite the civil war if he lost the election. But Taylor didn't rely on his reputation as a warlord; unlike his competitors, he made the transition from warlord to candidate relatively smoothly.[43] He was able to transform his armed faction into something resembling a political machine. His radio station, KISS-FM, dominated the media in the country, and despite his well-documented brutality as a warlord, the station ably amplified his credentials as a liberator and the administrator of Taylorland during the war's early years. His party distributed bags of rice emblazoned with slogans. Taylor's teenage daughters, Charen and Charlyne, even stumped for their father, proudly wearing T-shirts and hats that bore his photo and National Patriotic Party slogan "Vote NPP!" It made things easier that Taylor's opposition was fractured and ineffective.

Soon after Lynn arrived, Liberians went to the polls for the first time in twelve years. Around the country, civilians trudged to voting centers under bright clear skies. More than five hundred international observers oversaw the process—including former president Jimmy Carter, whose democracy organization, the Carter Center, later judged the proceedings to be "a uniformly excellent election process."[44] There had been irregularities, but none were significant enough to obviate the result: Taylor won 75 percent of the vote.

For critics, the vote didn't reflect the will of the Liberian people so much as the recognition of who—among the candidates—truly held the power in the country. As one commentator wrote, "Taylor's overwhelming victory most likely derived from a heady brew of electoral rules and irregularities, a huge campaign, a backbone of support, a divided and weak opposition, and his apparent dominance over the security question."[45]

The day after the election Howard Jeter, a Clinton administration envoy and the chief of mission at the U.S. embassy, visited Taylor at White Flower.[46] The American delegation walked into the middle of a party, where sixteen members of Taylor's entourage surrounded the president-elect, sipping champagne. Taylor welcomed them in a "natty 'swearing-in suit,' " greeting each man and boasting that he'd won even within the ethnic strongholds of his chief rivals.

Taylor and his followers were ecstatic at the result, but the U.S. government was in a tough position. Its distanced approach to the crisis had resulted in a semblance of stability and political process but not a desirable outcome. After making elections its continuous diplomatic refrain for more than fifteen years, Washington would now have to live with the Liberians' choice. Taylor made it clear that he intended to use the mandate to seek the sort of economic assistance his predecessors had enjoyed. Despite Liberia's desperate need, officials in the Monrovia embassy knew that Washington was not planning on rewarding Taylor's victory with increased aid.

Taylor likely understood this, so he issued a warning. "If Liberia does not get international economic assistance quickly, it will descend into chaos," he told the diplomats. He pressed for a state visit to Washington, and briefly the Monrovia embassy advocated his position—even receiving assurances from the Department of Justice that Taylor faced no actions related to his escape from Plymouth twelve years earlier. When it became clear that local authorities in Massachusetts would offer no such guarantees, however, the new president scrapped the request.

But for a moment, Monrovia seemed euphoric.[47] Chucky and Lynn drove through the city in awe of the adoring crowds lining the streets, celebrating his father's victory. The long war had yielded not only the office Taylor desired but also his legitimacy as a politician. His inauguration conjured a splendor that many Monrovians had long forgotten. Heads of state from Nigeria and Ghana traveled to the broken capital to see Taylor take the oath of office. He stood at the lectern clad in immaculate white flowing robes, a matching skullcap sitting atop his head.

"We are one people, one blood, one nation, with one common destiny indivisible by God," he told the crowd. "Let us never, ever permit ourselves to be divided again by anyone, either from within or from without."[48] It was a remarkable statement from a man who had fash-

ioned his career around exploiting the divisions within Liberian society. His regalia and oratory played to his indigenous audience, but his
enemies and critics saw him not only as a warlord but also as the con-
tinuance of the tradition of rule by the Congo elite that had been inter-
rupted by Samuel Doe. For all the bloodshed, the nation was stepping
backward to the settler hegemony.

Taylor's victory meant a personal victory for Lynn. Her parents
looked at Chucky differently now, and Lynn was grateful to be with
the man she loved, halfway across the world, without feeling the disap-
proval of her family. Although they were still very young, life seemed to
be taking shape. The war was over, and Chucky had the sort of vague,
hopeful plans for their future expected of a young man his age. The difference was that he had the opportunity to bring his ideas to life. The
couple celebrated Lynn's birthday in Monrovia in late summer, when
she turned eighteen.

Chucky introduced Lynn to his extended family in the capital.
Charles Taylor had nine children—by several wives—including a
younger son, Philip, with whom Lynn would eventually become very
close. With such a large crowd, much of the socializing occurred
at White Flower, where Taylor lived and also conducted his official
business.

Oftentimes the women and children would spend their days there
waiting for their moment with the new president. Taylor's daughters,
from his wives Tupee and Agnes, adored him, and he did not spare them
affection or generosity.[49] But outside the occasional birthday party, the
family didn't sit for daily meals or meetings.[50] If anything, Charles Taylor typically ate upstairs in his meeting room, alone or with the small
children, rather than with his wives and girlfriends.

One thing that struck Lynn was the absence of animosity or jeal-
ousy among Taylor's women. Despite their shared histories with this
man, they seemed to get along fine. "They would just all vie for his
attention, so whenever you could get to him was when you would get
to him," she said. "It wasn't a typical family environment."

Meanwhile the distance between Taylor and Chucky was palpable;
they rarely ate together or spent time together outside official functions. "[Chucky] always felt that he had to always impress him, you
know, or make him proud," Lynn said. He would talk to Lynn constantly about his father; he confided in her his fear that his father didn't

love him. But as Lynn began to spend more time with Taylor, she saw how he felt about his firstborn son.

Chucky's growing interest in his father's affairs dovetailed with Taylor's primary concern as a new president: his personal security. National security remained an important but secondary consideration. The existing government forces were structured accordingly. When Taylor came into office, he had an array of security forces at his disposal: the Special Security Service (SSS), the Special Operations Division (SOD), the Liberian National Police (LNP), and the Armed Forces of Liberia (AFL). These forces remained riddled with members of rival factions and vestiges of Doe's regime. Taylor had reason to view them as a threat.

Even the fighters who had helped bring Taylor to power posed a lingering danger. Many had put down their weapons to campaign for him, and after he won the election, they flooded the capital seeking their reward. Liberia had nearly $3 billion in external debt and only $25,000 in the bank.[51] Taylor knew that if he didn't pay his fighters, they would find a way to pay themselves. With such an unruly crowd, his personnel issues held a unique potential for disaster, a fact highlighted in an incident soon after the election, when one of Taylor's SSS commanders, a former NPFL executioner named Jack the Rebel, pulled a gun on the foreign minister's brother.[52] This wasn't a case of wartime rivals settling a score but rather a far more banal conflict: as the embassy reported, it was "either an armed robbery, or a drug deal gone bad."

With the chaos of war so recent, Chucky shared his father's concerns about safety. He viewed the men surrounding his father with suspicion, including the security officers charged with protecting him. But Chucky was at a distinct disadvantage among this crowd. While he was the president's kin, some of Taylor's most loyal fighters—like Benjamin Yeaten, who had followed him to Libya as a young recruit and become a feared rebel fighter—shared bonds that father and son did not: those forged through the crucible of the revolution.[53]

Chucky appeared to have no interest in working under the authority of anyone else. Instead he sought his father's approval to create a dedicated force, one unattached to the civil war and independent of the Liberian state—a force that would serve the sole purpose of protecting his father's power.

6

Gbatala

Frontline all the time, pain of my mind, documentated in the
book of life, Jah knows, try to keep a steady dome.

— *United States vs. Belfast*, EXHIBIT CE-4

On the evening of March 23, 1998,[1] President Clinton picked up the
phone aboard *Air Force One*. Clinton was two days into a ten-day presidential visit to Africa, the first of its kind in nearly twenty years, that
would take him to six nations. He had been greeted by an estimated
crowd of half a million in Ghana's capital, then proceeded on to Kam-
pala and meetings with the leaders of nine nations. Unlike similar trips
taken by Presidents Jimmy Carter and Franklin D. Roosevelt, Liberia
was not a destination. Charles Taylor would have to settle for a twelve-
minute phone call.

"Hello, President Clinton. How do you do?" Taylor asked when
connected to the U.S. president.

"President Taylor, how are you? It's nice to hear your voice."

The men shared little in common. They were both heads of state,
but each was the product of fundamentally different politics. Taylor was
a warlord who had induced his own election through revolution, a facet
of his political trajectory that he described to Clinton as "unfortunate."

At that moment, the U.S. government was hedging its bets with
Taylor. The Clinton administration hoped he could pivot from being
an "unrepentant but legitimized factional leader," as Secretary of State
Madeleine Albright wrote, to a true national leader.[2] A few months earlier U.S. policy on Liberia had formed with two objectives: encourag-

ing domestic reforms and discouraging foreign interference.[3] The latter became a focus of the first conversation between Presidents Clinton and Taylor: the Liberian leader's continued involvement in Sierra Leone.

After seemingly endless cycles of atrocities in Sierra Leone, the violence had become politically difficult for the Clinton administration, which had sat largely idle during the Rwandan genocide just four years earlier. The bloodshed in Sierra Leone culminated in February 1998, when Nigerian peacekeepers ousted the rebel government and reinstalled President Ahmed Kabbah. The junta leaders, not surprisingly, almost immediately fled to Monrovia. Taylor had long been viewed as the primary agent driving the violence. Washington understood this but also felt he might be able to help end the violence. President Clinton had appointed Reverend Jesse Jackson as a special envoy on the issue; in the background, the U.S. military staged Special Operations forces in Freetown, Sierra Leone.[4]

For months prior to the call, American diplomats had met Liberian officials and President Taylor to discuss concerns regarding human rights, freedom of the press, and Liberia's ambitions in Sierra Leone. Reporting by the State Department indicated that Taylor was receiving weapons shipments from Taiwan and had also been involved in the assassination of a political opponent, Samuel Dokie.

Yet Clinton told Taylor he was "very pleased" with his progress on human rights, even saying, "Some of the difficulties we had in the last few years have probably been our fault as well."

Clinton did not accuse Taylor of supporting the rebels in Sierra Leone. But he made clear where the Liberian leader fit within the crisis. "You can be of particular assistance in building the relationship with the Revolutionary United Front and urging all factions to disarm and demobilize in a peaceful way," he said.

Taylor listened as the president worked through his talking points. It was a softened reiteration of the message that the Liberians had received from State Department officials just days earlier.[5] But Taylor didn't let the world's most powerful leader off the phone without making his own request, as outlandish as it might have been.

"I'd like to get your assistance in the military situation here, training our army and helping train our police force," Taylor asked.

President Clinton parried the request. But it didn't matter: Charles Taylor had his own plans for reclaiming his military might.

.   .   .

Gbatala is a tiny quarry village along the Kakata Highway, three-quarters the distance from Monrovia to Gbarnga. The name, which means "near the creek Gba" in the Kpelle language, is pronounced BAH (and is not to be confused with Gbalatuah, the stopover along the St. Paul River). The village appears first as a collection of tin-roofed market shacks with hand-painted signs hugging the roadway. A hundred meters above the roadway, past a stand of narrow trees, sits the Gbatala homestead: a huddle of gray zinc huts clustered around a thatch-roofed A-frame palm-leaf shelter that serves as the community kitchen. A bush path overgrown with yawning green leaves and hibiscus flowers leads up a rocky hillside to a shaded overlook, revealing an unobstructed view of the roadway below. Farther on up the hillside looms a tall, granite cliff where the locals—men, women, and children—take part in the local industry: rock breaking. Overgrown and largely abandoned during the early stages of Taylor's revolution, the central but isolated overlook was once called Cobra Base.

It was on this vacant span of rocks that Chucky would make his imprint on Liberian history. Charles Taylor handed this location over to his son to fashion a training camp for what he hoped would become a new elite security force. Years earlier in the midst of the civil war, at a moment when Nigerian Alpha jets were targeting Taylor's other encampments, Taylor's forces had decamped to the quarry.[6] Gbatala was isolated and relatively secure, and importantly, it sat in the Taylor heartland. The Gbatala locals belonged to the Kpelle tribe, traditional supporters of Taylor, who could be counted on to not betray the base's existence. The location was also proximate to Taylor's headquarters a short distance up the highway at the nearby Center for Agriculture Research Institute, yet it was concealed enough to not draw attention from enemy forces passing along the highway or from the jets searching out targets.

In the mid-1990s Taylor's fighters began training at the base—not only Liberians but also Sierra Leoneans enlisted by the warlord to fight a proxy war in their homeland.[7] The fighting in both conflicts ebbed and flowed for nearly a decade before Taylor ascended to the presidency. For a time Cobra Base was left to the elements, a clandestine artifact of Taylorland that had no apparent use to Charles Taylor's new government in Monrovia. But when Chucky set to the task of creating a new unit, the site was selected as the ideal location.

When Chucky arrived there in 1998, Liberia was enjoying a degree of peace for the first time in several years. But peace did not mean security. President Taylor saw himself as surrounded by threats and living under the thumb of Nigeria, the regional power. Even after the election, Nigerian regional peacekeepers remained. This force was intended to act as a buffer between any armed groups that sprang out of the postwar chaos. Chucky's father remained bitterly at odds with the Nigerians, whom he viewed as an imperial power in West Africa. The Nigerians also played a significant military role in Sierra Leone, fighting the Taylor-backed RUF. Liberia's official military force, the Armed Forces of Liberia, presented another liability for Taylor: of the thirteen thousand soldiers who mustered following the election, more than half were untrained conscripts who had been brought in by President Doe to fight Taylor.[8] Taylor's victory at the polls hadn't converted his political rivals. Many of them were in exile in Guinea, Europe, and the United States. Forces within the scattered Liberian opposition began to galvanize behind a common goal: removing Taylor from power.

Taylor also had reason to be wary of external threats. Guinea, which boasted a large conventional military, was a largely Muslim nation with strong tribal ties to Liberia, including a significant population of Mandingos sympathetic to those marginalized by Taylor. Ivory Coast had its own fomenting tribal conflict that would lure fighters from Taylor's faction to attempt to depose that government. But Sierra Leone remained Taylor's chief regional adversary; and he remained deeply allied with the insurgent RUF and its leaders, Foday Sankoh and Sam Bockarie.

The idea of a new security force became common ground between Chucky and his father. Taylor felt the pressing need for a loyal presidential security detail. He could not trust this responsibility to any of the legacy security forces. Instead, he decided to build a new force, man by man. He consented to his son's involvement but did not entrust the task to him alone. Instead, to lead the effort, he chose someone who had been with him throughout the civil war, a mercenary known as Gambian Jacques.[9] Gambian fighters were a fixture of Taylor's inner circle—they were loyal to him rather than to a tribe or to the nation of Liberia. Many were holdovers from revolutionary camps in Libya, where Liberian rebels trained alongside counterparts from throughout

Africa. Chucky appeared to share one quality with men like this: he could be counted on for his loyalty.

The first task was recruitment. In 1997, after the election, a small group gathered at Chucky's house, near the KISS-FM radio station in Congo Town.[10] The men were Taylor loyalists, former fighters including Montgomery Dolo, Benny Warner, Eddie "Murphy" Karpolea, and Alex Voker, as well as a former commander of the Small Boys Unit named Zupon Johnson; the Small Boys Unit was a protective detail, comprised exclusively of children, that carried a reputation for brutality. Chucky hosted the inaugural meeting, but it was clear that Jacques was leading the effort. The men discussed how to go about forming a unit, deciding that they would need to proceed covertly. At that time, Liberia remained under a UN arms embargo, established by the Security Council in 1992 and held over from the civil war.[11] Any militarization that Taylor pursued would draw scrutiny from the Security Council and, potentially, sanctions.

Typical of the recruits was Christopher Menephar, a fifteen-year-old Kpelle boy from Yekepa, in Nimba County.[12] Few outside his family knew him by that name—since he was a child, he'd taken the nom de guerre "Cooper Teah," for a legendary commander from Taylor's militia who had fallen during the war. Menephar had been taken as a child soldier in the opening months of the war, when he was just seven years old, by a Taylor commander he could only identify as "Reagan." Eventually he was assigned to the Small Boys Unit. Separated from his parents and sisters, Menephar became a child of the war, finding a father figure in his commander and spending much of the fighting tasked to a BM-21, a Soviet-made forty-barrel truck-mounted multiple-rocket-launching system. After the war ended, he drifted back to his home village, where his one surviving parent welcomed him—his mother. There he received a letter asking him to join Chucky's unit. He had seen Chucky during the summer of 1992, though "he did not know me because I was a kid like him," Menephar recalled.

Menephar traveled to Monrovia and reported directly to Taylor's residence. Other former fighters had gathered outside the compound. Gambian Jacques scrutinized the recruits as they passed through the compound's entrance. Menephar recognized Chucky standing with him, no longer the boy he'd seen in Gbarnga five years earlier. Chucky now stood taller than his father. He was barrel-chested, with strong forearms and biceps. The recruits were processed individually; Jacques photographed them and asked a series of questions about their experiences during the war and their understanding of "VIP protection" and security issues. Chucky remained as this process inched forward. Menephar was only fifteen, but he had had experience with all these things.

Soon afterward Menephar received word that he had passed the first recruitment screening. Training would begin in July. Menephar and the other recruits were considered among the best of Taylor's forces, but in fact, by and large they were untrained fighters in their mid-teens to early twenties drawn from Taylor's NPFL or the Small Boys Unit. Many of the men were Kpelle, the tribe that Taylor continued to enjoy support from. In July the men would be returning to Taylorland, to Gbatala, in the heavily Kpelle Bong County. When Chucky arrived early in the spring of 1998, little or nothing remained of the former base; it was simply a rocky, barren hillside, a blank canvas.

From the safe remove of Chucky's house in the capital, Lynn watched him being swept up in creating the unit.[13] As a couple, they seemed to be growing up extraordinarily quickly. She had two lives: one in Orlando, where little had changed since she'd left for high school, and the other in Monrovia, where she and Chucky lived essentially as a married couple, albeit in the cloistered reality they were allowed to create. The days took on a familiar rhythm: they would wake up and eat a breakfast prepared by their cook, and he would head out for the day. She rarely accompanied him, spending much of her time with the cook.

Even as Lynn was being exposed to a remarkable new world, she began to catch glimmers of the reality under the surface. After the election, a circle of strange personalities began to surround Charles Taylor: former rebel commanders from his forces looking for official roles, the faithful party hacks seeking concessions from his newfound fortune, the foreign businessmen—Israelis, French, Russians, and Americans— looking to strike deals with the new head of state. Taylor did not discourage any of it. Liberia was finally open for business.

Taylor had experience working with organized crime from his time as a warlord. As early as 1992, he had forged an arms-for-diamonds network with international conflict profiteers.[14] According to the tran-

script of an interrogation with Italian investigators, an American named
Roger d'Onofrio Ruggerio had partnered with Taylor; so had Nicholas
Oman, a Slovenian-Australian arms trafficker; Ibrahim Bah, a former
mujahideen; and an Italian attorney, Michele Papa, in the benign-
sounding International Business Consult.[15] (None of the men would
be convicted for crimes related to Liberia.) According to *The Shadow
World* by Andrew Feinstein, the partnership opened a pipeline of weapons from Bulgarian manufacturers to West Africa, using a semilegiti-
mate trade in timber to mask some profits; later it would dissolve under
the scrutiny of international authorities.[16] The traditional weapons
pipeline into Liberia ran through Burkina Faso, where Taylor remained
closely allied with President Blaise Compaoré. At times during the civil
war, Qaddafi, who had built a massive arsenal of Soviet weaponry, provided arms directly to Taylor through Burkina Faso. Following the collapse of the Soviet Union, arms dealers from Eastern Europe began to
flood West Africa with weapons, replacing the quasi-official channels of
state-sponsored support with a robust black market. After the election,
Taylor faced the task of rebuilding his network.

One foreigner in particular began spending a noticeable amount of
time with the president, a man who went by the name of Dave Smith.[17]
He was white, in his forties, and much younger than many of the other
businessmen surrounding Taylor. Lynn presumed he was American—he
claimed to live in Boston—but he spoke with a "European accent."
Lynn knew that he had been introduced to Chucky through his father.
Beyond that, much of Smith's background remained a mystery. Even as
an admittedly naïve American teenager, the name "Dave Smith" didn't
strike her as a very inventive pseudonym.

"I thought he was CIA or ex-CIA," she said. She assumed, at first,
that he was there to monitor Taylor, to figure out his next move: Would
he assume the role of a statesman? Or would he prepare for the next
stage in the battle? Initially, she said, Chucky shared this view, but later
Chucky came to see Smith as a mentor. He portrayed himself as pos-
sessing a broad base of military knowledge—not the type Taylor's commanders had gleaned from fighting a bush war for more than a decade,
but a sophisticated understanding of intelligence and warfare.[18] This
was a world that Chucky had access to only through Hollywood action
movies and Tom Clancy novels. Smith taught Chucky the fundamentals of combat, how intelligence agencies like MI6 and the CIA oper-

ated, and how to correctly operate a firearm. He provided him with books on warfare and tactics. The two men also discussed the Geneva Conventions, the treatment of prisoners, and what qualified as torture.

Chucky had shown no interest in schooling, but when it came to security issues, he was a devoted student. "He was never in the military here. He was never militarily trained," Lynn said, but "he became more military-oriented."

One afternoon Smith arrived at the house to see Chucky. While Chucky kept him waiting, Smith and Lynn were alone. The scene was strange: an American girl barely out of high school waiting awkwardly with a middle-aged soldier of fortune. Despite the amount of time this man had been spending with her boyfriend, Lynn still had very little idea who Smith actually was. She had grown to doubt that he was CIA, given his involvement with Chucky—now she suspected that Smith was involved in trafficking weapons into Liberia.

Smith dropped his amiable facade when he found himself alone with Lynn. He asked her point-blank: "What are you doing here?"

The question caught Lynn by surprise. She didn't know how to respond. It was pretty clear to her why she was in Liberia, but she did not feel the need to justify it to a stranger, particularly in her boyfriend's home.

"You really shouldn't be here," he said. "You shouldn't be in Liberia. You shouldn't be mixed up with these people."

Lynn was taken aback. *These people?* Did he mean Charles Taylor? Chucky, a boy she had known since junior high? She felt she could rely on her own experience. The president she knew was a warm, fatherly figure—not the depraved warlord portrayed by his enemies. As for, Chucky—what could Smith know about him that she didn't?

She knew Chucky was surrounded by killers, but she believed he had never killed anyone. All she could think was: *What the hell is he talking about?*

There were aspects of Chucky and his father's lives that Lynn did not see, either willfully or because they kept her in relative isolation at Chucky's villa. But the fact was, Taylor's use of violence to maintain power had changed little since his warlord days. During his first year in power, his newly installed security forces were associated with robberies and killings.[19] Before long their crimes became difficult to conceal from the public. In one case, on June 28, 1998, a thirty-seven-year-old market woman disappeared in Paynesville, a suburb of Monrovia.[20] Local residents last saw her being led away by members of the president's Special Security Service, a unit commanded by Benjamin Yeaten, a loyal and notorious commander who had followed Taylor to Libya as a teenager and risen through the ranks during the civil war. Soon afterward the woman's remains were found, hastily buried behind her home. The U.S. embassy reported that "Mrs. Flomo's throat had been slit and her heart and breast had been removed in what was purportedly a spur-of-the moment ritualistic killing."

Hers was not an isolated case—nor was it distinct to Taylor's forces. Murders like this had long been shrouded in mystery, acts ascribed to secret societies that took place far out of sight of the community. Yet their existence merited only routine mention in annual State Department human rights reports. The extraction of organs was traditionally ritualistic, but, according to Stephen Ellis's *Mask of Anarchy*, over the course of the civil war, these killings became associated less with the traditional societies than with politics.[21] "So-called 'heartmen,'" Ellis writes, "defined by one modern Liberian newspaper as 'groups of organized killers often contracted by political aspirants and businessmen to kill people and extract their body parts to perform rituals.' Heartmen are said to supply hearts to 'juju men to make their clients succeed in life for high jobs in government or in private employment or for protection against enemies.'"

Within six months of his inauguration, Taylor was implicated in a killing for the first time as president. On December 4, 1997, a burned-out truck was found along a rural road deep in Nimba County. Inside sat three bodies, burned beyond recognition.[22] At first glance, the deaths appeared to be the work of bandits, who often stalked the remote, unpoliced roadways. But one sign indicated that this was more than a simple highway robbery. Close to the vehicle lay the severed head of a former Taylor loyalist, Samuel Dokie.

Dokie had made the mistake of publicly criticizing the newly elected Taylor. Like other former NPFL leaders such as Tom Woewiyu, Dokie could no longer stomach Taylor's style of politics and had actively campaigned against his old ally. Shortly after the election, Dokie was emphatic about the implications of Taylor's victory.[23] He told a *New York Times* correspondent that "Taylor is Qaddafi's surrogate" and that his popular election was "Qaddafi's biggest victory in Africa." Unlike other leaders, including election rival Ellen Johnson Sirleaf, Dokie did not leave the country following Taylor's election. His statements and continued presence in the country suggested he felt he had no reason to fear Taylor, now that his estranged ally had been elected president.

On December 3 Dokie's family was detained at a checkpoint in Nimba County. The next morning a small convoy arrived at the station where they were being held. SSS director Benjamin Yeaten appeared from one of the vehicles and approached the local commander. A wan, spectral man with bloodshot, searching eyes and cheekbones that rose out of his face, he viewed Taylor as a father figure as much as Chucky did. Hailing from Nimba County, he had come of age amid the bitterness of Doe's repression there. He had been one of the youngest but most determined trainees at Tajura, Libya—just eighteen years old in 1987—and eventually rose in the ranks of Taylor's militia.[24] He had distinguished himself as a loyal and brutal follower throughout the civil war. For his service, Taylor as president granted him a coveted role in his new government: head of the Special Operations Division and Special Security Service, the president's black-fatigued immediate ring of bodyguards known as "ninjas."[25] Yeaten often appeared alongside Taylor, an ill-fitting suit hanging off of his gangly frame, holding a leather briefcase with an automatic weapon inside. Despite his newly official status, the U.S. embassy noted, dimly, that Yeaten was among "known human rights abusers."[26]

At the Nimba County checkpoint where the Dokie family was being detained, Yeaten and the local commander began arguing, according to witnesses. The commander refused to hand over the family to Yeaten, but eventually allowed Yeaten to take custody of them. Instead of proceeding to Monrovia, the SSS vehicles turned toward Gbarnga. The family was never again seen alive. Soon afterward graphic photographs of the family's remains appeared in Monrovia newspapers.[27] The corpses were unrecognizable with the exception of Dokie's head.

The publicity following the killings complicated things for the president. Taylor addressed the nation, ordering an investigation and indicating that he would punish whoever was responsible. Yet he seemed to preempt a conclusion, suggesting that the killings were likely a botched robbery. Anxiety heightened, and in the weeks that followed, the inves-

tigation failed to find a perpetrator. Rumors, which Taylor would vehe-
mently deny, began to circulate that Taylor had ordered Dokie killed
and had himself eaten his liver.[28]

Unexplained killings were becoming more common around the
capital. Even figures who had survived the bloodiest days of the civil
war were disturbed by them, yet neither Taylor's opponents nor his
insiders had any authority to appeal to, fearing—accurately or not—
that the president and his forces were behind the violence. They aired
their fears to embassy officials.

Further details of Dokie's death drifted back to Monrovia. The
family had been brought to the Bong County residence of Charles Taylor's mother and had been tortured, their eyes gouged from their heads,
an embassy report stated. Grace Minor, a senator and close confidante
of Taylor's, toed the party line that the investigation should determine
who was responsible.[29] With an embassy official present, she said, "Let
justice be done." Then she stunned the room by muttering, "Even if it
is his mother who is involved."

Taylor was following a familiar script as a sub-Saharan Africa
leader. Having assumed control of the government, he was consolidating power through the use of violence. The choice of his son as the
leader of one of his security forces was also typical. Even Smith himself,
the shadowy mentor who appeared at the right moment to lead the
protagonist forward, seemed a stock character.

Despite the guidance he'd received from Smith, Chucky could barely
qualify as an amateur military leader. But there was a logic to the choice:
a son would obey his father, would act in his father's interest, and would
remain loyal. He fit neatly within the patronage system at work in Liberia. The question was how an American son would respond.

Chucky set about creating the new security unit, bringing a specific vision of what this force would be: disciplined, well trained, and
not given to the petty corruption and thievery typical of armed men in
Liberia.[30] The men would be well paid to ensure their professionalism.
Arguably, Chucky wanted a more Western military force—one that was
accountable to the chain of command and could rely on the presidency
for support. In this respect, he was working against the grain. While
young recruits like Menephar were eager to join an elite force to make

a living, the older-generation fighters had known only one system: the top-down tribal patronage networks that both rewarded and were supported by bribery and theft.

Chucky's first significant task was to convert the hillside at Gbatala into a training base for the new unit. He turned for help to Smith. The men determined what they would need: a classroom, a kitchen, officers' quarters, barracks, an ammo dump, a guardhouse, obstacles, and a firing range. The group that had originally met at Chucky's house drove out to Gbatala to begin construction. The buildings were spare by necessity, constructed from brick and cinder block; they were threadbare but functional. There was no electricity or plumbing at the site; the men relied on a generator for power and drew water from a well.

Building by building, the base began to take shape. One of the few earlier structures still standing was the base commander's house, atop the first overlook above the roadway. It was a single-story white-walled structure with "Executive Mansion SSS Cobra Base" painted in faded block letters on the exterior. Behind it sat a smaller barracks consisting of several separated rooms. A shed nearby would serve as the ammo dump. Farther up the hillside, a building consisting of a classroom and three adjoining offices was erected. Like several other structures, it was painted in a cartoonish forest-camouflage print that did little to conceal it. If anything it drew attention to the fact that it was a military structure. In white block letters, it read "College of Knowledge."

A narrow path threaded through the brush behind the classroom over a wooded berm, down a slope toward a swamp. Just beyond the water, the men dug more than a dozen holes, each barely larger than a grave, then covered the pits with bars and sheets of steel. They called the place "Vietnam," a name meant to inspire fear in the recruits: the holes were where they would be thrown for indiscipline. The location would also serve a secondary purpose: to house prisoners.

The first group of recruits arrived in June 1998, some thirty-five men, many of them teenagers, but also old-timers from Taylor's militia.[31] The two white men, Dave Smith and a man known only as "Robert," met the arriving recruits. Several fighters would later identify Dave as British and Robert as American; none recalled either man's last name. "We're going to teach you guys how to become a SWAT force," the trainers announced. Each man was given a mattress, eating utensils, a bucket, towel, soap, and a set of civilian clothes. The training was rigid and organized. The white trainers drilled the men on conducting patrols, clearing houses, freeing hostages, building cordons, carrying out searches, and setting up and manning roadblocks. Much to Menephar's surprise, none of the recruits were beaten.

What also surprised Menephar was the equipment laid out for the men. He'd come of age as the arms embargo was established in Liberia, fighting with Soviet-style hand-me-downs of varied vintage and origins. But nearly everything on the base was brand-new. The men had access to an array of firearms—M-16 and MP18 rifles, MP5 9mm submachine guns, MP22 automatic pistols—as well as RPG-7s. Chucky ferried the weapons and ammunition to the base in his jeep, Menephar said.

Typically these arms were Soviet-bloc military variants, but other weapons provided to the recruits, the MP5 and the Smith & Wesson–manufactured MP22, were favored by NATO nations. Robert had purchased much of the nonlethal gear in the United States, Menephar came to learn, including uniforms, boots, camouflage tents, and night-vision goggles. "All was American made," he said.

The trainees already knew how to fire weapons, as well as clean and reload them, but few, if any, had had any training in marksmanship. While conducting weapons training, Dave demonstrated how to fire accurately by hitting the stars on an American flag. Menephar, who confessed to being unable to strike a target from ten yards out, had never seen accurate fire. "He's making magic!" he recalled exclaiming. "Wow, we have a witch!"

The influx of weapons wasn't limited to the new security unit. The defense attaché at the U.S. embassy began tracking rumors that the RUF in Sierra Leone was continuing to receive support from Taylor.[32] In one incident, the attaché reported, peacekeepers in eastern Sierra Leone had "exchanged fire with soldiers disembarking from a Mi-B helicopter." The fighters, wearing green battle uniforms not typically seen on rebels, began firing before the peacekeepers could identify them. The U.S. embassy had been tracking reports of a "phantom rebel helicopter" in Sierra Leone fitting the Mi-B's profile; it believed one of Taylor's generals and "an American citizen who is a former UK Special Air Services officer"—a description consistent with Smith—was "providing arms and recruits for the RUF."

After a month at Gbatala, the recruits received orders to return to Monrovia. The men suited up in their new black uniforms and traveled to White Flower, where Chucky met them. The group then convoyed to Hotel Africa, where the president was hosting the All Liberia Conference, a perennial gathering that had sought to bring together the various tribes and political groups. Taylor wanted to take the opportunity to make a show of strength. When Menephar and the other recruits arrived at the hotel, they were ordered to spread out in formation. The group was given a name: the Executive Mansion Special Security Unit (EMSSU).

Taylor appeared from the hotel to review his new force, in pressed uniforms, holding new weapons. Menephar, in the formation, stood at attention before the man he'd been fighting for since he was a child. "He was proud," Menephar recalled.

Lynn too could feel the momentum of the unit. Many of the recruits were drawn from the Small Boys Unit, which gave them reputations from the civil war "as killers and murderers," but she simply saw a lot of them as "boys." Everyone referred to them that way, even though a number of the "boys"—like Menephar—already had young families. As the recruits passed through the house, she came to know some of them. "All these people know is war," she later said, "and now they had an opportunity to be a part of something special. Like a special unit. Protecting the president. They'd jump at that. They were very proud of it."

Chucky's role was changing as well. He was no longer simply the president's son. He had begun to command his own men. Liberia was a fiercely hierarchical and nepotistic society; the authority Chucky had over new recruits reflected that. What he lacked in experience, he made up for in familial ties and proximity to power. Lynn saw what this meant to the young men who were deeply experienced in the civil war but otherwise disenfranchised from the society.[33] "They loved him," she recalled.

Yet in order to lead an elite unit, Chucky needed to command respect from his men—a task accomplished among the younger recruits more easily than among the older NPFL veterans. In Taylor's inner circle, respect often went hand in hand with fear—Yeaten was the quintessential example. But unlike Yeaten, Chucky brought very little fear to the command position. He was just twenty-one, an American citizen who had spent only a handful of years in Liberia. He had no military training to speak of. Whatever love his men felt for him would not be enough to sustain them through training and eventual combat. He

needed to find a reason for men who had already seen some of humanity's worst behavior to fear him.

Taylor had fortified himself with myriad security forces, but he had not
purged the capital of his former enemies. His chief domestic antago-
nist was the Krahn leader Roosevelt Johnson, who had several hundred
followers, including former members of his ULIMO-K faction as well
as their wives and children.[34] They had holed up in a one-block-long
apartment compound on a crowded stretch of downtown Monrovia,
hard between the Executive Mansion and Mamba Point, called Camp
Johnson Road. There the group was guarded by a platoon of Nigerian
peacekeepers.

Johnson's presence was a persistent reminder of Taylor's lack of
complete authority over the capital—and the country. He had been
given an ornamental role in Taylor's administration—as the rural development minister—but he remained a faction leader who pursued his
own agenda. In February 1998 Johnson took a trip to Nigeria, where
he met with President Sani Abacha.[35] Taylor saw the visit as evidence
of a plot between the Nigerians and Johnson to destabilize his new
government. Upon Johnson's arrival back at Robertsfield, the Liberians
sought to arrest him. A physical altercation broke out between Taylor's SSS members and Johnson's retinue. Eventually the Krahn leader
was escorted back to Monrovia by a convoy of heavily armed Nigerian
peacekeepers. Johnson's followers clashed again with the SSS in late
March, and when the Krahn leader took a medical trip to the United
States, Taylor again suspected that he was plotting to overthrow the
government.

Shortly before dusk on September 18, 1998, more than one hundred
uniformed soldiers—an unruly conglomeration of Special Operation
Division fighters and members of Chucky's newly formed outfit—
approached the Camp Johnson Road compound from both sides.[36] The
peacekeepers had withdrawn, leaving Roosevelt and his followers vulnerable. Taylor's forces began firing on the compound with automatic
weapons and RPGs, according to the embassy. Throughout the night
the Krahn were under fire. They phoned the U.S. embassy, pleading
for the remaining West African peacekeeping detachment to intercede

and create a buffer zone, but to no avail. By daybreak nearly three hundred Krahn had been killed, including dozens of women and children.

The target of the assault, Roosevelt Johnson, slipped the cordon with a handful of followers—armed Krahn fighters—and bolted for the U.S. embassy to ask for shelter. The embassy gate lay several hundred meters away, but by the time Johnson and his fighters made it there, Taylor's forces were upon them.[37] The confrontation thrust the United States into the center of a domestic power struggle between Charles Taylor and his last significant factional rival. If the Clinton administration had hoped that Taylor would shed his warlord instincts, the unfolding drama at their embassy gate proved otherwise. The United States had had little interest mediating between these warring parties during the civil war—and even less during an active firefight.

The embassy guards refused Johnson's men entry into the compound. But when it became clear that the lives of the fighters were in imminent danger, U.S. security officers allowed the men behind a retaining wall shielding the entryway. They were safe for a time, but Taylor's forces gathered outside demanding their release, ratcheting up the pressure on the diplomats.

That tension quickly boiled over. According to a State Department account, Taylor's police chief ordered his forces to "go get them."[38] The soldiers' fusillade of fire cut down three of Roosevelt's men in an instant, while a fourth died moments after slipping through a turnstile into the embassy compound. Two American contractors were hit in the exchange—one returned fire, killing two of Taylor's men. In the frantic fire, a lone RPG arced over the embassy compound, falling harmlessly into the ocean. Six survivors—Roosevelt Johnson included—leaped through the turnstile to the safety of the embassy grounds and, effectively, into the care of the United States. (The U.S. government would later evacuate the men to Ghana, despite Taylor's government's calls for them to be turned over into Liberian custody.[39])

The U.S. government responded forcefully to the assault on its embassy, demanding an apology from Taylor's government and seeking a UN investigation.[40] A detachment of seventeen Navy SEALs was sent to take up a position two thousand yards offshore, poised to intercede in any further threats on the embassy.[41]

American officials directly implicated Taylor's fighters in the incident. "There is a concern that Liberian security forces are ill-disciplined and potentially dangerous," Deputy Secretary of Defense for Africa Vicki Huddleston told Taylor's foreign minister.[42]

It was the first public atrocity connected to the president's son. The incident illustrated both the breadth and the limits of Taylor's new power. The force that assaulted Camp Johnson Road had easily overwhelmed the Krahn opposition, although it was not an elite security unit. In the days afterward, witnesses reported executions of Krahn men carried out in broad daylight near the U.S. embassy. Members of the Krahn community accused Chucky and his men of "killing hundreds of innocent people including women, children and the elderly."[43]

The firefight at the gates of the embassy demonstrated not only Taylor's lack of control over his fighters and commanders but also their complete lack of respect for the international law that protected the embassy from such assaults. The embassy quickly evacuated much of its staff, including those wounded in the attack. American officials spent the next two months soliciting a reluctant apology from Taylor for the behavior of his security forces. The question of whether Taylor could convert his militias into professional fighting forces—and whether his son was in any position to be a leader—became particularly acute.

But shortly after the incident, the training cycle at Gbatala, so recently begun, ended. Once the initial batch of recruits had been deployed to Monrovia, Dave and Robert never returned to the base.[44] One senior commander insisted that the men had quit out of frustration. Lynn learned that there had been an altercation—Chucky and Dave had come to blows—though Chucky wouldn't reveal exactly what had happened. When Christopher Menephar later returned to Gbatala, he was told that Taylor had provided Dave and Robert with $3 million to purchase additional equipment and weapons. They disappeared, never to be heard from again.

7

Uprising

So when you see in the streets with the killers dat be, have your mother fuckin soldiers reportin to me.

— *United States vs. Belfast*, EXHIBIT CE-4

A bell sounded across the camp. An order was shouted: "Movement, cease!"[1] This meant to those training at Gbatala that Chucky had arrived. Word passed quickly over the rocky hillside, and recruits mustered in a field at the foot of a granite cliff face, standing to attention as they were addressed by their commanding officer, the president's son.

By early 1999, Chucky had emerged as the leader of the unit—the "Chief," as he was referred to. He began sculpting the group's identity. Initially it had been named the Executive Mansion Special Security Unit, but it took on a new name that reflected more than a protective detail: the Anti-Terrorist Unit, or ATU. Chucky oversaw the creation of an emblem that each fighter would wear: a crest with a cartoonish rendering of a red-eyed cobra and a green scorpion under the unit's name.[2]

The departure of Dave and Robert had left the ATU without the professional military training it badly needed. Chucky's father moved ahead anyway with the clandestine recruitment of both low-level fighters and new trainers. When the members of the unit returned to Gbatala in January 1999, they were accompanied by a new class of recruits and met at the base by a squad of white South African mercenaries, hired to shape them into a professional force.

In the 1990s military expertise was just another item for sale on the

West African black market. Violence in Angola and Sierra Leone was standard fare, within essentially illicit economies. Mercenaries thrived, enjoying quasi-legitimacy as weak governments like that of Sierra Leone hired professional soldiers to succeed where their own military forces had failed.

The South Africans whom Charles Taylor had hired as trainers included Oscar, a short man with an awkward hopping limp from a bullet wound; Menno Uys, a tall, muscular former member of the South African Special Forces Brigade ("the Recces") with a cleanly shaved head and a slightly twisted sense of humor; and Phelps, a barrel-chested bantam with enormous hands. Two others, Faber and Gerry, oversaw the training program and syllabi.[3] These men came to the job as veterans of Angola and Sierra Leone, having served in both the regular South African military and in the infamous mercenary group Executive Outcomes.[4]

Taylor had learned a painful lesson about the effectiveness of mercenary forces in Sierra Leone. The Sierra Leonean government engaged in a novel solution to confront the RUF: it contracted Executive Outcomes to mount an offensive against the rebel group.[5] Comprised largely of apartheid-era veterans of the South African Defense Forces, Executive Outcomes achieved a quick victory. It overwhelmed the rebels through a decisive combination of superior tactics and firepower, including the use of helicopter gunships, armored vehicles, and tanks. In 1997, when Taylor started looking to improve his own security forces, according to UN investigators, a business associate suggested a former South African Defense Force colonel named Fred Rindel who was not connected directly to Executive Outcomes but shared a similar background and experience.[6]

Rindel had become a fixture in African countries where war and diamonds found a nexus.[7] He had fought in Angola with the South African Defense Forces in support of an anticommunist rebel group, UNITA, which was also supported by the United States. That conflict reflected the typical Cold War antagonism, as Cuba and the Soviet Union threw their arms and expertise behind the Socialist People's Movement for the Liberation of Angola. After the fall of the Soviet Union, the diamond trade drove the economics of the war. In 1994, according to a book by Executive Outcomes founder Eeben Barlow, Rindel graduated from fighting to serving as a liaison between the diamond giant De

Beers and the Angolan rebels trafficking gems out of the war zone. Later he, like many of his colleagues in search of diamonds, gravitated toward Liberia and Sierra Leone.

The South Africans' experience in Angola provided an example for the crises he encountered there: both were resource-rich nations enduring upheaval after being detached from their international patrons. These men brought with them not only combat experience but business acumen—especially in the diamond business. Many former members of the apartheid-era military were urgently seeking economic opportunities outside South Africa in the postapartheid mid-1990s.[8]

These private military companies were also controversial: the South African government responded to their emergence by passing the Foreign Military Assistance Act in 1998, requiring the outfits to register for authorization to provide military training to other governments.[9] The Mandela government effectively put overt mercenary operations out of business. Yet there remained some gray area for the groups to continue operating. When Charles Taylor hired Fred Rindel, the South African did not seek authorization because, in his view, "his services were purely of a protective nature and did not include any combat training, or training of armed forces in Liberia."[10]

The scene at the Gbatala training base directly contradicted this assertion. The South Africans attempted to re-create conventional military-quality basic training, beginning with a course on hygiene, drill and ceremony, and self- and regimental discipline.[11] After a breakfast of oatmeal or Cream of Wheat and hot tea, the recruits sat for lectures on codes of conduct, communications, and marksmanship—what recruits called "sniping." For weeks, the training was limited to physical conditioning and classroom instruction. Eventually, the trainers permitted the men to handle weapons, training them in how to clean and disassemble AK-47s, Heckler & Koch MP5 submachine guns, and American-made Glock 9mm pistols.

Ultimately, the South Africans split the recruits into two companies: Alpha and Bravo. The training progressed with squad, platoon, and company leadership courses. The objective was not only to develop a well-trained force but also to create a leadership pool that could train future recruits.

But these fighters weren't fresh-faced volunteers—they had already experienced combat, of the chaotic, disorganized, and brutal type char-

acteristic of Liberia's bush war. Their experience on the battlefield was
a liability: they were not disciplined fighters and had no proficiency
with their weapons and minimal understanding of tactics. Many had
witnessed, if not committed, atrocities unbecoming to any member of
a professional fighting force. Violence bound these men together, and
it would be the primary language in which Chucky communicated to
them. On one visit to the base, Chucky warned his recruits, "Gentlemen, this is training base. When you come here, you abide by our own
law. When you go above the law, the law will lay hand on you."[12]

Western militaries favored humiliation, intimidation, work, and
exercise as tools to control the behavior of recruits, but Chucky's preferred method was corporal punishment. He wanted the ATU to be
held to a higher standard than the previous security forces surrounding
his father, but lacking any military training himself, he did not understand the deleterious impact of force. As a result, the Liberian commanders employed a training regimen even harsher than that of the
South Africans. Recruits arriving at Gbatala were subjected to "Zero
Week," a combination of starvation, intense physical training, and
dangerous—and in some cases fatal—obstacle courses. Sometimes men
were mowed down in live-fire exercises; others, according to one former fighter, were burned alive during rope drills over flaming barrels
of gasoline. Still others were beaten as they were forced to carry massive logs. One recruit described receiving twenty-five lashes from his
own best friend, on Chucky's orders.[13] His crime: failing to hit a bottle
during target practice. It was violent hazing under the guise of military
training. The trainees came away with little more than fear of Chucky.

Veterans of Taylor's revolution who underwent the training at
Gbatala didn't take the president's son seriously, but they were obligated
to follow his orders.[14] He was young and inexperienced and seemed to
have little idea of the realities of fighting a bush war in West Africa.
At one point, he appeared on the base with DVDs of the Hollywood
action movies *Delta Force* and *Air Force One* and made the men watch
the films to give them something to emulate.

The NPFL veterans weren't the only ones skeptical of Chucky.
Fred Rindel also had little regard for the president's son.[15] He didn't
let that feeling get in the way of his business interests, however. When
corresponding with Chucky, he struck a respectful tone—though likely
out of deference to Charles Taylor rather than the son.[16]

Despite the ongoing arms embargo, President Taylor hoped to grow and arm the force quickly, but Rindel cautioned Chucky against this expectation: "I think we need to sit down and plan this through for the government so that we have a total approach. You are the client and we will supply what you request but in the last 7 months we have gained insight and experience of the situation so we too have a far better idea on how to approach the situation. We are also aware of the restrictions that you have to live with and we now know ways and means of assisting you in getting around them."[17] While Rindel wouldn't comment in detail, the "restrictions" that both he and the Taylor administration faced were clear: neither man could allow the military training to become public while it was active lest it draw scrutiny from the South African government and from the UN Security Council, which was monitoring Liberia's compliance with the arms embargo.

For Taylor, domestic political concerns also drove the secrecy. First and foremost, the creation of a new unit was a clear violation of the Liberian constitution. In December 1999 Taylor opened a personal account to bankroll arms purchases and pay his security forces.[18] Years later he would testify before the Special Court for Sierra Leone that he had done so with the acquiescence of the legislature. But by creating, operating, and funding his own unit, the president circumvented the government payroll, avoiding the politically sticky fact that his new recruits were being paid salaries of $250 per month—more than most government ministers made at that time. He also avoided the issue of the Armed Forces of Liberia. The AFL had the legal authority to act as the nation's military force, but it remained staffed by traditional opponents of Taylor.[19] Rather than dissolve the AFL and provoke a potential public clash, he sought to emasculate it by forcing veterans into retirement and depriving the remaining combatants of funding, training, and weapons.

The source of the money flowing into Taylor's account for the Anti-Terrorist Unit was also necessarily covert. To bankroll this account, he relied on timber revenues, taxes, and donations from the Taiwanese government.[20] The Taiwanese motives were plain: they sought official recognition of their statehood from Liberia.[21] Taiwanese officials had contributed approximately $1 million to Taylor's political campaign to this end, and as Taylor assumed power, Taiwan became the largest international donor to the Liberian government (a position for which there was little competition).[22]

International aid was intended for infrastructure and relief costs, but some of it was diverted to Taylor's increasingly expensive covert security program. The South African trainers alone cost more than $100,000 each month.[23] Even so, the training program suffered from what Rindel saw as a lack of internal leadership.[24] "I only have one concern that I would care to highlight and that is the leader group . . . they do not have the necessary leadership skills and this is something that is essential." Rindel, who tolerated Chucky only because President Taylor wanted his son involved, thought the problem extended up the chain of command.

"Taylor Jr. had no capabilities as anything," he later said.[25]

Charles Taylor, meanwhile, hadn't yielded leadership of the new unit entirely to his son. In late 1998 or early 1999, he appointed a base commandant to work under Chucky and oversee the day-to-day training of the two companies at Gbatala.[26] But he did not choose a Liberian. Again, as with Jacques, he relied on a Gambian, a mercenary named David Campari, to live at the site and serve as the disciplinarian. Campari, formerly posted to Maryland County, had a reputation for being "wicked"—a Liberian word for extreme evil. In his forties, more than two decades older than many of the recruits, Campari was nonetheless menacing. To the consternation of the South African trainers, he announced his arrival on base by firing off a fusillade of live rounds over the recruits' heads.

Campari soon further set the tone for his presence on the base. He had brought two other Gambians with him, an aide and a personal medicine man. He believed strongly in juju, and as the recruits watched, the medicine man prepared his quarters by slaughtering a goat and spreading the animal's blood over the doorway. Campari was suspicious of other spiritual practices on the base. Many of the recruits were Christians, but he would allow them only thirty minutes for Sunday morning services, posting a military police detail to watch over them, weapons ready. "You are praying against me," he accused the men.

Campari shared one belief with Chucky: the necessity of harsh punishment. He enforced discipline using recruits designated as military police, or MPs. These soldiers were responsible for carrying out any order given by the commanders. Many recruits tried to avoid this type of detail, as well as serving at checkpoints and acting as a bodyguard, because as one trainee explained, you were required to "implement orders that I may not want to implement and I [would] be forced to implement them."[27]

The structured training regimen that the South Africans had established at Gbatala soon gave way to the arbitrary and impulsive whims of Campari. Daily life was governed by his moods and the amount of liquor he had consumed. On some days recruits were ordered to stand at attention for four or five hours at a time, but the punishment didn't lead to better discipline in the ranks. Some fighters sneaked off into the village to drink or consort with local women; when one senior officer, Morris Gbleh, returned to the camp drunk, walking up a darkened path, rather than identify himself to the sentry, he simply shot the man.

The true face of Chucky's leadership became apparent not long after Campari's arrival. In early 1999 Taylor entrusted his son with $50,000 in cash to cover the expenses of the base: construction, food, and payroll for the fighters. This infusion was necessary to maintain the secrecy of the training program, but it came with inherent risks; before long, Chucky discovered several recruits pilfering funds.

Christopher Menephar was posted at Gbatala sometime later when he received a call from an aide to Chucky named Tarnue Gizzie. The aide asked Menephar who was on the base at that time. Menephar responded that at that moment, he was the ranking officer, since the other leaders were absent. Gizzie told Menephar he would be driving from Monrovia, bringing prisoners.

Several hours after Menephar received the call, Chucky's jeep appeared on the base. Gizzie climbed out and told Menephar, "Chucky said that these guys should be put into the prison—into the holes." Menephar was unable to see any prisoners through the truck's tinted windows. Still, he climbed into the car and drove the short distance to the shooting range—down the hillside, behind the College of Knowledge, where he climbed out and opened the jeep's rear gate.

A thick pool of blood appeared, Menephar recalled, covering the trunk of the vehicle. He still couldn't make out any prisoners, but he saw three tarpaulins. The men had been wrapped in the tough canvas and thrown into the vehicle for the two-hour journey to the base. Menephar unloaded one of the men, and when his face came into view, he recognized him as a bodyguard of Chucky's named Obadiah Henry.

Henry had been beaten so severely that his eyes were rolling into the back of his head. The second prisoner was a boy Menephar didn't know but estimated to be about sixteen years old. The third prisoner Menephar also knew: another bodyguard of Chucky's, Justin Parker. When Menephar pulled the tarpaulin from his face, Parker appeared to be barely clinging to life. "He took these deep breaths. He just breathed one or two times," Menephar recalled, then died.

The other men were also near death, and Menephar knew they would not survive very long in the holes. He jumped into the jeep and drove back to the base to call Monrovia. He reached a bodyguard of Chucky's and told him that Parker had died and that "these guys have to go to the hospital because they are almost to the point." He received permission to deliver the men to Phebe Hospital, a short distance up the highway.

Menephar was accustomed to commanders beating their recruits, but the violence of this incident was alarming. He eventually learned what had happened to the men, but he couldn't understand what would drive Chucky to such a rage. According to that account, Chucky discovered that Henry and Parker had been stealing cash from the reserves President Taylor had provided for the unit. Over time, and with the help of a third thief—the sixteen-year-old boy—the trio had taken more than $23,000. Chucky immediately ordered that the three men be arrested and brought to his home in Monrovia. With the men in his custody, he ordered them into a room. Until now, there had been little record of violence carried out by the president's son. He was a relative newcomer to the security scene and, as a few of the recruits understood, an American. Whether those factors had encouraged the recruits to risk stealing from Chucky is not clear. But if the crime became public and went unpunished, it would badly undermine him.

As the captives waited, Chucky turned on music, then cranked up the volume on his stereo. He began beating and stabbing the men, Menephar was told, the screams concealed by the music. (A senior ATU commander who asked not to be identified said that Chucky did not directly participate, but "he gave the order."[28]) When the beatings ended, Chucky ordered the men to be taken to the base at Gbatala.

The next day Chucky rolled into Gbatala in a convoy. He was escorted by Benjamin Yeaten, who had become known to most of the fighters simply as "50"—his radio call sign. Yeaten had little direct involvement with the ATU at that time. If anything, his own unit—the SSS—competed with Chucky's for the president's attention. Yeaten served Taylor directly, overseeing his bodyguards and executing his personal orders, including the assassination of opponents. (The SSS had carried out the grisly assassination of Samuel Dokie.) But on that day Charles Taylor did not know that his commander was with his son at Gbatala.

"They decided to bring him in to find a solution," Menephar would later say of Yeaten.

Yeaten said little while he was on the base—he did not need to.[29] Despite his small stature, Yeaten was one of the most feared figures in Liberia. Though Chucky was larger, he appeared cowed by the SSS commander. Menephar escorted the visitors down a path behind the College of Knowledge to the spot where Justin Parker's body had been buried. It lay halfway between the base and the prison holes. (The fate of the two men taken to the hospital is not known.)

When the group returned to the base, Chucky ordered the recruits to fall in. News of Parker's death had quickly passed through the ranks, including to several young fighters who had grown up with Parker in Yekepa and were also members of his Mano tribe. According to Menephar, Parker's killing had angered many of the recruits. At muster, rather than join the others, a recruit named Thomas Quoa stepped out of formation to confront Chucky. He shouted that Chucky had killed "his brother" and said that "he was going to make sure that the president hears about it."

Quoa's decision to call out the president's son in front of Campari, Yeaten, and the rest of the recruits was reckless and nearly suicidal. Campari immediately placed him under arrest and dragged him across the gravel and into the bush toward where Parker was buried. He wasn't killed but was thrown into one of the holes at Vietnam. For Chucky, it had been an embarrassing public rebuke of his authority; he and Yeaten climbed into their trucks and eventually returned to the capital.

News of Parker's death nonetheless reached Chucky's father. The story had not leaked to the press in Monrovia; it would have not only shed light on yet another killing by Taylor's security forces but also revealed the secret training occurring at Gbatala. Taylor took no public action against his son, but the incident only contributed to the belief among veteran fighters that Chucky was not fit for command.

"Chucky, he was a little boy," said the former senior commander, who had served in Taylor's NPFL and was appointed deputy to the president's son.[30] "He was not mature. Inexperienced. Not educated. It was a tough time to work with him." Chucky was gullible, he said, given to taking gossip at face value and acting on it without investigating further. His erratic behavior made it difficult to accomplish anything. "Chucky was very untimely. He could behave very well. In two or three hours time, he [would] change," he said. "[When] he comes back he's abnormal."

Even as these deputies struggled to handle the president's son, recruits began to fear Chucky and his impunity. Commanders worried that he was using drugs and alcohol. Menephar noticed something else that he couldn't quite explain: Chucky appeared to be frightened by his own actions.

Regardless of its origins or causes, Chucky's behavior became both unpredictable and of ever-greater consequence to the ATU. This was apparent in an incident that federal investigators would focus on nearly a decade later, when he encountered Sulaiman Jusu at the St. Paul River bridge. It was on April 21, 1999, and Jusu, the refugee from Sierra Leone, had witnessed Chucky execute his brother-in-law and several other unarmed men.[31] Jusu had little insight into the mind of the president's son, but he saw Chucky's anger and knew that he considered the prisoners responsible for the attack on Voinjama that marked the first challenge to his father's government. Still he could make little sense of the killings or what immediately followed.

Jusu's ordeal did not end with the killings. The ATU fighters thrust the remaining prisoners onto their stomachs, bound their elbows together behind their backs, and wrapped their ankles with plastic Zip Ties, threading the plastic cords across their backs and around their necks. This practice was known as *tabay*—a manner of immobilizing prisoners common in West Africa. An indescribable pain shot through Sulaiman Jusu's body. He and ten to fifteen others were thrown into the back of a truck, unable to either stand or sit, as the convoy rolled away from the bridge and deeper into Liberia. With each mile, the men were carried farther from the help of their family, friends, or the international community.

Like Jusu, several of the other prisoners taken from the bridge also hailed from Kenema, Sierra Leone. Momoh Turay, a twenty-four-year-old, had fled the fighting months earlier after rebels killed his father and burned down his family's home.[32] He'd crossed into Liberia and registered as a refugee before reaching Voinjama, where he found work as a security guard for the World Food Program. While Voinjama was a city of more than 25,000, the group of refugees from Kenema was small enough that Turay could recognize others who had been detained at the bridge, including Jusu, his brother Maada, and another refugee, Foday Conteh. Turay had also watched Chucky shoot Albert and the others. (He would testify later, however, that only two other men had been shot.) The killings had terrified him. He had seen Chucky once before, at a meeting in Voinjama, where the group of refugees were offered the opportunity to train in Gbarnga. Both Turay and Jusu, who had fled the fighting in Sierra Leone, did not jump at the opportunity to return as combatants—a choice that didn't register with Taylor and the commanders he was traveling with.

Jusu, Turay, and the other prisoners lay in the back of the trucks, hog-tied, as the convoy wound down the broken bush roads toward Gbarnga. The men were in intense pain. Some cried. They could see nothing, and their cries were met with the butt of a weapon or a boot from the darkness.

The convoy arrived at a police station at Gbarnga after dark. Turay's blindfold was pulled from his face and a flashlight briefly shone into his eyes. Despite the late hour, police officers, Special Operations Division, and ATU fighters filled the station. The scene turned chaotic. The prisoners were brought in, and the fighters set upon them, thrashing them with sticks. The violence of the beating was so intense that Turay lost control of his bowels. After the officers finished, the police locked the Sierra Leoneans into a cell, without any charge or indication of why they were being held.

Chucky arrived at the police station the next day and, following some discussion, sought to conceal Jusu, Turay, and the surviving prisoners. The men were pulled from the cell.

Chucky again ordered them bound and blindfolded. When Jusu realized they were going to be *tabay*ed again, he fought and struggled. He felt a gun slam into him; the fighters started kicking him. Chucky struck him, forced him to the ground, and stepped on his head before tying him up.

The men were driven out of Gbarnga on the road through Charles Taylor's heartland. It was narrow and tidy, cleared of fallen palms by the local Kpelle people. After an hour, the truck reached Gbatala. Even if they had been told it, the name would have meant very little. The convoy slowed, pulled off the road, and wound up a gravel incline into the forest.

It was night when the men were pulled from the trucks. They could hardly see through the blindfolds. Flashlights flickered across the ground, but otherwise the only light was from the moon and stars overhead. The group walked to a small plateau. Turay heard Chucky tell Campari, the Gambian, to "take care of them."

The blindfolds were pulled from the prisoners' faces. Turay could finally see the other prisoners who had been brought with him: Sulaiman Jusu, Foday Conteh, Abdul Cole. Chucky walked away, and the group was forced to march down a sloping path into the bush. They passed through a small swamp and were led to a set of holes in the ground.

In the darkness, Turay was forced into a hole. A guard lowered a makeshift cover, heavy iron bars wound with barbed wire; his left hand was bound to the grate. It forced him to crouch; the hole was too shallow to stand, and fetid water filled the bottom, making it impossible to sit or lie. The cries and shouts of the other men punctuated the quiet of the night.

Sulaiman Jusu found himself in a similar hole—with a rotting corpse. It was just two and half feet deep and filled with water. The water rose so close to his mouth that he was forced to crane his head upward to avoid drinking it.

Even with the men in the holes, the abuse continued. Guards jabbed bayonets through the bars, stabbing the prisoners; one burned sheets of plastic, letting the molten drippings fall down on Turay's naked body. Jusu was forced to eat a burning cassava stem that had been pulled directly from the fire. At one point a guard stood over Turay, aiming his rifle into the pit, threatening to open fire. This persisted through the night into daylight. Eventually Turay fell asleep.

The next night a steady rain pounded the hillside. The guard watching over Vietnam left his post to find more shelter than the thatched lean-to offered. Jusu heard something outside his hole. It was Abdul

Cole, one of the other prisoners—he had freed himself. Jusu begged Cole to release him. Once Jusu climbed out of the hole, he went to Turay, prepared to release him. Turay refused, terrified of getting caught.

Jusu and Cole tore off into the dark, unfamiliar terrain. Dense forests surrounded the base, which was set back from the main road. Neither man had any idea where they were or where they should go. They passed through a cassava patch and then into a rubber plantation, following close to the road. They didn't realize it, but they had not ventured far beyond the perimeter of the base.

A guard almost immediately discovered the escape. He confronted Turay, still in the hole, demanding to know where the other prisoners had gone and why he hadn't alerted the guards. Several fighters—who Turay referred to as "Demons" for the group's popular moniker "Demon Forces"— began punishing him, tying his wrists to the gate, stepping on his hands, burning plastic over his body, jabbing pointed truncheons into the pit. As the night dragged on—and the prisoners remained at large—the abuse continued.

After daybreak, Turay heard men crying. He peered out and saw Chucky and several Demons smoking. Jusu and Cole had been caught. Chucky appeared over Turay's hole. He could see the anger in Chucky's face. Turay's hands remained bound to the bars above his head. Chucky removed a cigarette from his mouth and crushed it into Turay's wrist. Turay squirmed in pain. Then he heard Chucky order him removed from the hole.

Jusu and Cole had been severely beaten after the guards recaptured them, the butts of weapons slammed into their faces, chests, and legs. The soldiers had restrained the men with plastic Zip Ties and continued to punish them back at the base. When Chucky saw them, he too beat them.

Jusu and Cole were brought to the center of the base, between two buildings and a mango tree. Turay and Conteh were brought down the hillside from their holes to where the other escaped prisoners were bound.

The prisoners could see the anger in Chucky.[33] He told them that "this [is] Gbatala camp, nobody should escape from here and when you escape from here, he's coming to teach us a lesson." Then he issued an execution order.

One of the Demons cocked his gun.[34] "No, no firing," Chucky told the soldier. "Silent." He then ordered a soldier to cut off Cole's head.

The soldier unsheathed a three-foot-long knife from a pouch. Another appeared with a plastic bucket. Several soldiers held Cole down. He began crying, shouting, begging for his life. The prisoners watched as one of the soldiers carried out the order, sawing off Cole's head, back to front. If anyone escapes, that is the punishment, Chucky said. He ordered the men back into the holes.

That night the men felt they had no choice but to try to escape again. Jusu and Turay had been thrown into a hole together; they were joined later that evening by a third prisoner, a former officer with an opposition rebel group who identified himself as Dumbaya Dokule. The new prisoner was crying in pain; he'd had all his toes severed.

"If you have the chance to escape," Dokule told them, "do that."[35] Dokule had heard the soldiers talking and planning to "kill us in the morning when Chucky returns."

After seeing Cole's murder, the men had little doubt what would happen to them. A steady rain fell again that night. The men quietly went to work, cutting their restraints using a metal spoon. (The guards had used the spoon to shovel food into the prisoners' mouths, but when it fell into the hole, the guard feeding them hadn't bothered to retrieve it.) Eventually the three men were able break their bonds and open the gate over their hole.

They climbed out into the night and broke into a run. Dokule lurched behind them, unable to keep up, crying in pain. Jusu and Turay were concerned that the sound would attract the MPs, so they ducked into the brush along the roadway, lying flat in the dirt.

It didn't take long for the MPs to discover their escape. Waiting in the brush, the two men heard ATU officers pass by and descend upon Dokule, who was only a few yards from them. He began crying, and from their hiding spot, the two men could hear the soldiers beating him. After several gunshots, Dokule fell silent.

Jusu and Turay waited until morning to set out again. They walked the entire day and into the evening. Along the way, they found an encampment where they were able to pull pairs of pants from a clothesline, so they wouldn't be naked. They were unsure where they were but felt they had traveled a good distance from the base and began walking along a rugged farm road.

The men soon came to a junction. Too late, they realized they were standing just a few feet from several ATU officers, who caught sight of them. Jusu froze in the middle of the road. Turay tried to pretend he was urinating along the roadside. The fighters rushed at them.

Jusu's mind fogged over; he didn't notice who the fighters were—he simply knew he would be killed. He put up no resistance. The soldiers threw him to the ground and tied him. Turay tried to run but was caught. He resisted, telling the fighters to kill him. He didn't want to be tortured again. The men were stripped naked, blindfolded, and driven back to the base, certain they would be killed.

Chucky was waiting for them at the base. Campari, the base commandant, argued for executing the men outright. The second escape had further humiliated the ATU fighters under his command. There was only one way to ensure that it did not happen again.

As soon as Jusu and Turay were pulled from the truck, the MPs set upon them. Jusu recalled Chucky standing over him, melting plastic onto his genitals, butt, and feet. MPs kicked him while the torture continued.

During the beatings, a man in civilian clothing appeared, pulling Chucky aside. "Papay wants to see these men," Jusu heard him say.

The assault at Voinjama had been a shot across Charles Taylor's bow. The perpetrators hadn't stated any motivation or objective, but since the rebels had the unfettered ability to move across the border, Taylor saw the assault as Guinea's first effort to put military pressure on his administration. Guinea's tense relationship with Liberia predated Taylor.[36] During the Rice Riots of 1979, Guinean troops had reinforced the Armed Forces of Liberia in Monrovia to ensure that the rioting didn't devolve into a sustained crisis.[37]

The Guinean detachment was limited to only seven hundred soldiers and departed Liberia after three weeks, but the incident lingered as an affront to Liberia's sense of sovereignty. By the time Taylor won the 1997 election, Guinea had been ruled for more than a decade by President General Lansana Conté, a former French military officer who came to power in a 1984 coup. Guinean forces were among the first to arrive in Sierra Leone to stem the RUF advances in the mid-1990s, but they suffered extensive losses and had been restricted in their ability to fight back. Conté viewed Taylor as responsible for this and not worthy of his position as a head of state.[38] In a meeting with Undersecretary of State Thomas Pickering, he called Taylor "a president of rebels."

"You can't submit Taylor to established rules—he's a mercenary and will stay one—he was a rebel attacking in Liberia and is now a rebel attacking the sub-region."

The Liberian government formally notified its Guinean counterpart, as well as the United Nations, of its concerns; the Guineans did not respond.[39] President Conté of Guinea had forged a complicated and intimate alliance with the rebels who were coalescing in Guinean territory under the leadership of a Mandingo used-car dealer, Sekou Conneh, whose wife, Aisha, served as a spiritual adviser to the Guinean leader.[40] Not only were they given access to the forest redoubt along the Liberian border, but Conté allowed his military to cultivate ties with the guerrillas.

Taylor viewed the attack as an emerging national security threat. Shortly afterward he uncomfortably acknowledged the assault and that members of his own forces had later looted Voinjama after the rebels disappeared.[41] He tried to calm nerves, stating that the fighting wouldn't result in a clamping down on civil rights. He recognized that some of his security forces had crossed the line but promised those caught doing so would be punished. Should there be additional attacks, Taylor warned, "every inch of Liberian territory would be defended to the last man."[42]

That month reports of retaliation against Taylor's ethnic rivals began to trickle into the U.S. embassy.[43] Some speculated that government forces, frustrated that they had not been paid, had actually staged the attack on Voinjama as a pretext for a looting rampage. Other sources told embassy officials of revenge killings against tribes deemed to be rebel collaborators. "A Krahn source told an emboff [embassy officer] the security services (particularly the president son's unit) had been killing Mandingos," an April 30, 1999, State Department cable from Monrovia to Washington read.[44]

This was one of the first direct references to Chucky's unit, but the information carried no specific weight at that time. Chucky had become more of a known quantity over the course of the prior year, but his nationality wasn't mentioned. That information may have been novel, but the interest in his unit's conduct was part of standard State

Department reporting on human rights abuses. Each year local embassies compiled human rights reports on host nations, in part to abide by the Foreign Assistance Act, which precluded the U.S. government from funding nations actively committing abuses. In 1999 there was no sign that the information on the ATU would inform a criminal investigation. The focus then was on whether the war in Sierra Leone was blowing back into Liberia.[45]

A small convoy of jeeps and pickup trucks from Gbatala pulled to the front gates of White Flower on an evening in late April or early May 1999.[46] In the back of one vehicle, bound, blindfolded, and gagged with tape, lay Jusu, Turay, and Foday Conteh. The journey had been long. At Gbatala, Turay's arms had been bound so tightly together, he thought his chest would rip open. Before the vehicle started, he rolled himself out of the cab, hoping the fall, or an angry soldier, would kill him.

"I want to die," he muttered as he was pulled from the dirt and thrown into the vehicle.[47]

Throughout the two-hour trip to Monrovia, ATU soldiers had continued to kick and beat them. Over the roar of the engine, Jusu could hear his friend Turay crying. The men did not know where they were headed or what would happen to them. After the trucks lurched to a stop, the prisoners noticed the bright lights glaring through their blindfolds. It was the glare of electric light; the men were no longer in the bush but in Monrovia.

A short time later Chucky and Campari appeared, walking out of the compound, which the men would learn was White Flower. The defense minister, Daniel Chea, and a shorter man with a round face and salt-and-pepper beard followed. The latter approached the prisoners and asked that the tape be removed from their mouths.

Are you the rebels who attacked Voinjama? the man asked. Jusu realized the man speaking was Charles Taylor.[48]

The men insisted they were refugees, not fighters.

Taylor then asked the men why they'd refused to fight in Sierra Leone when offered the chance to.

Turay said, "We are just refugees. If you want to kill us, kill us."[49]

Jusu tried to explain this again but was struck across the mouth with a gun.

Taylor grew frustrated, according to the men; he threatened to have them brought to the beach and buried alive.

The defense minister interjected. "The killing should have been done where they're coming from."[50] He suggested that the men be brought to Barclay Training Center (BTC), the military training ground along the coast in downtown Monrovia. The opportunity to conceal the killing of these men had passed.

Indeed, an action they'd taken several months earlier—long before they ever encountered Chucky or his unit—would save the men's lives: they had registered as refugees. This status provided them legal protections under the UN High Commission on Refugees that even the Taylor government was sensitive to—protections that they otherwise lacked as Sierra Leoneans in Liberia. UNHCR was a persistent presence in West Africa after the outbreak of fighting in Liberia and Sierra Leone, running camps, repatriating refugees, and processing asylum claims. Africa accounted for more than 3.2 million of the 11.5 million worldwide refugees that year, but unlike nearly every other region in the world, the population of refugees on the continent continued to grow at a rate of 7 percent each year.[51] Liberia faced a twofold crisis of refugees: the 96,000 refugees flowing in from the fighting in Sierra Leone and the nearly 300,000 Liberian returnees arriving from exile in Ghana, Guinea, and Ivory Coast.

These shifting populations gave the Taylor government reason to fear that combatants could slip in as refugees from Voinjama. In Turay and Jusu's case, both were military-age males who had gunshot wounds from several years earlier, which could be read as evidence that they had fought at one point in their own country.[52] But given their refugee status, they couldn't simply be disappeared without leaving a record of their presence in Liberia. UNHCR closely monitored all the displaced populations along the frontier areas in Liberia, Sierra Leone, and Guinea. The commission had little power other than to report to the United Nations and donor governments, but the disappearance of refugees would potentially pose a political problem.

After leaving President Taylor's compound, Turay, Conteh, and Jusu were brought to the BTC. The base commander initially refused to accept the badly abused prisoners, but Campari and several ATU soldiers beat the commander bloody and dragged their prisoners to a shared cell. The other prisoners were horrified by the men. One told

Jusu that he didn't believe they had been at the ATU base for the simple fact that they survived. "No, nobody would go to Gbatala and come from there," he said.[53]

Conditions at the BTC were primitive and grim but nonetheless an improvement on Vietnam. The men's wounds had begun to rot and stink, so they were separated from the other prisoners and forced to sleep near the open bucket that served as the toilet. For several weeks, the men remained imprisoned, eventually able to walk and attend to themselves. But news of their presence spread out from the BTC. (Prisoners in Liberia are traditionally brought food by their family, so the existence of these new prisoners would be difficult to conceal in a small city like Monrovia.) Soon Jusu's wife and brother learned that he was alive. Eventually, an official from UNHCR visited the men. He asked whether they had registered as refugees. When he learned that they had, he promised to return.

The men heard nothing for weeks. Then one day the defense minister, Daniel Chea, arrived at their cell. They immediately recognized him as the man who—whether he'd intended to or not—had spared their lives. There was no reason for him to be there unless a decision had been made. Chea ordered their cell opened and demanded that Turay, Conteh, and Jusu be cleaned. The evidence of the abuse they had suffered was written across their bodies. Jusu and Turay refused—though it was unclear whether it was out of fear or out of understanding that the regime wanted to conceal their abuse.

The three men were led from the cell to a nearby office. A protection officer from UNHCR named Caroline Van Buren sat in the room, waiting for them.[54] When she took sight of the men, she couldn't restrain her anger. The defense minister had no choice but to free the men and, with them, their stories from Gbatala.

It was, perhaps, the most high-profile exposure of abuses carried out by Chucky's unit at that point. Yet even as their story became public, those closest to Chucky found the accounts of killings difficult to believe. The former deputy ATU commander who had dealt with Chucky's volatility (and was present for at least one journey with him to Gbalatuah) said of the April 1999 executions, "Chucky did not do anything ugly there."[55] For Lynn, it was even more difficult to reconcile the allegations.

"I don't think he did that," she said.[56] By that time she didn't doubt that he was capable of other acts of violence. His personality exhibited traits that suggested a deeper origin to his behavior. While there is no clinical definition of a psychopath, the term is lumped into a broader diagnostic classification—antisocial behavior disorder. According to the American Psychiatric Association's *Diagnostic and Statistical Manual on Mental Disorders*, it is characterized by "a pervasive pattern of disregard for, and violation of, the rights of others that begins in childhood or early adolescence and continues into adulthood."[57] A derivative classification, narcissistic personality disorder, is further defined by "a pervasive pattern of grandiosity, need for admiration, and a lack of empathy." The condition has a neurological foundation, according to Steven Pinker, psychologist and cognitive scientist, who writes, "The regions of the brain that handle social emotions, especially the amygdala and orbital cortex, are relatively shrunken or unresponsive in psychopaths."[58] The inclination toward revenge has been linked to a region of the brain called the rage circuit, which Pinker describes as "the midbrain-hypothalamus-amygdala pathway, which inclines an animal who has been hurt or frustrated to lash out at the nearest likely perpetrator." In humans, he notes, the impulse for revenge is fueled by the perceived reward it offers—and it requires a lack of empathy.

"I didn't see him as a murderer," Lynn recalled.[59] "Did he do some of those things? I'm pretty sure he did. Did he do all of those things? No."

Meanwhile the ongoing violence demonstrated that the international community could do little more than monitor the excesses of the Taylor government. Washington was failing to achieve either of its primary policy goals: minimizing the violence in Sierra Leone and curbing the abuses of Taylor's security forces within Liberia. The Clinton administration had charged Reverend Jesse Jackson and Ambassador Howard Jeter, special envoy to Liberia, with the task of bending Taylor to Washington's will with the promise of aid dollars. Their efforts had little impact; instead the State Department was reduced to reporting the grim drama playing out in Monrovia and the Liberian countryside.[60] "Human rights violations by the government persist. The security forces continue to be the worst offenders," one such report from the Monrovia embassy relayed early in the summer of 1999.[61] "Taylor's son Chuckie [*sic*] is particularly vicious and is accountable to nobody."

8

Danger

I'm livin in a bubble, bound for insane pourin fucken lava out my
brain father clear my path cause satan's in my way.

— *United States vs. Belfast,* EXHIBIT CE-9

Lynn Henderson pulled off of Tennessee State Route 18 later that summer. The car eased onto a private dirt road marked only by a handful
of weathered fence posts. The closest town, a hamlet of five thousand
named Bolivar, lay four miles down the road along the Hatchie River
in the southwestern corner of the state. Her destination was set back at
the far end of a mowed field: the house and barn that made up Rolling
H Farm, a tiny breeder.[1] This would be her last stop on a journey to
find the perfect gift—something fit for a president—for the man who
would be her father-in-law.

A year earlier Lynn's relationship with Chucky nearly came apart.
Her visits were infrequent and brief, and when she arrived in Liberia
on one trip, it became clear that he had been cheating on her.[2] Fed up
and disgusted, she confronted him.[3] She was prepared to leave him and
Liberia forever, but he wasn't ready to give up the relationship. Before
she could leave, he appeared at the Hotel Africa, on the far side of
Monrovia, where she had holed up. She recognized that getting out of
the country wouldn't be easy—at least not without his help. As angry
as she was, she agreed to take a drive with him to the beach. When
he stopped the car, he presented her with a small, nondescript pouch.
Inside was a piece of folded paper. Inside, she found a handful of dull,
uncut diamonds.

Chucky asked her to marry him.

It was a decidedly unromantic moment; for Lynn, the raw gems only contributed to the unreality of it. (They "probably came right off the river," she recalled.) She wasn't holding a ring but instead artifacts emblematic of the dysfunction of the place and situation she found herself in. Lynn was eighteen years old, very far from home, and without Chucky, very much alone. Her emotions collided in waves of happiness and sadness. She wanted many things in life that she could not have in Liberia. But she also wanted Chucky. If her future in the United States was relatively predictable—she would go to college like her older sisters—Liberia was not. There was the promise of wealth—Chucky always talked about his plans—but also the real possibility that everything would fall apart. Lynn made the decision that she felt made the most sense: she said yes.

So finding a gift for Charles Taylor carried new significance. She had flown in from Orlando to collect something unique, a purebred white German shepherd. Charles Taylor already had several dogs, but he had asked Lynn for the specific breed to complement his spotless white safari suits. A purebred was a sign of status, since the animals had to be imported; dingos and mutts could be found all over Monrovia and the countryside. Chucky had also asked for a dog—one more suited to his personality. Lynn found a pit bull puppy for him in Titusville, a city on the coast, an hour's drive from Orlando.

Even though she had not been back to Liberia in several months, Lynn felt closer to Chucky's father with each visit. The more time she spent with him, the more she came to see him not as a warlord—or even necessarily the president of Liberia—but as a well-educated, well-spoken father figure.[4] In moments of volatility and crisis with Chucky, she felt she could always turn to his father for comfort and support.

"He really loved me," she said. She began to feel the same toward him.

Liberia remained far from the home she had once hoped it could be. There were some signs that Chucky's station had improved—such as a Land Rover provided by prospective diamond miners who wished to curry favor with his father. Despite his growing responsibility with the ATU, however, Chucky hadn't progressed significantly into building a life for himself there.

His father had made little headway on addressing the devastating problems most Liberians faced every day: the lack of clean water, electricity, medical care, educational opportunities, and jobs.[5] The nation remained fragile. It was at peace, but the specter of war loomed large—and the donor states from the international community who had an interest in rebuilding postwar Liberia were wary of partnering with Charles Taylor, the man considered the author of much of the destruction in the first place. The only clear progress he had made was toward establishing Liberia as a security state—and positioning himself for the outbreak of another war.

This was cause for increasing concern among American officials.[6] On a Sunday afternoon in late June 1999, U.S. chargé d'affaires Donald Petterson arrived at White Flower to meet with Charles Taylor. The Liberian president's relationship with the U.S. government remained cordial, despite increasing disgust from Washington over his role in the Sierra Leonean conflict. Taylor hoped to restore the political, economic, and military connections of his predecessor, Samuel K. Doe, and an opportunity had presented itself. President Clinton had named a new ambassador to Monrovia, Bismarck Myrick, a career Foreign Service officer who had done stints throughout Africa—Lesotho, Somalia, South Africa—even Liberia in the mid-1980s, where he served in Monrovia as a political officer.[7] He, like Liberia's first president, was an African-American, from Norfolk, Virginia.

In the weeks following the August 1998 embassy bombings in Kenya and Tanzania, the embassy in Monrovia was one of several closed by the State Department out of security concerns—a fact that troubled Taylor.[8] He told Petterson that the U.S. government should not be concerned about a similar incident in Monrovia, saying that "foreign experts had been training an antiterrorist unit in Ganta and that if in the future the embassy needed support, this unit would be available." But these very forces were among the concerns Petterson wished to address. The embassy had been receiving reports about Taylor's security forces being the source of *insecurity*—being attached to violence, looting, and intimidation on the border. Though Petterson already knew the answer to his question, he asked: is the unit under Chucky Taylor?

The president acknowledged this obvious fact. Chucky had become a visible figure in Monrovia, tearing through traffic in a Land Rover with a license plate that read "DEMON."[9] Direct appeals to Taylor to protect human rights might not be effective, but Petterson knew that he might be receptive to the argument that his soldiers' excesses ran counter to his interests and could, for example, scare away foreign investors and donors. Taylor listened for a moment, then offered the diplomat the familiar solution to the problem of his undisciplined security forces: training support from the U.S. military, but problems of indiscipline and human rights violations among Taylor's force had worsened, rather than improved since Taylor made the same request of President Clinton months earlier. Petterson made it clear that the United States would not be taking on this project and that Taylor "needed to take the initiative to improve the quality of his forces."

Over the course of 1999, the U.S. embassy had learned increasingly more about Chucky and his unit—not only the news emerging out of Voinjama, but the sudden, unannounced presence of his fighters outside their compound. Yet his nationality figured into none of the reporting on him. The evening his father met with Petterson, Chucky's soldiers took control of three checkpoints located near the embassy.[10] Whether this was a deliberate show of force is not clear. The move, nonetheless, immediately sparked concern among American officials.

What followed was a series of confrontations between embassy security and Chucky's unit. His intentions were never clear, but the ATU fighters at Mamba Point heightened tensions, and Chucky further alarmed embassy security when he personally conducted a search patrol along the beach at the south perimeter of their compound, explaining obliquely that he was searching for "criminals."[11] Chucky's commanders, meanwhile, began harassing Liberian security officers working for the embassy, prompting the American regional security officer's intervention. Eventually Chucky met with the embassy's temporary defense attaché, Michael Bajek, and handed over a copy of the orders he'd given to ATU officers to set up checkpoints, search vehicles, and detail the occupants.[12]

This offered little comfort to the embassy or the local staff responsible for guarding the compound's entryway. Chucky did little to clarify why he was engaged in this game of chicken with the embassy. "At present, some embassy personnel are expressing concerns about having this unit on the compound's perimeter because of their lack of discipline and training," a cable reported. "According to one embassy officer, mercenaries have trained this group."[13]

Chucky's men kept up the pressure on the embassy into July 1999. "The Liberian government continues to deploy elements of the so-called Anti-Terrorist Unit," the embassy noted, as it began to learn more about these fighters.[14] "The ATU is the new name which the Liberian government has given to Chucky Taylor's notorious 'Demus Force' (also known as the Demon Brigade)."[15] Embassy officials continued to implore senior Taylor officials, including Jonathan Taylor, the minister of state and first cousin of the president, and Freddy Taylor, the head of the National Security Agency (not related), to turn the checkpoints over to the Liberian National Police. The requests went nowhere; the Liberian officials were not "willing to cross President Taylor or his son, Chucky, on the issue," an embassy official wrote at the time.[16]

Lynn was aware of the fearsome reputation Chucky and his men had developed. "Some of those boys were pure evil," she recalled.[17] Many of the fighters were drawn from the Small Boys Unit. Chucky's bodyguards bantered openly about cannibalism—shocking her by describing how human hands were the best part of the body to eat. Yet most interactions with Chucky's men gave her no reason to fear them. "I never saw the evil side of them, but I suppose it was there when [they were] confronted with the enemy. Killing, torture, I'm sure it takes a toll on the soul. I'm sure my boys [bodyguards] like Humphrey, Bobby, Tarnue, were considered evil. But I loved them, and they loved me."[18] Lynn understood why people feared Chucky: "He kind of had, I don't know, maybe a Dr. Jekyll/Mr. Hyde personality."[19] But she had been immune from his outbursts. She says that he had never harmed her; in fact, she always felt safer around him. "I always thought I brought out the better side in him because I'm a good person. I always thought that I made him a better person."[20] The truth was that Chucky led a separate life, characterized not only by the violence of the ATU but by his lying and womanizing.

Lynn wasn't the only person in Chucky's life to feel a pull to Liberia. Bernice regularly shuttled back and forth between Florida and Monrovia, living with her son and carrying out semiofficial duties—like visiting orphanages—typically associated with the first lady.[21] As Bernice's attachments to Liberia grew, her marriage to Roy Belfast began to splinter.

The exact nature of her renewed affection for Taylor wasn't clear; nor was it entirely remarkable. Taylor's wives, current and past, orbited around him, drifting in and out of his residence and benefiting from being connected with him. Bernice eventually openly associated herself as a member of the Taylor family. She went as far as adopting an alternate identity: Yassazoe Emmanuel Taylor.[22] The name drew from Charles Taylor's mother's first name. Liberia was a break from the other narratives in her life: middle age, divorce, suburbia. Monrovia offered a different sort of drama, the petty jealousies and affections of Taylor's wives set against the backdrop of political intrigue.

Lynn's view on it was clear: "She was obsessed with Charles Taylor. . . . She wanted to be there. She wanted to be Liberian."

Lynn arrived with her sister for another summer vacation in Monrovia in early August 1999, bearing two puppies as gifts.[23] Charles Taylor named his German shepherd "Rex," while Chucky chose to name his pit bull "Danger," borrowing the middle name from *Austin Powers*, the Mike Myers spy comedy.

Chucky indulged the two women in the little sightseeing Monrovia afforded: the dense business district along Broad Street where tailors and jewelers crafted their wares in open-air storefronts; the embassy neighborhood on Mamba Point, which centered on the American compound; the sprawling markets along the Mesurado River in Waterside and Duala, where tin-roofed shops hawked essentials: dried fish, bush meat, plastic bottles filled with gasoline, tiny bundles of hot peppers. The group walked along the beach in Congo Town, near Chucky's villa, snapping photos, with his bodyguard, Bobby Dixon, standing in the distance. Wherever he went, Lynn noticed, boys and young men saluted him, saying, "Yes, sir, Chief."[24]

The group ventured out of the city on day trips, even dropping in on a chimpanzee-testing facility near Harbel, operated by the New York Blood Bank—a strange artifact left over from pre–civil war Liberia—for an unannounced tour.[25] On the way back to Monrovia one afternoon, the group pulled off the road to an isolated berm littered with broken bottles.[26] Chucky retrieved a pistol and sawed-off shotgun from the truck for impromptu target practice. He filmed Lynn and her sister with a camcorder as they took turns firing the weapons, providing commentary.

At night, the group hit the clubs in downtown Monrovia, like the

Pepper Bush, a threadbare spot on Warren Street that attracted those who could afford to drink—foreign businessmen, government officials, Lebanese merchants, and security officers. Chucky had a reputation for throwing his weight around at clubs. In one incident, on September 22, 1999, he walked into a nightclub and noticed several members of the National Police's Special Operations Division (SOD) drinking with three clean-cut Americans—U.S. Marines attached to the embassy.[27] He approached the table where the men sat in front of their beers and drinks and demanded to know why the SOD officers were drinking on duty. He then looked at the Americans and asked the men "why the U.S. ambassador would allow Marines to drink late at night?" and demanded to know their names and rank. Rather than engage, the table of Marines stood up and walked out of the nightclub.

The threat of violence was constant. Chucky wore a sidearm on his hip at all times; his bodyguard, Bobby, with him, an AK-47 at the ready. On August 11 a second rebel attack struck Voinjama.[28] Shortly afterward the BBC's Africa Service broadcast an interview with a rebel calling himself "2nd Lieutenant Mosquito Spray."[29] The leader made it clear that his group was not aligned with any faction from Liberia's dormant civil war. (Rebels who had captured several aid workers referred to themselves as "the Joint Forces for the Liberation of Liberia," a previously unheard-of group.) "Mosquito Spray" gave little indication of the group's aim other than that it had formed to oppose Charles Taylor's government.

The gravity of the news didn't sink in initially for Lynn, who ran around Chucky's house in the pitch black wearing night-vision goggles, laughing off the ridiculous name of the new rebel leader.[30] Details of the assault trickled back to Monrovia—unlike the April incident, the fighting was sustained. Taylor described the forces as "very heavy, well armed and equipped."[31] He suspected Guinea's hand in the fighting, which appeared to originate in the neighboring nation. Taylor declared a state of emergency and called up his militia to deploy forces toward the border. It was time for Lynn to go home.

Lynn returned to Orlando in late summer, the daydream of Liberia over for a moment. Chucky called her when he could—but was vague, rarely discussing the fighting in the bush, which had started with the first assault on Voinjama that spring and resumed after she departed.[32] Beyond his security role, he hoped to start making money, dabbling with timber and diamond-mining ventures. In times like these—when everything was going well—he never mentioned coming home. He was content with the idea that America represented his past and Liberia his future. Lynn loved him, but she couldn't leave her life, her family, and her friends in the United States entirely behind. For better or worse, the couple had grown accustomed to living across the Atlantic from each other.

Lynn filled in the distance between them with suspicions about his philandering. They had been engaged for more than a year, but now the stakes had changed. That autumn she told Chucky that he was going to be a father.

If she had known what Chucky was doing in Liberia, it might have given her pause before moving ahead with their marriage. He had stepped to the fore in the ATU as a punisher and enforcer—of both prisoners and his own recruits. This didn't endear him to his men. Many trainees at the base were still seething with anger over the killing of Justin Parker, when they learned of another punishment Chucky had meted out in Monrovia.[33]

The incident involved an ATU soldier Chucky discovered drinking at a nightclub. This violation, while minor, was significant to Chucky. He was incensed that the man—a young, strong fighter from the Mano tribe named Kougbay Dunuma—was in uniform.[34] Chucky ordered the man arrested and brought to the Executive Mansion, to be locked in a cell located near the seawall behind the building. Punishments varied for prisoners. Sometimes they were forced to cut grass in the sun using a machete—which Liberians called a cutlass. Others were imprisoned without any legal or disciplinary proceeding. But Chucky had decided to make an example of this young fighter. At daybreak the morning after his arrest, Dunuma was pulled from his cell and tied to a pole.

Chucky ordered a punishment that amounted to a death sentence: one thousand lashes. (To give context, in antebellum Alabama slaves found in possession of a weapon could receive no more than thirty-nine lashes; those who forged "free passes" for other slaves could receive one hundred lashes.) An officer from Benjamin Yeaten's unit, Bartuah Gbor, recounted seeing the commotion from his office.[35] Dunuma was bound and restrained. For the better part of an hour, two men took turns striking the prisoner with a stick and a rubber truncheon. Gbor stepped out from his office to see what was happening. When the officers had finished, Dunuma looked at Gbor and said, "Can I have water to drink?" But Dunuma didn't live much longer. Gbor recounted that without making another sound, the man died. Chucky and the others removed the body to bury it outside town.

The ATU was becoming notorious for human rights abuses. Gbatala became a prison camp as much as a training facility. In early August 1999, as unrest continued near the border, several new detainees arrived at the base from Monrovia and were sent to Vietnam.[36] Among them were two men who had been transferred from cells at the Executive Mansion: Nathaniel Koah, a prominent diamond miner in Lofa County, and Anthony Sonkarlay, one of his employees.

Koah's story embodied the kleptocratic bent of the Taylor government.[37] While he'd been detained by the ATU, his arrest had little bearing on national security. Instead, by Koah's account, its purpose was to shake him down for a five-carat diamond. Koah, a prominent diamond miner and former supporter of Taylor's, had been in this position before. In 1994 he had mined a nine-carat stone in territory held by Taylor's rebels. As he made his way toward Ivory Coast, where he intended to sell the diamond, Taylor's fighters intercepted him, instructing him to detour to Ganta in northern Liberia because "Charles Taylor wanted this diamond." That stone, Koah said later, went to the purchase of weapons that helped Taylor retake his stronghold in Gbarnga. But Koah did not have any diamonds this time.

When Koah arrived at Gbatala, he would later testify, he'd already been subjected to several days of intense abuse and interrogation about a diamond he was allegedly carrying. He'd seen firsthand the person the president's son had become. Soon after his detention at the Executive Mansion, Koah witnessed the beating death of Duduma. (The two men had briefly been tied to the same pole.) He'd also seen his own wife stripped naked and beaten in an attempt to elicit information. He'd even been brought across Monrovia to White Flower where, he said, President Taylor himself interrogated him about the diamond and an alleged coup plot. Koah told the president nothing—by his account there was nothing to tell. He was turned over to President Taylor's son.

Chucky was interested not only in the diamond but also in Koah's political affiliations. The president's son directly questioned the prisoner, but Koah could offer no response, he would later testify. The change Chucky had undergone in his few short years in Liberia was alarming. "He came as an innocent child and he saw his father in power and they handed him [a] gun," Koah recalled. "When he handled gun, he was happy, he was power drunk. He could do anything when his father was president."[38]

When Chucky received no response from Koah, he ratcheted up the pressure, ordering his prisoner to pour a two-pound bag of salt into a cooking pot and begin eating it while he watched. Several days later Koah was taken to the third floor of the Executive Mansion where, he testified, Chucky ordered him to be suspended above a smoking fire. Several fighters stoked the fire below him with cotton and what Koah called "acid liquid," sending plumes of acrid smoke upward. Koah passed out quickly from the smoke. When he eventually came to, he found himself in a bath of ice water with Chucky standing over him, demanding to know if he was still alive.

Koah was then delivered to Gbatala. It was at a tenuous moment; indiscipline pervaded, even among the commanders.[39] Trainees continued to arrive from Monrovia and surrounding areas, only to find themselves menaced by David Campari. The Gambian would wake the trainees several times over the course of the night to assemble for roll call and deprived them of food, while entertaining women and drinking heavily on the funds set aside for the recruits. He trusted none of the Liberians and would draft vulnerable new recruits as spies to monitor dissent. All this behavior occurred out of Chucky's sight. When he would arrive on the base, Menephar and the others were too afraid to report Campari to him.

"Nobody wanted to get hurt," Menephar recalled. "And this guy is surely going to hurt you, he's going to hurt you seriously." The ATU recruits that did cross Campari were ordered held in the same holes as other prisoners. "He send you there. And you're not going to come [back] from there," he said.

With more prisoners on the base, Campari's attention began to shift to the detainees. Gbatala was a nightmare, Koah and Sonkarlay would later testify, where the prisoners experienced daily beatings and were forced to eat cigarette butts and drink their own urine, scarred with molten plastic and covered in voracious driver ants. The men claimed they were even forced to witness the killing and mutilation of other prisoners.

At the time of Koah's arrival, access to the holes was limited to the MPs, but the guards permitted Menephar to visit his former commander from the days of the civil war—a man named Morris Gbleh—who had also been imprisoned in a hole following the incident where he shot a sentry after returning from the village drunk. Gbleh was treated as a pariah within the ATU after that, but Menephar brought cigarettes to Gbleh's hole, "because he was like my dad."

There Menephar witnessed some of the abuse the prisoners would later recount, including being raped and forced to rape others. (Menephar refuted accusations about prisoner executions: "I never saw that. I never heard it."[40]) Word of the sexual assaults made it back to Monrovia, where it crossed a boundary with Charles Taylor. He sent his son to investigate at the end of the rainy season in 1999, between late August and October. Chucky arrived on base shortly thereafter and marched down to Vietnam, where Koah, Sonkarlay, and another man Chucky had ordered detained at the St. Paul River bridge—a furniture maker named Rufus Kpadeh—were being held.

When Chucky arrived, Koah complained about the rapes, according to testimony Kpadeh later provided.[41] Chucky didn't share his father's concern over the assaults and instead told the men that "he wanted to see if it was the truth." The men were then pulled from their holes and forced to rape one another again. Chucky said nothing, the men recalled. Instead, he and the other ATU soldiers stood there shooting photographs. Chucky's behavior defied explanation, but the mistreatment of the prisoners had real consequences for his father.

In early October 1999 a Monrovia-based human rights group, FOCUS, filed a petition for a writ of habeas corpus on Koah, after receiving a tip about the diamond miner's detention. Even as Taylor consolidated his power in Liberia, there remained a community of influential local human rights workers. The largest, longest-standing human rights group was the Justice and Peace Commission, a group backed by the Catholic Church with offices connected to the archdiocese of Monrovia and Gbarnga. Taylor had an adversarial relationship with these organizations, as he had with the media. He preferred to target outspoken human rights leaders and journalists individually through intimidation and arrest, rather than outlaw their organizations. Critics of the government had to consider their own safety before speaking out.

At that time, FOCUS was actively engaged in a campaign to have the Gbatala base destroyed because of the alleged human rights abuses taking place there. The next day *The News*, a Monrovia daily, published a front-page story with Koah's picture, indicating that he'd been detained by the ATU and brought to "an unknown location without charge and . . . subjected to torture, denied proper meal [*sic*] and safe drinking water."

The petition was surprisingly successful. Koah was almost immediately removed from the base and brought to nearby Phebe Hospital for treatment, before being delivered to President Taylor and Chucky. At that meeting, according to Koah, both father and son warned him to remain silent about the abuse he had endured, especially to the media. Chucky warned him that should he reveal anything "contrary to our advice, the government won't guarantee your safety."

Koah went directly to the press. Through FOCUS, he revealed the location of the ATU base at Gbatala and decried "gross human rights abuses ranging from forced sodomy to intense torture and other forms of inhumane treatment," singling out that "the Anti-Terrorists Unity [*sic*] are reportedly perpetrating these acts which [are] commanded by Chucky Taylor, the son of the President of the Republic of Liberia." It was an attempt not only to lend credibility to his allegations but to provoke outrage in Taylor at the actions carried out by his son's men.

"If I lie before God and man, you may kill me, Mr. President," he said at the press conference.[42]

Previously, Taylor had shown little interest in addressing allegations of abuses among his security forces—chronicled each year in the State Department's report on human rights violations in Liberia. But following Koah's statements, he ordered an investigation into the incidents of rape. One of the soldiers who had participated in rape was detained on the base, Menephar said, but shortly thereafter escaped. With both the president's and the public's attention suddenly focused on Gbatala, Menephar noticed that Campari had grown uncharacteristically afraid. If Taylor was truly intent on pursuing consequences, Campari had some reason to be: the Gambian had issued the order that the detainees should be raped, Menephar said, and fearing this would be discovered, he had allowed the soldier to slip away so he couldn't implicate his commander any further.[43]

The incident also became a rare rallying point for human rights groups to direct international attention to Taylor. On November 7, 1999, the Justice and Peace Commission sent a letter to Desmond Parker, the UN human rights officer, indicating that Koah had been "detained and tortured at the ATU Base in Gbatala, Bong County, from July 26 to October 18, 1999," and asking that the UN safeguard his rights, person, and provide health care for him.[44] Parker, a Trinidadian who was social with Chucky and his mother, took no immediate public action in the case, and the issue failed to rise above the din of local politics to put pressure on Taylor.[45] (Parker, who was named chief of protocol for the United Nations in 2010, declined comment, citing UN regulations.[46]) Koah, a diamond trader, hardly cut a sympathetic figure, particularly in light of the increasingly negative attention toward conflict diamonds. And in relative terms, Charles Taylor's government had been accused of far worse than what Koah alleged occurred at Gbatala.

Yet Koah represented a persistent problem for Chucky. Even though he had been warned of the consequences of not remaining silent, he continued to speak out, in an effort to humiliate and shame both Chucky and his father. In Liberian society, when an individual is publicly accused of wrongdoing, there is an expectation that if that person is innocent, the accused will rebut the allegation publicly. Chucky chose not to use the press to respond to Koah: he decided to deal with the man himself.

Several days later ATU soldiers arrived at Koah's home outside Monrovia, fired several shots through his front door, kicked it in, and poured into the building searching for him.[47] Koah hid in the ceiling, leaving his wife, Esther, and his seventeen-year-old daughter to deal with the gunmen. When the fighters couldn't locate him, they arrested Koah's wife and daughter.

The women weren't spared. Chucky interrogated them in his office at the Executive Mansion, according to testimony the wife and daughter later provided, demanding to know Koah's whereabouts. The women refused to tell him anything. After several hours, he turned them over to two soldiers, who led them apart and raped them. The women suffered serious injuries during the assaults but were released the following day. They couldn't easily turn to the press or human rights community, as sexual assault carried with it a severe stigma in Liberia—and going public offered no guarantee that the women would see justice served in Taylor's nation.

For his part, Koah climbed into a cargo truck and slipped across the border into Ivory Coast, abandoning his country and family. Chucky's former prisoner had been forced into exile, but not before exacting a huge cost to the ATU's reputation as a new, highly trained force. Yet Taylor had not abandoned the project. In fact, he hoped it would be a showpiece for his administration.

On December 17, 1999, Charles Taylor's convoy arrived at Gbatala base for a graduation ceremony.[48] The president was finally ready to unveil his secret training program. Accompanying him was a small group of dignitaries, including Daouda Malam Wanké, the president of Niger, and Maj. Stefan Arredondo, a representative from the office of the defense attaché with the U.S. embassy. Chucky, dressed in military fatigues, escorted his father, clad in a white safari suit, onto the base. Despite the events of the prior months, Taylor wanted to use the Anti-Terrorist Unit's graduation to show off the unit to outsiders, to showcase the advent of a professional fighting force in Liberia. The nominal purpose of the unit was for "VIP protection"—but the day's proceedings were meant to be a show of force and a projection of Taylor's power. The unit performed a live-fire demonstration and, at one point, launched an RPG-7 at the target range, surprising the audience.[49] President Wanké hastily excused himself to go to the bathroom, apparently unsettled by the missile's detonation.

While it was meant to be a public demonstration, some things had to remain concealed for the graduation ceremony. The South Africans and Gambians were ordered to leave to avoid linking the unit to any mercenary units. "The government did not want any foreigners on the base, because journalists from all over were going there," Menephar said.[50] A new commander, a Liberian named Jason Wennie, was brought to stand in as the base commandant.

Despite the success of the graduation ceremony, tension had been mounting between Chucky and his father. Beyond the Koah case, his son's leadership style troubled Taylor: Chucky kept strange hours, sleeping throughout the day and rising at night to begin his work. He was impulsive and reactionary, quick to punish and lock up his own men, but rarely equipped with anything resembling a plan. His personal life was sloppy as well. Commanders surrounding Chucky noticed that he had begun to drink, use drugs, and womanize more openly.[51]

Moreover, the vision Chucky had at the outset for a small, well-disciplined unit collided with the demands facing his father to build a force sizable enough to carry out Taylor's military agenda. After graduation, another batch of recruits traveled to Gbatala, including seasoned NPFL fighters sent by President Taylor to undergo ATU training. Many of the NPFL holdovers were veterans of the civil war and members of Taylor's Special Security Service; they were considered to be "militia"—shorthand for untrained, undisciplined, and unaccountable. While months earlier, the South African mercenary Fred Rindel had stressed the importance of quality fighters, the addition of these new fighters showed that quantity had become more important to Charles Taylor.

While President Taylor's action did not surprise the recruits already on the base, the next round of trainees he ordered sent did. Late in December 1999 a green Mercedes cargo truck lumbered up the gravel roadway leading onto the base grounds, delivering a new contingent of men.[52] The gunmen were fresh from the front lines along the border with Sierra Leone and Guinea, but Menephar noticed something different about them—they were not Liberians but Sierra Leoneans. These men were from the Revolutionary United Front, belonging to the commander Sam Bockarie, known by the nom de guerre "Mosquito" (not to be confused with the rebel "Mosquito Spray" who had attacked Voinjama). Journalists covering the war in Sierra Leone noted his decidedly unmilitary background: he had reportedly been a disco dancer and hairdresser before becoming a militia commander.[53] Bockarie was a feared leader, in large part due to the savagery of the RUF, which had cut a swath of terror across Sierra Leone, killing civilians and amputating limbs of survivors. This reputation preceded him and his men when they arrived in Liberia.

"It was my first time seeing Sierra Leoneans," Menephar recalled.

Months earlier, in March 1999, the RUF had struck a peace deal with the government of Sierra Leone, which called for a disarmament and demobilization program for rebel fighters.[54] The RUF leader Foday Sankoh called for combatants to abide by the terms of the peace, but only 4,217 of an estimated 45,000 fighters put down their weapons.[55] Sam Bockarie defied Sankoh and refused to disband his militia. The arrival of these insurgents at Gbatala signified Taylor's lack of support for peace in Sierra Leone—not only were the rebels permitted safe passage into Liberia, they were provided housing and military training. Whatever deniability Taylor had cultivated regarding his involvement in Sierra Leone, he was now willing to jeopardize it with the presence of the fighters.

He continued the expansion of the ATU, sending Yeaten's soldiers with the SSS and SOD to Gbatala base for training in late December and early January 2000.[56] Campari returned with a retinue of bodyguards from Maryland County to again assume control.

The new round of fighters at Gbatala were a motley bunch: older, battle-hardened factional fighters. The extent of their training prior to Gbatala was limited to what was called *balaka*—a brutal variation on endurance training that had been introduced to the NPFL in Libya.[57] Recruits had to survive beatings and live-fire obstacle courses to prove their mettle. Menephar, who had been tasked to assist the South Africans in training this new batch of recruits, looked down on them but set about the task of training them. "They were not properly taught. They needed to be taught professionally," he later said.

Taylor required a strong offensive force, capable of cross-border raids. Taylor did not seek an overt military conflict with any of his neighbors—but he felt the best way to defend Liberia was to weaken his neighbors.

The international community saw other motives in Taylor's pursuit of mayhem in Sierra Leone. He profited from trafficking in "blood diamonds" plundered there, using the proceeds to bankroll his lifestyle and war machine.[58] This practice had drawn the scrutiny of international human rights organizations and the United Nations, which began to explore the potential for sanctions on the precious stone trade. UN investigators linked a ferocious RUF assault and siege on Freetown in January 1999 to arms shipments that had been transported through Liberia at Taylor's behest.[59]

By February 2000, the Sierra Leonean presence in Liberia had become an open secret.[60] For American officials looking to stop the bloodshed in Sierra Leone, the fact that the RUF was not demilitarizing but instead strengthening its alliance with Taylor represented trouble. Late that month Liberia's foreign minister admitted to the U.S. embassy that Sierra Leonean forces were in Liberia. The following month, in a meeting with the ambassador, Taylor denied that the men were receiving training, but he appeared uncomfortable doing so. In fact, Bockarie had traveled in Taylor's entourage on a recent trip to Libya. The RUF fighters were now yet another military element fully under Taylor's aegis.

There was method to the disorder of Taylor's security forces.[61] By redrawing the divisions among the armed groups surrounding him, he prevented any single group or commander from attaining too much power and influence—including his own son. Their relationship—like most relationships in Chucky's life—was extremely volatile. In his father's presence, Chucky played the obedient son, showing Taylor respect in front of his peers.[62] Beyond his sight, Chucky often ignored his father's orders, according to a senior ATU commander who asked to not be identified.

Chucky's day-to-day behavior veered toward the unpredictable—he was "sometimey," as Liberians said, meaning that he often acted normally but could explode. He drove manically and went nowhere without his bodyguards. He conducted his liaisons with women at the Hotel Africa and the Boulevard Hotel rather than at his home. One hotel employee recalled Chucky emerging from his room, enraged at an electrical outage and holding the staff at gunpoint until the generator could be restarted.[63] A manager at the Boulevard said, however, that unlike most members of Taylor's inner circle who frequented the hotel, Chucky always paid his bill.[64]

On January 28, 2000, Monrovia hummed with activity. Official convoys raced through the streets and helicopters buzzed over rooftops, as dignitaries and not-so-dignified hangers-on to the regime arrived for the marriage of the president's son. Chucky and Lynn had no interest in having a state wedding (Lynn had envisioned a small affair for close friends and family), but Charles Taylor insisted on an event in line with his position.[65] The event could only take place in Africa—both Chucky and his father remained fugitives in the United States, so the couple would marry in Monrovia. The date set for their nuptials was also his fifty-second birthday.

Liberia had little reason to celebrate the wedding of the president's son. At the beginning of 2000, the country ranked 174th out of 175 nations listed on the Human Development Index.[66] Only 15 percent of the adult population could read and write, and the average life expectancy of a citizen was just over forty-two years, according to State Department estimates. The government provided few, if any, services to the people, most of whom lived without reliable access to electricity and running water. Many teachers went without pay for months and even years. State-sponsored schools and universities barely functioned. The legal system also withered for lack of funds, and when the courts did operate, judges ran the risk of being assaulted and tortured by security forces for unpopular rulings, while others insisted on receiving bribes to simply hear a case. International donors—including the United States—had all but abandoned the country, leaving Taiwan nearly alone in its monetary support for the Taylor government. The United States offered Liberia only $13.1 million in aid for 2000, much of it to provide food to the population, many of whom lived on the edge of starvation.

The U.S. ambassador, Bismarck Myrick, pleaded for money from Washington to support civil society programs—including opposition groups—which had been blocked by the Senate Foreign Relations Committee.[67] Myrick recognized that Taylor's conduct as president, particularly his human rights record, was viewed with "repugnance" in Washington, yet he touted progress on governance issues and noted in a letter to Susan Rice, the assistant secretary of state for African affairs, that "Taylor is not the total of Liberian society. He is the duly elected president of the country."[68] Myrick envisioned using State Department funds to bolster internal checks on Taylor's power, but Washington had no plans to invest in Taylor's government or programs that could, even indirectly, provide him support. "Only if the other parties are strengthened will the Liberian electorate have an alternative to Taylor and his ruling National Patriotic Party," Myrick wrote.

As lavish as the wedding was to be in Liberia's current context, Lynn nearly missed it.[69] She departed with Chucky's mother in late December on a KLM flight from JFK to Ivory Coast, but even as it approached Abidjan, Ivorian military officers were staging a coup in the capital. The aircraft rerouted to Togo, where Lynn and Bernice disembarked, then faced the challenge of traveling overland across three West African nations—one of which was in the midst of political collapse—to reach the Liberian border. Lynn was nearly four months pregnant and had with her the beautiful, white sleeveless wedding gown she had selected at a bridal boutique in downtown Orlando. The two set out by car across Togo, crossing the border into Ghana and driving to an airfield, where Charles Taylor had chartered a small, propeller aircraft to pick them up. The two hazarded Ivorian airspace and soon touched down in Liberia. There were just a few short weeks to finalize wedding preparations and ready everything for the arrival of Lynn's parents and sisters, as well as Chucky's cousins from Georgia and Massachusetts.

Conducting a luxurious wedding in this environment suggested a few logistical obstacles. For example, flowers. It wasn't a matter of simply hiring Monrovia's top florist: there wasn't one. President Taylor had to import the flowers from Ivory Coast. Travel for the wedding party was no simple matter, either. Liberia remained hard to reach not only because of carriers and weather but, as Lynn had seen, because of the region's politics. By January, however, the situation in Ivory Coast had stabilized sufficiently for regular air travel to resume between Monrovia, Abidjan, and the rest of the world. Lynn's parents and sisters and several of Chucky's cousins arrived just days before the nuptials.

Providence Baptist Church on Broad Street in downtown Monrovia was selected for the ceremony. The stone sanctuary sat a short distance from Providence Island, where the church had been originally founded in 1822 by Liberia's first émigrés. Chucky was dressed impeccably in a black tuxedo, a white boutonniere pinned to his lapel. President Taylor looked on from a wooden pew, smiling. Chucky's mother, Bernice, wore sunglasses throughout the ceremony. Their wedding party reflected a sampling of Liberia's elite: Chucky's best man, Israel Akinsanya, was a Liberian political operator who had spent much of the past decade in the Twin Cities before returning to his homeland; Wisam Fawaz, a groomsman, was a friend and business partner prominent in the Lebanese community and had connections to one of the country's largest timber companies. Lynn's family, by and large average Americans, disconnected from the world of politics and power, watched as their daughter and sister exchanged vows with Chucky. The child

Lynn carried would be born between these worlds, which were steadily growing apart.

But that night they celebrated. Chefs had prepared "Barracuda à la Lynn" and an ornate wedding cake.[70] Lynn's father gave a short toast to the audience, but the room clearly belonged to President Taylor. Taylor knew of the struggles Lynn had endured in her relationship with his son. She had sought consolation from him in the face of Chucky's dalliances. Taylor had little to say on the subject of fidelity, but he offered Lynn words of advice on how to deal with his son. "The patient dog gets the biggest bone," he told her in private.[71]

At the reception, Taylor offered a toast. He referenced a passage from the Old Testament, recalling the story where Ruth, a widow, promises loyalty to her mother-in-law:

> Don't ask me to leave you and turn back. Wherever you go, I will go; wherever you live, I will live. Your people will be my people, and your God will be my God. Where you die I will die, and there I will be buried. May the Lord deal with me, be it ever so severely, if anything but death separates you and me.[72]

In April 2000, four months after the wedding, Lynn went into labor in Orlando. Their honeymoon had taken the couple briefly to Trinidad, then they went separate ways: Lynn returning to Pine Hills, Chucky to Liberia. His absence was a reminder of some of the unchanged truths about him. He was a fugitive in Florida and at odds with the nation of his citizenship. Chucky listened to the birth at the other end of the phone line from Monrovia. They called him Charles Heman Taylor III. For his middle name, they chose the Hebrew word for "faithful."

If you laid out the facts of their marriage, it seemed impossible: They lived across an ocean; Chucky was unfaithful and volatile. Then there was Liberia, with its harsh tropical climate, the exposure to violence and disease, and the strange palace politics surrounding Chucky's father. Chucky hoped to make his own money like other children of the elite. Despite all this, Lynn hoped for normalcy.

She brought the boy to meet his father six months later. The trip was her first visit since the wedding and the first occasion for their small family to be together. As she settled into the house, she noticed that Danger, the pit bull she had purchased for Chucky, was nowhere to be seen. When Lynn asked one of the house employees what had happened, she received an implausible response. ("Oh-Ma, a coconut fell on her," the woman said.[73])

She could only suspect that something had happened while she was back in the States—and she knew what Chucky was capable of. When she confronted Chucky, he simply told her that "he shot the dog."[74]

9
Resources

Real talk no shame, as this game is the same, hold my beef any day despite da risk and the pain.

— *United States vs. Belfast*, EXHIBIT CE-9

Charles Taylor expected his son to earn his living, to not rely on handouts for his survival, to be a loyal and effective leader. By February 2000, when the newest fighters completed their training at Gbatala, those expectations collided with the realities of his son's disastrous tenure as the leader of the ATU.[1] Chucky had accomplished little more than develop a reputation for brutality and indiscipline. The allegations that surfaced in the press following Nathaniel Koah's detention translated into a popular fear that defined public opinion of him. In one highly publicized instance, a local newspaper ran a story with the headline "Chucky Shows Compassion."[2] It detailed Chucky's heroic efforts to rush a gravely injured child to the hospital, but as the embassy reported: "Only by finishing the article did a reader learn that Chucky had hit the child with his vehicle and that the victim was dead on arrival at the hospital."

For Charles Taylor, this reputation was a liability. The newest recruits who arrived at Gbatala in late 1999 were men loyal to Benjamin Yeaten, not to Chucky. The competition between Yeaten and Chucky became palpable. Both looked to President Taylor as a father figure. While Chucky was Taylor's flesh and blood, Yeaten had known Taylor longer—he was a child of the NPFL, coming of age at Tajura and following the revolution into adulthood. When the ATU absorbed

Yeaten's fighters, Chucky did not emerge a more powerful commander of a larger unit. In fact, the president fired his son.

Chucky wasn't entirely unprepared. Before losing his command, he had set out to establish himself in business. Liberia's economy and political system had always operated on a patronage system, where familial and personal relationships were rewarded with jobs, contracts, and positions, and in that respect, Chucky was born into incredible privilege.[3] To outsiders, Taylor's government bore all the markings of a traditional organized crime family: the state-run industries and major export businesses were rackets that Taylor allowed his loyalists to exploit in exchange for a percentage of their earnings.[4]

When Taylor took office, he began sculpting legislation that would legalize the wholesale theft of natural resources from Liberia, eventually pushing three laws through the legislature to accomplish this—the National Forestry Law, the broader Strategic Commodities Act, and even the Petroleum Law, which governed any discovery of fossil fuel deposits.[5] As strong as he was, Taylor could not always overrule the organs of government and simply impose his will on the nation. He often worked within the legal bounds of an established, if not necessarily functional, government, including a theoretically independent legislature and judiciary. Taylor was even taken to task by the legislature for procedural minutiae. In one instance, after representatives complained that the president had not formally submitted the nominations of several senior appointees, he complied. Most of the time, however, Taylor used these institutions to confer legitimacy on his actions. If he could achieve his political and economic objectives with the mien of propriety, his critics, domestic and abroad, would have less fodder.

Timber was one of the industries traditionally managed by the nation's elite.[6] To make room for his son, Taylor revoked a number of timber concessions with VH Timber Companies and several Spanish and French logging groups, allowing Chucky to move ahead with a fledgling timber venture, United Timber Company.[7] He connected Chucky with the Fawaz family. Two of the patriarchs of the family, Hussein and Abbas Fawaz, controlled a massive timber operation in southeastern Liberia called Maryland Wood Processing Industries. As Chucky made inroads into the business, he found a friend and business partner in Wisam, a son of the family.

The Strategic Commodities Act effectively handed the state's assets

over to Taylor, designating "all mineral resources especially gold, diamonds, all natural forest resources including logs and timber, unique
and rare species of vegetation and wildlife as strategic commodities and
grants the president the sole power to execute, negotiate and conclude
all commercial contracts or agreements with any foreign and domestic investors for the exploitation of any of these commodities."[8] Taylor
would control the necessary checks and balances with respect to trade;
the act noted that commercial agreements "shall become effectively
binding upon the republic as would any treaty to which the republic
is a party, upon the sole signature and approval of the president of the
Republic of Liberia."

This was bald corruption, giving Taylor unilateral authority to loot
the nation's resources. Nearly all Taylor's predecessors—Tubman, Tolbert, Doe—had used the office as prerogative to grab resources from
the Liberian state to maintain their parties and personal empires, but he
took it one step further and made corruption the law. He could not be
called a criminal, because he had legalized all the rackets.

But Chucky and his father could not carry out business without
international investment. For all Liberia's wealth in timber, iron ore,
gold, and diamonds, the barriers to entry into the international markets
for these commodities were significant. Taylor required not only capital
and logistical support but also international partners willing to market Liberian resources. For the most part, it was European and Asian
investors, willing to navigate the dangerous and controversial business
environment, who stepped into this gap. American investment had not
entirely dried up in Liberia. Firestone Rubber, which had been acquired
by Bridgestone, a Japanese competitor, continued to extract rubber sap
from its vast plantation near Harbel and remained very much represented by the U.S. embassy in Monrovia. Beyond the corporate sphere
lay a different class of entrepreneur: independent investors seeking
riches in Liberia's gold and diamond reserves. The chief asset many
of these investors could bring to the table was the willingness to turn
a profit on the back of a wounded and traumatized nation. This was
where an investor like Jeff House fit in.

House was a businessman from Minnesota whose connection to
Liberia had been forged in the Twin Cities.[9] Thousands of Liberians
had migrated there since the beginning of the crisis, making the Twin
Cities—next to Staten Island, New York—the largest concentration of

Liberians living outside of Africa. House had built a comfortable fortune in real estate and had the reputation as someone who could line up investors. In late 1999 and early 2000, an acquaintance from Minnesota connected him to diamonds and gold in Liberia—an investment opportunity far afield from strip malls and parking structures in suburban Minneapolis.[10]

Before traveling to Liberia, Jeff House had been introduced to Israel Akinsanya, the Liberian entrepreneur who stood as Chucky's best man.[11] Then thirty-one years old, he had worked for a small marketing firm in the Twin Cities, where he set down roots.[12] Akinsanya, who later became the head of public relations for Liberia's national oil company, had decided to return to Monrovia following President Taylor's election. It was there that he struck up a friendship with Chucky, he says, after a mutual friend invited him to a dinner at Chucky's house.[13] Akinsanya knew of Chucky's reputation but withheld judgment; having a connection with the president's son would only help him. Akinsanya was startled to find that, despite Chucky's lack of education, he presented himself as articulate and well read.

The two eventually grew close, Akinsanya said, though he never viewed Chucky as a peer. When Chucky needed investors to help back mining plans, he partnered his new friend with American connections. The two began working together under the mantle of a company called Resources International. Soon after hearing from Akinsanya, Jeff House was flying to Liberia.

While both Liberia and Sierra Leone boasted diamond reserves, the two nations differed geologically. Stones from Sierra Leone were pit-mined—dug directly from the rich clay—often by hand. These stones tended to be both larger and more abundant than those found in Liberia, where the majority of mining was alluvial. Miners in Liberia worked the riverbeds sorting through rock and dirt in search of precious stones that had over centuries been washed into the waterways.

Liberia had developed another revenue stream: illicitly trafficking stones mined in Sierra Leone. This practice, which predated the Liberian civil war of the 1990s by several decades, had been a way for traders to circumvent laws and taxes in Sierra Leone, which did not become independent from the United Kingdom until 1961.[14] Traders along the border—many of whom shared familial and tribal backgrounds— moved the stones from the mines in Sierra Leone's Kono District through northeastern Liberia on to Monrovia, where they were shipped to Antwerp, the global center of the diamond trade. In early 2000, as UN investigators began looking into conflict diamonds, they noticed that Liberia exported quantities of stones that far exceeded the capabilities of its mostly artisanal mining industry and undeveloped geological reserves.[15]

Chucky believed that Liberia had vast, yet-to-be discovered diamond resources that could be pit-mined with the right equipment. He looked to Fred Rindel, the South African mercenary who had helped facilitate the ATU training, to obtain investment for the mining venture, drawing unwanted attention to both men.[16] In early August 2000 Chucky received faxed copies of several press articles that discussed, in accurate detail, his relationship with Rindel.[17] An *Africa Confidential* story noted Rindel's presence at the Mamba Point hotel in Monrovia, saying the ex–South African Defense Force colonel "styles himself a mining engineer" even though he was instrumental in training RUF units used to retake large swaths of Sierra Leone's mining areas. Rindel distanced himself from Chucky, insisting his involvement in mining in Liberia was strictly for "the benefit of the people of Liberia." Dealing with Chucky "was his father's wish" Rindel said when contacted regarding their relationship, "perhaps with the intention of keeping him away from the fleshpots and drugs."[18]

For an investor like House, however, Chucky offered the influence of being the president's son, access to untapped diamond and gold concessions, and detailed satellite imaging that would help guide their exploration. Chucky needed capital—and hoped House could provide investors.

House returned to the States and embarked on a road show to seek out backing for the venture. He immediately encountered resistance; after speaking with the corporate finance arms of multiple "junior mining ventures in the US and Canada," he wrote to Akinsanya in mid-August, "it is impossible to attract investment capital in Liberia. There were no exceptions. They stated no exceptions. They stated many reasons but mainly the threat of war, political instability, and the terrible PR of conflict diamonds."[19]

This was an unwelcome revelation. Inside his father's inner circle, there was little reliable information about how the government was perceived. But doors were beginning to shut—from the inability to attract foreign donors to the increased scrutiny of the United Nations. This posed a fundamental challenge to Taylor: without wealth, he would rapidly lose strength.

House now had serious misgivings about the project, but he told Akinsanya that he would move ahead with his own money to purchase the concessions and begin alluvial mining, hoping that if they hit "the right spots in the river this will generate a substantial cash flow which will allow us to bootstrap" the later stages of exploration.[20] Chucky wanted to assuage House's concerns about working in Liberia. He responded directly to House's note to Akinsanya, somewhat incoherently, with a note that read, "As for the question of threats of war, political instability we must remember that the 100 (hundred years) of peace that the world had enjoyed, Africa has not experienced the same and is the last continent of conflict. So it is the ability of a [*sic*] administration through its political part and National Security Measures that one should analyse and African Administration."[21]

"As for the banning of conflict diamonds," Chucky wrote, "not only I as an individual but the Government of Liberia fully supports UN Resolution 1306."

The resolution Chucky referred to had passed in the Security Council in early July, banning the sales of rough diamonds from Sierra Leone without authorization of the government of Sierra Leone. To give the ban some force, the Security Council created an investigative body—referred to as the Panel of Experts—to report on compliance of parties believed to be involved in the trade.

The decision was a blow for Chucky and his father, effectively criminalizing a significant source of revenue for the regime. The diamonds flowing from Sierra Leone through Liberia onto the world's market were estimated to be at 31 million carats between 1994 and 1998.[22] This made the need for Liberia to develop its much smaller diamond resources all the more urgent. In his negotiations with House, Chucky eventually acknowledged that the South Africans wouldn't be able to provide any help for further phases of exploration. House sought out his own geologist, attempting to hire a Czech scientist who was familiar with the region and could provide an assessment independent of the preliminary findings of the South Africans. (It's unclear whether that relationship ever materialized.)

To equip the operation, House turned to an ex–Green Beret and veteran diamond hunter based out of Indiana named Daniel Pohle, who had traveled throughout Africa and South America, outfitting diamond- and gold-mining operations with mechanical dredges that automated the laborious operation of separating out precious stones and metals from dirt and mud.[23] "I build the toys and make sure people know how to use them," he said.

Pohle was also a veteran of West Africa—he had spent time in Sierra Leone during the 1990s, setting up mining equipment in the Kono District while it was under RUF control. As a former U.S. Special Operations soldier, he was dismissive of the severity of the fighting between the Taylor-backed rebels and government troops. ("I was there when they were playin' cowboys and Indians," he recalled with some bravado.)

Pohle arrived in Liberia in September 2000. He was there to do the actual labor of mining and to oversee the operation of two pieces of machinery the men had purchased: an excavator and what was called a "diamond and gold plant," a machine that could move through forty yards of riverbed each hour. He hoped to prove whether diamonds existed in any quantity and had brought along another American to help operate the equipment. House did not make an appearance; instead the group's local contact was an attorney from the Twin Cities named Ben Houge who ran a school for the deaf with his hearing-impaired daughter deep in the bush.[24] Houge was a character that could emerge only in Liberia: a charity worker with a sideline in diamonds. Houge said if all went well, the mining would bankroll the charitable school.

Pohle claims the mining operation was Houge's real reason for being in Liberia and that "basically the cover was a school for the deaf." With the blessing of the authorities, the group set up their machinery in a creek along the Lofa River, near the border of Lower Lofa and Grand Cape Mount Counties. Pohle noticed that nearly everywhere he went in the bush, he found armed men and boys—a sight familiar from his experiences in Sierra Leone.

"Everybody had an AK, some of 'em just in short pants. Those were the throwaways from Charles [Taylor]," he recalled, saying the fighters never interfered with him. "I didn't never have to get rough on anyone." But Pohle decided not to stay around long enough to see whether the operation began yielding diamonds.

Meanwhile Liberia's tenuous political situation was an increasing concern for Jeff House. In Monrovia, confrontations between Taylor's forces and American diplomats were becoming more frequent.[25] In the bush, ATU forces lost ground to insurgents in Lofa County, then staged a retaliatory cross-border attack into Macenta, Guinea, where Taylor believed his enemies were operating with American support. For an American businessman, all signs pointed toward a collapse in the relationship between Liberia and the United States. "Vic," an unidentified business partner, relayed to Akinsanya some of House's fears, saying that House

> was a bit nervous when he heard that the President had been quoted as saying that the US and Britain are trying to assassinate him. I told him that most of what is on the news is mostly overblown. . . . You should hear the stories that he has heard about CT [Chucky]. How he has these drug parties, and that he runs drugs from Columbia [*sic*] and that he hires these $1000 a day hookers from Columbia [*sic*] that are flown in to service him and his friends. He also has the killing sprees. He said he does not believe these stories and that he really likes CT and that he is an intelligent and articulate man and is very impressed by him. I think it was because of these stories that he wants to help improve the image that the outside world has of CT. He really wants to help. Talk to you later.[26]

A handwritten note on a faxed copy of the e-mail read:

CT,

Just got this from Vic. As you can see this is why i say that you need to call him every now and then. I will see you later to talk about this.

Izzy[27]

It isn't known whether Chucky tried to address House's concerns, but House grew even more distressed. In August 2000 Charles Taylor responded to the allegations that he had been trafficking diamonds with the RUF by accusing the American government of funding a $2 million plot to assassinate him.[28] The charges, broadcast over his KISS-FM radio station and published in newspapers sympathetic to Taylor, ratcheted up festering anti-American tensions in Monrovia, particularly among Taylor's security forces.

In October, President Clinton signed an executive order barring the entry into the United States of "President Charles Taylor, senior members of the Government of Liberia, their closest supporters, and their family members," citing the Liberian government's role in sustaining the crisis in Sierra Leone through the diamonds and weapons trade.[29] Akinsanya received another e-mail to an account that he and "Vic" shared, detailing House's concerns:

> I've been trying to call you all morning. I spoke with Jeff yesterday. . . . Someone has been telling him that going over there would be the dumbest thing he could do since THEY will be removing the chief by force in 30 or 60 days and that they are after CT also. He was also told that there were 11,000 troops waiting at the border that they are planning to send in.[30]

By mid-October, however, even as the operation got off the ground, the lawyers continued to finalize the deal. House and Chucky had agreed to incorporate in Nevis, a tiny Caribbean nation—also a tax and regulatory haven—but the Minnesotan objected to several provisions requiring him to report gold and diamond discoveries to the government, while being offered no guarantees of future mining rights.[31] Leslie Anderson, the attorney who reviewed the contract for House, recalled his understanding of how profits were to be distributed: "The state of Liberia or the country of Liberia would've got the proceeds, part of the proceeds would go to Taylor, part would go to Jeff, and, I think, it was supposed to be very, very lucrative, if they ever hit the diamonds."[32]

They never did, though. According to Anderson, the deal suddenly fell apart. House had been unable to deliver the investors that Chucky required to launch the effort. Anderson said that Chucky had retaliated by kicking the American workers out of the country and taking the only thing left of value: the mining equipment. It was a classic bait and switch, executed perfectly on the unsuspecting Americans who had been "dumb enough to bring all this equipment over," as Anderson said.

It was a bitter lesson of dealing in Taylor's Liberia. House, despite the appearance of official sanction, had been hustled; he returned to Minnesota and filed for bankruptcy.

Jeff House was not the only business partner whom Chucky threw in with. In early 2000 another opportunity presented itself in an underworld figure named Leonid Minin.[33] Minin represented a new type of organized crime figure that had emerged with the fall of the Soviet Union: a global gangster and conflict profiteer unaligned to any ideology. To international law enforcement agencies, his nationality remained a mystery. Minin was believed to be an Israeli citizen born in Ukraine, who leveraged his connections within Russian organized crime and the former Soviet military and intelligence services to provide weapons and equipment to conflicts around the globe. This type of chimerical identity reflected the flux of the post–Cold War world, with diplomatic passports, dual citizenship, and an array of aliases—Minin had thirteen, including "Wolf Breslan," seemingly ripped straight from the pages of a spy novel.[34] Figures like Minin—and Victor Bout, the Russian arms trafficker dubbed "The Lord of War"—had the agility to exploit weak borders and out-of-date international enforcement standards. But most significantly for Taylor—and Chucky—criminals accepted payment in a currency favored in West Africa: diamonds and timber.

Timber first drew Minin to Liberia in 1998, but by 2000 he began shipping weapons to Robertsfield for Taylor's government. Liberia had been under an arms embargo for most of Taylor's political career.[35] When he was an insurgent warlord, arms procurement had been a clandestine process, and little had changed now that he was an elected president living under the same arms embargo. Taylor was still required to purchase weapons for his forces on the black market, which required working with men like Leonid Minin.

Over the first year and a half of his presidency, Taylor relied on an ad hoc pipeline for transitting weapons from Eastern Europe to West Africa. The system was built on the willingness of brokers in well-armed former Soviet bloc nations to sell off weaponry to the highest bidder and on the disarray of the West African aviation infrastructure, which permitted illicit air traffic. Weapons flowed into Ivory Coast and Burkina Faso en route to Liberia, along the way relying on the shared

profit motivations of the traffickers, the government, and military officials willing to transit arms to Taylor. The weapons served Taylor's foreign policy objectives, whether that meant arming his own forces or
providing weapons to the RUF in Sierra Leone. In some cases, shipments were driven directly from the airfield to White Flower, where
they would remain firmly in his control.

The flood of Soviet bloc weapons—which were primarily small
arms and light conventional systems—had a transformative effect
for the rebel groups throughout Africa. Cheap, durable, and—most
important—easy to operate, small arms became the engines of the wars
not only in Sierra Leone and Liberia but also in Angola, the Democratic Republic of Congo, Uganda, Rwanda, and Sudan. As violence
had become a way of life in the region, weapons trafficking became an
essential industry, one synonymous with power—a line of business into
which Chucky sought to insinuate himself.

Robertsfield became a hub of regional weapons trafficking. Some of
Minin's shipments were small enough to be ferried aboard a BAC-111,
a 150-seat passenger jet that had once belonged to the Seattle Super-
sonics, on flights from Ouagadougou.[36] Others arrived in larger Soviet
cargo aircraft. In May 2000 another aircraft, an Ilyushin, landed in Robertsfield with a load of Strela and Igba surface-to-air missiles—weapons
that far exceeded both the capabilities of Taylor's forces and the immediate threat he faced. With the prospect of a long war developing in Lofa,
Taylor sought to acquire greater amounts of sophisticated weapons to
counter the threat.

Over the preceding year, Minin had become a familiar face for
Charles Taylor. Minin was trying to sell to the government of Liberia
the aging BAC-111 jet he'd been using for weapons shipments to serve
as a presidential jet, but the cost was prohibitive. While Charles Taylor relied on Minin for connections to arms networks throughout the
world, for Chucky, Minin represented an opportunity to make money.
Chucky had the valuable timber and diamond concessions his father
had assigned to him but little means to convert them into profits. When
he sought, despite worsening security conditions in the region, to get
his ventures off the ground, he turned to his father's friend.

The two began meeting in Monrovia in 1999, often with Minin's
partners, including Erkki Tammivuori, from a Finnish family in the
export business, and Fernando Robleda, a Spaniard.[37] Timber was the

shared interest. While Chucky brought little to the table in terms of business experience or financial acumen, he did have proximity to his father. As the foreigners pursued their logging ventures, Chucky would use them as a sounding board for other moneymaking schemes.

Unlike much of his work with the ATU, Chucky's business life touched more directly on Lynn. Minin had covered some of the costs of the couple's honeymoon. Nonetheless, he hadn't made a positive impression on her—she remembered him as "nasty, dirty-looking," a functioning drug addict with a taste for heroin.[38] "I remember thinking: *gross*," she said.

Minin and Chucky soon partnered in a timber company, Exotic Tropical Timber Enterprises, following the model of the large-scale timber efforts his father had partnered with Dutch, Malaysian, and Lebanese investors on exploiting concessions. The National Forestry Law had passed in January 2000, handing over all old-growth forests to the government without regard to land ownership claims. President Taylor allocated these concessions on a case-by-case basis, granting a limited term for the recipients to turn a profit on a given tract. The practice encouraged hasty clear-cutting and resulted in considerable damage to Liberia's rain forests.

At one point, Chucky pitched Minin's business partner, Fernando Robleda, on a fuel oil deal. The Spaniard faxed a note to his boss afterward: "I'm just coming from Chucky [*sic*] house. He called me this morning for a business proposal and, for the first time, I think it could be interesting."[39] It would give Minin the sole rights to import crude oil into Liberia for the duration of two to three years at an estimated $3 million profit per month. The profits from this monopoly, presumably, would be charged to the Liberian consumer.

Chucky pressed Minin to invest in the deal, but he had already paid $2 million in "taxes"—the personal tribute required to do business in Liberia—to Charles Taylor for the Exotic timber venture. Robleda put Chucky off, asking whether the money they had provided to Charles Taylor could be applied toward Chucky's venture—in effect, asking the son to borrow from the father. "He told me, again, it's not possible because it's a matter of respect in front of his father," Robleda wrote to Minin.

That deal never went forward.[40] But Chucky did manage to insert himself into an Ukrainian arms shipment coming through Minin: a vast load of 7.62mm rifle ammunition and various other arms purchased by his father set to transit through Abidjan, Ivory Coast. The deal represented a $1 million investment for Taylor, from which Chucky could collect a commission. The payments flowed into accounts in Cyprus and New York that belonged to Minin's company, Aviatrend; they had identical references with Minin's timber ventures—"Buying Technical Material/Wood Extractions Tools"—to provide cover for the transaction.

That July an Antonov AN-124, a hulking 446-ton Soviet-era cargo aircraft, took off from Gostomel Airport outside Kiev, loaded with armaments, most notably the five million cartridges of 7.62mm ammunition, bound for Abidjan. The flight had all the markings of an official and legal weapons sale; authorities in both the originating and destination countries had signed off on the export. A Ukrainian military officer accompanied the shipment to Ivory Coast to ensure the cargo was delivered, and when the plane touched down in Abidjan, an Ivorian military officer met the aircraft.

Nearly all the authorizations provided by the Ivorian government, however, had been forged; the Ivorian general who appeared to have initiated the purchase was, in fact, in hock to Taylor because of arms the Liberian had provided him following a coup a year earlier. Nearly as soon as the weapons hit the tarmac in Ivory Coast, a smaller Ilyushin, similar to the aircraft that had arrived two months earlier, took off from Robertsfield, outside Monrovia. Touching down in Abidjan, the arms were loaded onto it, whereupon it began ferrying the cargo back to Liberia, to deliver it to the actual purchaser.

As large as the shipment was, it was not complete—the arms accounted for only $250,000 of the order purchased through Minin. What had been meant to be a lucrative and successful weapons transaction between Minin, Chucky, and his father quickly fell apart.

The next month Italian police officers stormed Minin's hotel room in a suburb outside Milan.[41] They found the short Ukrainian surrounded by prostitutes and in possession of more than 58 grams of cocaine, more than $35,000 in cash, and nearly $500,000 in diamonds. More than fifteen hundred pages of faxes spelled out in incriminating detail his ties to the companies and individuals underwriting a variety of weapons deals—including the Ivorian deal. Several documents directly referenced Chucky, including one from Erkki Tammivuori that mentioned "special packages for Junior." The Italian investigators surmised that this referred to missiles, though it could have been drugs.

In either case, the arrest was a huge humiliation for Chucky, who cut his ties with Minin, faxing him a handwritten note that read: "From this day forward never in your life ever contact me again." Chucky never discussed arms deals, Lynn said, though she didn't doubt he tried to engage in some. Other Taylor insiders insist that Chucky never had a hand in any weapons deals. "Chucky was irresponsible so his father could not trust him for bringing in weapons," one of Chucky's deputies said.

All the advantages of being the president's son yielded very little in the way of easy profits for Chucky. Even with the deck stacked entirely in his favor, he failed to distinguish himself in the field of hustlers, entrepreneurs, and monopolists in Taylor's Liberia. In business, as with the ATU, Chucky seemed to be the biggest obstacle to his own success.

10

War Business

I tote dat gunn dat, feelin fear as I blast spreadin rumors with your ruger.

—*United States vs. Belfast,* EXHIBIT CE-4

Lynn had been married just four months before she became a mother; six months later she packed up her newborn son and embarked with him on his first trip to Africa and his first meeting with his father. She was just twenty-one years old—an age when many of her friends were focused on graduating from college—but she hoped to settle down and start a life with her husband. Their teenage romance had barely survived the years they'd spent apart; it was unclear how their marriage would last when they were finally together.

It was October 2000 when she returned to Monrovia. Until then she had been connected to Liberia only through conversations and e-mails with Chucky. While she remained in the dark about much of his life, she knew that in the year he had been without his unit, he had made very little money off his various schemes and ventures. More important, she knew that the pressure on his father's government had increased significantly. What she did not know, when she finally arrived, was that Chucky had given up on the idea of being a husband and father.

"I never wanted her there," he said, even though he'd lured her to Liberia as a teenager, begged her forgiveness after she discovered his infidelity, married her, and fathered her son.[1] It was characteristic of Chucky's personality to discard people when he no longer felt they served a purpose in his life.

Indeed, having a child had not been the catalyst for change in Chucky's life that Lynn had hoped for; if anything, it pushed him away and did nothing to change his behavior. As much as she still loved him, she couldn't deny that his darker side had become more present. His temper flared with his bodyguards, as he was constantly yelling at them. Then there was Danger; he never acknowledged what had happened to the dog.

When Chucky mysteriously injured his hand, Lynn understood that he'd broken it hitting someone. But as with many of the shrouded details of his life outside of their home, she didn't pursue it. "All through my time in Africa, I really believed he hadn't killed someone," she said.[2]

The end came quickly and without incident, she recalled: "One day he just decided he didn't want to be married anymore." She knew all the failures in Chucky's life were weighing on him, but the more fundamental problem was that "he just became a different person." She returned to Florida and filed for divorce. For nearly a year, the couple did not communicate. She remained in Orlando raising her son as a single mother, hearing little of Chucky's life in Monrovia and receiving no financial support for their child.

Eventually, Chucky wanted their two-year-old son to travel with Bernice to Africa to accompany him on a medical trip to South Africa to receive surgery on his hand. She refused. Furious at being denied access to his son, Chucky called Lynn in Orlando and reached her sister. When Lynn refused to get on the phone, Chucky grew enraged, according to a member of her family.[3] He threatened the family member and parents in specific terms: "He told me that he was going to line me and my mom and dad up and shoot us in the back of the head." (The family member asked to not be identified, given the nature of the threat.)

Lynn called President Taylor, hysterically crying. Taylor had grown accustomed to these phone calls from his daughter-in-law, according to Lynn. But he grew upset when she relayed Chucky's threat. Chucky was even more enraged when he heard that Lynn had contacted his father. Taylor warned his son that "he cannot go threatening me or my family, period," according to Lynn.

But Charles Taylor's hands were tied; he could place his son under house arrest, but this was a temporary solution. Taylor was the most powerful man in Liberia, but his power was increasingly limited. He had no influence with or leverage against the foreign powers seeking to isolate him. He had little control over the countryside, where rebels operated relatively freely. And he had even less control over his son, who followed his own violent whims.

In late 2001 Chucky invited Israel Akinsanya to join him on a trip to Singapore. According to Akinsanya, Chucky told him little about the nature of the trip other than that "he has his business partners he wants to see."[4] Chucky often kept things compartmentalized, Akinsanya said, but his account defies credibility. Not only had Akinsanya been closely involved with the Jeff House deal, he had good reason to deny knowledge of the details of Chucky's trip. At that time, Chucky, along with dozens of members of Taylor's government and certain associates, had been barred from international travel under new UN sanctions targeting the regime's involvement in Sierra Leone.[5]

For all his unpredictable behavior, Chucky remained loyal to his father in the face of the sanctions. The travel ban represented the first time the international community tied Chucky to his father's regime, even though it made no mention of his nationality, which was not a well-known fact. For much of 2001, he simply withdrew from public life, making only occasional appearances at some of the late-night haunts that Taylor's officials were known to frequent.

Akinsanya had grown accustomed to Chucky's tendency to drop out of society, holing up at his house, keeping nocturnal hours, and cutting himself off from outside contact. "I really didn't have any close friends," Chucky said. He felt culturally isolated as an American and suspicious that those around him saw something to gain in his friendship.

Even as Chucky isolated himself, Akinsanya befriended Bernice, whom he described as something like a stage parent. "She was a very nice person, but you could tell that she was manipulative," he recalled, saying that she was more than happy to use the fact that she was the mother of the president's son for leverage.

Mother and son fought bitterly, Akinsanya recalled, often about Chucky's father. By both Akinsanya's and his own account, Chucky was the lone voice of truth among the "sycophants" surrounding Charles Taylor. As the end of Taylor's five-year term loomed, Chucky was candid with his father about the future. "There's going to be elections in this country," he told him, according to Akinsanya. "And if there are elections, you're not going to win."

Taylor likely understood that. His administration had accomplished little or nothing in improving the lives of Liberians. The violence of the civil war had devolved into a low-grade conflict that he met with persistent repression of political enemies, dissidents, and journalists. And fear that war would return in force set in.

When Chucky and Akinsanya landed in Geneva for a stopover en route to Singapore, it was a rare respite outside the region. He filled the few short hours between flights splurging on clothes and luxury watches. While Akinsanya said he wasn't clear on whom they were traveling to see, a former Defense Department official said that Chucky made multiple trips to Singapore on the dime of Joseph Wong, a businessman connected to the Oriental Timber Company.[6] Wong was linked to arms-for-timber transactions by UN investigators in a 2001 report to the Security Council that described large quantities of Liberian timber moving to Asian markets and moving weapons, which eventually fueled RUF offensives in Sierra Leone, to Liberia.[7] "Chucky would go there [to Singapore] and drink and play with the girls," the official said. "It got to the point that he was embarrassing Mr. Wong, so he told the president that he would not pay for [his son] anymore."

As the two men arrived in Singapore, Chucky began receiving phone calls from Liberia. Since March 2001, rebels had staged several attacks in Lofa County, and President Taylor was growing concerned. The fighting in the bush was chaotic—government forces engaged the rebels and then, at times, fought one another to secure looting rights over an area. By October the situation briefly stabilized, but the damage was significant. The town of Zorzor was razed, UN investigators passing through the area noted, and on the rural back roads, armed young men crammed into the beds of Isuzu pickups.[8]

Taylor wanted his son to return, not just to Liberia but also to his security forces. According to Akinsanya, Chucky—who was typically emotionally reserved—opened up to him for once. He wasn't comfortable with the identity he had created for himself in Liberia.[9] "I didn't realize how much people were afraid of me until after I left the military," Chucky told him.

"How did you realize that?" Akinsanya said.

"I started to hear about myself . . . that people were generally afraid of me," he said. Chucky thought his reputation as his father's enforcer was unfair. It was a self-serving—if not outright dishonest—response, given how he had gone to great lengths to create an aura of intimidation. Akinsanya nonetheless took the comments at face value.

"I just sit here, and I'm jealous of my sisters," Chucky told Akinsanya. "Do you think I don't want to be in Switzerland going to college?" At least one of Chucky's stepsisters attended Collége du Léman, an exclusive boarding school in Geneva. "I want to tap into those fruits of the tree." Chucky appeared like "a wounded animal" to Akinsanya as he explained the impossibility of being relied upon as a military commander, while wanting more from life than war and the struggle for power. "I'm caught," he told Akinsanya, "between loyalty to my dad and having to protect this thing here and watching my other siblings progress."

Akinsanya didn't know what to tell him. He could see that Chucky was in pain. "This was just a twenty-two- or twenty-three-year-old kid with immense power and responsibility—what was he supposed to do with it?"

But Chucky didn't just have power and responsibility—he had privilege and access. He never evinced a crisis of conscience, and he publicly took issue with his father's failures only after it was too late. He relished his role as a military adviser and strategist, but he wanted no accountability for the results of his father's policies. As the two prepared to return to Liberia, Chucky told Akinsanya that he didn't want the path that his father had laid out for him.

"I want to move on with my life," Chucky told him "and he's calling me back to war."

ABOVE: Chucky Taylor (right) appearing with his father before reporters at an unknown location in Liberia

LEFT: A defaced photograph of Charles Taylor found among Chucky's personal effects

BELOW: President Charles Taylor meets Reverend Jesse Jackson, a Clinton administration special envoy, on February 11, 1998, in Monrovia. On the visit, Jackson told Taylor that his purpose was not to "scold Liberia for the excesses committed during the war," but "to revive the warm partnership relationship that has always existed between the two countries."

Taylor in Buchanan, Liberia, on May 29, 1990, on the offensive against
the Armed Forces of Liberia en route to securing vital port access

Chucky Taylor in Monrovia in 2003, celebrating his visiting son's birthday

Chucky in Liberia at an unknown date and location

A torn photograph of a teenage Chucky at his childhood home in Orlando in the early 1990s

Chucky wearing body armor (center, left) and others
at an unknown date and location in Liberia

Chucky with his personal firearm at an
unknown date and location in Liberia

Chucky on an unknown date and location in Liberia

Chucky with Anti-Terrorist Unit (ATU) and other security in
Gbatala, Liberia, on an unknown date

Chucky with Benjamin Yeaten at the funeral of a colleague at an
unknown location in Liberia

Chucky discussing maneuvers with ATU comrades in Monrovia in 2003
with his brother, Philip (far left), looking on

INSET: The ATU emblem, designed in 1998, depicting a cobra with a scorpion, which the National Patriotic Front of Liberia also used in their insignias

MIDDLE: Chucky with security forces at an unknown location in Liberia

BOTTOM: What remains of the Executive Mansion: the Gbatala base, Bong County, Liberia

Assistant United States Attorney Karen Rochlin of the Southern District of Florida, one of the prosecutors who obtained the Chucky Taylor conviction

Immigration and Customs Enforcement Special Agent Matthew Baechtle in Kle, Liberia, investigating Chucky Taylor in 2007

11

Satan and The Prophet

Wit my tru war soldiers, Army Thugs United, aint no time we divided.

— *United States vs. Belfast*, EXHIBIT CE-4

In the summer of 2001, Robert Ferguson, an operations coordinator hired to work for the U.S. embassy's defense attaché, arrived in Monrovia.[1] Ferguson, an ex–Air Force mechanic, had served in the Gulf War maintaining A-10s, but he had seen more action at his prior posting in Jakarta, where he had been when Suharto stepped down in May 1998, causing the capital to erupt in rioting. Apart from receiving a State Department country briefing and doing some of his own research, he arrived in Liberia with limited knowledge of the country. He had never been to sub-Saharan Africa, knew little of the war in Liberia and the developing conflict, and had only a cursory sense of the cast of players he'd encounter in Monrovia. But almost as soon as he landed in town, he heard the name Chucky Taylor.

Ferguson—whom nearly everyone referred to as Fergy—arrived at a tense moment between the embassy and the Liberian government. The man he was meant to replace had been shot by Taylor's forces weeks before. Earlier that summer Taylor's security forces had begun enforcing a curfew throughout Monrovia. In June, Ferguson's predecessor, Sgt. James Michael Newton, had been driving through the capital shortly before dawn when, according to the Liberian government, he burst through an ATU checkpoint at high speed.[2] The ATU officer on duty opened fire, wounding the sergeant. Newton was later evacuated to Ivory Coast for medical treatment. The U.S. embassy issued a statement saying it "was an isolated incident that was not related to any anti-US sentiment." Former ATU officers and an American diplomat blamed Newton for disobeying the order to stop. But one former ATU commander, Gen. John Tarnue, said the shooting had been "premeditated" and that Benjamin Yeaten, Momoh Gibba, and Chucky had authorized it because "the US military attachés were spies."[3] The State Department released no further information. So Ferguson had reason to be cautious, but he also had to get close to the leadership of the security forces.

The Clinton administration had cemented its view of Charles Taylor—the continuing violence in Sierra Leone, not the repression of his own people, had been the breaking point. Several months earlier, in a December 9, 2000, cable titled "Liberia: Undermining Charles Taylor," Washington indicated that it was working on a "long-term campaign" against Taylor and solicited the Monrovia embassy's "assistance in developing information required to weaken and discredit the Taylor government internationally."[4] The United States hoped to rally support for sanctions against Taylor's government, the cable explained. "The success of our efforts at the UN will depend in large measure on our ability to convince other UN members of what we already know—that Charles Taylor is instigating cross-border conflict, trafficking arms, looting resources (Liberia's and neighboring nations) and, in general, sowing instability throughout West Africa."

Washington asked Monrovia for evidence "demonstrating conclusively that Taylor is the driving force behind much of the violence and deepening human misery in the region"; obtaining it "is an important, ongoing [U.S. government] priority," according to the cable. The author of the cable, William M. Bellamy, the deputy assistant secretary of state for African affairs, said the request was not connected to a prosecution of Taylor; rather, "it was specifically to find a way to stop the bleeding, to get this crisis under control in West Africa."[5]

Not long after his arrival, Ferguson ventured out to test the Monrovia nightlife. Nighttime in Monrovia was unlike nighttime in most capital cities around the world: the lack of electricity turned the streets into black, darkened lanes illuminated only by lights from the homes and apartment buildings that were fortunate enough to be fed by generator power. During the rainy season, a bolt of lightning would momentarily sear the darkness with white light, capturing luminescent still lifes of the urban landscape; then the streets would return to darkness. Night was also the time of activity for Taylor and his son.

The Pepper Bush, a Monrovia nightclub, was a favored spot for Taylor insiders. And it was there that Ferguson had his first run-in with Chucky. The incident, which would eventually become a part of popular lore, was a clash between two strong personalities. Ferguson made little effort to keep a low profile at the Pepper Bush; he stepped out onto the dance floor and began dancing with one of the women in Chucky's entourage. The American diplomat had clearly—and perhaps deliberately—crossed a line. Chucky's colleagues saw it as a gutsy provocation, to which the president's son was obligated to respond. Chucky called Fergy across the club to threaten him.

The diplomat was unfazed. "I don't give a shit," he recalled telling Chucky. "Look, you're not going to do anything to a U.S. diplomat. Your daddy would have you killed quicker than shit."[6]

The interaction ended there. Ferguson had quickly established a reputation as an American diplomat who wasn't easily intimidated. His response was particularly bold given the fate of his predecessor. Liberia was becoming a more dangerous place by the day, and the pressures on Taylor were increasing. Ferguson was dismissive of his role—he called himself "a secretary"—but few diplomats were willing to engage these men as closely as he did, and he would remain engaged through Taylor's fall from power.

Taylor's concerns were larger than his son's run-ins at nightclubs. By May 2001 insurgents had overrun much of Lofa County. The Taylor government was unable to ascertain who the fighters were or the exact nature of their grievance. It was clear that the rebels had military support from Guinea, which—in comparison to Sierra Leone and Liberia—more closely resembled a conventional military power. The attacks in Lofa showed a level of sophistication and matériel not typical of a bush army. A Lebanese merchant who witnessed an attack reported to the embassy that an organized ambush on an ATU truck had killed six fighters and wounded more than a dozen.[7] In the past, Taylor had retaliated against incursions from Guinea both with Liberian forces and with RUF proxies, attacking towns in Guinea like Macenta and

Nzérékoré, killing and forcing the displacement of thousands of civilians. Even if there was something of a moral equivalence to the tit-for-tat fighting, the violence provided the Guineans with a grievance to air to the international community.

Not surprisingly, this uptick in violence flowing across the Guinean border coincided with an increase in U.S. support for the government in Conakry, Guinea's capital. American Special Forces began training members of the Beret Rouge, an elite Guinean military unit.[8] Earlier that year the Conakry embassy had asked Secretary of State Colin Powell to "put some money on the Guinean forces."[9] It drew the situation in dramatic terms: "Guinea has been under attack by forces consisting primarily of RUF and Liberian combatants but including an assortment of mercenaries and dissidents, orchestrated by Charles Taylor, the root cause (to use USG phraseology) of instability in the sub-region." The Defense Department ultimately authorized a "lethal (offensive) training" program involving a detachment of U.S. Special Operations forces.[10]

William Bellamy, the State Department official who had worked on a strategy to isolate Taylor, visited the Guinean border regions, which suffered from an influx of refugees following cross-border assaults from Liberian and RUF forces. He saw the U.S. Special Forces training missions as a "morale booster" to the Guineans who had reinforced the area. The training, which occurred at Nzérékoré, a Guinean border town closer to Monrovia than to Conakry, alarmed Taylor. Insurgents who were captured by Liberian forces, Taylor later testified, acknowledged that they'd received training by U.S. military personnel in Guinea before staging attacks in Liberia.

The United States was able to maintain deniability of involvement with the rebels. In his memoir, *My Friend the Mercenary*, British journalist James Brabazon wrote that an American defense intelligence official known simply as "Frank" directly brokered his access to the rebel group seeking to oust Taylor.[11] The Americans were, in part, motivated by the fact that they had no visibility into rebel activities in Liberia and wanted to see the footage Brabazon returned with. The one condition, Brabazon said, was that he "agree not to disclose the details of the armaments the rebels received from the American-backed government in Guinea."

But defense officials in Guinea did little to conceal their relationship with the anti-Taylor faction. President Lansana Conté was incensed by the continued assaults on his territory from Liberian-backed Guinean dissidents—they had briefly overtaken the town of Guékédou in December 2000. Conté repudiated the action in a statement to the United Nations, accusing the RUF and Liberian forces of direct responsibility for "625 deaths, 293 seriously wounded, 127 missing and 59,604 displaced."[12] For Conté, Taylor was not a man with whom you could negotiate.

"Satan has his role to play," Conté, a Muslim, told the American ambassador to the UN, Thomas Pickering. "But Satan and the prophet don't understand each other."[13]

The fighting pushed Conté closer to Liberian dissidents in Conakry who sought to depose Taylor. When the group sought Guinean military assistance, Conté insisted that he have a hand in who would be named the leader of the new faction. His favored choice won out: Sekou Conneh, who was married to the president's spiritual adviser. The dissidents formed under yet another acronym in Liberia's seemingly endless civil war: LURD (Liberians United for Reconciliation and Democracy).

Around this time, the United States dramatically increased weapons sales to Guinea. Arms sales jumped from $500,000 for 2001 to $3 million for 2002.[14] It was a drop in the bucket in terms of overall global military assistance, but in a region where small arms drove much of the conflict, it was significant. The Defense Department also loaned Guinea $3 million under a low-interest grant and loan program to purchase the weapons. All this support was overt. Taylor was well aware of the United States' sudden interest in his neighbor and suspected the training program provided cover for a covert American support for the rebels attacking Liberia.

In early 2001 the U.S. military's objectives in Africa were extraordinarily vague. The official policy was "to increase the number of capable states in Africa . . . to build stability and peace within their borders and their sub regions," as the Unified Command Plan for Sub-Saharan Africa stated. There was little room for Taylor's Liberia within this vision; for Taylor, politics was about war, not governance. He had drawn power not from the people who elected him but by keeping his enemies on their heels and allowing his followers to take financial advantage of regional insecurity. This was entirely at odds with the American vision, which sought stability above all else.

After September 2001, the U.S. military interest in Africa would shift toward combating terrorism. Taylor historically had never been linked to terror groups, although a December 2002 *Washington Post* report based on Western intelligence reports alleged that the summer prior to the 9/11 attacks he had hosted two Al Qaeda operatives at the ATU's Gbatala base. The men—identified by the *Post* as Ahmed Khalfan Ghailani and Fazul Abdullah Mohammed—were allegedly converting Al Qaeda cash to diamonds in anticipation of an American crackdown. A former ATU commander who learned of the men's presence said that their motives were apparent only in hindsight. "Nobody knew anything [about] the guys that we were helping them—what their intention [was], who the identity of the guys were," he said, doubting that Taylor understood the gravity of his involvement with them.[15] "Taylor at that time worked very hard to be in America's favor, so for him to work with Al Qaeda would not have been smart." In fact, when he met with Ambassador Myrick on September 14, 2001, Taylor appeared "emotionally shaken by the terrorist attacks on the United States."[16] The apparent connection to the terrorist group—as ephemeral as it appeared to be—would only further damage Taylor's reputation in the eyes of the West. He began to fear that the United States and its allies sought to physically take him out of the equation.

When Taylor met with a European Union delegation in June 2001 regarding the violence in Lofa that summer, he did little to restrain his growing anger. The United Nations had just slapped Liberia with a round of sanctions on travel of senior officials, as well as on the trade in diamonds and arms; it further boxed Taylor in, ratcheting up the tension between his administration and Western powers. The U.S. embassy source present at the meeting, whose name has been redacted from the cable, noticed that "Taylor appeared tired and his face puffy."[17]

Taylor stopped short of directly accusing the Americans of supporting the rebels, instead directing his allegations to the British, who had taken an active role in enforcing the peace accords in Sierra Leone. To make his point clear, he placed a spent mortar shell and empty ammunition box on the table with what appeared to be British markings—though the embassy source present questioned their authenticity. This was not the first time Taylor had made this accusation, but the response to it in the past had been tepid.

"If Guinea wants war," Taylor warned the European delegation, "we will give it to them." As he stormed out of the meeting, the embassy officer noticed the president was wearing a bulletproof vest.

After receiving the call in Singapore, Chucky had returned to the war effort as the general officer commanding the ATU, an impressive title but of no real military significance. The responsibility of managing the war against the insurgents had been given to Benjamin Yeaten, leading a set of former militia commanders.

By early 2002, Taylor's options were rapidly diminishing; he had underestimated the enemy. The group that Conté backed had quickly graduated from a loose band of exiled dissidents to an existential threat to Taylor's presidency.

The rebels' confidence proved that Taylor's war effort in Lofa had not gone well. To a visiting U.S. congressional delegation in April 2002, Taylor acknowledged that his militia fighters were ill trained and, on good days, given more to harassing and looting civilians than to fighting.[18] Rather than take responsibility, however, he sought to tie the threat of war to the lack of support from the international community. The United Nations had launched a program to disarm, demobilize, and reintegrate Liberian rebels in 1997, but it was ineffective. Yet similar programs in nearly a dozen other African nations including Congo, Angola, Mozambique, and Rwanda had had more success in disarming and redirecting the fighters who had made civil war a way of life. It was a vintage Taylorism: he had created the war machine that had initiated the destruction of his country, including his son's ATU, but he couldn't be held responsible for the ongoing consequences.

As the countryside began to fall to rebel control, the war consumed Taylor's presidency. At times he summoned the language the Bush administration had introduced following 9/11, referring to the rebels as "terrorists" and calling prisoners "illegal combatants," hoping to paint his fight against the insurgents with the antiterrorist brush.[19] In February 2002 he declared a state of emergency. He justified it by pointing to an ambush that had occurred at Kle Junction, less than twenty miles from Monrovia, but some saw it as an effort to forestall the elections that were scheduled to take place the following year.

Taylor was also making drastic defense decisions. Much over Chucky's objection, he reconstituted the civil war–era militia divisions under commanders he could trust: Roland Duo, Benjamin Yeaten, and Coocoo Dennis.[20] Years later Chucky would point this out to distance himself from the increasingly disorganized military force backing Taylor. "I held no authority over the reinstated untrained militia division commanders and there [*sic*] men," he wrote in a letter. "Nor was I responsible for the mixing of trained & untrained forces, the hyperexpansion of ATU, dismissal of stringent recruitment standards, total breakdown of discipline and return of some ATU personnel back to fight under these various untrained, structurally unsound militia commands."

The reemergence of the militias represented something of an abdication for Taylor. Other than Yeaten, these men had played a marginal role in the early years of Taylor's administration. But now as frontline commanders, they were given the mandate to reactivate the network of fighters they had led during the civil war. These men had brought him to power but also caused great destruction to Liberia. "I held the presidents [*sic*] ear as many others did," Chucky reflected in a letter. "I along with others should have pushed for a strong mandate of greater discipline, oversight among the forces engaged in the war."

Even as they grew apart strategically, father and son were driven together by circumstance. In only a few months, the sanctions had depressed the already ravaged economy, and defending the capital became the priority. Neither man could leave the country without defying the travel ban. The limitless opportunity that both had seemed to relish when Taylor entered office five years earlier had been reduced to a binary choice: fight or surrender. The men were in a position to do neither.

Over the prior year, the collapse of his father's power was mirrored by Chucky's personal decline. He would periodically binge on drugs—what those close to him believed was cocaine and heroin—then sleep for days on end, disappearing from public view. His already small circle of friends dwindled to the handful of men who did not fear him. But even those friends willing to endure his company were not immune to his violent temper. One day his car broke down in traffic while he and a friend, Wisam Fawaz, were driving in downtown Monrovia.[21] As they inspected the engine, the hood accidentally slammed down on Chucky's head. Humiliated and furious, Chucky lashed out, beating Fawaz in the middle of traffic.

As trivial as the incident seemed compared with other acts of violence, the beating marked the watershed moment for those surrounding Chucky. According to Samuel "Pi" Nimley, an ATU commander and confidant of Chucky, Liberians who had read about the abuses at Gbatala and heard rumors of Chucky's predatory behavior came to view him as categorically evil. They believed that "he was born a demon. . . . He was just born bad. He make the people fear him so much," Nimley recalled. "They have a saying, 'When his mom gave birth to him, he slapped the doctor instead of the doctor slapping him.'"

The notion that Chucky bore a curse became popular in Monrovia, reinforced by the birth of a disabled son by a Liberian girlfriend. Chucky and Lynn remained estranged, and she had no knowledge of the child. Many took the boy's birth defect—a shortened arm—to be a mark of his father's transgressions. Chucky rejected the boy, refusing to acknowledge that he was the father; the mother later left the country, to raise the child in England.

In April LURD rebels launched another attack on the capital, surprising Taylor's forces with an assault that swept down from Bomi Hills to Bushrod Island within Monrovia in a matter of hours. The rebels quickly withdrew, but the attack had demonstrated how vulnerable the capital was.

Chucky and an ATU unit of approximately two hundred fighters scrambled to assess the damage that had been done to one of President Taylor's properties.[22] A convoy of trucks departed Monrovia, including a pickup truck with an antiaircraft weapon mounted in the cab, following the Bomi Hills highway into the bush. Ferguson, the American diplomat, trailed the group out to the countryside.

A larger force awaited the ATU, and a firefight broke out. Very quickly, the ATU members realized that the rebels outgunned them and that they were on the verge of being overrun. "We need to go," Ferguson, who witnessed the fight, recalled one of the fighters shouting.[23] But Chucky continued firing on the enemy, either oblivious to or unconcerned with the danger.

In the confusion, the ATU convoy staged a hasty retreat, fleeing back toward Monrovia, stranding Chucky. Fearing the consequence of the president's son being captured, the unit turned back into the fire to retrieve him. By the time they reached him, he had been hit in the hand with a ricochet. Nimley, an ATU commander who was present, laughed as he recalled how the situation quickly deteriorated and Chucky and his men found themselves fighting for their lives.[24] "He handled himself well and took control of the day," he recalled. "That saved lives."

Ferguson disagreed, saying that Chucky had been "playing Rambo." He considered the mission in Bomi Hills an ill-advised armed adventure characteristic of the slipshod and unprofessional approach of Taylor's military. He had an equally withering assessment of the ATU: "This was just a bunch of people who had weapons in a country that nobody cared about."

The incident was too much for Charles Taylor; fearing the propaganda coup should his son fall into enemy hands, he forbade Chucky to return to the front. The ATU also learned from the incident. No longer would it run headlong into a fight with an unknown number of enemy. Later, when the rebels attempted to breach the city again, the ATU drew them into an effective ambush along the road leading into Bushrod Island; attacking from the rear, they trapped the rebels. But the victory was modest. It did little to forestall the inevitable rebel march on Monrovia.

In May 2002 a Washington, D.C.–based security company, Global-Options, approached President Taylor forwarding a "Proposal for Services."[25] Taylor's ascendance to power had lured plenty of opportunists seeking to make money off of Liberia's misery, but GlobalOptions stood out as an American company with a unique pedigree. The company's proposal offered the services of Tom Coulter, "a former Commanding Officer of SEAL Team Three, and Chief Staff Officer of Naval Special Warfare, Group Two"; and of Randy Lubischer, "a retired US Marine combat veteran with 20 years of service." Lubischer's biography listed experience in conducting "numerous vulnerability and force protection assessments of many U.S. Embassies and Military facilities throughout the world"—a point Chucky underlined. The proposal put forward a three-step approach to Taylor's security situation: an evaluation of Liberia's fighting forces, a sixty-to-ninety-day intensive training course, and a reevaluation and appraisal of next steps. "Conflict does not take place within the sterile confines of a classroom and our training will reflect this," the proposal read. The company proposed training in "sniping," "demolitions," and "parachuting" but was also—paradoxically—careful to indicate it wished to "assist President Charles Taylor and the Government of Liberia, in a manner consistent with United Nations directives."

Chucky's father needed to find an upper hand against the new rebels. It wasn't clear whether a team of American ex–Special Operations would provide that. Nor was it completely clear that these men could be trusted. From his earliest days as a warlord, Taylor had sought an official U.S. military presence in Liberia; GlobalOptions was the antithesis of that—private, ideologically opaque, and of little political value. And it was expensive: GlobalOptions quoted several proposals, from ninety-day to one-year engagements involving from six to twelve trainers at a cost of $373,462.50 to $2,437,310. On the last page of the proposal, Chucky underlined a recommendation that Taylor should "at least consider entering into preliminary negations [*sic*] with Liberian United for Reconciliation and Development [*sic*]," saying "these negotiations will allow the Liberian government time to train and equip its forces for defensive purposes, with the assistance of GlobalOptions."

That recommendation, tucked at the tail end of the document, neatly dovetailed with the developing strategy of the U.S. embassy to head off an armed fight for Monrovia with a political solution. Taylor came to suspect the American contractors were working with his enemies, so the engagement never went further, and Taylor was left to prosecute the war on his own.[26] The fighting persisted with a familiar cadence: the rebels would overrun a town, and then Taylor would send in the ATU to flush them out. The rebels, however, wanted more than a seat at the table—they wanted Taylor gone. In Liberia the options for Charles Taylor—and Chucky—had narrowed to one: a fight for survival.

The war, as it had in the past, became an end unto itself—a paycheck for the rebels, opposition leaders, and freelance militia fighters. The rebels used their gains against Taylor to rally support from outside governments, who wished to keep the pressure on him leading into the elections scheduled for 2004. The rebels, while politically geared toward deposing Taylor, hardly represented a force for good in Liberia: they sacked villages and massacred civilians just as the government forces did. Taylor also faced internal pressure. Members of the militias that had been brought in to augment the ATU were not loyal to him. Many saw the fighting as a platform to pillage—and switched sides as soon as the momentum shifted against Taylor.

In June 2002 the war took a more personal turn for Taylor.[27] The rebels overran and sacked his home village of Arthington, where Chucky's ancestors had first arrived more than a century earlier. The rebels torched a home belonging to Taylor's family. The fighting in the president's ancestral home was both a strategic and a symbolic defeat, but the fear it created in Monrovia was real—the distant sound of the mortars could be heard within the capital, which was already swollen with civilians fleeing the fighting in the countryside. The ATU swept into Arthington soon afterward to flush out the LURD fighters, but the psychological damage had been done. The town had nearly been destroyed.

That month Charles Taylor's convoy appeared on the horizon in Margibi County, just outside Monrovia, a menacing train of tinted-window sports utility vehicles and trucks bristling with more than one hundred fighters clad in black fatigues. The procession was bookended by two pickups outfitted with Soviet-vintage antiaircraft guns. As much as these convoys represented a show of force, they also signified Taylor's weakness as a head of state: he could not travel within fifty miles of his home without enough firepower to hold back a battalion.

In an address to the nation, the president offered a candid, if not entirely sincere, perspective on the violence plaguing his country: "This government has no desire for conflict and violence, neither war. We do not wish to fight our own brothers and sisters nor do we believe that military success of the troops will bring lasting peace. We believe that dialogue through the process of reconciliation will bring peace through the grace of almighty God."[28]

Taylor's choice of language was appropriate; yet again Liberia had turned on itself. Legions of disenfranchised men and women— particularly from the Mandingo and Krahn tribes—eagerly joined in the fight to unseat the president, while others were forced into servitude by the new faction. Within Taylor's inner ring of security, there was also tension: Taylor did not trust the ATU and relied instead on the black-clad "ninjas" from the Special Security Service for close protection.

· · ·

Chucky sat shotgun in his BMW along the roadside in Kakata, a market town east of the Monrovia suburb of Paynesville.[29] His and several other vehicles full of ATU officers waited to escort the president back to the capital, through the rubber plantations and glowing green plains of Margibi County, into the choked commercial district of Red Light at the edge of Monrovia. An ATU lieutenant named Isaac Gono sat behind the wheel of Chucky's car, watching the convoy approach. Gono—known as "Papa"—had been by Chucky's side ever since he was a troubled American teenager venturing into Africa for the first time. He was just one of a handful of drivers Chucky trusted to carry him throughout Monrovia and on trips like this, a rare and increasingly dangerous trip out of the capital.

President Taylor was en route from Gbarnga, Bong County. At one time, Bong County had been the center of his power, but it had since suffered assaults by LURD forces raiding from Lofa County. Just days earlier the rebels had staged a tactical retreat from Gbarpolu, an inland town that had once served as the NPFL headquarters after fighting with government forces left hundreds of civilians dead.[30]

As Taylor's convoy approached, the waiting ATU vehicles cut a slow U-turn across the roadway to join it, Gono following the other vehicles. A dog darted across the road, and Gono hit the animal with full force, killing it, smashing the car's headlight.

It was an accident, perhaps careless, but it nonetheless enraged Chucky. On the journey back to Monrovia, he seethed. When the convoy arrived back in Congo Town, the ATU detachment peeled off toward Chucky's beachfront villa. As the group dismounted from their vehicles, he surprised many by his response to the minor incident: he ordered Gono placed under arrest.

He could have had his driver thrown into the cell behind the Executive Mansion for a few days—that sort of punishment wasn't uncommon in his father's forces. But Chucky wanted something more immediate—he wanted to see Gono punished. According to a human rights report detailing the incident, he ordered his men to beat the lieutenant "'til you see his bones and shit."[31] Two ATU officers—Maj. George Davis and Capt. D. Histine Teaiyer—complied, thrashing the driver with long sticks. Before long Gono lay in the grass in front of Chucky's house, dead.

Chucky would later insist that he did not intend for his driver to die, but the evidence showed that he did nothing to stop it.[32] As soon as he realized the gravity of what he had done, he began making panicked phone calls to other ATU officers. The Liberian National Police arrived on the scene and arrested the two ATU officers who had carried out the order. One ATU commander recalled Chucky's state when he arrived at the villa: "He was dejected. He was confused. He couldn't believe it. That Isaac was dead. I'm sure he was under the influence of something. I'm very sure. . . . He was sweating. . . . [He] couldn't get over it."[33]

More officers converged on the scene. Samuel Nimley, who had also received a call from Chucky, was incredulous to learn that someone so close to Chucky could be killed for such a trivial reason. Nimley had been part of the convoy when the accident occurred but had returned home rather than follow the unit to Chucky's house. "Just the damn [head]light," he said. "Can you imagine?"

Like the killing of Justin Parker, the death of Isaac Gono became a mess for those around Chucky to clean up. When Gono's brother-in-law, George Wortuah, went to claim the body at John F. Kennedy Hospital, he found that the driver had been trundled into a bag by the ATU officers and brought to the hospital morgue. When the officials showed him his brother-in-law's body, he saw that Gono's clothes had been shredded with the force of the beating.

Soon afterward the family learned that it was Chucky who had given the order that resulted in Isaac's death. They wanted everyone involved to be held accountable, including the president's son. While Gono's wife hoped for justice, his brother-in-law Wortuah privately contemplated retaliation. Eventually the family sought one of the few means of recourse available in Taylor's Liberia: the Catholic Justice and Peace Commission (JPC), a human rights group connected to the Archdiocese of Monrovia. The JPC still enjoyed a degree of protection over its activities through its affiliation with the Catholic Church. Liberians victimized by the Taylor government often turned to the organization, which also served as a liaison to international human rights groups researching violations in Liberia.

The JPC had continually received reports of ATU abuses ever since the unit's creation. But the letter from Isaac Gono's sister, which arrived a few days after the killing, was among the first complaints it had received about violence committed by the ATU against one of its own. The JPC issued a statement about the murder to the press. Taylor briefly succeeded in pressuring one paper to bury a story on the killing, but eventually the Monrovia dailies ran with the story, which quickly leaped to international wire services—some outlets erroneously reporting that Gono had been tortured to death.

The press coverage forced the Ministry of Defense to issue a response. The ATU officers who had acted on Chucky's orders were to blame, the ministry said, noting that they had killed the driver "during the process of interrogating 1st/Lt. Gono over the accident, used unusual harsh methods, rendering 1st/Lt. Gono unconscious," and that Chucky "awoke and came downstairs to only find his chief driver lying unconscious. He immediately ordered an ambulance to rush the Lt. to the nearest hospital."[34]

President Taylor ordered a military commission to investigate the case. At a press conference, he distanced his son from direct involvement in the killing. He qualified that statement, saying, "in military term he's responsible. As a General Officer commanding that unit he's responsible for what his men do or fail to do; to that extent, he's responsible."

The U.S. embassy monitored the situation from a remove. "Although there is clearly a bit of showmanship in these allegations," a cable reported, "the fact is that a man is dead. The reason for the beating was trivial and the decision to do it capricious and egregious.... The incident shows how blatant disregard for human life is among the security thugs of the ATU. Meanwhile, given the personalities involved, the call for justice is a courageous one."[35]

The military commission never proceeded beyond charging the two ATU commanders who had carried out the beating. They were held for several days, then conveniently "escaped." After the family stopped cooperating, the JPC abandoned its investigation.

The police director eventually delivered a message to Gono's family: Chucky wished to see them. "He was afraid," Wortuah recalled of their meeting. "He assured us he ordered his bodyguard to punish Isaac, [but] he [didn't] say you should beat him to kill him. And that was [a] mistake."

Before the meeting ended, Chucky gave the family $1,000. Eventually, the family received $16,000 to cover funeral expenses and to provide for Gono's two children. "All the assistance was done through President Taylor," Wortuah said.

Charles Taylor's government was struggling to defend itself against the most serious threat to its power that it had faced in five years, yet the president was reaching into his own pocket to pay for his son's senseless excesses. If Taylor couldn't count on the commanders closest to him to be disciplined enough not to kill their own men, he had little reason to hope that they could stop the rebel advance.

Taylor began to fear that rebels were infiltrating the capital, stashing weapons and preparing for the assault. One of the men who came under his suspicion was a student and dockworker, Varmuyan Dulleh.

Dulleh lived in Paynesville, outside Monrovia, and worked for the National Port Authority while attending school at the University of Liberia. His uncle was Alhaji Kromah, the former leader of ULIMO-K—the faction that had nearly wiped out Taylor's army during the war. Kromah, Taylor's nemesis, now lived quietly in Arlington, Virginia, but Taylor feared that he and his young nephew were part of a plot involving the Americans and his neighbors in Guinea to remove him from power.

That July, shortly after two a.m., Dulleh heard a familiar voice calling to him from the darkness outside his house.[36] He recognized the voice—it belonged to a man named Abraham Kelleh. As strange as the request was, coming in the middle of the night, Kelleh asked Dulleh whether he could stay at his home. Annoyed, Dulleh opened his front door. The only light illuminating the night came from Dulleh's neighbor's home, across the swamp. Kelleh stood stock-still.

Dulleh immediately sensed something was wrong. As he stepped out to ask his friend what had happened, he noticed several men bounding across the yard toward him. They were carrying weapons. He turned and bolted along the exterior of the house toward a mango tree at the edge of the property. He wore only his bedclothes and no shoes. Before he could make it any farther, soldiers surrounded him, training their weapons on him. He glanced over his property. There seemed to be more than one hundred soldiers, most wearing solid black uniforms bearing the distinct badge of a cobra and scorpion.

"So you want to overthrow the papay?" one of the voices barked at him.

The men set upon him and threw him into a vehicle, to be carried to the president's residence. After a short drive to Congo Town, Dulleh was brought before the president at White Flower, wearing only the white T-shirt he had been sleeping in and a pair of black trousers.

"Mr. President, we have got him. This is him," the police director said.

Taylor was seated in his office at his desk with two Liberian flags perched behind him, a Bible near his hand. A young man who bore a distinct resemblance to the president waited silently among the security personnel in the room.

"I have a few questions to ask you," Taylor said to him. "How many rebel soldiers have [you] been able to smuggle from the bush into the United States Embassy? Where do you have the arms?"

"President Taylor, I have no idea what you are talking about. I have no idea absolutely," Dulleh responded. He began to weep out of terror.

Taylor continued questioning Dulleh. Had he ever been to Guinea?

Dulleh had lived in Guinea, which was an unremarkable fact. Many Liberians, particularly Mandingos, had fled to Guinea at some point during the war. But the LURD rebels had enjoyed relatively free access to Guinean territory throughout the uprising and, presumably, military support from President Lansana Conté.

Dulleh looked at the president and lied.

President Taylor flipped through his passport and paged through the numbers on his cell phone. Then he looked up at the prisoner and said, "Look down that man."

Dulleh turned around and saw a slight, wan man with bloodshot, spectral eyes standing behind him.

"That's General Benjamin Yeaten," Taylor said. "I'm going to turn you over to General Benjamin Yeaten, and he's going to beat you until you tell the truth."

Dulleh had never seen Yeaten before that night, but he knew the man's reputation as a murderer—he was one of the men Taylor turned to to carry out his execution orders. Yeaten reached down, yanked Dulleh to his feet, and dragged him from the room.

Dulleh called from the hallway, "President Taylor, can I make a statement?"

"Yes, come in," the president said.

"President Taylor, my life is in your hands—" he pleaded.

The president cut Dulleh off. "No, your life is not in my hands. Your life is in God's hands."

Dulleh was loaded into a jeep full of gunmen and driven down the darkened hillside to a single-story home with an adjoining wall. He was led inside by Yeaten, past a group of men dressed in civilian clothing. Yeaten then produced a small box.

"This box you see is a box filled of money. We're going to give you money and do nothing to you. Just tell us the truth," he told Dulleh.

He was presented with an impossible situation: confess to a crime he had not committed or face interrogation that wouldn't end until a confession was reached.

"I am not involved with anything. The information about me was not true," he pleaded.

Yeaten's countenance shifted. The statement clearly enraged him. Armed guards then led Dulleh into a garage, where men stuffed a filthy rag into his mouth and forced him to the floor. Yeaten appeared, holding an electric iron. Behind him was the young man resembling the president—Chucky. Yeaten grabbed Dulleh's right arm and pressed the hot iron into his flesh.

The torture continued for some time. Several gunmen held Dulleh down as Yeaten seared the prisoner's other arm, his stomach, his leg. Dulleh struggled to cry out, but the rag stuffed in his mouth muffled the sound. He was helpless.

Yeaten yanked the rag from his mouth. "Are you ready to talk?" he asked.

"Yes," Dulleh responded.

Yeaten stared at him. "So why you involved with the rebel movement to overthrow the president?" he asked.

Dulleh could only say, "No."

A fighter appeared in the room with a pot of steaming water. Yeaten filled a cup and poured it over the prisoner's head; he filled a second cup, dousing Dulleh's back.

The pain was unbearable for Dulleh. He heard Yeaten order him to cup his hands together. The general poured the scalding water into Dulleh's hands. Dulleh began screaming so loud, he could hear nothing else.

Yeaten raised a shotgun to the prisoner's head and ordered him not to spill the water. Dulleh saw Chucky stand up and raise a gun to his head. He recognized him only as the young man he'd seen with President Taylor.

Dulleh could think about little more than the pain. The burns on his hands, across his back, and on his leg throbbed excruciatingly.

The young man addressed him. "Do you remember the man you talked to in the office not long ago?" Dulleh heard him say.

Dulleh could only nod his head.

"That man has the Holy Bible in his hands," the young man said. "I don't have it in my hands."

Dulleh finally realized who the man speaking to him was. He was the president's son, Chucky.

Several soldiers then forced Dulleh flat onto his stomach. He caught a glimpse of Chucky with a short, round object in his hand. Suddenly a jolt of electricity burst through Dulleh's body. He had felt Chucky press the stick again to the back of his neck; the shocks continued across his back. The soldiers flipped Dulleh over and pulled his pants down. Dulleh looked down to see Chucky jabbing the stun gun at his penis.

It was an image that would remain with Dulleh long after he was disappeared into state custody, without charge or trial, another victim of Charles Taylor's paranoia and his son's sadism.

Despite Taylor's fears about rebels in Monrovia, the real threat remained on the front lines. In July 2002 Chucky had sent Christopher Menephar to assess the fighting as it neared the capital.[37] He was no longer a hardened child soldier but a lieutenant colonel in the ATU, a commander who took his responsibilities seriously. Menephar prepared a memo titled "General Front Line Report Bomi, Gbojay, Arthington Mont., Bomi Co. Liberia."

The report reflected the military formality as well as the lack of formal education among the elite ATU fighters: "On the 24th of July, I was mandated by GOC to assests [*sic*] the various front lines," it began, then went on to describe the fighting in Bomi County, including assaults by small groups of lightly armed rebels and ambushes carried out by government troops. The report painted a positive picture of the counteroffensive by Taylor's troops: "We observed that the enemy are on the run in Bomi" by a "joint" operation on the evening of July 19, 2002, involving the AFL and ATU.

The rebels sought to establish a headquarters in Tubmanburg, an old mining town with a population of less than twelve thousand, that would put them within striking distance of Monrovia. The memo reported five men wounded, one hundred fifty enemy dead. The numbers were impossible to verify—whether the count was accurate and whether the dead were, in fact, the enemy. Menephar's report noted that the ATU was fighting alongside militias throughout Bomi County and that there was a "good working relationship between the local pop and government."

It is unlikely that Menephar was completely candid or accurate in his account of what happened in Bomi. He had little incentive to provide a leader as volatile and ill equipped as Chucky with any information that would reflect badly on him or his father.

In fact, a few old men would emerge from Tubmanburg to tell a different story. According to that account, government fighters did "liberate" the town.[38] Rather than fight, the rebels disappeared into the bush, leaving little sign of their presence. The government commander then assembled the civilians and explained to them that they would be evacuated to Monrovia. A truck carried away one group of men, women, and children. When it returned to Tubmanburg a short time later, the residents noticed that the vehicle's cab was soaked in blood. The remaining civilians who could not fit on the first journey were forced into the truck and driven to a bridge overlooking the Mahel River.

The ground there was littered with bodies. Babies with their skulls bashed in. Women with their bellies slit open. The fighters were busily dumping the dead into the river. When the truck stopped, the soldiers forced the civilians out. One fighter pulled a man's wife aside, shot her, then set upon mutilating her body. The fighter then turned to the husband. All the man could do was beg to say a final prayer.

"We are not here for God business," the fighter said.

War as Taylor knew it best had returned to Liberia. He had entrusted Benjamin Yeaten, his most relied-upon enforcer, to confront the threat. The methods were familiar to those who had survived the civil war. Terror stood in for military might. Rebels were the enemies, but too often civilians were the targets. As long as foreign powers supplied weapons—as Guinea did to the rebels—the underequipped and ill-trained government forces could do little to maintain their monopoly on the use of force and defeat their enemies.

12

ABT

Real as chrome, march and we hone, hand to hand, man they no, flip at the birth of a fight.

— *United States vs. Belfast*, EXHIBIT CE-4

In October 2002, Charles Taylor granted the new American ambassador, John W. Blaney, a rare private audience.[1] Exhausted by the sanctions and the fighting over the summer, the Taylor government was left with very few resources. His inner circle was collapsing in on itself. Isaac Gono's gratuitous murder was only the latest symptom of the decline, but the problems ran far deeper than indiscipline in his security forces or his murderous son.

For months the Taylor government had been screaming itself hoarse to the international community over the growing insurgency. The West's covert support for the rebels was growing clearer: white helicopters with no official markings were reportedly seen transporting and resupplying the rebels near the front, and captured enemy fighters reported that they had been trained by U.S. Special Forces. Meanwhile, the rebels' public relations arm operated freely in the United States. Whatever support the rebels enjoyed in Washington, covert or otherwise, ran contrary to the State Department's objective of stopping the violence in West Africa. In the background, American diplomats lobbied the government in Conakry to close the border to Liberia and cease the traffic of fighters into Liberia. Publicly State Department officials made a clear distinction: they did not back the rebels, but they did support the opposition. This policy was summed up as "ABT"—Anyone But Taylor.[2]

The ATU continued to be a menacing presence near the U.S. embassy compound. In one incident, heavily armed fighters carrying AKs, RPKs, and RPGs appeared along the compound's northern perimeter.[3] When confronted, the fighters explained that they were "conducting a routine weapons search of the area," despite the proximity to the diplomatic compound. With increasing frequency, dismounted ATU patrols appeared on Mamba Point, approaching the embassy gates to berate the local guards. At one point a disoriented civilian attempted to climb onto the embassy property.[4] The local guards who detained him noticed that he had been severely beaten. The man told them, "ATU commander Chucky Taylor and associates were chasing him."

Charles Taylor's behavior had taken a turn for the strange over the course of the year. Despite the fact that he was already married, he was rumored to have wed a recent high school graduate who was seven months pregnant in a tribal ceremony.[5] The rumor infuriated the first lady, Jewel Howard Taylor, and drew questions from the press. Taylor said that he was entitled to four wives and that it was his wife's responsibility to help find appropriate matches.

If Taylor was comfortable or calm, given the tumult of the year, he didn't show it when he met with Ambassador Blaney. Sitting alone with the ambassador, Taylor fidgeted noticeably. His relationship with the United States had grown so tense and distrustful that the ambassador found it necessary to assure Taylor that the United States did not seek to physically harm him.

Taylor appeared reassured by the statement. He visibly relaxed, then tried to explain away the behavior that led to the rift with the United States. "Yes, he had been involved in Sierra Leone, and deeply regretted it," the ambassador reported Taylor as saying. "But Washington did not understand the context of that involvement." Taylor had chosen to arm the Sierra Leonean rebels out of fear that "these forces would have been turned on himself and Monrovia." Now he desperately sought to rescue his relationship with the United States, offering use of Robertsfield for the U.S. military and future rights for yet-to-be-discovered Liberian oil fields.

Taylor was convinced that there was an "ocean of oil" to be discovered offshore in Liberia.[6] The entire Gulf of Guinea remained largely unexplored at that time—the result of the region's instability and the costs and technical challenges associated with deep-water drilling. Two years earlier Taylor had commissioned a 2-D seismic imaging study by a Houston-based company, TGS-NOPEC, which suggested the potential for significant deep-water reserves offshore.[7] The notion that war-wracked Liberia could transition to an oil-producing nation might seem far-fetched, but Africa was a continent of transformation, where many impoverished and violent states altered their global positions with the discovery of resources.

Taylor's offer seemed genuine to the ambassador, yet his actions suggested that he was committed to his path as a warlord. Liberian forces were involved in the renewed conflict in Ivory Coast, completing the troika of insecure states bordering Liberia. Even after their positive meeting, Taylor continued to publicly suggest that the U.S. government sought to forcibly remove him from power using "American funded assassins."

"No one should trust Charles Taylor," the ambassador reported back to Washington, later concluding that "we need to make another move in order to keep Taylor corralled or we may find ourselves in an even bigger and rougher rodeo."

By early January 2003, Charles Taylor had stepped into the twilight of his political career. The preceding summer a new, more abstract threat than the rebel army had emerged in Freetown: the tribunal created out of a UN Security Council resolution, known as the Special Court for Sierra Leone.[8] Prosecutors had spent years investigating crimes related to the civil war that had destroyed Liberia's neighbor and brutalized the populace. The investigation invariably led to Liberia, not only to Sam Bockarie, who still unofficially enjoyed refuge in Monrovia, but also to Taylor. As the rebel commanders whom Taylor sponsored from Sierra Leone atomized throughout the region—a few looking to cut a deal with the new court—the Liberian president's role in the conflict became more and more difficult to conceal.

Taylor had real reason to fear being brought before an international tribunal. International justice had become more forceful in the late 1990s. Yugoslav president Slobodan Milošević's indictment and arrest demonstrated the international community's willingness and capability to put a head of state on trial. If the investigators were able to assemble enough evidence to charge him, Taylor knew, his elected position would offer no immunity.

The truth of the matter was, Liberia was dying from the inside. Displaced Liberians poured into Monrovia fleeing the fighting in the countryside, while others fled into Sierra Leone. Meanwhile Liberians in Ivory Coast began to return en masse to southern counties in Liberia, running from that country's civil war. The situation would have been alarmingly complex for any nation to face, but for a government that had devoted none of its energy to the well-being of its people, the crisis threatened a humanitarian disaster. Taiwan, motivated by Liberia's recognition of its nationhood, had again stepped into the breach for Taylor, shipping approximately ten thousand tons of rice and undertaking projects to restore water and electricity to the capital.[9]

By February 2003 the rebels were headquartered in Voinjama, having pushed government forces out of Lofa County. The rebel group had taken control of Robertsport, a picturesque oceanfront village midway between the border with Sierra Leone and Monrovia, securing a potential port should their supply line through Guinea be cut. Two senior officials in the State Department met with rebel representatives to hear their demands and gauge their willingness to participate in peace talks.[10] The rebels made it clear that they could assault Monrovia but didn't believe it yet necessary to achieve their goals. For Taylor, this refrain eerily echoed his own as a rebel leader a decade earlier, when he had sat down with Ambassador Kenneth Brown to discuss the terms of Samuel Doe's departure. Just as Taylor had demanded then, the LURD representatives were emphatic that any deal the rebels cut had one requirement: the president must leave power.

For Lynn, Liberia remained a loose end. She had not spoken to Chucky for nearly a year and a half. She had left him and his world behind, for the comparatively anonymous existence as a single mother putting herself through school in Orlando. But their divorce did not move forward, in part because Lynn wasn't ready to let go of what she called her "African princess fairy tale."[11] The prince in that fairy tale had been replaced by a man who had threatened to execute her family. The boy she had fallen in love with seemed to have disappeared completely into the madness of the civil war. She still cared for that person, but she wasn't certain whether he still existed.

Bernice eventually broke the silence between the two of them. She still lived a few miles from Lynn in the Pine Hills home where Chucky had grown up, though she spent much of her time in Monrovia. One day, as Lynn recalls, her mother-in-law called out of the blue. Chucky was killing himself with drugs, she said, and she needed Lynn's help to save his life. Lynn couldn't ignore her mother-in-law's plea. She picked up the phone and reached out to him—not only because Bernice had asked her to but also because she had yet to let go of her husband. "Even though he was a shitty father and a shitty husband, I didn't want him to die," Lynn said.[12]

The two talked. For a moment, Lynn set aside the past and agreed to return to Monrovia, despite the dangers. She was compelled by simple reasons. "I missed him," she recalled. "I missed Liberia."

When Lynn landed again at Robertsfield in early 2003, Chucky barely resembled the person she had married. He appeared wan, strung out, and emaciated; his well-built frame had withered. As troubling as the sight was, she was happy to be there and happy for her son, who was nearly three years old, to be with the father he scarcely knew.

As they drove toward Monrovia, Lynn entered a new Liberia. In the two years of her absence, it was not only Chucky who had deteriorated—so had the world immediately surrounding him. Gone was the euphoria that had followed his father's election. Gone was the privilege and freedom of movement that came with being part of the presidential family. Gone was the sense that the small country had a future. Sanctions and the war had whittled away all those things. All that remained was Monrovia, a city distended with refugees and, as the fighting overtook much of the countryside, growing more desperate by the day.

"I specifically remember asking why they had to let strongholds on some of these places go," Lynn recalled. Chucky explained to her that securing the country "just wasn't logistically possible."

By choosing to join him in Monrovia, Lynn had willingly entered into the siege, though she could not have known how precarious the situation in the capital was. "Holding Monrovia was the crucial element in any of their wars," he told her, as she recalled. "Once Monrovia fell, it [would be] over."

Lynn tried to create some semblance of normality. Shortly after arriving, she put together a small birthday party for her son. Streamers were hung. A few balloons decorated the table near a glass of beer. Chucky even doffed a golden, cardboard cutout crown, tilting it low over his brow and mugging for the camera. But he never removed his fatigues. His sidearm always lay nearby.

The tension of the war surrounded Chucky's villa. His usual retinue of bodyguards lingered outside the house, men who had remained by his side for years—Bobby Dixon, Tarnue Gizzie, Humphrey—and who had always respected him. But Lynn noticed a change in how Chucky treated his men. "He would get angry a lot and he would yell at the men a lot," she said.

Eventually she learned of Isaac Gono's killing, which despite the press coverage had been treated as a secret. When she asked Chucky about it, he refused to talk about it other than to say that he "absolutely did not do it."

Chucky had always shielded her from his world outside the house. As the war approached, that separation became more and more difficult to maintain.

After nearly a year of investigations, prosecutors with the Special Court for Sierra Leone fired their opening salvo. On March 3, 2003, the court issued a set of indictments against leaders from various Sierra Leonean factions, including Taylor allies Foday Sankoh and Sam Bockarie.[13] If Charles Taylor felt he'd dodged a bullet, the relief was temporary: he grew increasingly concerned that Bockarie and his men would cooperate with the court in building a case against him. The Sierra Leoneans constituted direct evidence that Taylor had supported the conflict in Sierra Leone—and as the war closed in on Monrovia and he had fewer resources to draw from, Bockarie and his men had become too powerful and difficult for Taylor to control.

Taylor's fear became real when one of Bockarie's men disappeared from his refuge in Liberia. One of the RUF leader's closest advisers, a fighter named Victor, feigned illness at Gbatala training base and disappeared upon returning to Monrovia.[14] Victor had trained Bockarie's fighters at Gbatala with the ATU and thus represented a direct link between Taylor and the charges outlined in the indictments released in

Freetown. Chucky had already taken the step of destroying the ATU rosters listing the Sierra Leonean fighters.[15] His father wanted to take that a step further: he wanted to track down and destroy all the Sierra Leonean fighters in Liberia—Bockarie included.[16]

Killing off the Sierra Leoneans became an urgent task that Taylor gave to Benjamin Yeaten. Bockarie's rebels had been hired out to fight against Ivorian government forces seeking to push out insurgent forces fighting for Alassane Ouattara in the north of Ivory Coast. This assignment had left the fighters temporarily out of touch with the developing intrigue in Freetown and Monrovia. Now Bockarie received an order from Monrovia asking him and his forces to retreat from Ivory Coast and regroup in Liberia's Nimba County to meet with Yeaten.[17] He was reportedly surprised but crossed the border into Liberia nonetheless. He trusted his Liberian counterpart enough to bring along his family, including his wife, mother, and son. The group arrived midday at the country compound belonging to Vice President Moses Blah, where they sat for a meal of rice and cassava leaf.

This would be the last meal of Bockarie's life. The official account would hold that Bockarie was killed in a firefight attempting to reenter Liberia. But eventually an ATU officer would testify to the actual details of the Sierra Leonean rebel's killing.[18] According to the officer, Mohammed Sheriff, following the lunch Bockarie was led into the bush and beaten to death. Bodyguards raped and killed his wife and executed his son and his mother. Yeaten's men fired several rounds into Bockarie's body to provide evidence to support the official account of his death. One of most dangerous potential witnesses against Taylor would now never be able to cut a deal with prosecutors.

Yet Taylor still had to deal with the distinct possibility that he would be overthrown. He flew to Accra in June 2003 to sue for peace. The LURD rebels had successfully backed him into a corner from the north. And now yet another faction, the Movement for Democracy in Liberia, or MODEL, was pursuing government forces from the south. After a brief lull in fighting, both rebel factions renewed their assaults that month. For months regional mediators had been negotiating to bring Taylor and the rebels to the table. Taylor now realized the loss of Monrovia was imminent, and he hoped that the regional leaders could use the promise of elections to broker a truce.

When the warring parties convened in Accra, the conference took on the air of a carnival—heads of state from around Africa converged on the city. Representatives from Taylor's government, the rebels, and Liberia's varied political constituencies shouldered into the conference center. International figures with little connection to the crisis, like Cornel West and Al Sharpton, waded into this crowd, hoping their voices would be heard above the din. The men wanted Taylor to leave power—but were also pressuring the Bush administration to intervene directly in the crisis. ("This administration's policy is different, absolutely different, when it comes to people of color," Sharpton said. "I can't imagine that there wouldn't be intervention in Europe if thousands were dying in war."[19])

In Accra, the international media temporarily fixed its glare on Liberia, hoping to document a potential turning point in the crisis. This audience was unparalleled in Taylor's political career. When he arrived at the conference, he intended to deliver a performance that reflected the significance of the moment. He was left with very little to negotiate; in fact, the only bargaining chip he had was himself and his future in Liberia. Nonetheless, the international attention focused on Accra made this conference the ideal forum for Taylor to proffer a solution to the crisis.

Back in Monrovia, U.S. embassy officials learned of a looming disaster.[20] For months, it had been an open secret in Washington that in March the Special Court for Sierra Leone had indicted President Taylor along with the other defendants. The indictment, which remained under seal, charged the president with a surfeit of counts, including terrorism, rape, looting, use of child soldiers, and slavery—all related to the war in Sierra Leone. It marked the first time in history an African head of state had been formally accused of crimes against humanity.

Events began to unfold simultaneously in Freetown, Accra, and Monrovia. The Freetown-based prosecutor for the case, an international law professor named David Crane, unsealed the indictment at an explosive moment—just as Taylor arrived at the Accra conference— serving the Ghanaian government with a copy of the charges, as well as a warrant for the Liberian president's arrest.[21] Taylor had known of the possibility of indictment, but like everyone else, he was blindsided by Crane's announcement.

The prosecutor explicitly aimed "to humble and humiliate him before his peers, the leaders of Africa, and to serve notice to Taylor and others that the days of impunity in Africa were over."[22] He hoped Taylor would not be returning to Monrovia with a cease-fire in hand but rather would be led in handcuffs to a cell in Freetown.

According to Robert Ferguson, the State Department had warned Crane against unsealing the indictment during the Accra conference— not only for the danger it posed in Liberia, but because of the unlikelihood that an African leader would assent to the arrest of a peer at an international peace conference.[23] In fact, the unsealing of the indictment put the Ghanaian hosts in a nearly impossible position: if they allowed Taylor to be apprehended on their soil, his friends and supporters would likely view the peace conference as little more than a pretext for the arrest. Crane could have waited until after the conference concluded, Ferguson said, to avoid throwing a wrench into the negotiations. "But he chose not to. He wanted to do it then, he wanted to make a political statement, he thought the whole world was watching this conference."

Officials at the U.S. embassy could have hardly imagined a worse scenario. As attenuated as Taylor's authority was, it remained the only power holding together the militias and security forces in Monrovia. His removal, officials feared, could send these groups into a death spiral, as competing armed bands loyal to Taylor fought over the last scraps of property, food, and power that remained in the capital. In the midst of the developing refugee crisis, civilians would undoubtedly suffer the brunt of the ensuing violence.

Embassy officials began working the phones in Monrovia. It wasn't clear who could step in should Taylor be arrested. Among those contacted was Moses Blah, Taylor's vice president. The Americans sought assurances from Blah that he could control Taylor's fighters should anything happen in Ghana. According to Ferguson, who attended the meeting, the vice president responded, Yes, we understand. We have total control over it. Blah was an ornamental holdover from the NPFL, with ties to Taylor dating back to the Libyan training camps—and according to the Liberian constitution, the succession of power fell to him. But in truth, he had control over nothing.

When Taylor learned of the indictment, he fled the conference, abandoning the negotiations for the more urgent task of consolidating his power. In Monrovia, once Benjamin Yeaten learned of Blah's meeting with the embassy officials, he notified Taylor that the vice president was plotting a coup with the Americans. Only hours after the indictment was unsealed, the vice president was placed under arrest. Yeaten, the incident revealed, held the power in Taylor's absence.

Crane's decision to indict Taylor amplified the crisis not only by backing Taylor into a corner but also by applying pressure to those around him. The tactic was akin to going after a mafia family in the midst of a gangland war. As the siege took hold in Monrovia, those close to Taylor found themselves not only confronting the enemy but also facing the choice of whether to turn evidence on their leader. This dilemma was particularly acute within Taylor's inner circle, including for Chucky. Cooperation would mean not only working with Crane but abandoning the war at its most critical moment.

That night Taylor returned to a Monrovia hovering near the edge of chaos, but his heavily armed motorcade was greeted by cheering crowds. The response was more complex than simple adulation. Taylor was a savior, even if he was a savior of his own design: he'd manufactured a form of chaos that only he could control; his people were utterly reliant upon him.

By early June, the front lines of the war had settled on Duala Market, a small city of tin-roofed shacks on the opposite bank of the Mesurado River. The market stretched out across Bushrod Island, a thumb of land that points southward toward where two bridges fork into downtown Monrovia. The island was the nation's Achilles' heel, home to the Freeport of Monrovia, the capital's lifeline to the world. If the port fell, the city would be under siege.

On June 3, Chucky made a rare appearance on the front lines, when he met his commander, Christopher Menephar.[24] Unlike Chucky, Menephar had spent much of the end of the dry season in direct combat, leading small ATU units into battle against the rebels. In May rebels had overrun his position in Gbarnga, forcing him to retreat along bush trails toward Charles Taylor's farm in Bong County. The next month Menephar led two platoons to assault the rebel headquarters in Bomi Hills, surprising the enemy with a midmorning assault. But as the firefight raged, the ATU fighters depleted their ammunition and were forced to flee through the jungle back toward the capital.

After the assault on Bomi, Menephar remained on the new front lines at Duala Market. The ATU regrouped in anticipation of another assault on the capital. Once the rebels hit Duala, the combat shifted: no longer were the rebels fighting the government soldiers along a single asphalt roadway and red dirt paths in the jungle; now they battled amid the maze of low-slung buildings lining the one road that led to Monrovia. Taylor's men had little with which to defend the city beyond small arms and antiaircraft guns mounted in the beds of pickup trucks.

That day Chucky drove his jeep to the front, approaching Menephar's position, a building off the road where ATU soldiers had sought shelter. The two men had a brief, confused conversation, in the midst of the fighting. Not far from their position, a rocket slammed into the middle of a roadway, cutting down two SSS officers. As Menephar helped load the wounded into a vehicle, Chucky told him, "Stay right here! I'm gonna get you more ammo."

That was the last time Menephar saw Chucky. Three days later, just after eight a.m., an RPG slammed into the building where Menephar had sought shelter. The explosion brought the building down around him, sending a shard of shrapnel into his forehead. Menephar lay there unconscious. The fighting around him did not stop. The rebels pushed on toward the forking bridges leading into Monrovia.

Instead of returning with ammo, Chucky retreated across the bridge to the relative safety of the capital. As the fighting encircled the capital, he holed up at his villa, on the opposite side of Monrovia, while his comrades were forced to retreat.[25] In the diminishing area of his father's control, the house was considered safe. Lynn remained there with their son. The city took on the air of surreal desperation. At night, after the generator cut off, Lynn could hear the all-night prayer sessions called "the tarry" going on until dawn, the neighbors praying together against some horrible future that seemed to be bearing down on the capital.[26]

One afternoon that June an ATU officer ran to Chucky's house demanding to see him. Rebels had breached the city, he warned. Mortars sounded in the distance, punctuated by the faint rattle of gunfire. Bushrod Island lay several miles away, separated only by some of Monrovia's most densely populated neighborhoods. It was impossible to tell how long it would take for the rebels to fight their way to Congo Town or what they would do once they got there. But Lynn didn't need to speculate; when Chucky appeared, she saw panic in his eyes.

Chucky rushed Lynn and their son into the back of his truck, haphazardly throwing a Kevlar vest over them, then tore out of his compound gate, down the mud roadway leading to his father's house. As they turned out onto the road, Chucky's bodyguard smashed the truck's rear window to clear a firing position. Lynn caught a glimpse of Monrovia out the window of the racing truck. Civilians pushed their dead along in wheelbarrows. The ground was littered with debris; inexplicably, bloodred corn syrup spilled across the road.

"Okay, we're going to die," Lynn said to herself.

Her son responded, "It's okay, Momma."

But when the family arrived at White Flower, all the panic they had felt rushed from the room. They were met, instead, with an almost surreal calm. Charles Taylor sat outside in the back of the house, the mothers of his children seated in chairs in a circle around him. Seeing Chucky arrive in a panic, with wife and child in tow, all Charles Taylor could do was laugh at his son for overreacting.

Taylor displayed outward calm in the face of the rebel threat, but the Special Court's indictment troubled him. He had warned the American ambassador that he would fight "to the death" rather than face trial in Sierra Leone. But he also recognized that he had other options. If he could outlast the rebels, he said, he would abide by the promise he had made at Accra to step down.

"I'm done gone," he told the American ambassador, but remained vague on the terms or timing of his departure.[27] While Taylor had alienated most of his neighbors in West Africa, some considered allowing him a comfortable retirement to be an acceptable compromise if it would spare the Liberian people further suffering. Each hour Taylor delayed and deliberated could be measured in lives. The cousins of war—starvation and disease—had followed the displaced into the capital. As stray bullets and mortar shells from rebel forces rained down on the capital, it forced Taylor to choose between his political future and the safety of the Liberian people.

Meanwhile Chucky had been disappearing into himself ever since his father's return from Ghana. It wasn't just the drugs—though he'd clearly gone over the edge—but also the painful realization that Lynn could see dawning over him: it was over.[28] The war. Liberia. His father. There was nothing left for him. And he had nothing to show. When Lynn found him shut inside the bathroom one day that summer, she stood outside the door, pondering whether she should open it.

Like many others who had tied their fortunes to Charles Taylor, Chucky was looking for a way out of Liberia. The UN travel ban had rendered his Liberian diplomatic passport largely useless. Even if consular services had been available at the embassy in Monrovia, the act of walking, hat in hand, through the embassy gates that the ATU had patrolled so menacingly would have been impossible for him. Chucky's mother pursued a workaround: she worked to secure him a Trinidadian passport that could, at least, get him to Port of Spain, Trinidad.[29] But even then—as the few airlines that serviced Roberts-field folded up local operations—the window to escape was quickly closing.

Lynn feared what would come next. Around Taylor, everyone scrambled to make arrangements to leave the country. Benjamin Yeaten, meanwhile, continued to do Taylor's bidding, liquidating anyone who "could turn on him and be witness," Lynn recalled.[30]

But even as the last hours of the Taylor government ticked down, Lynn still knew very little of what Chucky had been involved in, or what specific role he had played in his father's power. She had no idea whether he was really the sadist and murderer that much of Liberia believed him to be. Chucky had learned two lessons from his father: keep things compartmentalized, and manage your liabilities.[31] "He taught me that without ever speaking of it," he said years later.

But as the war raged around them, these boundaries became more difficult to maintain. One afternoon an ATU officer appeared at the house with a handful of photographs. Chucky made no attempt to hide them from Lynn—he barely registered them. But when Lynn glanced over at them, she saw "dead bodies. There were at least six or seven of them, they were all layed down and all shot in the head." The images stunned her.

That afternoon as Chucky holed up in the bathroom, she found the courage to push open the door, startling him.[32] He held something in his hands—drugs—she couldn't tell whether it was cocaine or heroin. But when she knocked it away, Chucky turned on her. He leaped toward her, wrapping his hands around her neck.

Despite all the violence surrounding him all these years, Chucky had never laid a hand on Lynn. But now it seemed as if he could kill her. Her screams carried through the house, sending her mother-in-law racing to the bathroom. The fairy tale had ended—the ugly reality was undeniable. This was not the future Lynn wanted for herself or her child. When she looked up, with her husband's hands around her neck, her three-year-old boy was standing there looking at his father.

"That's my son's last memory of his dad," she recalled.

As the siege threatened to finally boil over into the city, Charles Taylor gave Chucky $50,000 in cash. Many government officials, Charles Taylor included, were making preparations to leave the country. According to Samuel Nimley, who spent early July 2003 with the president's son, Chucky burned through $10,000 on drugs, even as staples like food grew scarce in the capital.[33]

One of the few places with reliable stores of food was the Mamba Point Hotel, situated several hundred yards from the embassy gates, where Chucky went to eat and drink. As the crisis grew and the final days approached, Robert Ferguson bumped into a paranoid Chucky at the hotel. "What are you doing here?" he recalled Chucky saying to him. "Are you here to kill me?"[34]

"I wouldn't waste my time," Ferguson told him.

Ferguson and the embassy staff had been living under fire for several weeks, bearing witness to—and receiving much of the outward blame for—the worsening humanitarian situation in the capital. Desperate Monrovians stacked their dead at the embassy gates in a plea for American intervention. Beyond its diplomatic efforts to stop the war, the U.S. embassy could do little to alleviate the suffering of the Liberian people. That power belonged to Charles Taylor.

Chucky was an American citizen, Ferguson knew, but he wasn't so desperate as to ask for his help. He was forced to consider his options: hold out with his father and risk his life, in the hope that the rebel advance would peter out; flee Liberia into the uncertainty of exile; or trade on his knowledge of his father's crimes to secure his own freedom. This was referred to as the Prisoner's Dilemma. Theoretically, the most advantageous course of action would be to hold out, though the most likely to succeed would be defection. In studies of the Prisoner's Dilemma involving psychopathic subjects, their choice was nearly always the same: they chose the option they felt served their best interests and ratted out their partner.[35] Chucky did not deliberate publicly. Within days, he simply disappeared.

PART III

13

Exile

Knowledge can't bear, nigga handle your fear.

—*United States vs. Belfast*, EXHIBIT CE-5

The mountains of Trinidad's Northern Range come into view first. Green cliffs drop directly into the churning Caribbean; then the peaks give way to steep, overgrown valleys decorated by houses and winding roadways. At the base of this descent lies Port of Spain, resting on the Gulf of Paria, the wedge-shaped inland sea that separates the island of Trinidad from its closest neighbor, Venezuela. Descending airliners cut a wide arc over the gulf lining up with Piarco International Airport. Ships litter the harbor below: fuel tankers and container vessels ambling away from port, fishing vessels gliding toward the coast, and, visible as the aircraft approaches land, shipwrecks sitting in the shallows, keeled to reveal their sun-bleached hulls basking above the milky blue waterline.

Chucky landed here in mid-July 2003. Two weeks earlier he and his mother had slipped out of Monrovia, chartering a flight to Ghana and eventually on to Lomé, Togo.[1] Lynn had left Monrovia shortly after their altercation, and Charles Taylor had begun preparations to abandon the presidency. Chucky and his mother remained in Lomé for several days before flying to Port of Spain via Paris. Just as when he'd fled Orlando as a teenager, Chucky told nobody that he was leaving Monrovia, not even his closest commanders, who were making a desperate last stand at Waterside Market on the opposite shore from Bushrod Island.

The CIA tracked his departure, noting that shortly after he fled, armed men overtook the guards at his villa.[2]

After Lynn's departure from Liberia, the end came swiftly. On June 26, President George W. Bush—on the eve of a five-nation trip to Africa—had called for Charles Taylor to leave Liberia immediately.[3] The president's statement surprised even the U.S. embassy in Monrovia, where the staff greeted the decision with enthusiasm.[4] Surprisingly, Taylor responded to President Bush's demand with neither defiance nor defensiveness. Instead, he replied, "The government of Liberia welcomes the interest that the U.S. President George Bush has taken in the Liberian conflict and urges the U.S. government to remain proactive in the peace process."[5]

But as Chucky fled Liberia, he knew that even though he was an American citizen, he was also clearly an enemy to the United States.

News of his flight spread quickly. In the end, his presence in Monrovia was immaterial to the resolution of the crisis. Several days later, as Christopher Menephar raced to the battlefront with a load of ammunition, his cell phone rang.[6] It was Chucky calling from outside the country.

"Why are you calling me for at this time?" Menephar said. After being wounded in Duala in early June, Menephar had brought himself to JFK Hospital, several miles from the front. The hospital was crowded with the wounded and dying and lacked food, medicine, or enough staff to treat many of the patients. Not a single commander or comrade visited him to bring him food or offer help. After five days he had the strength to walk out of the hospital on his own. The war was still raging just blocks from his home, so he returned to the battle, shrapnel still embedded in his skull.

On the phone Chucky stated the obvious—that he had left the country. "I wanted to say sorry for what happened," he told the commander, promising to send him money.

The call annoyed Menephar. Chucky wanted to talk, but he was in the midst of a fight. He had been a loyal fighter all his life. He respected the chain of command and performed as he had been trained to. But none of his training or experience prepared him for how to confront the cowardice of his own commander. In the end they had each been fighting for something very different: Liberia was Christopher's home, the home of his ancestors, and the home of his children. Liberia was a chapter in Chucky's life that had come to end. There was little Menephar could say to him, so he told Chucky to call him back later.

Chucky's disappearance disappointed even his most loyal commanders. "He panicked, he panicked. He couldn't take the pressure anymore," recalled Samuel Nimley.[7] It also surprised Charles Taylor, according to Nimley, who despite providing his son with money to escape, hadn't expected that he would leave while the battle for Monrovia still raged. "That was a cowardly move. To leave your father in the fight," Nimley said.

Taylor's options rapidly diminished as the war zeroed in on the capital, not only from the north but also from the south, where the Krahn faction, MODEL, had taken Buchanan. The warring parties, meanwhile, continued to treat the peace talks in Accra as a paid vacation, idling the hours away, attempting to negotiate ministerial positions in the government to follow Taylor's departure.

His departure seemed a forgone conclusion in Liberia, but it did not take away any of the sting of his son's abandonment. "All that helped to break the old man," Nimley recalled.

In Port of Spain, Chucky and his mother arrived at the Hilton, a forty-year-old hotel and convention center that sat on a hillside shrouded behind a wall of açaí trees opposite the sprawling Queen's Park Savannah at the center of the city.[8] From there, mother and son watched the end of Charles Taylor's presidency play out as much as the world did: on CNN. In a desultory ceremony at the Executive Mansion, Taylor handed over power to Moses Blah, then boarded a chartered plane to his exile in Calabar, Nigeria. Although his capitulation marked a final humiliation, he had succeeded in something his two predecessors had not: leaving office alive. Before his departure, he feebly told those gathered, "God willing, I will be back."[9]

In Trinidad, mystery immediately surrounded the mother and son staying at the Hilton. Not long after their arrival, rumors began to circulate that they had fled Liberia and were in hiding. Reporters began appearing at the hotel. Chucky knew better than to talk to the press, but his mother agreed to speak with one journalist, offering a stunning and strange interview to a reporter with Trinidad's *Guardian* newspaper.[10] Calling herself Liberia's "special envoy for presidential affairs," Bernice told the paper that she had been married to Taylor and had two children by him, a daughter, Zoe, and a fourteen-year-old son, Charles Taylor Jr. She claimed to be a trained Foreign Service officer. Despite being an American citizen of Trinidadian descent, she told the paper that she "didn't get this job because of Charles Taylor."

She also tried to deflect rumors that she had arrived with laden with diamonds from West Africa. "If I had these diamonds, honey, trust me, I would have a mansion somewhere in Trinidad," the *Guardian* quoted her as saying.

Bernice offered a defense of her son's father, claiming that Taylor had never been given the opportunity to govern. When questioned about his human rights abuses and the allegations of war crimes, she insisted that he was being held responsible for others' actions and that the efforts to bring him to court traced "all the way back to the United States."

The money dried up soon after their arrival, and eventually Bernice returned to Florida, while Chucky, remaining in Trinidad, was forced to move from the Hilton to a studio apartment in Carenage, a hillside ghetto overlooking the Caribbean.[11] He had few connections in the country—an aunt who lived in Glencoe, a neighboring, upscale community, and a cousin who worked as a cop in downtown Port of Spain.[12] When it came time to find work, the best Chucky could muster was a job as an unarmed security guard.

Trinidad, a tiny, relatively insulated island, had very little to offer Chucky. He could not follow his mother home to Orlando because he no longer had a valid U.S. passport. Having been out of the country for nearly a decade, he remained a fugitive in Orange County, Florida. The island quickly became a place stuck between the Liberia of Chucky's past and the United States where he hoped to build his future.

He began plotting his return to the United States. The UN travel ban made it impossible for him to travel under his Liberian passport, but he held out hope that his name could be removed from the sanctions. At one point he contacted the head of the UN mission in Liberia, an ex–U.S. Air Force major general named Jacques Klein, to see what redress he had. Klein, who had been in Monrovia only a short time, had struck up a romantic relationship with Linda Fawaz, who stood as a bridesmaid in Chucky's wedding. In the end, the connection yielded nothing. Klein never returned his calls.

Chucky had little to negotiate with, but he still hoped his connection to his father could avail him something. In October 2004, he dialed the telephone number of the defense attaché at the U.S. embassy in Monrovia.[13] Major Ryan McMullen was new to the post, having arrived earlier that month. He had spent nearly fifteen years in the army, including a two-year stint as the desk officer for sub-Saharan Africa for the Pentagon, where he had covered more than forty-three countries. He had a good idea what had transpired in Liberia before his arrival.

When McMullen picked up his phone, the caller asked for Major Butler, the former attaché.

"This is Chucky Taylor, Jr.," the caller said. The major knew who Chucky was, but he wasn't clear on why the former president's son would be calling. McMullen explained that he was the new attaché and asked what he could do for him.

Chucky launched into a meandering proposal. He explained that he wanted to join the U.S. Marine Corps. His experience in the ATU and the skills he'd acquired as a commander, he reasoned, would be of use to the Marines. Moreover, he said, he was an American citizen. He simply needed a new passport so that he could return to the United States to enlist. He then asked McMullen whether his name remained on the UN travel ban for Liberia.

McMullen wasn't entirely surprised by the call—Chucky had been in touch with the post prior to the major's arrival. But his expectation that the embassy would assist him was strange. The ATU, after all, had antagonized embassy personnel from the outset. Nor did Chucky's reputation comport with the Marines Corps values. McMullen saw the request as a pretense. Chucky was clamoring for a way—any way—back into the United States.

Chucky continued calling for the next several months. The major showed no interest in his offer, but Chucky had few options at that moment. He explained his situation to McMullen: he was running low on money, he needed a change of scenery, and he wanted to travel to Iraq to work as a contractor for the U.S. government. McMullen asked him to put his request in an e-mail.

Two months later McMullen received an e-mail from "Charlie Tango," an online alias Chucky used. The note revisited the request to return to the United States. "Legally I have all the right to go back home if I want to," Chucky wrote. "I will say again I am an American first before anything."

Chucky was correct—nothing was preventing him from applying for a U.S. passport. But he did have reason to be concerned about the blowback from his connections to the Taylor government, so what he sought was to open a channel to the federal government to pave the way for his return home.

Other members of Taylor's inner circle—Gen. John Tarnue and Cindor Reeves—had successfully converted their willingness to talk about Charles Taylor into temporary immigration status in the United States and elsewhere.[14] (While Chucky was aware that both men had disappeared, he unlikely knew the extent of their cooperation.) His knowledge of his father's activities was far more intimate, and in the e-mail he made an offer to speak to the government about what had gone on in Liberia. The remainder of the e-mail remains classified, so it isn't clear what level of cooperation Chucky was offering.

But after reading the contents of the e-mail, Major McMullen printed it out and jotted a note at the top of the paper.

"He wants to talk," it read.

What went wrong? Why am I in this situation?[15] In early 2005 these were the questions that dogged Chucky. He'd been in Trinidad for nearly two years since he'd left Monrovia, but the collapse of his father's regime remained raw in his mind. The memories were reinforced by his isolation. He was marooned on the island, cut off not only from family and friends but also from his identity.

Lynn had visited him once, but by the time she arrived in Trinidad, there was nothing left of their marriage.[16] In June 2005, she filed for divorce, seeking full custody of their son, indicating in court papers that the "Father has no relationship with the minor child of the marriage. . . . It is in the child's best interest that the Husband/Father, who is a fugitive from justice, have no access" to him. [17]

Trinidad remained foreign to him, but he began to make connections to the culture. At first, it was a girlfriend—a schoolteacher who lived in his apartment complex—and, eventually, a child. While living there, he was drawn to some of the island's spiritual practices.[18] He sought out advice from an Obeah woman, the type of sorceress who could cast spells or read his future. According to Lynn, the fact that her son was not relying on her advice drove Bernice to jealous anger.

But island life proved small and claustrophobic. Chucky sought an outlet. If he were stuck on the island, he at least could make something of the experience. Just as he had insinuated himself into Liberia's national preoccupation with politics, he waded into the cultural lifeblood of Trinidad: music.

It began in his tiny apartment. A cousin from Lithonia, Georgia, had sent Chucky CDs of instrumental music she had composed and then layered over with hip-hop beats. He would flip on a track, set it on repeat for thirty or forty minutes, and, as he explained, allow "the track to speak to me instead of me trying to impose my concept or approach on it."

He began filling legal pads with pages and pages of lyrics, gutting the past of images and ideas, giving memories shape and form between drum breaks and oscillating keyboard lines. Months passed. Chucky's cousin continued to send music. He continued to write. Eventually he decided it was time to put it all down in the studio.

Eclipse Audio was a small, four-room recording studio run by three friends on Maraval Road, a tidy, shadeless residential street not far from Saint James, Port of Spain's nightlife strip. The studio's proprietors, Dion Camacho, Phil Hill, and Sean Poland, were musicians in their late thirties making a living tracking everything from radio jingles to local calypso and Soca legends. Hip-hop wasn't Eclipse's particular forte— Dion and Phil played together in a Britpop band—and when Chucky arrived at the studio, his presence immediately raised questions.

"What is an American dude doing in Trinidad recording rap?"[19] Camacho recalled asking his colleagues.

Chucky booked a few forty-dollar-an-hour sessions, several hours at a time, always paying in cash. But he remained vague about himself, explaining only that "he had family" in Trinidad and "was down here chilling for a while."

Chucky would usually arrive at the studio alone, carrying his lyrics and a few bottles of Guinness. For the most part, Dion and Phil remained downstairs working in the office while Sean Poland, the studio's engineer, ran the sessions. Poland, a soft-spoken, heavyset Indo-Trinidadian, sat upstairs at the controls in the mixing room, which looked across a narrow hallway into the isolation booth. Chucky handed him a CD that he wanted to lay vocals over, stepped into the booth, and put his headphones on.

Poland sized Chucky up. He seemed nice, direct, and confident. He always showed up in name-brand shoes and clothes, but didn't necessarily look or carry himself like a rapper—no bling, no entourage. Chucky gave him the instrumental music for a track he called "Brains." Poland was not anticipating what came through the speakers the moment he hit "record." A frenetic, Cypress Hills–esque loop kicked in. Chucky paused a measure, then let loose:

ATU boy, ATU fought in the
Streets, where you at man?
You know
You gonna make me call your names out
Beat your brains out
Bust your fuckin' ass, got you laid out

Poland focused on the levels on the board, not giving the lyrics much thought. The initials ATU—which Chucky called out as "Alpha Tango Uniform"—meant nothing to him. If anything, he figured it was Chucky's clique back in the States. This sort of bravado and bluster went hand in hand with hip-hop. Poland queued up another track, one Chucky called "Beef."[20] It bumped without instrumentation and a stripped-down, midtempo, four-four beat. Chucky rolled into the verse with a clunky, put-on dance-hall patois, then switched back into his American accent, growling through the lyrics:

True beef I make you stitch up your top lip
True beef make me blow off your face bitch
True beef I bring case murder one bitch

Between takes, Poland and Chucky would step out onto a small balcony directly outside of the isolation booth, smoking cigarettes and sipping beers as the low sun washed over the rooftops of the surrounding pastel concrete homes. Chucky didn't project any of the violence he described in his lyrics. The two men made small talk about music—Chucky had a love for Method Man and Biggie Smalls—but Poland never pressed him for any insight into the lyrics. It never occurred to him that Chucky could be rapping from experience.

One day Chucky showed up at the studio and asked Dion and Sean whether they had seen a new movie called *Lord of War*. Neither of the men had. Chucky explained to them, somewhat incensed, that one of the main characters, "Andre Baptiste Junior," was based on him. The character was the son of the bloodthirsty dictator "Andre Baptiste," based, more or less directly, on Charles Taylor. Chucky confided to the men that he was Taylor's son.

It was an unbelievable claim. The men said nothing until Chucky left. But then Poland asked the obvious question: "Why would Charles Taylor's son come to Trinidad to record hip-hop?"

Camacho rented the film and returned to the studio dumbfounded. When he found Poland, he said, "Sean, Chuck talking shit."

He couldn't believe that this guy who had walked in off the streets of Port of Spain into their studio could be who he said he was. "Impossible," he recalled saying.

Chucky stopped by Eclipse Audio one morning in March 2006 and told the men he was preparing for a flight to Miami. He had asked Sean to burn several copies of the CD he had recorded, explaining that he was going to the States to shop his music for a record deal. It was the sort of big talk they had come to expect from him—just like the confession that he was Charles Taylor's American son.

In the studio, Chucky asked Dion and Sean for help choosing his demo's cover. He spread out a set of photographs on the table. The men gathered around to look through them. In the pictures they saw rebels, clad in uniforms, clutching AKs; Chucky with them, drawing troop movements in the sand; Chucky in full camouflage standing with Charles Taylor, dressed in white, clutching his walking stick. The men were dumbstruck, speechless.

"I'll see you guys in a month," Chucky told them as he left. "I'm just going away to chill, get some vibes, come back."

After he walked out, Dion took stock of the year this American had spent cutting tracks at their studio.

"Oh, Jesus Christ," he thought to himself. "This fella tellin' the truth the whole time."

14

ICE

Tru urban soldier man only feast with my clan, bread with my killers, that's the code as it stands.

— United States vs. Belfast, EXHIBIT CE-4

.

For Special Agent Matthew Baechtle, it began with a stack of papers on his desk in Washington, D.C.[1] Grimly titled dispatches from NGOs and human rights groups like Global Witness, Amnesty International, and Human Rights Watch. Newspaper and magazine articles dating back through the last decade. Reports from investigators with the UN Security Council. In the fall of 2003, this was the history of the Liberian civil war: a disjointed maze of names, dates, acronyms, incidents, and allegations. The first step was to make sense of it. Only after doing that could he even think of walking out the door to do the job he'd been trained to do: to investigate crimes, to find suspects, to bring back cases that could be prosecuted. As beginnings go, it was a just that—a beginning—and not much else.

Baechtle was a rookie who had only recently joined Immigration and Customs Enforcement, or ICE, as it was then becoming known. He'd been assigned to the Arms and Strategic Technology Investigations Unit (ASTI), housed in the agency's Washington field office. When he walked into work, he looked like a clean-cut, well-mannered fraternity brother, twenty-three years old with jet-black hair, a place-kicker's build, and a bemused smile. Customs enforcement wasn't the obvious career path for Baechtle. None of his family members were in law enforcement. (Nor were any of his fraternity brothers, for that matter.) He didn't expect to get rich in this line of work, but he'd always had an interest in solving crimes. He split his childhood between Kingston, Jamaica, where his father worked for Colgate-Palmolive, and Monmouth County, in what he fondly called "the greatest state in the union," New Jersey. When it came time to go to college, he already knew the direction he wanted his life to take. He enrolled at the University of Richmond, majoring in criminal justice.

As graduation approached, he considered his next steps. He ventured with a group of friends to a job fair in Washington. Walking through the booths, he came across a recruiter for the U.S. Customs Service. The agent, at six foot seven, stood about a foot taller than Baechtle; in fact, he was an ex-NFL player who'd blown out his knee before joining the service. He delivered his pitch explaining that the customs service was the investigative arm of the Treasury Department, with a mandate that covered everything from confiscating counterfeit goods to drug interdiction. For many criminal justice majors, the FBI was the obvious dream job, but Baechtle saw that customs' crime base was broad and varied—it seemed an ideal opportunity to break into federal law enforcement. He applied on the spot.

Shortly after September 11, the government's investigative agencies had entered a period of uncertainty. The terrorist attacks in New York and Washington represented a systemic failure not only of intelligence but also of law enforcement. As the Bush administration was forced to confront this, the foundations began to shift underneath the sprawling infrastructure of agencies and administrations charged with enforcing American laws. Bureaucracies that had hardened into territorial and self-perpetuating entities now had to reassess how best to protect the United States. President Bush hastily created an Office of Homeland Security, appointing Pennsylvania governor Tom Ridge to head up the effort.[2] Until the summer of 2002, Bush resisted creating a cabinet-level homeland security position, as he sought to balance national security imperatives against the politically unwieldy notion of a massive bureaucratic overhaul. Eventually, the overhaul won out. In November, the Homeland Security Act was passed. When Bush signed the act into law, more than twenty federal agencies and offices were subsumed into the Department of Homeland Security, ballooning into the third-largest government department, with more than 180,000 employees and an annual budget upward of $33 billion.

The changes in Washington had a direct impact on Baechtle's career. When he entered the Customs Basic Enforcement School in the spring of 2003, he joined the final class hired into the service. By the time he graduated, the service simply no longer existed. He would be joining the principal investigative arm of the new Department of Homeland Security, an agency with a sprawling mandate called Immigration and Customs Enforcement.

Baechtle showed up at the Washington field office for his first assignment. It was a grim seven-story box-shaped federal building that had housed the Immigration and Naturalization Service (INS). The drab surroundings contradicted the urgency of his first assignment with ASTI. The unit's priority, especially important following 9/11, was investigating the transfer of weapons of mass destruction or any related sensitive technologies, from fissile material, chemicals, and germs that could be weaponized to materials that would be potentially used to construct centrifuges. At its disposal was a set of extraterritorial laws that allowed ICE to pursue crimes that were committed outside the United States.

Unwittingly, Baechtle had been placed not only on the front lines of the post-9/11 domestic security effort but also at the cusp of American law enforcement. Just as terror threats had to be addressed at their source, criminals falling under the increasingly broad jurisdiction of U.S. laws had to be confronted where they operated. This presented an exciting, if daunting, challenge for junior agents. It certainly beat raiding poultry plants in Iowa to roust illegal aliens. But in terms of the career he was undertaking, it also broadened the crimes that the rookie could pursue. Baechtle had little idea of what sort of cases he'd be working or where they would take him. The answer to that lay in the stack of papers his boss had tossed on his desk.

"Hey, why don't you look at what's here," the supervisor who handed him the stack of papers said, then walked away.[3]

Baechtle started reading through the pile. One common link that ran through the documents: Liberia, a country that was barely familiar to him but would define his career for years to come.

Baechtle's assignment did not simply appear from the ether. After Charles Taylor stepped down, American policy continued to isolate him in his exile in Nigeria. This position was articulated as policy several months later with Executive Order 13348, in which the White House had identified Taylor as an "unusual and extraordinary threat to the foreign policy of the United States" and declared "a national emergency to deal with that threat."[4] The order forbade American citizens or businesses to have dealings with Taylor or his insiders and family members, including Chucky. It was one of 291 such orders Bush issued during his presidency that were promulgated to the departments and agencies responsible for enforcing the provisions.

Meanwhile Agent Baechtle started to absorb information about Liberia.[5] He would eventually refer to this process as "schooling up": he pored through every available document and public source report to develop an expertise. The process was imperative. He knew very little about Liberia, having caught his first glimpses of the country just months earlier in between summer classes at the Federal Law Enforcement Training Center at Glynco, Georgia, where he was finishing his training. That summer fighting in Liberia had, for a moment, shouldered aside images of the war in Iraq on CNN. Reports on the violence were otherworldly—footage of T-shirt-clad fighters haplessly spraying automatic weapons in the middle of the deserted streets of the capital. Baechtle had no reason to believe that his career would have anything to do with it.

In some regards, his assignment—to sort through the shattered pieces of the Liberian crisis to determine whether any American citizens bore any responsibility for the suffering there—was strange. Washington's attitude toward Liberia had long been marked by indifference, inaction, and ineptitude; Liberians, on the other hand, had looked to the United States to solve problems that were uniquely theirs. But the civil war had married the two countries in a manner that a century of relative stability had not. Over the course of the 1990s, thousands of Liberian refugees had fled to New York, Minneapolis, Philadelphia, and Providence under temporary protected status, a designation that recognized their unique need for haven during the crisis.[6] Those who arrived could be counted as fortunate. Hundreds of thousands of others remained behind in sprawling refugee camps in Guinea and Ghana, waiting to be resettled in any Western nation that would take them.

The name "Charles Taylor" loomed large in all the research Baechtle had been provided. Taylor had long thrived in an impunity gap, where neither the laws of his own nation nor those of the international community could touch him. Even after he had been pushed from power, he and his followers were indignant at the accusations levied against him. What was the crime? Where was the evidence? Had he ever been convicted in a court of law?

The answer was simple: Taylor's wars had destroyed nearly all mechanisms of accountability in Liberia. The nation's legal institutions had collapsed during the civil war; the brightest legal minds had fled the country or been forced to the periphery of political life. After the Special Court in Freetown indicted Taylor, it appeared he'd remain comfortably out of reach in his exile. Meanwhile his isolation proved something of a success for U.S. policy makers, the culmination of a two-year campaign by State Department officials to marginalize him.

Yet as Taylor settled into exile in Nigeria, and as Liberia found an uneasy peace, the deposed leader remained a threat to U.S. interests in the region. He enjoyed considerable support in Liberia, particularly among an entire generation of recently disarmed combatants. His ex-wife quietly assumed a place in the country's legislature. As many continued to feel his influence over affairs within the country, it seemed a distinct possibility he would keep his promise to return to Liberia.

What was at stake in Liberia for the United States? Officially, the government would cite "regional security." Taylor's continued freedom was clearly incompatible with this goal. He and his inner circle, however, read darkly into American motives: the United States wanted Liberia's resources—not just its rubber and iron ore, which were known quantities, but its yet-to-be-discovered oil, which they believed lay offshore in the Gulf of Guinea. In either case, the White House's executive order directly targeted Taylor and the threat he posed.

Still, Taylor could never be Baechtle's target. Federal statutes clearly spelled out the rules of engagement for his investigation: he could pursue American citizens regardless of where they had committed a crime, or he could pursue foreign nationals who had entered the United States. A typical ASTI case involved an individual or a company located in the United States that was attempting to sell weapons or technology to another country, whether that meant assault rifles for a Colombian drug organization or nuclear detonators for engineers in nations trying to develop the bomb. Taylor had clearly and repeatedly violated UN sanctions with multiple parties, but ICE had no clear jurisdictional claim in any of these cases; the weapons hadn't passed through the United States, and Taylor was not American.

Other countries had undertaken cases involving timber-, diamond-, and arms-trafficking violations in Liberia. Italy attempted to prosecute Leonid Minin for trading in conflict diamonds and timber following his 2001 arrest near Milan. That prosecution was made possible only by the fact that Minin had entered Italy. Nonetheless, the court found that since none of the contraband transited through Italy, it had no jurisdiction. Minin received a two-year sentence for narcotics offenses and disappeared soon after his release. Meanwhile Dutch officials began targeting one of their own citizens, Gus Kouwenhoven, who had operated a hotel in Monrovia and a timber company in the bush before fleeing Liberia in 2003. Both Greenpeace and Global Witness had linked Kouwenhoven not only to the trade in timber in Liberia, in violation of UN sanctions, but also to providing weapons to Taylor's forces.

There was no corollary target for Baechtle and the United States. While a few American businessmen had tried their hand in Taylor's Liberia, none graduated to the president's inner circle. But in the tangle of material before Baechtle, there were two references that could be easily overlooked. Deep in a report by UN experts, there was a curious mention:

> Leonid Minin also stated that the son of President Taylor, Charles "Chucky" Taylor (Jr.) had tried to become part of some of these arms transactions, in order to collect commissions. Another business partner of Leonid Minin, a Finnish national with companies in Turkey and Switzerland, had dealt with Charles Taylor Jr. and documents found in Minin's possession show that this individual was sending documentation on different types of equipment to Minin.[7]

Then, in a separate report, Chucky and Minin were linked in an ammunition shipment originating in Ukraine. "The final delivery to Liberia was arranged between the military at Abidjan airport, Sanjivan Ruprah, Mohamed Salamé and Charles Taylor Jr. Minin said a special plane was organized from Monrovia to pick up the ammunition," according to a report by UN investigators. The name "Chucky Taylor" was one strand among many to follow. Taylor had nearly a dozen children, and the reporting on Chucky was scant. But Baechtle thought that, if anything, Chucky might be a potential source for information to further his investigation.

His focus remained on arms and trying to determine whether a violation of U.S. law had occurred in any of the weapons transactions that kept the civil war in Liberia going. The UN Panel of Experts and NGOs like Global Witness and Amnesty International had reported extensively on weapons trafficking and sanctions busting in Liberia, but this work had not produced relevant evidence of any crimes.

The concerns of the human rights investigators differed from Baechtle's; NGOs worked primarily to generate publicity and political pressure. Law enforcement agencies, however, needed to focus on specific elements of a crime. Moreover, they were not at liberty to discuss the status of any investigation without authorization. Federal agents like Baechtle thus maintained cordial but not particularly close relationships with independent investigators and researchers, who eagerly submitted reports and facilitated contacts with potential witnesses.[8] In this case, the third-party reporting on Taylor's rise to power filled in the historical record on Liberia, but none of it identified a specific target that he could hope to put in front of a grand jury.

Charles Taylor's rule over Liberia had generated not only a decade of instability but also more loose ends than could be accounted for. As the Taylor government spun out, it jettisoned individuals from its orbit and with them the secrets they held. Taylor's castoffs would often land in the hands of foreign diplomats, NGOs, and intelligence and law enforcement agencies. ICE worked with the Organized Crime and Racketeering Section of the Department of Justice to assemble a roster of contacts who could provide context and background on Liberia and Taylor's government.

Two individuals eventually came to light: Hassan Bility and Brig. Gen. John S. Tarnue.[9] Both men were Liberian exiles who entered the United States in 2003 and 2001, respectively. Hassan Bility had worked as an editor at the Monrovia weekly newspaper *The Analyst* and, according to critics, was a former spokesmen for an anti-Taylor rebel faction.[10] General Tarnue had served as a commander first in the Armed Forces of Liberia, then within Taylor's militia.[11] While both men had spent much of their lives in Liberia at opposite ends of the conflict, they shared the experience of falling out with Taylor.

One strand in particular connected the men: both alleged that the ATU had physically brutalized them, and both had eventually fled Liberia. The men provided investigators with testimony in the case involving Gus Kouwenhoven, the Dutch timber baron, who was later charged in the Netherlands for aiding Taylor's war machine.[12] Kouwenhoven was convicted of arms smuggling in 2006, only to see his case overturned in 2008; in 2010 judges ordered that he be tried again, but the case remains pending. The two men also offered evidence of Taylor's involvement with rebel leaders who were being prosecuted by the Special Court in Freetown, Sierra Leone.

Even though Tarnue was an American-trained military officer, he had served at Taylor's side from the earliest days of the civil war, before coming under suspicion by Taylor.[13] His crime, he says, was that he had cooperated on security measures with officials in the U.S. embassy in Monrovia. His own soldiers eventually arrested him and incarcerated him behind the Executive Mansion. The treatment he received there was similar to what Nathaniel Koah and Kougbay Dunuma had endured: he was beaten and stabbed by ATU fighters. Eventually he was located in a hospital in Ghana by Dr. Alan White, a former Pentagon official acting as the chief investigator for the Special Court, where the Liberian general was receiving medical care. Realizing Tarnue's potential value as a witness, White spirited him out of West Africa to the United States; he was permitted to bring his family with him.

Bility had been arrested many times in the course of his career, but in June 2002 he was detained a final time in Taylor's Liberia.[14] He was confronted by plainclothes security officers as he stepped from his downtown Monrovia office with his four-year-old son to buy popcorn. He was brought to Taylor, who accused the editor of plotting to overthrow his government. Taylor's forces disappeared Bility for nearly six months, detaining him in secret facilities around the country, in filthy conditions with a string of other prisoners. Taylor, always keen to the political moment, referred to Bility and the others using the Bush administration's favored term "enemy combatants."

Among the "enemy combatants" with whom Bility was imprisoned in Liberia was the student activist Varmuyan Dulleh, who had been arrested and tortured by Benjamin Yeaten and Chucky in July 2002.[15] Dulleh had been brought to a hole at Kle Junction, outside Monrovia, where Bility and other men were being held. Arriving with injuries over his body, he recounted, still terrified from the experience, how he'd been tortured and interrogated by Taylor, Yeaten, and Chucky. Bility knew Dulleh from childhood but could do little to help him. The men were eventually separated, after the U.S. embassy publicly pushed for Bility's release while the Taylor government held him. As a journalist, he arrived in the United States to something of a hero's welcome— earning recognition from the Press Union of Liberia and Amnesty International. Tarnue's arrival, as a regime insider, was a more delicate transaction.

Both men had resettled in the United States: Bility outside Boston and Tarnue in Baltimore. After landing in the United States, both were eventually put in touch with Baechtle. Baechtle acknowledges that around this time, while conducting background interviews related to his arms-trafficking investigation, he met with a Liberian who had recently relocated to the United States, though he could not disclose whether this man was Bility or Tarnue. During the course of the interview, Baechtle asked the individual "Why are you in the United States?" The source recounted the ordeal that had forced him to flee Liberia, offering as an aside that he'd been tortured by Taylor's son Chucky. (Bility said he did not provide this initial tip to Baechtle.) On its face this was an unremarkable charge. Allegations of human rights violations were almost the norm in Taylor's Liberia and a recurring theme in refugee claims. The charges were not central to ASTI's focus, and Baechtle filed the accusation away in his memory.

Yet he was working within an agency that had a strong tradition of pursuing human rights violations. In the 1970s the service had been given the authority to pursue former Nazis in the United States. One such case involved Anton Baumann, a carpenter who had lived quietly in Milwaukee for nearly a half century; an INS investigation implicated him as a former SS guard at a concentration camp and resulted in his deportation in 1991. During the 1990s the focus shifted to investigating more recent crimes against humanity. The INS targeted immigrants arriving from the Balkans, Central America, and Africa who might have committed human rights violations, such as Juan Angel Hernández-Lara, a former member of Battalion 3-16, a CIA-trained Honduran military unit accused of killing nearly two hundred leftists.[16] Hernández-Lara settled in West Palm Beach, Florida, before being discovered and pleading guilty to immigration charges that resulted in his deportation.

After the formation of Immigration and Customs Enforcement under the Department of Homeland Security, Assistant Secretary Michael J. Garcia pushed the mission of seeking out human rights violators.[17] In 2003 he created a unit within the Office of Investigation called the Human Rights Violators and Public Safety Unit, as well as a specialized unit of attorneys called the Human Rights Law Division. The unit pursued historical crimes like the Srebrenica massacre in Bosnia in 1995 and the ethnic cleansing of Hutus in Rwanda in 1994, where individuals implicated in the violence had sought haven within the United States.

But Baechtle had come to ICE through U.S. Customs. His training did not explicitly cover how to investigate human rights crimes; nor had he received specific training in how to interview victims of violent crime. As he began to interview individuals who had emerged from Taylor's Liberia, it became clear that many were just that: survivors of trauma perpetrated by criminal security forces. He felt compassion for these people, but he eventually returned to the allegations that Taylor's son had participated in weapons transactions, hoping to find an American connection. This accusation had been introduced in the reporting from the UN Panel of Experts in 2001. Italian prosecutors had also uncovered reams of documents implicating the younger Taylor with Leonid Minin, but as we have seen, their case had evaporated for lack of jurisdiction, and Minin disappeared soon afterward. Chucky Taylor remained a dangling thread in all this.

Baechtle still knew very little about him. Chucky carried a notorious reputation among Liberians, but it was not substantiated by detailed public reporting. Baechtle began to hear about random assaults and acts of violence against women carried out by Chucky and his bodyguards from the Liberians he interviewed, behavior that mapped to the prototypical characteristics of a dictator's son: decadent, violent, and unaccountable. But it was difficult to sort truth from fiction. Even the UN travel ban on Liberia was surprisingly vague on Taylor Jr.; it listed no date of birth or nationality, just that he was an "associate, adviser and son of former Liberian President Charles Taylor with ongoing ties to him."

There was some intelligence on Taylor Jr. developed by other U.S. agencies. The CIA had reported on his presence in Liberia (but has declined to declassify its findings).[18] As early as 1995, diplomats in

Monrovia also noted him. A 1995 cable between the U.S. embassies in Monrovia and Ouagadougou, with the subject line "Taylor's Domestic Affairs," says, "Taylor has a son, Chucky, Junior who is 19-20 years old, we believe by an American citizen now resident in Florida."[19]

Amid confusing accounting of Taylor's wives and children, the reference did not appear entirely out of place. But for Baechtle, there was something crucial in this cable. The fact that Taylor Jr. had been born to an American citizen held the potential to change everything. That wouldn't necessarily give him a target or a crime, but it could yield something his investigation needed to move forward: an American connection to Liberia.

Earlier in that spring of 2005, the name "Charles Taylor Jr." began cropping up in cable traffic between State Department headquarters and embassies in Monrovia, Jakarta, Lomé, Beirut, and Port of Spain.[20] Much of the discussion concerned former officials of Charles Taylor's government sanctioned under the UN travel ban. In tandem, the United States had moved against Taylor insiders, placing them on the Office of Foreign Assets Control (OFAC) list, prohibiting U.S. citizens and companies from transacting with those subject to U.S. sanctions. Unlike most of the Taylor insiders included on the OFAC list, Chucky's personal information was limited. His name appeared misspelled as "Chuckie" with no passport number and, beyond his date of birth, little other identifying information. Yet the OFAC designation strung up Chucky's life and livelihood perhaps more than any of the other insiders, because it isolated him financially from his family in the United States.

Various parts of the federal government began to stitch together some of the pieces of his identity and picked up on Chucky's trail. While he had been in touch with the Monrovia embassy a year earlier, the State Department sought confirmation of his whereabouts. "The Department would appreciate receiving information from Embassy Port of Spain on whether Taylor is, indeed, resident in Trinidad, and, if so, information on his current activities," one cable requested.[21] The embassy in Port of Spain approached Trinidad and Tobago's Ministry of Foreign Affairs, the Counter Drug-Crime Task Force, and the Central Bank's inspector to find further information on him, but reported that "these sources are unable to ascertain the whereabouts or the financial records of Charles Taylor, Jr., who reportedly resides in Trinidad."

Port of Spain reported back a surprising detail to Washington. "Post understands that Charles Taylor, Jr. may be an American citizen by birth," a cable noted, asking for "guidance before proceeding further."[22]

Baechtle had heard rumors about Chucky's nationality from sources he interviewed during the course of his arms-trafficking investigation. He eventually zeroed in on the evidence of Chucky's citizenship that his case needed. It was a copy of a birth certificate from St. Margaret's Hospital in Boston, dated February 2, 1977, for a child named Charles McArther Emmanuel born to Bernice Yolanda Emmanuel.[23] No father was listed on the document, but the certificate provided proof that Charles Taylor's son, Chucky, was an American.

For Baechtle, it was a revelation.[24] "I assumed that he was just a Liberian," he recalled. The birth certificate was an irrefutable piece of evidence. It helped Baechtle begin to confirm the complicated picture of Chucky's identity: that he had changed his name to Roy M. Belfast and that he had lived, for at least part of his life, as a typical American child.

In June 2005 Baechtle flew down to Orlando to meet with Chucky's mother and stepfather. Roy Belfast had been estranged from both Bernice and his stepson for years by the time he sat down with Baechtle. Roy, who lived in a ranch home on a quiet cul-de-sac, provided some detail about Chucky's childhood, filling in the years between Charles Taylor's departure and Bernice and Chucky's reunion with him. But Roy hadn't heard from his stepson in years and knew very little about his experiences in Liberia.

Baechtle also ventured out to Pine Hills. He hadn't given much consideration to the circumstances of Chucky's childhood, but as he drove through the neighborhood, he began to connect this drab, unremarkable suburban landscape with the stunning political trajectory Chucky followed in Liberia. He learned of Chucky's petty criminal past—the assaults and robberies—joining a snapshot of the person he was becoming when he left the United States with who he became after his father's election in Liberia.

It all struck Baechtle as improbable and weird. "It's not necessarily the normal way you see somebody spend five years," he said. "That's an understatement."

Two days later Bernice agreed to meet with Baechtle. He under-
stood that Chucky's mother had spent a considerable amount of time in
Liberia and could illuminate her son's activities there. She consented to
meet him in the presence of her lawyer, a local attorney named Wayne
Golding.[25] As their interview began, according to an affidavit later filed,
Baechtle asked Bernice to clarify the nature of her son's role in Charles
Taylor's government. Bernice had little choice but to respond truthfully. If she lied to Baechtle, she ran the risk of being charged with
a felony. If she told the truth, it was unclear what, if any, jurisdiction
the U.S. government would have over anything that had occurred in
Liberia. (Later, when asked about this interview, she would deny ever
meeting Baechtle.)

In the interview, Bernice repeated a fact that was well known to
those in Liberia: Charles Taylor had directly appointed his son to lead
his personal security force, the ATU. Any number of witnesses could
have established that fact, but for Chucky's mother to corroborate it
was powerful. Baechtle left Orlando with the thing that had eluded him
since he began his investigation: a viable target. He needed to determine whether Chucky had played a role in any of the crimes his father
had been implicated in. The answer wasn't in the stack of documents
on his desk in Washington, and it couldn't be established solely by the
testimony of exiles living in the United States. He would have to go to
the scene of those crimes.

Baechtle landed at Robertsfield several weeks later, setting foot on
West African soil for the first time. Over the course of his investigation,
he had conjured a mental picture of Liberia from his own experiences
growing up in Kingston, Jamaica, and passing through its impoverished
Third World corridors. But Liberia was different. Even after two years
of relative peace, it remained one of the poorest nations on earth, with
a weak interim government propped up by a legion of international
donors and NGOs and secured by a UN peacekeeping force. The airfield was a single, cracked concrete runway, bordered by fields of palms,
a handful of white Soviet-era UN choppers, and a lone single-story
terminal. He climbed down the stairwell to the tarmac, stepping into
the dense humidity.

Driving into Monrovia for the first time, the absence of infrastructure was immediately apparent. Each UN checkpoint he passed through revealed the desperate conditions—the teeming crowds at ELWA Junction at the edge of the capital, the air thick and sweet with decaying vegetation and generator exhaust.

Monrovia, it became apparent, was a small town, both geographically and politically. Baechtle received a briefing from the regional security officer at the U.S. embassy, who sketched the current security situation and dramatis personae. The ATU had officially disbanded, but many of the men remained tied to the leadership—in particular, Momoh Gibba, one of several Taylor enforcers who had survived and remained in Monrovia.[26] (Benjamin Yeaten had fled to Togo, where he was given a role in the presidential security force. He eventually agreed to cooperate with the Special Court, according to the court's chief investigator, but was barred from leaving the country by Togolese officials.) Word of foreigners in Monrovia, particularly those asking questions about members of the Taylor family, traveled fast. But the not-too-distant past remained concealed.

Baechtle was struck by one facet of Liberia: how friendly and open those he met were. Eager to meet an American federal agent, many contacts dove in with the Liberian handshake, the fluid sequence from a traditional clasp to an arm wrestler's palm grip punctuated by a forefinger-to-thumb snap. It was not easily mastered, but once the agent got the movements down, it helped him begin to establish a rapport with the Liberians he met. In conversation, he found that even though he'd introduce himself as "Matt," more often than not he became "Mac." The resilience of the people also resonated with Baechtle. The impact of the war was clearly felt in Monrovia, but he noticed a remarkable strength in those he met—the will to pick up and move on. Baechtle began establishing contacts within local law enforcement, many of whom were former police officials run out by Taylor. Baechtle began to develop a sense for the culture and people, something that would prove critical to his investigation.

On March 16, 2006, the embassy in Port of Spain issued a passport to Chucky in the name "Charles McArther Emmanuel."[27] He had appeared at the Port of Spain embassy with a notarized copy of the same birth certificate from St. Margaret's Hospital that agent Baechtle had obtained and applied for a passport, explaining to a consulate worker that his had been stolen. Chucky filled out an application to renew his passport under his birth name. The form also asked for the name, birth date, and birthplace of his parents. When it came to the identity of his father, Chucky lied, listing his parent as "Steven Daniel Smith," born on June 4, 1952, on the island of St. Vincent.[28]

For years, Chucky had sought a negotiated return to the United States, offering himself to State Department officials in hopes that they could remove him from the UN travel ban. At any time he could have applied for an American passport, although it would alert officials to his presence and his intentions to return. In the end, Chucky took a risk, not because of events unfolding in Trinidad but rather because of developments in Washington, Monrovia, and Abuja, Nigeria, where his father's fate was being decided by officials in the respective governments.

Liberia's newly elected president, Ellen Johnson Sirleaf, had landed in the United States for the first state visit of a Liberian leader since Ronald Reagan hosted Samuel Doe in 1983. Her candidacy and election represented a rare piece of good news from Liberia. She had the pedigree of a Harvard-educated, former World Bank economist, which immediately set her apart from her predecessors. But more than that, she carried little outward baggage from the civil war. Even though she had been an early supporter of Taylor, she was considered her own person.[29] The United States hoped to persuade her to solve the most pressing problem they saw in Liberia: Charles Taylor.

Even before Sirleaf arrived in the United States, Washington made clear the terms of U.S. support for her government—principally that Taylor had to be brought to justice. In order for that to happen, she would have to formally request that Nigeria renege on the terms of Taylor's exile. This was potentially explosive for Sirleaf. Taylor's influence still reached into the fledgling postwar government, where his ex-wife, Jewel Howard Taylor, was a legislator and his former son-in-law, Edwin Snowe, served as the speaker of the House.[30] Thousands of former fighters, most unemployed, remained in the capital, easily organized and incited by their former commanders. Sirleaf was forced to calculate the risk of aggravating Taylor's base against the loss of up to $50 million in supplemental funds that Congress was considering.

On the day Chucky arrived at the embassy, Sirleaf addressed a joint session of Congress.[31] She thanked the members for the $445 million the

United States had given to Liberia in the prior two years. Liberia would need more U.S. aid, she knew, and she was willing to make concessions.

The clock then began ticking for Charles Taylor. With arrest imminent, the former president plotted an escape from his exile in Nigeria. Like Chucky, he faced restrictions on flying internationally with a Liberian passport; he felt his best chance was to flee Nigeria on the ground. Meanwhile in Trinidad, Chucky was plotting his next move. He decided this was the moment, regardless of the risks he faced returning.

On March 29 one of Chucky's aliases popped up on a Department of Homeland Security list of individuals scheduled to fly into the United States.[32] ICE immediately phoned the regional security officer at the U.S. embassy in Port of Spain to confirm that a passport had been issued. According to his itinerary, Chucky planned to arrive in Miami on an American Airlines flight from Trinidad the following evening. Exile, for Chucky, was finally coming to an end.

Chucky's imminent arrival forced Baechtle to react. Despite the abundance of allegations in the press, in nongovernmental organization reports, and in the rumors that had become part of Liberian lore, he wasn't prepared to charge Chucky with a crime more significant than an immigration violation. In front of him was potentially the only opportunity he would have to interrogate Chucky and develop evidence for another charge. But it was possible that Chucky could land in Miami and drive up Florida highway 91 all the way home to Pine Hills unimpeded and then disappear.

Baechtle needed to find another clear violation of U.S. law. While Chucky had left twelve years earlier with four felony charges, the statute of limitations for those had long expired. Any new charge would have to have occurred outside the country. Turning over the question with another agent of whether there was a crime that would potentially interest a prosecutor, Baechtle recalled one witness—a Liberian—he'd met with a year earlier. The man was one of many refugees from Taylor's Liberia who had found sanctuary in the United States. Baechtle's meeting with him had been almost coincidental—they weren't discussing his investigation into weapons trafficking.

"There was this one guy who said he was tortured by Chucky," he recalled to his colleague.[33] It was an interesting allegation, but was it a crime? The alleged act had occurred in Liberia, not in the United States. It seemed a somewhat strange question, but the agents wondered aloud whether American citizens could be charged for committing torture outside the United States.

Baechtle retrieved a copy of Title 18 of the U.S. Code, a car battery of a volume, detailing crimes and criminal procedure covered under U.S. law. He rifled through the pages, searching for a reference to "torture." Deep in the text, between chapters on terrorism and another on trafficking in contraband cigarettes and smokeless tobacco, he found chapter 113C, section 2340, on torture. The entry was brief—just under four hundred words—and Baechtle began reading:

> "torture" means an act committed by a person acting under the color of law specifically intended to inflict severe physical or mental pain or suffering (other than pain or suffering incidental to lawful sanctions) upon another person within his custody or physical control;[34]

To Baechtle's mind, the statute applied directly to what the witness had suffered. The crime carried severe penalties: a twenty-year sentence for each count or, in instances where death resulted, the potential for life imprisonment or the death penalty. But the most significant language in the statute described the jurisdiction:

> (1) the alleged offender is a national of the United States; or
> (2) the alleged offender is present in the United States, irrespective of the nationality of the victim or alleged offender.

In that bland phrasing, the statute provided for "extraterritorial jurisdiction," meaning it gave Baechtle the authority to pursue any crime of torture that Chucky might have committed in Liberia.

Suddenly countless avenues opened for an investigation, but prosecuting torture was complicated. It had simply never happened. Congress had enacted the law in 1994, yet the government had never brought a case under the statute.[35] Its origins lay in the UN Convention Against Torture, a treaty that the United States had signed on to in 1984. The treaty had obligated the federal government, among other things, to create and enforce an antitorture law. After Congress passed the law in 1994, it became a little-known but significant component of human rights law. The statute's obscurity changed soon after September 11, 2001.

As the FBI and CIA responded to the attacks, the Justice Department confronted the implications of this law on the War on Terror. Alberto Gonzales, then working as White House counsel, oversaw the team of lawyers laboring away toward an official opinion on the legal definition of *torture*.[36] In reviewing the federal antitorture statute, Justice Department lawyers found that "acts must be of an extreme nature to rise to the level of torture . . . certain acts may be cruel, inhuman, or degrading, but still not produce pain and suffering of the requisite intensity." Their work would provide a foundation for the "enhanced interrogation techniques" that the CIA would employ in its secret prison program.

In the years that followed, specific allegations against CIA officers and defense department contractors—civilians who could be prosecuted under this law—would surface related to charges of abuse and wrongful deaths at Guantánamo Bay, Abu Ghraib, and Bagram Air Base in Afghanistan. In some cases these allegations were supported by photographic evidence, investigations by human rights groups and the U.S. Army, testimony from victims, and, in the case of Abu Ghraib, American military personnel who were also accused of abuse. None of these allegations resulted in an indictment under this law.

There was no legal distinction between Chucky Taylor and the CIA officials accused of committing torture: all were American citizens who, if charged with a crime, were entitled to a trial before a jury. The precedents that could be set by a trial were as much political and moral as legal. A line of argument rationalized the CIA's techniques as justified in the face of an imminent terror threat directed at the United States; Chucky could similarly argue that the insurgency cohering against his father had posed an existential threat to the Liberian government and people, and, despite his methods, the moral difference was in the eye of the beholder. The most relevant distinction between Chucky and the CIA officials was political: the agency had allies in Congress, but the son of an African dictator stood alone.

Special Agent Baechtle knew that he would need support from the Justice Department—he'd be asking its attorneys to do something that they had never done before.[37] Over the past two years, he'd developed a relationship with one attorney in the Criminal Division of the Justice Department. A federal prosecutor would have to sign off on any case that Baechtle brought, so he needed an indication that he wasn't chasing a charge that was—either politically or legally—impossible to pursue. He reached out to the attorney to see whether he could stop by his office a few blocks away, at Justice Department headquarters. The prosecutor had the day off but instructed Baechtle to stop by his home. Baechtle lugged the code over to the Xerox machine and copied the statute. With the law in hand, he climbed into his government-issued vehicle, which agents referred to as their "G-ride."

Baechtle was not the only ICE employee grappling with this unique law. Mona Ragheb, ICE's chief of the human rights law division, had come up against the issue of torture many times, covering allegations out of Latin America, the Balkans, and even Liberia.[38] But when she received a call from Baechtle's supervisor advising her that they were considering a potential charge using this law, she didn't jump out of her seat. "Hold on—it's not that easy," she thought.

One experience stood out in her memory as a lesson on the impractical nature of bringing human rights cases. ICE investigators had unearthed information that implicated a Bosnian Serb living in Boston in acts of torture committed in the Balkans. The U.S. attorney's office in Boston strongly supported that charge, but in order to move toward an indictment, the prosecutors needed approval from the Justice Department. The Boston assistant U.S. attorneys prepared a memo detailing their case for the Criminal Division—the attorneys in D.C. who would review the questions of law raised by the potential charge. The prosecutors even flew down to Washington to present their evidence to the division. Ragheb's office felt that this was a strong case—sufficiently strong to justify the use of the statute for the first time.

But Justice disagreed. Its finding wasn't based on the quality of the evidence; it was political. The preferred method for dealing with human rights violators living in the United States was not to put them on trial but to find an administrative charge—such as lying about their involvement in human rights abuses—with which to commence a deportation proceeding. The decision came down to a matter of policy, not law. When prosecuting "an individual that's not a native-born U.S. citizen, then you run into the realm of exerting universal jurisdiction," Ragheb said of the case. "That's something that, from a policy standpoint, the government may not want to pursue."

Underlying the statute was the controversial legal principle of "universal jurisdiction." Based on the notion that some crimes are so abhorrent to international interests that all states are obligated to prosecute them regardless of borders, nationality, or relation to the crimes, universal jurisdiction wasn't an entirely new idea. It had been the underpinning for prosecutions of pirates in the nineteenth century, the trials at Nuremberg, and, in recent history, Spain's warrant that led to the arrest of former Chilean dictator Augusto Pinochet in 1998.[39] Nonetheless, it remained largely untested in the United States. Former secretary of state Henry Kissinger, in an essay in *Foreign Policy* in 2001, warned that it would "risk substituting the tyranny of judges for that of governments; historically, the dictatorship of the virtuous has often led to inquisitions and even witch-hunts."[40] The U.S. government had not pressed any universal jurisdiction cases, wary of opening American officials to potential prosecution.

Ragheb reviewed the initial evidence. The allegations typified the scenarios envisioned by the Convention Against Torture. But the identity of the alleged criminal distinguished this case from others. "This guy was a native-born U.S. citizen," she said. "So all the arguments about universal jurisdiction that had been a concern in people's minds were thrown out."

Baechtle pulled up to the house of the Criminal Division attorney.[41] He explained the sequence of events unfolding, the details he'd turned up within his investigation, and his belief that he could build a case against Chucky. The attorney read through the material Baechtle provided and saw how the pieces fit together. Baechtle couldn't expect the Justice Department to indict Chucky at that moment, but he hoped to get some indication that he was headed down the right road.

"Yeah," the attorney told Baechtle. "This looks about right."

For the team preparing for Chucky's arrival back at ICE headquarters, the case looked more than right.

"It was the perfect case," Ragheb said.

15

Flight

Possibility of feds rushin on me, it's vice versa my nigga, when they questioning me, cause we coming.

— *United States vs. Belfast,* EXHIBIT CE-9

Two suitcases and one carry-on bag.[1] For all his hopes, plans, and schemes, for all his father's conquests and ambitions, for all the suffering, humiliation, and pain he'd caused, he was returning home just as empty-handed as he'd left more than a decade earlier—all his belongings stashed in what could easily be loaded into the trunk of a car.

It was approaching seven p.m. on March 30, 2006. Shortly before sunset, as the 767 dropped below the clouds, Chucky sat among the passengers waiting to land. At that time of day, the black waves of the Atlantic boiled down into the shoreline in long white ripples. As the cabin lights dimmed and a noisy hush set in, Miami's skyline came into view.

Chucky hoped to step off of that flight, into this crowd, retrieve his bags, and climb into an old friend's car for the three-and-half-hour drive north to Orlando. He hoped to disappear from his actions in the past and from the person who had committed them. These hopes weren't unreasonable. Few Americans knew where Liberia was or what had transpired there during the civil war. Even fewer understood the legacy of suffering that Charles Taylor had left on the region. Only a handful knew that Taylor's American son bore some role in it. Special Agent Baechtle and his colleagues were among them.

Chucky, meanwhile, almost hadn't made it out of Trinidad. Even after obtaining the passport, he faced a more immediate challenge to return to the United States: he had no money for airfare.[2] He turned to his few remaining friends in Liberia, according to a former commander, asking for $1,500. It wasn't the first time he had reached out for help; he seemed perennially broke, having squandered the opportunity to make money while his father was in power. "He was too much involved in this killing and fighting and fighting. He never put in the time to make some money for himself," commander Sam Nimley said. Eventually a Lebanese friend fronted the cash for Chucky, no questions asked. "We didn't know he was going to use it for a ticket," Nimley said.

Before departing, Chucky had a final piece of unresolved business to attend to. It's not clear what contact, if any, he had maintained with his father while in Trinidad, but on March 25, as he prepared to leave, he called him in Calabar, Nigeria. Without the protection of Nigeria, it was only a matter of time before UN authorities tracked Charles Taylor down. Taylor warned his son against returning to the United States, his attorney later said, though it's unlikely the former president had any inkling of the efforts coalescing to detain his son.[3] Chucky reminded his father that, regardless of what happened, he had children to take care of. It was strange counsel coming from his son who had neglected his own children. The irony was that it wasn't his father's abandonment that had destroyed Chucky's life but their reconciliation.

"You've lived your life," Chucky told his father. "Have you provided for all these other people?"[4]

The morning of Chucky's arrival *The Washington Post* ran a story buried on the sixteenth page with the headline "Liberia's Taylor Found and Arrested":

An immigration official in Gamboru, in northeastern Nigeria, spotted Taylor in a jeep with diplomatic tags that was attempting to cross into Cameroon about 7:30 a.m., according to Nigerian authorities. Under orders from President Obasanjo, who for years had resisted pressure to deliver Taylor to the Special Court for Sierra Leone, Taylor was taken into custody and, in the confines of a sleek green-and-white government jet, flown to Monrovia.[5]

With his attempt to escape Nigeria scuttled, Charles Taylor appeared hours later at Robertsfield, draped in a flak jacket, being led down a stairwell from an airliner by an armed guard, his hands cuffed in front of him. Gone was the cool, magisterial expression, with eyes hidden behind Ray-Ban aviators; it was replaced by a look of numb shock. He was returning to Liberia, as he had promised, but with his hands bound, being marched across the tarmac to a UN helicopter waiting to carry him to Freetown. He would be the first African head of state in history to face trial before an international criminal tribunal.

That morning Special Agent Baechtle put on a pressed suit.[6] He typically wore blue jeans and a collared shirt, but he had dressed up for no particular reason. Nearly as soon as he arrived in the office, he turned around and raced to Reagan International to catch a flight to Miami. He had hurriedly assembled his team to leave Washington to meet the flight. One of his ICE colleagues would follow him to deliver the warrant to Miami. Baechtle put a call into the Customs and Border Protection supervisor at Miami International Airport, asking him to meet in the international terminal. As Chucky's flight taxied to the gate, Baechtle stood at the end of the jetway in the airport's Concourse D.

As crowds of vacationers and business travelers streamed past, adrenaline coursed through the agent. All the work of the last two years had coalesced in the prior thirty-six hours. The moment came to seem all but inevitable.

Yet aspects of it didn't make sense. For one, why would Chucky risk coming home when he knew federal agents were investigating him? The United States had successfully pressured Liberia and Nigeria to remove their protections of his father, but it was unlikely to make the same efforts with Trinidad. As long as he remained there, he was relatively safe from prosecution; but once he set foot on U.S. soil, everything would change. For the first time in nearly fifteen years, he would face the full force of American law. Baechtle could only wonder "Why?"

He had spent the prior day on the phone with the regional security officer at the Port of Spain embassy trying to determine whether Chucky had applied for an American passport. That information was privileged; in order for the embassy to pass the lead on to ICE, the

Diplomatic Security Service had to open a case on Chucky, which it did almost immediately.

At the gate, Baechtle watched American Airlines flight 1668 taxi to the jetway.[7] Jacques Smith, an antiterrorism officer with Customs and Border Protection, stood a few steps ahead of him. He would be the one to initially detain Chucky. Baechtle made it clear that he did not want Chucky to be handcuffed.

A banal quote had been on Baechtle's mind—"Failure to prepare is preparing to fail."[8] It wasn't something he'd picked up in college or in ICE training, for that matter. This shred of wisdom had hung on the kitchen wall of the Elberon Bathing Club, where he'd worked summers on the Jersey shore flipping burgers and waiting tables. It had stuck with him over the years. Going into Miami, he'd worked through a mental checklist of what he wanted to accomplish, what needed to happen. He'd thought through contingencies and how he'd react to them, preparing for what could be his only shot at speaking to his target one on one.

Aboard the plane, an announcement alerted the cabin that customs would be checking passports at the gate. Passengers around Chucky readied their documents. The passport he held was virtually untouched. As he filed out of the aircraft with the other passengers into a carpeted hallway, enclosed by panes of glass on each side, Smith, down the hallway, scanned the crowd.[9]

Smith let a stream of passengers pass, then stopped a man clutching a single carry-on bag. Baechtle, watching from a remove, caught a glimpse of the man's face—he looked like a younger version of Charles Taylor.

There are some people here who'd like to speak with you, Inspector Smith told Chucky, pointing to Baechtle, standing farther down the jetway. The customs officer led him over, holding on to the passport. Another agent took Chucky's carry-on bag. As they approached, Baechtle presented his badge.

Would you mind speaking with me? Baechtle asked him, indicating that they could sit privately in an office.

Chucky agreed. He wasn't compelled to talk with anyone; at any moment, he could have requested his lawyer and waited out his arrival in silence. For some reason, he did not. As the men walked, they made small talk—chatting about Carnival, which had just passed, and the weather.[10] The men stopped at a window marked "Special Services." Smith handed over Chucky's passport to be stamped. After nearly twelve years, he had entered the United States.

The agents led Chucky into a windowless office in the lower level of the terminal. In one corner sat a humming photocopier, at the opposite end a doorway. Special Agent Christopher Malone unlocked a door and led him into a smaller room with two desks and four chairs. Baechtle introduced himself again and explained that he was the agent who had planned on meeting him in Trinidad in 2005.

Normally customs would cuff you, Baechtle said. But I asked them to waive the policy since in the past you've indicated that you'd like to speak.

Chucky acknowledged the agent's gesture.

At the outset, Baechtle wanted to establish a rapport with him as he would any suspect or witness he was interviewing.

I have to advise you that you are the subject of a federal arrest warrant, Baechtle said. It's necessary that I advise you of your rights.

What's the warrant for? Chucky asked.

Baechtle referred to the penal code, 18 U.S.C. 1542, making it a crime to make a "false statement in the application and use of passport."

"You have the right to remain silent, anything you say can . . ." Baechtle began. Chucky recited along with him, as any child raised on American television could.

Do you understand these rights? Baechtle asked.

I do, Chucky said, asking how long it would take.

Outside the interrogation room, Inspector Jacques Smith pulled surgical gloves over his hands and opened up Chucky's bag.[11] He removed the notebooks one by one and laid them across a table. He opened one notebook. Page upon page was filled with neat, almost feminine handwriting. A sample of the lines read:

> Just know when we step out killers upon the street, so more out any time of the night, boy watch out. ATU pan da scene. So cool out. ATU niggas on the scene. Body bag is all you see. So tell me what's it going to be.[12]

Farther down the page, it was signed "Charles Taylor II." He pulled out a book from Chucky's bag—*Guerrilla Strategies*—a survey of insurrections around the world written by French theorist Gérard Chaliand.[13] The cover displayed Goya's *And There's Nothing to Be Done*, an etching depicting a blindfolded prisoner bound to a pole awaiting execution, the corpse of a comrade at his feet. Inscribed on the inside cover was "Return to G 2 section after reading instruction by GOC" signed "Brigadier Charles McArthur Taylor, II."

Inside the interrogation room, Baechtle began questioning Chucky.[14]

You were born Charles McArthur Emmanuel on February 2, 1977, at St. Margaret's Hospital in Boston, Massachusetts, he said.

Chucky nodded. Baechtle continued through other vital information: his Social Security number, other names he was known by as a student.

Your mother's name is Bernice Yolanda Emmanuel? Baechtle asked.

Correct, he said.

You indicated on the passport application you filled out in Trinidad that your father's name is Steven Daniel Smith. Is that correct? Baechtle asked.

I think it's one of the names my pops used, Chucky responded.

Did he go by any other names? Baechtle asked.

Charles McArthur Taylor, he replied.

The former president of Liberia? Baechtle asked.

Chucky congratulated the agent. "You're making a jump."

Chucky had done what little he could to conceal his connection to his father. But the measure he took, providing the false name "Steven Daniel Smith," instead provided ICE with a valuable break: this seemingly minor obfuscation was a felony under federal law. Baechtle now had a charge to detain Chucky on: passport fraud. The crime carried a maximum sentence of twenty years in prison, though it was unlikely he would receive that much time. Chucky could be arraigned on that charge and, given his history fleeing criminal charges, held as a flight risk until trial. This sort of administrative charge had been used in recent years on a variety of cases against drug traffickers, fugitive murderers, and outlaw radicals, like a former member of the Symbionese Liberation Army. For Baechtle and his colleagues at ICE, it provided a good starting point—but they were after much more.

As the evening dragged on, Chucky spoke with a sort of detached confidence. When the two men sat down, Baechtle had planned to work chronologically, covering the timeline of his suspect's life, then circling back to events he wanted more details on. Chucky wasn't self-conscious or evasive about the milestones of his past: his reunion with his father in 1992, his return to West Africa two years later, the fighting of April 6, his father's election. Baechtle knew this story line, but as soon as he began asking about Charles Taylor's security apparatus, Chucky distanced himself.

Were you a member of the Executive Mansion Special Security Unit? the agent asked.

No, Chucky replied.

Were you the head of any unit? Baechtle asked.

No, he responded, but I was privy to their activities.

Do you know what the initials ATU stand for? Baechtle asked him.

Anti-Terrorist Unit, Chucky said.

Did you command the ATU? Baechtle asked.

No, Chucky responded. I had an advisory role.

It quickly became clear that this federal agent had more than superficial knowledge of the ATU—his questions suggested knowledge of information that couldn't easily be gleaned on the Internet or from reports published by Amnesty International or Human Rights Watch. The information suggested that Baechtle had had direct contact with individuals familiar with the unit. His questions had started broadly, but as the interrogation continued, he winnowed down to particulars. *Who constructed Gbatala base? Did you have ATU bodyguards? Who commanded those bodyguards?*

Chucky initially equivocated about his involvement. But Baechtle's questions quickly cut through his efforts to obscure the past. Eventually Chucky admitted that the ATU was his "pet project." Yes, he had helped build the base, and, yes, he had provided support.

Baechtle circled in on two incidents that had received wide press coverage in Liberia: the death of the little girl who had been run over by Chucky's truck and the murder of Isaac Gono.

These were unfortunate incidents, Chucky said, but the deaths were accidental. The responsibility for both fell on his driver and his bodyguards, not on him. His bodyguards could be overzealous at times, he said.

Baechtle switched tacks and focused on Chucky's role with the "pet project."

You had the ability to order people to be arrested and detained, he said. You took command functions such as arranging for food and clothes and fuel to be brought to this base. You helped build this base, and you say you were not a commander?

No, Chucky maintained.

The thrust of Baechtle's questions became apparent: had Chucky been involved in human rights abuses in Liberia? Chucky readily denied that he had ever served on the front lines during the fighting, had ever beaten or shot anyone or witnessed the death of any person. Nor, he said, had he tortured or ordered the torture of anyone.

What's the worst behavior you saw by the ATU? Baechtle asked.

I saw someone slapped with an open hand, he replied.

Going into the interview, Baechtle had sensed that Chucky would talk, but after several hours, the man had yet to refuse to answer a single question. Instead, he chose to directly deny allegations and talk around certain issues—the command history of the ATU, for example. Then Baechtle would follow up with a detailed question, making it clear that ICE already had independent knowledge of the subject.

Eventually, after Baechtle pressed him on human rights abuses, Chucky offered something up. Now I know what you must be referring to, he said. That incident with that "press guy."

Chucky recounted a situation where he had been present for something violent: a prisoner had been beaten and burned with an iron. *I did not take part in any beating or torture*, Chucky insisted.

Special Agent Malone stepped into the room and took over, giving Baechtle a chance to sit back and observe for a moment. Malone took a sharper tone with Chucky, reeling off allegations against the ATU— that the unit had raped women, stolen cars, tortured and killed people.

He asked whether Chucky had ever seen anyone killed.

He denied that he had.

Have you ever been taught about the Geneva Conventions?

Chucky responded that he had.

Did you learn about what torture was during that training?

Chucky acknowledged he had.

The agents explained to Chucky that they had already spoken to one man who claimed that he'd been tortured by him, as well as corroborating witnesses. ICE would continue identifying witnesses, they explained, as well as more victims who had been tortured by him.

Chucky had been back in the United States less than three hours, but his decade in exile in Liberia was collapsing in on him.

"I didn't do any of that," Chucky countered. His enemies were after him, he said. "I'm being framed."

16

18 U.S.C. § 2340

From da days we was kids been restin bids, thru hands nuff times over firvaless shit.

— *United States vs. Belfast*, EXHIBIT CE-4

News of Chucky's arrest broke immediately, but only as a footnote to the larger story of the capture of Charles Taylor. *The Miami Herald* and wire services picked up on the fact that within twenty-four hours of Taylor's arrest in Nigeria, his son had been detained in Miami. The Homeland Security chain of command also took notice—while ICE was developing a record for tracking down human rights violators in the United States, Chucky's status as the son of a former head of state put him in a separate category from the individuals they had arrested to date.

Baechtle's ICE team had developed a strong case on the passport fraud charge, but they didn't have much else against Chucky. From nearly the moment he was arrested, demands to bring him to justice for human rights violations grew. Human Rights Watch and other organizations pressed Homeland Security to charge Chucky with crimes committed in Liberia. Almost overnight the case developed from a body of potential evidence that Baechtle and his colleagues had been quietly exploring out of public view into an investigation with international implications. Soon after the arrest, the decision was made to loop in the FBI.

The Department of Justice paired Baechtle with Special Agent Gregory Naples, an ex–Army Ranger and West Point graduate assigned to the extraterritorial counterterrorism squad in the Washington, D.C., field office.[1] While competition between federal law enforcement agencies could be expected, Baechtle knew that the complex and logistically challenging task of tracking down further evidence would require the FBI's support and expertise.

Chucky remained locked up in the Metropolitan Detention Center in Miami awaiting trial on the passport fraud charges. It was unlikely the present charges would result in significant jail time; any sentence he received would be reduced by his time in pretrial detention. But he learned soon after his incarceration that Baechtle and the federal investigators were continuing to probe his activities in Liberia.

Chucky had few resources to contest any charges. He had claimed indigence upon his arrest and, to defend his passport fraud case, had been assigned an experienced attorney out of Miami's federal public defender's office, Miguel Caridad.[2] Yet even with Caridad representing him, Chucky had reason to wish to avoid a trial.

He eventually agreed to attend a proffer session with the prosecutors and agents in Miami, a meeting typically used to negotiate immunity from prosecution in exchange for information. In drug and organized crime cases, prosecutors often leaned on defendants to implicate others higher up the rung in order to avoid jail time; for that reason the vast majority of criminal cases terminate in a plea—avoiding prosecutors the costly and time-consuming process of a trial and securing reduced sentences for the guilty defendants.[3] Negotiating a proffer, also called a "Queen for a Day" agreement, presented an inherent risk to both parties. On the one hand, a suspect could leverage his knowledge of crimes to avert prosecution, but on the other, anything the suspect disclosed during the session could be used as a potential lead for investigators. If the prosecutors caught any inkling that a suspect was lying or omitting information, any deal would be taken off the table. Chucky's proffer was unique—he didn't belong to a traditional criminal enterprise, and any crimes in which he could implicate anyone would likely be of little interest. He thought the session signaled that the government's real interest in him was to elicit intelligence on his father rather than pursue a conviction.[4] But his case involved crimes of impunity where the process of a trial served justice better than a plea would.

For the agents and prosecutors recently assigned to the case, the session provided the first opportunity to meet with Chucky outside a courtroom. The U.S. attorney for Florida's Southern District had assigned two of his most accomplished prosecutors, Caroline Heck Miller and Karen Rochlin.[5] Miller ranked among the most experienced federal prosecutors in Miami. At fifty-eight, she had been with the office since 1980.[6] A tiny figure with a diminutive presence, she could have passed for an elementary school principal. But she'd litigated some of the U.S. attorney's office highest-profile cases in Miami, including the criminal prosecution surrounding the 1996 ValuJet crash that killed 110 people in the Everglades and the trial of the Cuban Five, intelligence agents for Castro's government living in Miami. The men had been implicated in spying and conspiring to commit murder after Cuban MIGs shot down two planes from the activist group Brothers to the Rescue.

Rochlin, forty-six years old, had seventeen years' experience in Florida as an assistant U.S. attorney.[7] Seeking out trial experience, she made the improbable leap from a Beltway corporate law firm to the U.S. attorney's office in Miami. Among the first cases she pitched in on was the Manuel Noriega prosecution. Over the next decade, she worked her way through major crimes, organized crime, public corruption, and eventually to the narcotics division of the office—a job that carried her to every continent except Australia and Antarctica. Along the way she developed a reputation as a formidable and effective prosecutor with the nickname "The Rock."

The attorneys and agents sat down in the stark conference room at Miami's federal courthouse for the session. Chucky walked into the room wearing a dun khaki federal detention center–issued uniform and took his seat. While Baechtle had spent time with Chucky during the initial interview, Naples had no firsthand experience with their suspect.[8] As Chucky began addressing the room, the FBI agent noticed something odd: Chucky spoke with confidence and didn't seem to recognize that those gathered in the room could incarcerate him for the rest of his life.

Naples thought, This is going to be a very interesting interview.

Chucky informed those gathered that he believed everyone assembled had been appointed directly by President Bush. He unpacked this idea, according to Naples, drifting into a quasi-legal argument, all the while trying to evince an educated air to the audience of attorneys and federal agents. He dropped phrases and terms that didn't fit with his intended meaning. It quickly became clear that he had no idea how to correctly assemble thoughts into words and was not at all self-conscious of this fact. In very real terms, he was out of his element. In Liberia, where the literacy rate hovered at 20 percent, he could pass for educated, parroting the language and ideas of his father. Those who did see through him wouldn't dare speak up. But here the charade did not hold up well.

"It was awkward," the agent said.

During a break in the session, Chucky ventured small talk with Agent Naples. In a preliminary hearing, he had learned about Naples's background. He told Naples he "wanted his [own] son to go to West Point."

By Chucky's account, he declined to cooperate with the government in exchange for a ten-year sentence; the U.S. attorney's office would not comment on any potential plea.[9] "There is intense anger based on my declines [*sic*]," he wrote in a letter from federal detention, with the same incomprehensibility, shortly after the session. "Now the question arises, am I a big fish in Liberia, and among panafricanists [*sic*] in the region, my response is I'm a mere tadpole in a vast ocean, filed [*sic*] w/ sharks, scavengers, and whales, pounded by hurricanes."

But the two sides failed to come to an agreement. Prosecutors typically cut a deal to either avoid the resource drain of a criminal trial or to trade up for information on other crimes. In this case, the government had every incentive to stage a public trial and little interest in eliciting information from Chucky on his father or the regime.

Meanwhile Chucky still had to confront the passport violation: either plead guilty or go to trial. Since he had implicated himself in the interview with Baechtle, a trial threatened to draw out the inevitable— a conviction and sentence. A guilty plea, on the other hand, could put a positive end to the proceedings. Figuring in his time served, Chucky could realistically expect to be released in months rather than years. The agents focused on the new investigation understood that the charges could put him behind bars for the rest of his life.

Early in December 2006, nearly eight months after Chucky's arrest, Agents Baechtle and Naples walked into a Starbucks in Chicago.[10] They had traveled there to meet a Liberian whom they had learned about some months earlier, Varmuyan Dulleh. While this was not the first time agents had met Dulleh, the success of their case hinged on the outcome of that day's meeting with him. A Department of Justice trial attorney accompanied the agents, while Dulleh had with him an attorney from one of Chicago's top law firms, Mayer Brown. The attorney, Lori Lightfoot, had taken on Dulleh pro bono, not as a target of investigation but as a potentially crucial witness in the government's case against Chucky.[11]

Agent Naples laid out a spread of mug shots for Dulleh to consider. The agents hoped he could locate an image of one of the men responsible for his exile.

Nearly four years had passed since he'd been forced to flee Liberia.[12] After his arrest in the summer of 2002, he'd been held for another year, shuttled from primitive prisons throughout Liberia. The following summer, as the regime collapsed and the Taylor era came to an end, he fled in fear for his life. The thirty-three-year-old Mandingo man had landed at O'Hare International Airport with his wife and son in 2005, the end of a long, tortuous journey from Monrovia via Guinea. He had been resettled in the United States as a refugee—one of nearly twenty thousand arriving from Africa that year. While thousands of other Liberians had been selected to resettle based on a lottery, Dulleh had been granted asylum as a victim of political violence. He spelled out the ordeal he had lived through to the Red Cross and UNHCR and, after receiving approval from the State Department, was paired with a charity in Chicago and sent to start his new life. He was given a small apartment and his son was enrolled in school, but Dulleh's health had been compromised by his experience.

A month after his arrival Dulleh traveled to Heartland Health Outreach, a nonprofit that provided health care to refugees and the homeless. A nurse entered the examination room and handed him a robe to change into. When she began taking his history, she noticed that he was anxious, responding to her questions in a dull monotone. When she looked at him, he averted his gaze. He removed his shirt. A large scar ran across his right arm. A series of smaller scars and abrasions spread across his legs, and two oval burn marks dotted his shoulders.

The nurse pulled out a body map to detail each one. How did you get these scars? she asked.

Later, at the Starbucks in Chicago, Dulleh told this story to the agents. He spoke in a quiet, sullen voice. It is unclear whether he knew how significant his memories were in the case against Chucky.

Dulleh stared down at the six photographs arrayed in front of him. They were booking shots, from the U.S. marshals, of African-American males. Naples watched Dulleh scan the images.[13] Dulleh was a proud, intelligent man, Naples could tell, but whatever had happened to him, he wore heavily. Most of the men in the lineup conjured nothing from him. But he recognized a light-skinned black man with a beard, his head cocked slightly, an annoyed look on his face.

When they met four years earlier, that same face had seethed with rage. In that moment, Dulleh had not doubted that this man would take his life. Chucky had called out to him, "Do you know I can kill you and nothing can happen?"

That was no longer true. Dulleh pointed to the third photograph in the array.

That is Chucky Taylor, he said.

Are you positive? Naples asked.

One hundred percent.

Dulleh's identification had an immediate impact. On December 6, 2006, the day before Chucky faced sentencing on the passport violation, the Justice Department unsealed a seven-page indictment accusing him both of conspiracy to commit torture and of the act of torture.[14] He had remained in federal custody at the detention center in downtown Miami as his charge for passport fraud made its way to court. But even as he and his attorneys prepared to enter a guilty plea, he looked forward to his release. The new indictment guaranteed that he would not be freed anytime soon.

In anticipation of his sentencing, Chucky had prepared a rambling letter to Judge Donald L. Graham.[15] It opened vaguely: "for the last 8 out of 10 years, I lived in a place where Western covert support was permanent, and isolation of an administration was an overt action." In the letter he admitted to lying on the passport application, described his failed efforts to mediate an agreement with the State Department, and made clear his willingness to discuss his experience in Liberia.

The statement seemed crafted for a wider audience. Chucky had designs on publicizing his story, hoping that someone would pay him money for an interview.[16] But he also seemed to want to preempt further legal action against him. He knew that his past was being investigated but knew little else beyond that. His mother had received a subpoena from federal prosecutors that suggested a broader investigation. Eventually, his lawyers learned of the intention to indict him on torture charges.

The new indictment detailed the events of the early morning hours of July 24, 2002, in Monrovia, referring to Dulleh simply as "the Victim" and to Yeaten as the "co-conspirator," but implicating Chucky, under his four aliases, as the son of Charles Taylor and the commander of the Anti-Terrorist Unit.

"This marks the first time the Justice Department has charged a defendant with the crime of torture," Assistant Attorney General Alice Fisher said in a prepared statement. "Crimes such as these will not go unanswered."

It was a strange quote coming from the Bush administration Justice Department—in particular from Fisher, who would later become embroiled in the scandal surrounding the Office of Legal Counsel's interpretation of the very statute that Chucky had been indicted under. Fisher's connections to the interrogation practices used on detainees in the war on terror stretched back to 2002, when she had joined a delegation that toured Camp Delta at Guantánamo Bay (incidentally just weeks after Dulleh was detained by the ATU). According to journalist Jane Mayer, the lawyers on that junket sat in on an interrogation of a detainee.[17] Later, in 2005, Senator Carl M. Levin, who was looking into detainee abuse allegations, briefly held up Fisher's nomination for assistant attorney general. Following her confirmation, the issue continued to dog her.[18] The Justice Department's Office of Professional Responsibility probed whether in her prior role as deputy assistant attorney general she had sanctioned the use of torture, or—as the Bush administration referred to it—enhanced interrogation methods on terrorism suspects.

But ultimately the Justice Department's own entanglement with the torture of terrorism suspects did nothing to stop it from pursuing Chucky's case. Human rights groups applauded his indictment, but Chucky thought he was being made a scapegoat. "It's evident that Washington," he wrote in a letter from prison, "cannot determine my precise involvement in business or any other sector in Liberia and has had to rely on streams of information, not intelligence, coming from shady questionable accounts by Human Rights Watch, who in turn got it from other human rights groups, Liberian opposition, UN reports, who some consider motivated by ethnic and trible [*sic*] also political reasons."[19] Yet he was also defiant, saying, "How do I prove my innocence, and not make this intelligence gathering excercise [*sic*] for these cocksuckers in Washington, that's the challenge presented."

At his sentencing for the passport violation—the day after the indictment was announced—Chucky addressed Judge Graham directly, striking a much more reserved tone. "I've been placed in a very difficult position over the years due to my father's role as former President of Liberia and my status as an American citizen," he explained. "Throughout all, I've maintained my loyalty to both family and country. I fully respected and observed the laws of Liberia during my time there. I remained neutral as strenuous diplomatic issues emerged between my father's administration and Washington. . . . It seems that there are attempts to make me pay for being the son of a former African leader who now stands as the second former head of state in history to be indicted for war crimes."

Chucky's assumptions about the federal government were wrong. Washington wasn't using the threat of prosecution to lean on him for intelligence. Both ICE and the Justice Department had one interest in him—gathering enough witnesses and evidence to ensure that he was the first person in history to be convicted under the federal antitorture statute.

On a Sunday morning in November 2007, Special Agent Baechtle and an ICE colleague, Special Agent Julian Doyle, climbed into a white SUV at the U.S. embassy in Monrovia.[20] Baechtle had become familiar with the journey to Liberia over several visits, but on this trip was Assistant U.S. Attorney Caroline Heck Miller, who accompanied him for the first time. Before departing the capital, the investigators and attorneys had a stop to make, to pick up their guide for the day, a man named Rufus Kpadeh.

Kpadeh had met the agents once before, three months earlier, inside the U.S. embassy.[21] The path that led the agents to Kpadeh illustrates the networks Taylor had inadvertently fashioned with his brand of authoritarian rule. Early in the investigation the agents had located Nathaniel Koah, the diamond broker who had been arrested and brutalized at Gbatala. Koah's vocal publicity campaign following his arrest by the Anti-Terrorist Unit had drawn considerable attention. A human rights group took up his cause and brought it to the attention of the U.S. embassy, which worked directly with the visiting ICE and FBI agents. But Koah was a complex witness: raw and excitable, a former Taylor supporter who had abandoned his wife and daughter to be sexually assaulted as retribution for his decision to go public. His primary motivation now was not to see Chucky and the other perpetrators punished but to be compensated for his ordeal.

In the course of the agents' interview with Koah, he mentioned that he'd been detained with another man from Lofa County. Unlike Koah, Kpadeh had never gone public with his story and had only recently returned to Liberia from refuge in Ivory Coast and Guinea. He made his living farming and building furniture. While he belonged to an opposition political party, his political affiliations did not run much deeper than that. He was, compared to Koah and Dulleh, relatively unattached to the parties involved in the civil war; most important, he wasn't interested in money.

When Kpadeh first met with the investigators, he told them his story: he fled Voinjama in August 1999, was detained at the St. Paul River bridge, and was brought to the office in the building alongside the road. There he met Chucky for the first time and on his orders was sent to Gbatala.

He spoke with a soft, raspy voice—when he paused, he wheezed audibly.[22] While Koah remained deeply angry and vengeful over the suffering his family endured, Kpadeh presented himself as calm and free from ulterior motives. When pressed, he acknowledged he wanted justice, but mostly he wanted to continue with his life in Liberia.

News of Chucky's arrest and indictment had made it back to Monrovia, but the indictment listed only one, unnamed victim. The secrecy was meant to ensure the safety of Dulleh and his family prior to trial. But whether through Monrovia's gossip mill or because of familiarity with the circumstances surrounding the accusations, Chucky's former commanders quickly learned the accuser's identity.

They did nothing, however; they had no incentive to help Chucky. Taylor-era figures, by and large, were keeping a low profile. Chucky's former fighters felt no loyalty to a commander who had abandoned them. Finally, there was no money in helping him.

Yet Kpadeh faced a risk going into his first meeting with the Americans. He lived in Voinjama but spent enough time in Monrovia to be targeted by former ATU members living in the capital. Despite this risk, he told his story to the agents. At one point he stood up to remove his shirt—revealing a trail of scars stretched across his torso. He agreed, upon the agents' return, to take them to the place where he'd received those injuries.

Some three months after that initial meeting, the agents prepared to travel into the countryside with Kpadeh and an attorney overseeing Chucky's new criminal case. The group left Monrovia before daybreak, threading through the capital's streets to Paynesville, where the typically overrun, trash-strewn marketplace of Red Light—named for the single, out-of-service traffic light—began to stir with activity. By the time the group reached Margibi County, an hour's drive outside the capital, the road pointed through the rolling green groves of the hinterland toward the rising sun.

Nearly one hundred miles from the city, the group passed over a small bridge into the village of Gbatala. On the left side of the road stood a hand-painted billboard dug into the mud shoulder. It depicted a reunion scene, set against a village backdrop: a sleeveless teenager with a headband discarded a machete and an AK-47 with one hand and shook the hand of a neatly dressed older man with the other.[23] In the background, a woman and two children—a boy and a girl—rushed out from a tin-roofed hut wearing jubilant smiles. In large block letters it read THE WAR IS OVER.

Their truck veered off the road, then went up a steep gravel incline, barely visible from the roadway. Within moments the vacant stretch of buildings that was once the Anti-Terrorist Unit base appeared. Kpadeh stepped out of the vehicle with the attorneys and agents. The site had returned to its original use: a quarry. The sharp white light of the sun refracted off granite boulders, and tidy pyramids of gravel interspersed across the hilltop. In the distance stood the College of Knowledge, faded but still identifiable. As the building came into view, they could see that the roof was missing; the rear cinder-block wall had collapsed; weeds had grown through the floors and the walls.

Kpadeh recalled to the prosecutors and agents how he had been carried here in the back of a pickup truck, laid across the bed of the cab with other prisoners.[24] How the soldiers had bound his arms, elbow to elbow, behind his back and tied his ankles together. And how he could see only what bled through the edges of his blindfold, as the sounds of others shouting for help filled the darkness.

When Kpadeh was first brought to Gbatala, he recalled, he had been pulled from the truck and brought into this building. He couldn't see faces, but he recognized voices; one was Chucky's—who had ordered his arrest—and the other belonged to David Campari, the base commander. Again Chucky had demanded to know if Kpadeh was a rebel. And again Kpadeh denied it.

That answer wasn't sufficient. He was pulled up to his feet and dragged out of the building to a nearby creek, where the questioning continued. Each time Kpadeh denied the accusations thrown at him, a soldier plunged his head under water. Finally the soldiers pulled him from the water. He heard Chucky's voice order, "Campari, cut under his nuts."

Campari, he recalled, pulled out his knife and carried out the order.

As the American team took in the surroundings at the base, Kpadeh wanted to lead them toward Vietnam, but the narrow dirt path that ran down the hillside toward the area was impassable. The rainy season had just begun, and a dull, green swamp had formed at the bottom of the slope. Kpadeh told the investigators there was an alternate route, a road that wound around the base. The group climbed into their SUVs to drive the short distance to the location Kpadeh pointed out.

When they arrived, he led them toward the dense undergrowth. The ground turned from gravel roadway to swamp, water soaking through the investigators' shoes as they moved into the bush until they could go no farther. Then one of the agents found two logs propped in the water as a makeshift bridge. The terrain ahead remained damp but navigable.

A tent-shaped thatched hut stood in a clearing ahead. As the group approached, about a dozen holes in the terrain became visible. The holes varied in depth and shape, the deepest approximately four and half feet. Many were overgrown with vegetation, looking like unused open graves. Kpadeh climbed into a hole to demonstrate its depth.

Kpadeh had been brought here, bleeding from underneath his testicles; soldiers guarding Vietnam had stripped him and thrown him into a hole near the riverbank. Filthy water had accumulated at the bottom of the hole. The guards closed the steel gate over his head. He discovered that he could not stand: he could only squat or sit in the stagnant water. The soldiers called this hole "Waterfall."

Kpadeh lived in this hole for several weeks. The other holes adjacent had names that he went through for the agents: one was called "Bella Yella" after the notorious prison in central Liberia; another was called "Advise Yourself"; another, "Survivor." Occasionally the guards would remove Kpadeh from the hole, he recalled. Once he was brought to a ring on the hillside and forced to run around it, carrying a heavy log: soldiers beat the log with sticks and bars as he passed by. This was a torture called "running the rim" that prisoners and recruits alike were subjected to. Another day he and other prisoners were forced to play soccer by kicking a large stone across the gravel, while Chucky and the soldiers stood by and laughed.

Chucky wasn't a constant presence on the base, Kpadeh explained, visiting only once or twice a week. In his absence the abuse persisted, particularly at the hands of Campari. Once when Chucky arrived at the base, a prisoner complained to him that the guards had raped him and other prisoners while he was away. Chucky, Kpadeh recalled, told the men he wanted to find out if this was true. He marched down to Vietnam and ordered Kpadeh and another prisoner pulled from their holes. Kpadeh was handed a bar of soap and ordered to sodomize the other man; the man was then forced to sodomize Kpadeh. Chucky sat and watched, Kpadeh remembered. Chucky didn't say anything; he only laughed.

Most of the time the prisoners remained in Vietnam. The guards subjected the men to strange, terrible abuses, Kpadeh explained: they jabbed the men's hands and bodies with the long rod used to clean the barrels of their guns, they poured driver ants—insects with jaws so strong that traditional healers used their bite to serve as sutures to close wounds—into his hole. Kpadeh had struggled to kill them all before they could bite him. Some soldiers burned sheets of plastic over Vietnam, so the molten drippings would fall on the prisoners.

One night, Kpadeh recalled, Chucky arrived at Vietnam and ordered four prisoners out of a nearby hole. Kpadeh recognized one of the prisoners as a Mandingo man named Richard Abu. The men were led off into the darkness toward the barracks. For ten minutes he heard nothing; then gunfire crackled over the quarry, and Abu's voice cried out, "Eh Allah! Eh Allah! Eh Allah!" Then there was silence. Kpadeh could see only a large fire burning on the hill.

Agent Baechtle took in the scene. He was surprised that the base had remained intact after so many rainy seasons, that the holes hadn't washed away or collapsed. For the purposes of the prosecution, the base provided a crime scene, one that corroborated the accounts of what had occurred here. More personally, walking into this environment and seeing the basic, physical reality of the base made the horrors that had occurred here resonate more deeply.

The other agent, Julian Doyle, inspected the surrounding area.[25] He came across a clearing, beyond the hut where three stakes stood in a line. Lodged in the copper-colored dirt amid the dead vegetation, he found rusted shell casings and an empty, three-pronged clip with the inscription "M 13," typical for housing 7.62mm rounds used in AK-47s.

Kpadeh's ordeal at Gbatala had come to an end in October 1999.[26] But now as he led the agents and prosecutors through the base, the memory of the day when he and other prisoners had been pulled from Vietnam came back to him. They were hauled toward the barracks, where they saw Chucky standing, waiting for them. Kpadeh was naked and filthy; his hair had grown thick and matted, and he'd lost a third of his body weight. Chucky conferred with Campari in front of the prisoners, telling him that "human rights people" were coming to the base to investigate abuses. The prisoners were given soap, clothing, and shower slippers and told to bathe and cut one another's hair. They learned they were being transferred to police custody at the Gbarnga LNP Station.

Do not tell any human rights groups that you were jailed at Gbatala, Chucky warned the prisoners. That was the last time Kpadeh saw Chucky Taylor, until he faced him nine years later at his trial.

The sun had already climbed high above the base. The team had quite a bit of ground to cover in order to return to the embassy before sunset. Kpadeh climbed from the hole and back into the truck with the Americans.

17

Testimony

Power move, try the best to believe you'll need nuff guns from
da feds, And a fuckin' armory, come clean, man we bombard your
scene, raise you up out your green.

— United States vs. Belfast, EXHIBIT CE-4

Vultures floated in slow rising circles over downtown Miami, chased by
their shadowy reflections in the mirrored glass of the skyscrapers. It was
September 29, 2008, a bright, hot Monday. A stream of people walked
across the open, concrete esplanade toward the entrance of the Wilkie D.
Ferguson Jr. Federal Courthouse.

Shortly after nine-thirty a.m. Chucky was led into courtroom 12-2
to take a seat with his defense counsel. Clad in a gray blazer and black
slacks, he resembled a museum security guard more than the former
commander of an elite paramilitary unit. He wore a trimmed beard
and a cowed expression as the room waited quietly for the judge to
enter. Law students, human rights attorneys, and a handful of reporters
filled in the gallery. Nobody—not Chucky's mother, not Lynn, nor any
of his family members—appeared to support him. He was nonetheless
defiant. "There is nothing in my past that I am afraid to confront," he
wrote in a letter before the trial.[1]

A year earlier the government had filed a superseding indictment
including the accounts of Rufus Kpadeh, Momoh Turay, Sulaiman Jusu,
and another man, Mulbah Kamara, making up eight separate counts
of torture, conspiracy, and firearms violations.[2] The additional charges
rendered the task of defending Chucky extraordinarily difficult, if not

impossible. The new victims were also unnamed, and every act they accused Chucky of committing would likely require a dedicated set of witnesses to refute. The defense team had already traveled to Liberia several times chasing the shadow of the unidentified first victim in the original indictment: Varmuyan Dulleh.[3] The new charges—and the string of unidentified victims attached to them—effectively multiplied their already insurmountable challenge.

Yet potential witnesses had arrived in Miami who could cast doubt on the government's case. The defense team located one potentially significant witness, an ATU commander who told them that he had accompanied Chucky to St. Paul River in April 1999 and that nothing had occurred there.[4] The commander, who would not speak for attribution, was also posted to Gbatala during the period of Kpadeh's detention. In an interview he appeared to offer evidence contradicting some details outlined in the indictment. Asked whether Chucky had ordered executions at Gbatala, the commander responded, "Oh, no. My God, no.

"He never ordered anyone's execution in my presence on the base," the commander, who asked not to be identified, said.

Yet the same commander confirmed certain aspects of the prosecution's case, such as the existence of the detention facility at Vietnam, the mistreatment of both recruits and prisoners, and Chucky's presence at the scene of the crimes alleged in the indictment. He readily acknowledged Chucky's role in the deaths of Justin Parker, the SSS officer Kougbay Dunuma, and Isaac Gono. He was far from an ideal witness. The commander remained on the UN travel ban, but he had been approved to enter the United States as a defense witness.[5] He ultimately declined to testify because he felt his testimony would be of little help to Chucky.

"Even if there was no travel ban, I could not have gone, because I was going to look Chucky in the face and tell the facts," he said. "Things he did wrong: I tell him. Things he did right: I praise him."

Several days before opening arguments, legal issues central to the conduct of the trial remained to be settled. Both parties in the case submitted proposed jury instructions, which figured significantly into how the jury would view evidence, but also how they would define the principal charge of torture.[6] In its proposed instructions, the defense chose a definition of torture as "equivalent in intensity to the pain accompanying serious physical injury, such as organ failure, impairment of bodily function, or even death." The definition stemmed not from case law but from the Justice Department itself, in a legal interpretation of the federal antitorture statute known as the Bybee Memo, authored by John Yoo of the Office of Legal Counsel.

It was an attempt to link the public debate over the use of "enhanced interrogation" to the alleged acts Chucky been accused of committing in the name of his father's regime. He held out hope that the government could be compelled to produce videotapes of the interrogation of Abu Zubaydah that the CIA acknowledged had been destroyed—perhaps to seize the moral high ground from the prosecutors. He thought these videos would reveal to the jury the hypocrisy of the same Justice Department that had legalized torture now prosecuting a defendant for it. The public debate over enhanced interrogation had little relevance to the trial, but Chucky saw a political connection between the two.

The U.S. attorney for the Southern District of Florida, R. Alexander Acosta, rejected the suggestion of moral equivalence between enhanced interrogation and the torture Chucky had been accused of.[7] "This case is in many ways *sui generis*," he said. "The acts that were committed were heinous. They were torture. They were committed not just once or twice, but repeatedly. . . . It's the first and only time the torture statute has been used and I would defend its use."

The judge, a Bush appointee named Cecilia Altonaga, appeared to want to prevent the case from becoming another platform for the Bush administration torture debate.[8] She tabled the most controversial issue—the definition of torture—until after each party had presented its case. But when asked to apply the controversial definition put forward by the Bybee Memo, she said, "I will not give an instruction that relies upon that memorandum as its authority."

Just as the trial was to open, the prosecution's case suffered a significant setback. The indictment's original witness—Varmuyan Dulleh—reversed his decision to testify. In pretrial arguments, Chucky's defense team had indicated that they would raise Dulleh's HIV status under cross-examination. (Dulleh had tested positive in 2005.) The stigma associated with HIV, particularly within the Liberian Mandingo community, made him fearful of being forced to disclose this information at trial.

Another prosecution witness, the former journalist Hassan Bility, pressed Dulleh to reconsider.[9] The two were old friends with strong familial and tribal ties, and they had been imprisoned together. When he reached Dulleh at home in Chicago, Bility found him distraught. Bility tried to convince him of the importance of his testimony, but by the time Bility hung up the phone, whether Dulleh would appear on the stand in Miami remained unclear.

On the first day of the trial, Assistant U.S. Attorney Christopher Graveline rose to address the jury. Graveline was a Department of Justice trial attorney who had joined the case earlier in the year. He carried himself to the lectern set up between the prosecution and the defense as if he were in uniform; square-jawed and broad-shouldered, he had spent much of his career as a judge advocate general in the 101st Airborne Division and V Corps, before joining the Department of Justice.[10] His last significant military case—prosecuting the American men and women accused of abusing prisoners in Abu Ghraib prison—provided one of the few discrete connections between Chucky's case and the political issue of torture engaged in by U.S. personnel; jurors would not be aware of this, however, unless they had followed the Abu Ghraib prosecutions closely.

Graveline's first words to the jury turned their attention toward the basic human brutality that this case would consider. "Burning flesh, beheading, fiercely stabbing men's hands with sharp metal rods, cutting a man's penis with a sharp blade, shocking a man's genitals with electrical prods, sodomizing that same man with electrical prods," he began in his opening statement.[11] These were just some of the crimes that the government would outline, all in support of the allegations that Chucky Taylor, referred to by his legal name, Roy Belfast Jr., had committed torture.

The stark, descriptive language took these acts out of any political or cultural context and presented them in explicitly physical and anatomical terms. Graveline's opening introduced one of the prosecution's themes—and telegraphed a challenge the government faced: that the evidence provided by the witnesses and victims, some of whom had never set foot outside Liberia, should be considered with equal weight and authority as if it were coming from an American.

The jury listened as Graveline recounted Chucky's family history and the creation of the ATU, and as he introduced the victims from the indictment by name, he described what they would testify to and ultimately how these acts tied back to violations of U.S. law. It was a dizzying summary of a case that would require the jury to make more than a simple determination of guilt or innocence. The jurors sitting in Judge Altonaga's courtroom would be asked to navigate a foreign culture and history to come to their verdict.

But as he concluded, Graveline grounded the government's case in a simple, understandable rationale: power. "Chucky Taylor conspired with others and tortured men in Liberia in order to keep his father in power," he said.

Developing a theory for Chucky's defense relied on exploiting the weaknesses in the government case. Chucky's statement at the airport to Agent Baechtle provided a strong admission of the core facts of the case, but he did not implicate himself explicitly in all the charges brought against him. That would be the role of the witnesses. Even though Chucky's team knew little information beyond the names of many of the witnesses, they could infer some motivations, particularly for those who no longer lived in West Africa. If the defense could discredit the witnesses against Chucky, they stood a shot at creating reasonable doubt.

Federal public defender John Wylie immediately made clear that that would be the focus of the defense.[12] "Desperate and disgruntled Africans accuse American to escape war-torn Liberia" was how he characterized the victims to the jury in his opening. He seemed to be cognizant of the media presence in the courtroom, explaining that that would be the headline if this case were a newspaper article. He portrayed the prosecution's case as a fraud perpetrated against his client and the American criminal justice system. It was a novel idea, turning Liberia's weaknesses into strengths for Chucky's defense. The broken, traumatized, and dangerous world of West Africa was motive alone to lie, cheat, and steal.

To illustrate this point, Wylie played a video to the jury. It was a handheld moving panorama of downtown Monrovia, shot from the front passenger seat of a vehicle. In it the jurors caught a glimpse of the elements of daily life in the capital: the crowded and chaotic streets, peopled with black Africans, many wiry thin, dressed in flowing robes, shorts, T-shirts, and flip-flops, peering out of tin-roofed shacks or impossibly smashed into the cramped backseats of yellow cabs. The point was clear: Liberia was nothing like Miami or the surrounding suburbs.

"Liberia is literally one of the poorest countries in the entire world," he began. "There is no electricity throughout the entire country. The wealthy have generators, and they get their power that way, but there's no power grid. There are no landlines, no telephone lines. So only the people lucky enough to have cell phones are able to communicate by telephone. Because there are no landlines, there are no ATMs. Unemployment is 85 percent. The life expectancy of a Liberian man is approximately forty years old. The infant mortality rate is one of the highest in the entire world."

Wylie cast the prosecution's case as the latest episode in a long-running conflict in Liberia. The witnesses who would appear were not disinterested victims, he stressed; they were enemies of Chucky and his father. Some had manipulated the international community to leave Liberia. All were manipulating the truth to attack Chucky.

"Someone once said the first casualty of war is the truth," Wylie said. "You are going to see that in this case." He reminded the jury of the prosecution's primary burden: to prove its case beyond all reasonable doubt. "The Government is asking you to take yourself back in time on the other side of the world, drop yourself in the middle of a war, and determine if these acts actually happened," he said. "That's impossible."

It was an impressive showing, but it didn't undo key setbacks that jeopardized the defense's case. Weeks earlier John Wylie had flown to South Africa to depose a witness who the team felt could potentially upend the government's case.[13] It was highly irregular for a federal judge to allow a deposition to be taken in lieu of live testimony, but the witness, a former military trainer, worked in Afghanistan and lived in South Africa. The defense argued that he was "present on the ATU training base at Gbatala throughout 1999 and can testify that none of the alleged acts of torture supposedly committed at the base ever occurred." The deposition required authorization from South African authorities, which the attorneys expected would be forthcoming within days after their arrival. But days turned to weeks, and the attorneys still hadn't received the necessary approvals. Wylie couldn't tell whether the reason was incompetence or willful neglect, but it didn't matter. The opening of the trial loomed large. The defense team was forced to pack up without ever sitting down with the trainer. Chucky's attorney would have to go to trial without one of his potentially most important witnesses.

To make matters more difficult, Chucky's defense team didn't receive the names of potential prosecution witnesses until late August, just weeks before the trial opened. With that list in hand, they realized the witnesses weren't only Mandingos and members of the opposition but insiders, fighters from the ATU and SSS who had served under Chucky and his father at Gbatala and on the Executive Mansion grounds. The list posed a frustrating problem for the attorneys. It wasn't clear to them which witnesses correlated to which counts in the indictment—the defense counsel pressed for further information prior to receiving the final witness list so they could anticipate each person's testimony and, as much as possible, investigate the allegations before the witness took the stand. At a minimum, the lawyers expected that regardless of who took the stand, they would have a chance to impugn their testimony based on ulterior motives.

Rufus Kpadeh appeared as the prosecution's first alleged victim.[14] He stepped into the courtroom in the late afternoon, clothed in an incandescent green and orange smock, ornately detailed with gold thread. Against the backdrop of the futuristic courtroom, a sort of asymmetrical moonscape of soundproofing, speakers, lighting, and flat panel monitors, his traditional African garb was jarring.

Before Kpadeh took the stand, the defense learned that the government planned to lead with a witness who would not only provide strong evidence but also would refute the defense theory. Chucky's counsel wished to portray the witnesses as opportunists willing to say anything to secure their immigration status, but Kpadeh lived in Liberia and had no intention of leaving. "We knew that he was the only one that . . . had not received some sort of asylum in another country," Wylie said.

Assistant U.S. Attorney Miller opened the questioning of Kpadeh. Her presence in the courtroom was unassuming. Her tiny, stooped frame and drowsy, heavy-lidded eyes were countered by a deep, authoritative voice. In conversation, she had a warm, natural presence that put people at ease—even when she was questioning them. Perhaps that could be attributed to her beginnings as a reporter—her first lessons in the law had come while covering trials for the *St. Petersburg Times.*[15] When she began questioning Kpadeh, she wanted more than a recitation of facts from him—she wanted the jury to understand who he was as a human being and what had happened to him. The credibility of his testimony depended on it.

"A trial is a dialogue—truthfulness and accuracy is of paramount importance," she said in a later interview. "A good witness is a witness who listens carefully."

Kpadeh returned in his testimony to the events of August 1999 at the St. Paul River bridge, the peremptory interrogation by Chucky, his arrest, and his being forcibly *tabay*ed and tossed into the truck. He retold these things in a quiet, raspy voice, wheezing softly. He spoke in English, though his accent made it difficult at times for the judge and the jury to immediately recognize what he was saying. Eventually Miller asked Kpadeh to show the jury the scars from the ropes.

He stood and stepped out of the witness stand, took several steps toward the jury box, and rolled his sleeves up. He held his arms straight out from his body, so that the jury could examine him. As a still life, the gesture might otherwise have registered as pleading, but the unfaltering purpose with which Kpadeh approached the jury box showed no such signs. Chucky watched, expressionless, from behind the defense counsel's desk, a yellow legal pad in front of him, as the display played out a few feet away. The secrets of Gbatala had crossed the ocean.

"Thank you, Mr. Kpadeh," Miller said. "You may take the witness stand again."

Kpadeh gave the clear impression that he had prepared to testify. When Miller probed the specific acts of torture, such as "running the rim"—where Kpadeh stated he was flogged while running in circles carrying a large log—the questions and responses circled around the statutory language that defined torture.

"Was it painful?" Miller asked.

"Yes," Kpadeh replied.

"In what way would the pain change?" she pressed.

"I would always feel severe pain running down my shoulders," he replied; the phrase *severe pain* was a direct echo of the statute.

But the government had to go further than matching witness statements with the law. It had to prove intent. Intent figures into the legal definition of any criminal act, but with the antitorture statute it remained especially muddy legal territory. Could an act be considered torture if it was not intended to be? For example, if the intent was not to harm a person but rather to elicit information, did that constitute torture? That was the *24* scenario. The Bush administration argued that intent was a pillar of interpreting the statute. That position opened the door to a universe of ugly hypotheticals, perhaps most graphically illustrated when Bybee Memo author John Yoo was asked whether the president could legally order a child's testicles to be crushed: he responded, "I think it depends on why the President thinks he needs to do that."

But for the defense, the primary issue was not the definition of torture but witness credibility. On cross-examination, John Wylie set about attempting to unearth inconsistencies in Kpadeh's testimony. He probed the allegations of torture and, focusing on "running the rim," asked how, given the abuse he had allegedly suffered and the conditions he had been detained under, he had been able to complete such an arduous task.

"You must have been feeling very weak after you had been at this base for two weeks?" the attorney asked.

But Kpadeh's matter-of-fact answer, if anything, bolstered his credibility. "It depends on the strength you have," Kpadeh answered plainly. "I am an African child. I am very strong."

Ultimately Kpadeh's testimony effectively stood the defense theory on its head. He had not considered seeking asylum or resettling in the United States. If anything, as Assistant U.S. Attorney Miller elicited on redirect questioning, he had spent his free time in Miami pricing out chain saws to bring back to his farm near Voinjama. For all the difficulties that went along with living in Liberia—and all the perceived advantages of living in a developed country—Kpadeh explained to Wylie during cross-examination, "My home is the best for me."

· · ·

Shortly after ten-thirty a.m. on October 1, 2008, Chucky's stepfather, Roy Belfast Sr., walked into the courtroom.[16] The prosecution had already demonstrated the brutality Chucky was allegedly capable of. Now they would show exactly who the person sitting at the defendant's table was. Belfast strode past the gallery in loose olive slacks and a faint gingham shirt, untucked. His presence appeared to catch the defense by surprise. Turning to see his stepfather, Chucky appeared stricken. He stopped writing on his notepad, as had been his habit throughout the trial; his mouth was slightly agape as his stepfather took the stand and recited his oath. Belfast had little choice in being there; he appeared under prosecution subpoena.

The government wanted to use Belfast to establish a fundamental fact: that Chucky was Charles Taylor's son. But it also asked him to help explain the complicated family history and the eventual disappearance of his stepson.

Belfast spoke in a soft, lilting Trinidadian accent. As he testified, he called his stepson "Charlie," recounting the first time he met the boy, when Chucky was just five. Chucky eventually came to call him "Pop." The family's migration south to Orlando, Belfast testified, was a deliberate act of protection. He and Bernice had intended to "put some distance" between Charles Taylor and Chucky, but as events unfolded in West Africa and Belfast's marriage unraveled, Bernice no longer felt the need to protect her son from his father. In fact, she chose to close that distance.

Chucky wiped tears from his eyes with a folded handkerchief. Wylie patted his back, as if to console him. On cross-examination, public defender Caridad made Chucky stand so that Belfast could identify him.

"Did you consider him your son?" Caridad asked.

"He was considered my son. I was his father," Belfast said. He stood and stepped down from the stand. As he passed the defense table, he nodded toward Chucky, who looked back at him, then leaned forward, holding his hand over his eyes, rocking slightly in his chair.

On October 1, 2008, two men milled about the fourteenth-floor lobby of the courthouse waiting to testify: Sulaiman Jusu and Momoh Turay. Baechtle had tracked them to Sweden and, after the U.S. attorneys interviewed them, determined that they would appear at trial. That day

Turay, a small, broad-chested man, wore a denim suit; Jusu, lanky and tall, donned more traditional linen garb. From the east, fragments of Biscayne Bay shone through the buildings and rooftops of downtown Miami as glints of cobalt. A calm quiet echoed through the hallway as they entered the courtroom.

Nearly a decade had passed since their ordeal ended in Liberia. After the United Nations secured their release in Monrovia in 1999, the men had received treatment in a clinic adjacent to the U.S. embassy for several weeks, then were relocated to a refugee camp outside Monrovia.[17] Eventually Taylor's security forces discovered the men there, harassing and beating them until they were forced to flee again. As horrifying as their ordeal had been, it proved helpful in establishing a case for resettlement. Finally, Sweden accepted both, along with their families, for resettlement, and they left Liberia in March 2000. Jusu settled in Stockholm, and Turay, farther north, in a small Swedish town just below the Arctic Circle.

It was there that Special Agent Baechtle had found them.[18] In interviews, they offered parallel accounts of arrest, detention, and torture at the Gbatala base, but more significantly, both implicated Chucky in killings. He had not been indicted for murder but faced potentially harsher sentence under an "enhancement" if murder were proved.

The government put both men on the stand and took the jury through each one's experience in painstaking detail. When Jusu testified, he recalled the executions the men had witnessed Chucky carry out at the St. Paul River bridge. He described the decapitation they had seen Chucky order at Gbatala. For the jurors, this testimony illustrated that there were no boundaries to the brutality the defendant had been accused of. It also lent credibility to the fear of death that other victims in the case would testify to.

Credibility was a problem for both men, though.[19] They had lied during the process of resettlement, to allow women who were not their wives to accompany them to Sweden. That made the men vulnerable under cross-examination. During cross-examination, John Wylie often talked over Turay, trying to raise any skepticism he could from the jury—drawing attention to the fact that he'd been convicted of hitting a child and pushing him to acknowledge past lies. Wylie was laying the groundwork for his closing, where he would seek to discredit Turay, portray him as an opportunist, and sow seeds of doubt in the veracity of his testimony.

On October 10, Varmuyan Dulleh took the stand; as the first victim to appear in the indictment, his testimony was crucial to the government's case.[20] If the idea of Charles Taylor's power, and Chucky's connection to it, had been abstract for the jury, Dulleh's account of his arrest brought the jurors directly into Taylor's inner sanctum. Assistant U.S. Attorney Graveline asked Dulleh to describe the scene at White Flower after he had been hauled there from his home. Dulleh related that Taylor's commanders Momoh Gibba and Benjamin Yeaten, along with his ministers, had been sitting along a wall, and he explained where Chucky fit within this group.

Wylie attacked Dulleh's credibility, pointing out that he had lied about his identity in order to escape Liberia. But just as with Turay and Jusu's fabrications on their refugee claims, Dulleh's lies were easily understood as necessary for his own survival. The defense counsel pursued Dulleh's motivations for testifying, trying to tie the funds that Dulleh had been provided and the health care he had received to his appearance before the court. Finally Wylie pressed the underlying politics between the defendant and witness, seeking to connect Dulleh to his uncle Alhaji Kromah, the leader of a faction at odds with Taylor. Dulleh responded calmly and clearly throughout.

Chucky's attorney eventually focused on statements that Dulleh had provided to the representatives for the UN High Commission for Refugees who had vetted his claim to be resettled in a host country. To be resettled in the United States, applicants either are selected by lottery or need to provide proof that they have suffered religious or political persecution in their home country. The defense attorney pointed out that Dulleh's accusations had particular currency because they involved a political figure: Chucky, the son of the president.

"Now, when you were telling the story to the United Nations, was Chucky Taylor present?" Wylie asked.

"No," Dulleh responded.

"Was his lawyer or a lawyer for Chucky Taylor present when you were telling the story to the United Nations?" he continued, raising the idea that the first time this story was told—and allegedly fabricated—Chucky could not defend himself from the accusation.

"No," the witness said.

On redirect, Assistant U.S. Attorney Graveline picked up Wylie's thread, emphasizing the ridiculousness of the line pursued in the cross-examination. He referred to the subterranean pit where the men were held for a time beneath a trucking weigh scale during their ordeal.

"Was Chucky Taylor's lawyer under the weigh scale at Kle when you accused him with those men of torture?" The defense objected, and Graveline rephrased the question. "What, if any, lawyers did you see under the weigh station at Kle?" he asked.

Dulleh responded, "Absolutely no lawyers."

The prosecution's case had been devastating. Much of the local and national media attention focused on the depravity of the accusations rather than the legal and political significance of the case. For Liberians following Chucky's story in Monrovia's dailies, the trial represented a stunning reversal of power. In the United States victims of violent crime take for granted that they have the right to face their perpetrator in court, but those who had been victimized during Liberia's civil war could have made no such assumption.

After the civil war, Liberia pursued its own type of reckoning through the Truth and Reconciliation Commission (TRC). The process was intended to give both victims and perpetrators the opportunity to air their experiences before investigators and at public hearings. Ultimately, though, the TRC process was toothless: hundreds of victims recounted the horrors they suffered, and dozens of perpetrators recounted in detail the torture, murder, and mutilation they took part in, yet nobody faced any criminal charges. While his father was being prosecuted for crimes he had committed in another country—Sierra Leone—Chucky Taylor, in fact, was the only participant in the entire fourteen-year conflict to be brought before a judge and jury.

For fourteen days the jury heard accounts of Chucky's brutality. They learned of his connection to his father's regime. They saw the scars on his alleged victims' skin. But one voice they hadn't yet heard was Chucky's. And his attorneys hoped to ensure it remained that way.

The prosecution sought to introduce the rap lyrics that the agents had discovered in Chucky's personal effects when he was arrested.[21] At sidebar, defense attorney Miguel Caridad fought vociferously to exclude the lyrics from the trial as irrelevant and prejudicial. He knew that, in the context of a criminal trial, they would not reflect well on his client.

"Rap lyrics are notoriously violent no matter who writes them," he argued before the judge.[22] "This is pure and simple character assassination. They want to make him look like a violent guy because his character is violent. That's a complete character smear. They do not need it for anything. It doesn't say anything about torture."

"It's probably good it doesn't from your perspective," the judge said, then overruled his objection.

In a flat, unaffected tone, a customs agent read the lyrics to the jury:

Ways and my heart dump stays all day as we plot and give way. We see the burst from your muzzle have ya bleedin for days. More sweat in my training means less blood in my life. So wit the shots from guns keep it dead and precise. Bull-doze ambushes in the midst of a fight. Try to cut my supply, you'll be losing your life. Heed this warning.

It required only a small, if circumstantial, leap to connect these lyrics with the allegations the jury had already heard detailed. The words had their own force: they provided a window into the imagination of the one person who had remained silent throughout the trial.

For Chucky's case, the admission of the lyrics was catastrophic— the image that he was a cold-blooded and violent killer wasn't simply a figment of the government's imagination—it was one that the defendant himself cultivated.

The last investigator scheduled to testify for the prosecution was Special Agent Baechtle. The defense had fought to keep his most compelling testimony—his account of Chucky's statements to him at Miami International Airport—out of the trial. Knowing that U.S. Attorney Miller would be questioning him, and familiar with her thorough, methodical approach to witness, Baechtle prepared to testify. Like other ICE agents, he'd been trained to do so, facing down stand-in prosecutors and defenders in a mock courtroom setting at the academy. But this case marked his first significant criminal trial, and his testimony held, potentially, the most incriminating evidence of the prosecution's case.

Baechtle took the stand on the afternoon of October 16, 2008.

U.S. Attorney Miller walked him through the events of the evening of March 30, two years earlier—Chucky's arrest and interrogation.[23] The agent recounted that the actual arrest was a small part of what turned into a three-hour conversation. Chucky, in the agent's retelling, detailed his experiences in Liberia from when he first met his father in 1992 until the moment he fled eleven years later. Baechtle's recollections of the conversation clung to the facts. He offered no opinion of Chucky, nor was any solicited by the prosecutor.

Based on Baechtle's testimony, what Chucky told him on the night of his arrest amounted to an admission that he not only had command responsibility for the ATU but was present for the torture of one individual at Yeaten's house, presumably Varmuyan Dulleh. The fact that these admissions were elicited only after Chucky was confronted by specific information and accusations created the impression that the defendant had hoped to obfuscate the details of his past. Most significant, based on the agent's testimony, Chucky had made all his admissions willingly, with little or no pressure from the investigators.

"Were you present for the duration of that three-hour interview?" Miller asked.

"Yes, I was," Baechtle responded.

"Was the defendant responsive to your questions?" she asked.

"Yes," he said.

"Were there any questions you asked that he refused to answer?" the prosecutor asked.

"Not that I recall," Baechtle said.

The trial broke for the day, and Baechtle returned to his hotel with his testimony scheduled to resume in the morning. The judge forbade him to speak to anyone until he concluded testifying, which gave Baechtle his first night off since the trial began more than two weeks earlier.

It provided him a moment to look back on the experience.[24] The trial had been a period of exhilarating uncertainty, but he felt confident in the evidence that the witnesses could provide and in the abilities of the prosecutors. The investigation had been long and meticulous, leaving very little to chance, but Baechtle recognized the inherently unpredictable nature of a criminal trial.

Chucky's public defender, John Wylie, had made an undeniable point when he laid out the challenge facing the jury: they were being asked to go back in time to determine whether the crimes Chucky had been accused of had actually occurred.[25] The government had provided the evidence and witnesses, but had they made the crimes real enough for the jury to convict Chucky?

Baechtle knew what had made the crimes real to him: Marching along a thread of dirt into the swamp at Gbatala and coming upon the water-filled holes of Vietnam exactly as they had been described to him.[26] Peering into the dark, fetid weigh station at Kle and feeling physically repulsed at the thought that men had been imprisoned for weeks on end in the garbage and filth. Interviewing the witnesses, not just hearing the details of their stories, but listening to the manner in which they told them. Noticing how their vivid memories of these brutal acts overlapped, and seeing how they punctuated their recollections with physical scars across their arms, legs, chests. And then realizing how all these moments, places, and people connected back to decisions made by a man who wasn't some supernatural monster but came from a Florida suburb. Chucky's story had been improbable and at times surreal, but its brutality was real, and he made this palpable at the trial.

More than a month after the trial began, Miguel Caridad, the senior federal public defender, delivered the closing, after calling eleven witnesses (including Baechtle and Naples).[27] The defense case had suffered a crushing setback when nine witnesses, primarily ATU members flown in from Liberia, disappeared the night before their testimony. To date the jury had heard a remarkable stream of testimony, much of it in Liberian- or Sierra Leonean–inflected English, delivered by witnesses who had never before set foot in an American courtroom. The defense played on their foreignness to thread together the witnesses' testimony under one theme of implausibility—the stunning escapes, the life-saving interventions. He asked them to consider these stories as if a resident of Miami was telling them.

"Ladies and gentlemen, what is going on in this country? What is going on in Liberia? How can you possibly understand such a tale? It seems like a different planet to me. Maybe a Liberian jury could make sense of this, but an American jury? How can you possibly evaluate the credibility of such a tale?"

It was a question that cut to the core of any extraterritorial case. When Congress ratified the Convention Against Torture and passed the federal antitorture statute, it had taken political and legal steps toward an idea of international justice. But ultimately the validity of that idea fell to an American jury to determine. Could an American jury deliver a just verdict on such an extraordinary and foreign set of facts?

Caridad returned to the familiar element in the case, the American and Floridian accused of the crimes. And even though his client had not testified, Caridad sought to use the statements Chucky gave Baechtle to support the defense. "Ladies and gentlemen, the only statement that makes any sense in this case is the statement made by Chucky Taylor, the American," Caridad said. "He sits with these agents for two hours, tells them all that they could possibly want to know."

Assistant U.S. Attorney Caroline Heck Miller attacked Caridad's attempt to set up an impossible cultural distance between the jurors and the victims in the prosecution's rebuttal. "Ladies and gentlemen, we submit that you should reject this," she argued. "Their bodies are not different. Blood is red. Knives cut. Fire burns. Pain hurts. That's what this case is about, and it is about that for all victims in this case."

She also attacked Caridad's notion that much of the testimony was implausible. She acknowledged that many of the witnesses had escaped near-death experiences to be able to testify, but the remarkable nature of their survival didn't impugn their credibility. "A survivor may always appear to be lucky by hindsight," she said. But survival—as miraculous as it might seem—was the miracle that all witnesses shared, she pointed out. "There was no miracle for Abdul Cole or no miracle for those people on the beach, certainly the luck for Albert Williams and the other men who were pulled out of the group and were shot was very bad. For them, also, there was no miracle."

Miller closed for the government with a poetic turn, referencing a fountain wall at the courthouse. "That wall reminds me of words that have been quoted at another time in our history, words of the Prophet Amos. 'Let justice roll down as waters and righteousness as a mighty stream.' It is time for those waters of justice now, ladies and gentlemen, for those waters to flush out and cleanse the filth of the pits of Gbatala, to short-circuit the dreadful electricity in Benjamin Yeaten's garage and to cleanse, finally, the tears of suffering by human beings at the hands [of] and caused by this man here, the defendant."

The jury deliberated for a day and a half. Shortly after two p.m. on October 30, 2008, the foreman notified the court's deputy that they were prepared to return the verdict.

Several months earlier Chucky had written a letter to his son telling him that he had some "things to take care of," asking him to write to him, to tell him about school, sports, his friends. "I've always loved you and always will your [*sic*] my first son my only son, I pray for you all the time and I want you to grow strong, smart, and disciplined," he wrote. Most significantly, he wrote that he was sorry "for not being there, and sorry for the times when you came to visit, I was not a better man, and Father." These were words that Charles Taylor could have just as easily written to Chucky a decade earlier, before their lives together spun out into the darkness of violence and power.

It took less than four minutes for the verdict to be read. The foreman responded to each count with the word *guilty*. Each count compounded the sentence he would face, until it became clear he would likely never be set free.

With the verdict read, the court officer asked those in the courtroom to rise for the jury to depart the room.

Chucky refused.[28]

Three months later, on the morning of January 9, 2009, Bernice Emmanuel stood outside courtroom 12-2 dressed in a trim black blazer and white blouse with teardrop pearls hanging from her ears, her silver hair smartly parted across her face. The hallway was subdued; only the thrum of the ventilation and clicking of footsteps punctuated the quiet. She clutched a yellow legal pad, giving the appearance that she might be one of the small group of attorneys preparing to enter Chucky Taylor's sentencing hearing. A reporter approached her and addressed her as "Ms. Emmanuel." She appeared startled for a moment, then smiled and said, "I'm sorry, you have the wrong person." She turned and walked inside the courtroom.

Emmanuel had appeared at the court that morning bearing a letter for Judge Altonaga. Chucky's mother had been absent from the trial, but this day, above all others, would determine her son's future. The contents of her letter to the judge will forever remain between those two women. Perhaps Emmanuel recognized her own complicity in her son's descent. Perhaps she chose to reiterate his claim of innocence. But one could reasonably expect that from woman to woman, mother to mother, it would be an appropriate moment to beg mercy for her son.

That morning Chucky did not ask for mercy.[29] In their presentencing comments, his attorneys struggled to distance him from his crimes. In an at times awkward presentation, Caridad leaned heavily on the "nurture" scale of the argument, pitting much of the brutality of his actions on the company Chucky had been introduced into in Liberia: David Campari, Benjamin Yeaten, and finally, his own father. But that rationale delivered Chucky to a pitiful conclusion, as offered by Miguel Caridad: "It's fair to say that if he had stayed in the United States, he wouldn't be a torturer."

Chucky rose to address the court, wearing his prison khakis, appearing more heavyset with his beard heavily grown in. He pointed out that he had expected to lose at trial, and even though the government had dangled before him a plea deal of thirteen years, he said, he had chosen to attempt to prove his innocence. He criticized the court as unable to adequately address the issues raised by the civil wars that his father had engineered.

"Every family has had some tragedy and trauma physically and mentally," he said. "No one was immune, whether the witnesses involved in this case or my own family, be it my grandfather, my uncles or my cousins whose lives were taken during the war. My sympathy and heart goes out to all of those families caught up in the former conflicts of Liberia and Sierra Leone."

He then addressed the witnesses gathered there that day. "As many consider these witnesses foreign, both in culture and speech, these witnesses are my African brothers and it is *wajib* [duty as a Muslim] that I extend my prayers to them and their families and will continue to do so even after this sentence is handed down. I also maintain Liberian and West African traditions by saying sorry. Sorry, my brothers, to what has happened to you during the fourteen-year civil conflict and the war that lasted in Sierra Leone."

He did not acknowledge his crimes. He did not offer any explanation for how he had found himself in this situation. He simply asked the judge to place him in a penitentiary proximate to his mother and his son. Had he expressed contrition, he would have jeopardized his chance of appeal. But by not doing so, his words came across as a final, passive act of defiance.

. . .

Judge Altonaga addressed the courtroom shortly before noon. "I have given careful thought as well to the history and characteristics of the defendant," she said. "While there is some appeal to saying he went to Liberia at a young, impressionable age and was surrounded by his biological father and that father's cohorts for whom this lifestyle was acceptable is to only look at one piece of the history and characteristics of the defendant."

Altonaga noted that Chucky had a "normal upbringing here and he left the United States for the incorrect reasons . . . the acts which he committed, and by the jury's decision he has been found to have committed, occurred when he was a young man in his twenties and occurred at his direction, occurred through his imagination, through his control, sadistic, cruel, atrocious acts, which may become commonplace after a time if one sees it occurring day after day after day and which immunize any shock or concern after one participates in those events day after day after day, but which, nonetheless, constitute unacceptable universally condemned torture."

The government sought a 147-year sentence, while Caridad had sought a "fair and reasonable" punishment. Judge Altonaga sentenced Chucky to 1,164 months—ninety-seven years in prison.

Throughout his criminal case, Chucky had fought divorce proceedings with Lynn. She did not follow his trial in any detail.[30] It was a painful reminder of the lost opportunities he had come to represent. Much of her life was now devoted to putting him and Liberia behind her. She worked as a nurse, raising her son outside Pine Hills, while trying to finalize her divorce.

Chucky argued in family court—somewhat fantastically—that the two had never been married, apparently to avoid any future claims that Lynn and his child were entitled to any of his assets. (To refute his claim, Lynn's attorney's introduced wedding photos and a copy of the menu at their reception.)

"It really saddens me," Lynn said after the verdict. "It saddens me because the only thing we'll ever be entitled to is a legacy of torture and murder along with some horrific memories."

Charles Taylor learned of his son's sentencing at the International Criminal Court at The Hague, where his own trial for crimes against humanity continued. Taylor offered no public comment, but his attorney told the press that the former president was distressed by the punishment meted out to Chucky.

On May 30, 2012, three and a half years after his son's punishment came down, Charles Taylor received a fifty-year sentence from the Special Court for Sierra Leone for crimes against humanity.

Despite the sentence, Chucky didn't consider his battle over. His attorneys appealed to the 11th Circuit, largely on constitutional grounds, asking the appellate court to throw out the conviction.[31] That process wound forward with very little involvement from Chucky—he could only wait for the determination.

Several of Chucky's victims, including Rufus Kpadeh and Nathaniel Koah, filed a federal lawsuit against him in Miami, seeking damages for the suffering they had endured at his hands and under the control of the ATU.[32] Chucky did not contest that suit, which resulted in a default ruling, but he later chose to represent himself in the penalty phase of the lawsuit. With his appeal pending, there was little contribution he could make to the proceeding without jeopardizing his criminal case. The judge eventually awarded the plaintiffs $22.4 million in damages, an amount that they could never hope to recover from an indigent Chucky.[33]

In letters from prison, Chucky drew more distant from his father, referring to him as "President Taylor" or simply "Taylor." He blamed his father for the collapse of discipline in the ATU. He insisted that he belonged in a separate category from the sycophants surrounding his father. Ultimately, he laid the entire tragedy of Liberia at his father's feet. "President Taylor my father has very little to be proud of 'a legacy of ashes' the death of the innocent and the brave can never be forgotten," he wrote. "I never wanted to see it play out like this."

After the fall of Charles Taylor, Liberia achieved a milestone it had not reached in more than a quarter of a century: a decade of peace. This was due, in large part, to the support of the international community and the presence of one of the largest UN military missions in history.[34] President Ellen Johnson Sirleaf accomplished something that none of her predecessors had: she changed the narrative of the nation from one of destruction to one of rebuilding. The international community embraced her as a reformer and an antidote to the warlord politics that had ruled the region for so long. In 2011 she was awarded the Nobel Peace Prize.

Yet beneath the surface little had changed in Liberia. Graft and bribery plagued the government and judicial systems even as President Sirleaf declared war on corruption. War criminals implicated by the nation's Truth and Reconciliation Commission went unpunished, despite official recommendations for prosecutions.[35] The rain forests continued to be harvested for timber, palm oil, and rubber with little oversight; the same NGOs that had reported on Taylor's pillaging of state resources now issued reports critical of the new government. As Chucky and his father had predicted, U.S. oil interests staked their claims in Liberia: both Chevron and Exxon purchased development rights for offshore prospects. In April 2013 Chevron drilled its first wells.[36]

Even the security apparatus in the Liberian government bore reflections of the Taylor era. While the ATU had been disbanded, former members of the unit were quietly integrated into the Liberian National Police and President Sirleaf's National Security Agency, which was led by her son.[37]

On February 22, 2011, the U.S. Supreme Court rejected Chucky's submission to hear his appeal.[38] When he received the news at Big Sandy United States Penitentiary in Kentucky, far from his mother's home in Florida, he was left to contemplate the facts that had determined his fate: the beginnings of his family history in slavery, the creation of Liberia, the injustice perpetrated by his forebears, his father's revolution. There were his crimes and the survivors who lived to tell their stories. Then there was his identity, defined not only by the fact of his birth but by how he had led his life.

"I personally won't be defined by my father's legacy. I'm an individual," he said in a call from prison.[39] "It's just unfortunate that my father's leadership was the way that it was. Disappointing not because he's my father or what the personal relationship we had was, but the fact that he failed so many people. My anger is directed at him for failing the people who committed themselves to his dream and those who died as a result of his dream."

Like his father, Chucky has never taken responsibility for his crimes.

A NOTE ON SOURCES

In June 2007, a few months before Rufus Kpadeh led the investigators there, I drove in a two-truck convoy for the first of several visits to Chucky Taylor's training base at Gbatala, Liberia. My guides were several human rights workers from Gbarnga whom I had met only hours earlier. These men had lived through the successive stages of the war and carved out a niche in the type of information valuable to international human rights groups, reporters, and, as it would turn out, law enforcement officers. When I arrived at their office—a single-story structure tucked behind the local archdiocese—the men sat me down for an unsolicited debrief on Chucky. As a group of former combatants went through vocational training outside the window, the men offered up a string of fascinating, if completely unverifiable, tales of Chucky's excesses and abuses. I was eager to get the day going but had been warned off of going to the base alone because, as one of the men explained, "people who lived in Gbatala were psychologically held hostage," and it wasn't clear how they would react to a foreigner.[1]

My driver for the day was Mr. King, a rotund man in his sixties with a toothy smile and wearing a neatly pressed charcoal jumpsuit. The truck reeked of rotten fruit, and, despite the heat, we drove with open windows toward the base. When I ventured small talk—Charles Taylor was about to be tried at the Special Court at The Hague—Mr. King simply said: "I don't like to hear about Charles Taylor, to be frank with you. When I hear it, it vex my nerves." Mr. King hadn't asked our specific destination, and I decided he might not really care to know. We continued toward Gbatala in silence.

Eventually we pulled off of the mud roadway and drove up an incline through a stand of trees, stopping outside a huddle of small mud-brick huts. We got out of our vehicles and walked past a community kitchen, an A-frame shelter built of palm and timber with a dirt floor coated in ash. One building we passed had the second hand-drawn etching of a kung fu fighter I had seen that day. Hibiscus seemed to pour out of every bush. Hens clucked nervously underfoot. A skinny dingo skittered past.

As I approached the center of the village, a small clutch of women in torn T-shirts and patterned skirts circled a set of wooden preschool-size chairs beneath a large mango tree. As they instructed me to sit down, a child ran off into the bush. Moments later a woman with chalky dust covering her clothing appeared from the tree line.

A small crowd gathered. The woman told me her name was Annie Perry. What was meant to be an interview quickly turned into something of a public performance. She knew Chucky, she told me. He would bring supplies to the women as they prepared meals in the kitchen at the base. She hadn't been forced to work. In fact, she was paid for her labor, she said, noting that things had been lean around Gbatala since Taylor left power. She and other members of the crowd searched my face for a reaction.

I had arrived at Gbatala with a set of wrong assumptions. I had assumed that the people I met there would eagerly pick up the historical thread that was popular in the West: that the collapse of the Taylor government should be followed by the pursuit of justice for the people who had been victimized by him and his son. But this idea, it turned out, had nothing to do with the interests of the desperately poor people in the village.

Sitting with Perry and her neighbors, I nonetheless felt obligated to ask about torture at the base. Unsolicited, one of the human rights workers translated my query into something of a statement in Liberian English: "The question is: 'Chucky is in the States now in jail. They accusing him for committing torture. Suffering human beings. Suffering people. Grabbing people. Sometimes they carried them there. They suffered there.'"

I could feel the crowd lean in to hear Perry's response.

"No, it never happened presently me being there," Perry said, smiling.

To wrap up the interview, I asked Perry her age—she was thirty-nine—then thanked her. And as I walked away, she said to one of the human rights workers, "I did that for nothing?"

Perry and another woman followed me, climbing into Mr. King's truck as we drove up the hillside to the base. When we arrived, they remained in the truck—I realized—because Mr. King had turned on the air-conditioning. One of the human rights workers pulled me aside and offered that with a little "motivation" the women might be more willing to speak. I tried to explain to him why I could not do that but felt like I was explaining the rules of hockey to someone who had never stood on ice.

The hillside at Gbatala was now a working quarry. At that time of day, with the sun hanging high in the sky, the ground was bathed in searing white light reflecting off the stone cliff face. There men, women, and children worked breaking large rocks into smaller rocks with medium-size rocks, a method that had likely changed little over the previous millennia. The youngest children—whom I estimated to be about three years old—carried stones in straw baskets to the adolescents tasked with cutting them down. A load of gravel, a pyramid about knee high, required three days' labor and could net seventeen dollars from an NGO or local business. But, as the locals explained, among the many casualties of the war was the local gravel market.

I spoke with a few of the villagers working at the quarry. In those conversations, it became clear that the locals had their own assumptions about me. They assumed that if I had traveled that far, I must surely be willing to offer a small sum of money in exchange for the information they had about the activities of the base. After a few more awkward exchanges, I gave up on gathering more than an image of this place. A small crowd of the rock-breakers had stopped working and gathered near our vehicles. I could sense a sort of festering rage frothing to the surface. Several people demanded compensation for their time, presumably wasted on me, and demanded that we bring NGOs here to purchase their rocks.

I climbed into Mr. King's truck. Whatever expectation the villagers of Gbatala had of me had shattered against my incomprehensible cheapness. I didn't give them any money, less out of any high-minded ethical rigidity than out of a more basic cowardice of breaking from professional convention—even in the face of grinding poverty.

We pulled back onto Kakata Highway. I sat silent for a few minutes, then Mr. King spoke. "Those women didn't want to tell you the truth," he said. "She was there. She saw everything. But she didn't want to say anything to you. That's the base. They grab you. They bury you alive."

"Did she tell you that?" I asked.

"Yeah," he said. "Most of those women over there were with Taylor. Especially that lady. She used to cook for Chucky and the soldiers. And she was there on the base. But she don't want to tell you everything. That's what she told me."

Chucky likely would have been amused by the obstacles I ran into at Gbatala. I can say that with some confidence, because in the seven years reporting this book, he became my most important—and least cooperative—source.

In April 2006, shortly after he was arrested at Miami International Airport on a passport violation, I wrote Chucky a letter requesting an in-person interview. Journalistically, this was a Hail Mary pass. There was no indication at that time that he was the target of a federal human rights investigation. Little was known about his identity beyond the sketchy biographical basics reported after his arrest. And the public source reporting on his activities in Liberia was vague and unclear. I'd heard the name "Chucky Taylor" only while reporting on Liberian émigrés living in housing projects on Staten Island, many of them refugees from one of the phases of his father's civil war. Chucky was always treated as an aside, an asterisk on his father's destructive campaign for power, a sort of bogeyman who inspired fear among many but whom few had ever seen or interacted with.

That sit-down interview never occurred. In the moments when he agreed to sit down with me, prison officials would not permit it. When prison officials appeared ready to relent, he refused. Instead I came to know Chucky through letters, phone calls, and eventually e-mails exchanged when I first began reporting on him for *Rolling Stone*. He even gave me a nickname: Glass Chin.

That is to say, I came to know several Chuckys in those years: the Chucky who was unaware that he would be subject to a federal torture indictment, the Chucky who was fighting to defend himself before a jury in Miami, the Chucky who was confronting a ninety-seven-year sentence. "Dwyer, true men of strength reflect and accept the past," he wrote me in 2010. "There's nothing in my past, I'm not prepared to confront."[2]

Yet he never once shared with me his version of the remarkable, strange, and at times unbelievable trajectory of his life. But he did unwittingly share something equally important: the revelation that he wasn't capable of being truthful with himself.

I pieced that narrative together with reporting on the ground in Liberia, Trinidad, Pine Hills, and at his trial, appeal, and civil case in Miami, speaking with family, friends, victims, and comrades. I used Freedom of Information Act requests to obtain more than a thousand documents from the State Department, Department of Defense, and National Security Council to write the diplomatic history behind Taylor's rise and fall. And after much pleading, I sat with the investigators from ICE and the FBI, as well as prosecutors from the U.S. Attorney's Office in the Southern District of Florida.

Chucky warned me in a letter from 2007 that "any attempts to gather information about me will be met with dead ends." That was not the case. In Liberia I met many people close to him interested in hagiography, but others who were willing to speak truthfully, without fear of retribution and without the aim of receiving compensation. Yet the ethical terrain there was extraordinarily challenging. I walked away from several important interviews and reporting trips because the sources demanded compensation. My most reliable sources were those who, despite the daily struggles to survive that they faced, sought nothing in return. In one case, without being asked, I spent fifteen dollars on toys and groceries for a source's family after being shaken at the sight of his hungry children. I knew that was wrong as a journalist, but I was willing to take the ethical hit so that I could sleep a little better that night. The endnotes that follow strive to be both a thorough and concise accounting of my reporting.

Throughout this process, I communicated with Chucky, not because I felt he would shed any light on the crimes he had been convicted of or that he would reveal the secrets of his father to me. I sought to understand him. I'd seen glimmers of emotion from him: at his trial when his stepfather testified, in his angry phone calls to me from prison, in the letter he wrote to his son. I held out hope that I would witness a moment of change that would illuminate his character in a way that his actions and words had not.

I'm still waiting for that moment to arrive.

ACKNOWLEDGMENTS

This book exists because of the dedication and support of others. I owe much of what is written here to my sources in the United States, the United Kingdom, Liberia, and Trinidad who tolerated my presence, answered my questions, and kept the lines open until my reporting was complete. This includes Chucky Taylor, who—despite the distaste he voiced for me and this endeavor—maintained contact until the end. My editor Andrew Miller at Knopf, and his assistants, Will Heyward and Mark Chiusano, built this book, draft by draft, providing thoughtful and demanding feedback through the revisions, encouraging me to realize the full potential of this remarkable story. Sean Woods, my editor at *Rolling Stone,* taught me that collaboration creates better work, a lesson I carry with me. Shawn Coyne looked past many of the outward impossibilities of this story and found this manuscript a home, while Eric Lupfer provided the needed support to see it through. In Liberia, my driver James made this journey possible, not only navigating the horrible roads, but enabling me to navigate the culture and painful history of each place we visited. While many others who helped me need to go unnamed, I'd like to acknowledge a few who lent a hand along the way, giving me a place to crash, assigning stories, helping me source documents, reading early drafts, or just picking up the phone: Howard Chua-Eoan, Mark Schoofs, Elizabeth Dickinson, Josh Keating, Rufus Arkoi, Tim Hetherington, Glenna Gordon, Barbara Medina, Nicholai Lidow, Yvette Chin, Ernestine Fobbs, Matthew Cole, John Bowe, Chris O'Connell, Peter Kline, and Chapin Clark. My mother, brothers and sisters, and children helped me through all of the hassles and heartaches, while the proud memory of my father carried me through the most difficult moments in telling this story.

Finally, for everything, I am grateful to Sarah.

NOTES

PROLOGUE

1. Matthew Baechtle, Investigation Report 2008, U.S. Attorney's Office, Southern District of Florida, p. 6.
2. *United States vs. Roy M. Belfast, Jr.*, U.S. District Court, Southern District of Florida, Miami Division, prosecution exhibits.
3. Ibid., Trial Transcript, October 2, 2008.
4. Matthew Baechtle, interviews by author, May 25 and August 16, 2010.
5. *United States vs. Belfast*, Trial Transcript, October 2, 2008.
6. UN Security Council, *Report of the Panel of Experts Pursuant to Resolution 1343 (2001), Paragraph 19, Concerning Liberia*, October 26, 2001, S/2001/1015, http://www.un.org/Docs/sc/committees/Liberia2/1015e.pdf.
7. *Prosecutor vs. Charles Ghankay Taylor*, Special Court for Sierra Leone, Case no. SCSL-2003-01-T, Trial Chamber II, Trial Transcript, July 14, 2009.
8. Ibid., Trial Transcript, July 16, 2009.
9. Chargé d'affaires of U.S. embassy in Monrovia to State Department, April 30, 1999, Cable code PTQ4617.
10. *Encyclopaedia Britannica Online*, s.v. "Saint Paul River."
11. *United States vs. Belfast*, Trial Transcript, October 7, 2008.
12. Ibid., October 2, 2008.

CHAPTER 1   Been-To

1. *United States vs. Roy M. Belfast, Jr.*, U.S. District Court, Southern District of Florida, Miami Division, prosecution exhibits.
2. Ellen Johnson Sirleaf, *This Child Will Be Great: Memoir of a Remarkable Life by Africa's First Woman President* (New York: Harper, 2009), p. 70.
3. *Prosecutor vs. Charles Ghankay Taylor*, Special Court for Sierra Leone, Case no. SCSL-2003-01-T, Trial Chamber II, Trial Transcript, July 14, 2009.
4. Constitution of the Republic of Liberia, Chapter 4, "Citizenship," Article 27(b), 1986.
5. *Prosecutor vs. Taylor*, Trial Transcript, July 14, 2009.
6. Bernice Yolanda Emmanuel, conversations with author, summer 2006; January 18, 2008; and January 9, 2009.

7. D. Elwood Dunn, *Historical Dictionary of Liberia* (Lanham, Md.: Scarecrow Press, 2000), p. 341.

8. Ibid.

9. Sirleaf, *This Child Will Be Great*, p. 67.

10. Ibid., p. 66.

11. Gerald R. Ford and William R. Tolbert, Memorandum of Conversation, November 5, 1974, http://www.fordlibrarymuseum.gov/library/document/0314/1552840.pdf.

12. Edward J. Perkins with Connie Cronley, *Mr. Ambassador: Warrior for Peace* (Norman: University of Oklahoma Press, 2006).

13. *Prosecutor vs. Taylor*, Trial Transcript, July 14, 2009.

14. Ibid.

15. Stephen Ellis, *The Mask of Anarchy: The Destruction of Liberia and the Religious Dimension of an African Civil War* (New York: New York University Press, 1999).

16. Margarite Fernández Olmos and Lizabeth Paravisini-Gebert, *Creole Religions of the Caribbean: An Introduction from Vodou and Santería to Obeah and Espiritismo*, 2nd ed. (New York: New York University Press, 2011), p. 155.

17. Lise Winer, *Dictionary of the English/Creole of Trinidad & Tobago: On Historical Principles* (Montreal: McGill-Queen's University Press, 2009), p. 733.

18. Emmanuel conversations.

19. Robert Gosney, interview by author, January 11, 2010.

20. Henry C. Dethloff and John A. Adams Jr., *Texas Aggies Go to War in Service of Their Country*, expanded ed. (College Station: Texas A&M University Press, 2008), p. 315.

21. *Prosecutor vs. Taylor*, Trial Transcript, July 14, 2009.

22. Ibid.

23. Republic of Liberia, Truth and Reconciliation Commission, testimony of Winston A. Tubman, "A Contemporary Personal History of the Liberian Conflict (1979–2003)," Monrovia, October 9, 2008.

24. *Prosecutor vs. Taylor*, Trial Transcript, July 14, 2009.

25. Mark Huband, *The Liberian Civil War* (London: F. Cass, 1998).

26. Emmanuel conversations.

27. *Roy Belfast vs. Bernice Belfast*, Ninth Judicial Circuit, County Court of Orange County, Florida, Case no. 2003-7541, "Husband's Answers to Standard Family Law Interrogatories," March 3, 2004.

28. Victoria A. Tolbert, *Lifted Up: The Victoria Tolbert Story* (Minneapolis, Minn.: Macalester Park, 1996), p. 138.

29. Gosney interview.

30. *Belfast vs. Belfast*, Case no. 05-CA-3693, "Amended Complaint to Partition Real Property," December 13, 2005.

31. James C. Clark, *Orlando, Florida: A Brief History* (Charleston: The History Press, 2013), p. 89.

32. Orange County Property Appraiser, Warranty Deed, April 1, 1987.

33. Lynn Henderson, interviews by author, January 15 and May 24, 2008; May 30, 2009; April 8, 2010; and June 2, 2011.

34. Lauren Ritchie, "Rise Seen in Drive-by Shootings," *Orlando Sentinel*, July 16, 1990.

35. Sharon McBreen and Karen Samsock, "Special Unit in Orange Will Battle Escalating Game Crime," *Orlando Sentinel*, February 19, 1990.

36. *Belfast vs. Belfast*, Case no. 05-CA-3693, "Plaintiff's Answer to Defendant's Counter Claims Counts I, II, & III," January 15, 2006.

37. Henderson interviews.

38. Emmanuel, conversations with author.

CHAPTER 2   Reunion

1. "Letter from Henry W. Dennis, Esq.," in *African Repository* (Washington, D.C.: American Colonization Society, 1872), 48:94.

2. Sir Harry Hamilton Johnston and Otto Stapf, "Portuguese Explorations," in *Liberia* (Dodd, Mead & Co., 1906), pp. 41–42.

3. David Stephen Heidler and Jeanne T. Heidler, *Henry Clay: The Essential American* (New York: Random House, 2010), p. 131.

4. Allan E. Yarema, *The American Colonization Society: An Avenue to Freedom?* (Lanham, Md.: University Press of America, 2006), p. 11.

5. Robert W. Thurston, *Lynching: American Mob Murder in Global Perspective* (Farnham, Surrey, England: Ashgate, 2011), p. 284.

6. U.S. Congress, *Report of the Joint Select Committee to Inquire into the Condition of Affairs in the Late Insurrectionary States* (Washington, D.C.: Government Printing Office, 1872).

7. American Colonization Society, *The African Repository and Colonial Journal* (reprint ed. Way & Gideon, 1889), vol. 45.

8. D. Elwood Dunn, *Historical Dictionary of Liberia* (Lanham, Md.: Scarecrow Press, 2000), p. 25.

9. James J. Hentz, ed., *Routledge Handbook of African Security* (New York: Routledge, 2014).

10. American Colonization Society, *The African Repository and Colonial Journal* (reprinted. Way & Gideon, 1889), 51–53: 92.

11. Frederick Starr, *Liberia: Description, History, Problems* (Chicago: n.p., 1913), p. 27.

12. Ibid., p. 28.

13. J. S. La Fontaine, *Initiation* (Harmondsworth, England: Penguin Books, 1985), p. 94.

14. Charles Spurgeon Johnson, *Bitter Canaan: The Story of the Negro Republic* (New Brunswick, N.J.: Transaction Books, 1987), p. 80.

15. *Prosecutor vs. Charles Ghankay Taylor*, Special Court for Sierra Leone, Case no. SCSL-2003-01-T, Trial Chamber II, Trial Transcript, July 14, 2009.

16. Bernice Yolanda Emmanuel, conversations with author, summer 2006; January 18, 2008; and January 9, 2009.

17. ABC News, *Nightline*, June 13, 1990.

18. *In re: Change of Name of Charles McCarthur Emmanuel to Roy McCarthur Belfast, Jr.*, Circuit Court of Orange County, Florida, Case no. DR-90-547, January 30, 1990.

19. *The Peace Keeper's War* (film), directed by Mark Stucke and Carlos Mavroleon, Journeyman Pictures, 1992.

20. *United States vs. Roy M. Belfast, Jr.*, U.S. District Court, Southern District of Florida, Miami Division, Trial Transcript, October 16, 2008.

21. U.S. ambassador to Liberia to U.S. secretary of state, July 7, 1992, U.S. Department of State, Document E24, National Security Archive, George Washington University.

22. Eugene Herring, interview by author, May 2009.

23. Christopher Menephar, interviews by author, June 18–19, 2009; August 2010; and December 12, 2010.

24. Emmanuel conversations.

25. Israel Akinsanya, interview by author, October 25, 2011.

26. Kenneth Brown, former U.S. ambassador to Ivory Coast, interview by author, 2008.

27. Ramsey Clark, former U.S. attorney general, interview by author, February 2007.

28. Cindor Reeves, interview by author, March 28, 2009.

29. Emmanuel conversations.

CHAPTER 3   Jailbreak

1. Thomas Devoll, interview by author, May 2007.

2. *Prosecutor vs. Charles Ghankay Taylor*, Special Court for Sierra Leone, Case no. SCSL-2003-01-T, Trial Chamber II, Trial Transcript, August 27, 2009.

3. Donald L. Horowitz, *Ethnic Groups in Conflict* (Berkeley: University of California Press, 1985), p. 482.

4. U.S. ambassador to Liberia to U.S. secretary of state, April 20, 1980, U.S. Department of State, Document E2, National Security Archive, George Washington University.

5. U.S. ambassador to Liberia to U.S. secretary of state, December 31, 1980, U.S. Department of State, Document E48, National Security Archive, George Washington University.

6. *Prosecutor vs. Taylor*, Trial Transcript, July 15, 2009.

7. U.S. ambassador to Liberia to U.S. secretary of state, October 16, 1982, U.S. Department of State, Document E103, National Security Archive, George Washington University.

8. U.S. ambassador to Liberia to U.S. secretary of state, August 3, 1990, U.S.

Department of State, Document E38, National Security Archive, George Washington University.

9. U.S. ambassador to Liberia to U.S. secretary of state, April 22, 1980, U.S. Department of State, Document E8, National Security Archive, George Washington University.

10. William C. Mithoefer to Assistant Secretary of State George Moose, October 13, 1980, U.S. Department of State, Document E31, National Security Archive, George Washington University.

11. Ibid.

12. U.S. ambassador to Liberia to U.S. secretary of state, January 8, 1981, U.S. Department of State, Document E49, National Security Archive, George Washington University.

13. U.S. ambassador to Liberia to U.S. secretary of state, March 12, 1981, U.S. Department of State, Document E55, National Security Archive, George Washington University.

14. Ibid.

15. U.S. ambassador to Liberia to U.S. secretary of state, September 24, 1980, U.S. Department of State, Document E29, National Security Archive, George Washington University.

16. Ramsey Clark, former U.S. attorney general, interview by author, February 2007.

17. *Charles M. Taylor vs. James B. Roche, et al.*, U.S. District Court, District of Massachusetts, Civil Action no. 85-1314-K, "Government's Response to Petition for a Writ of Habeus Corpus re Extradition," April 25, 1985.

18. Ibid.

19. U.S. ambassador to Liberia to U.S. secretary of state, September 1, 1984, U.S. Department of State, Document E30, National Security Archive, George Washington University.

20. Denis Johnson, "The Small Boys' Unit: Searching for Charles Taylor in a Liberian Civil War," *Harper's*, October 2000.

21. Timothy Dwyer, "County Jail Squeeze; in Norfolk Facility, 214 Live in 72 Cells," *Boston Globe*, May 7, 1982.

22. Devoll interview.

23. Richard G. Stearns, judge at U.S. District Court of Massachusetts, interview by author, March 19, 2010.

24. *Prosecutor vs. Taylor*, Trial Transcript, July 15, 2009.

25. Ibid., August 25, 2009.

26. Ibid., May 14, 2008.

27. Quentin Outram, "'It's Terminal Either Way': An Analysis of Armed Conflict in Liberia, 1989–1996," *Review of African Political Economy* 24, no. 73 (1997): 355–71.

28. *Prosecutor vs. Taylor*, Trial Transcript, May 7, 2010.

29. U.S. ambassador to Ivory Coast to U.S. secretary of state, January 28, 1990, U.S. Department of State, Document E2, National Security Archive, George Washington University.

30. Nicholai Hart Lidow, "Violent Order: Rebel Organization and Liberia's Civil War," dissertation, Stanford University, 2011.

31. William Reno, *Warlord Politics and African States* (Boulder, Colo.: Lynne Rienner Publishers, 1998), p. 88.

32. U.S. ambassador to Liberia to U.S. secretary of state, January 1, 1990, U.S. Department of State, Document E175, National Security Archive, George Washington University.

33. Political officer for U.S. embassy in Freetown to U.S. secretary of state, July 14, 1990, U.S. Department of State, Document E5, National Security Archive, George Washington University.

34. Neil Henry, "Doe to Bush: 'Help Your Stepchildren,'" *Washington Post*, August 9, 1990.

35. Republic of Liberia, Truth and Reconciliation Commission, *Partial Empirical Inquiry Mission Report Nimba County*, Monrovia, February 2008.

36. U.S. secretary of state to U.S. delegation, June 8, 1990, U.S. Department of State, Document E43, National Security Archive, George Washington University.

37. Ibid.

38. Ellen Johnson Sirleaf,. *This Child Will Be Great: Memoir of a Remarkable Life by Africa's First Woman President* (New York: Harper, 2009), p. 179.

39. Ibid., p. 171; *Prosecutor vs. Taylor*, Trial Transcript, July 15, 2009; Jucontee Thomas Woewiyu, "An Open Letter to Madam Ellen Johnson-Sirleaf," *Liberian Dialogue*, September 15, 2005.

40. U.S. ambassador to Sierra Leone to U.S. secretary of state, July 14, 1990, U.S. Department of State, Document E5, National Security Archive, George Washington University.

41. Sirleaf, *This Child Will Be Great*, p. 175.

42. U.S. ambassador to Liberia to U.S. secretary of state, July 25, 1990, U.S. Department of State, Document E36, National Security Archive, George Washington University.

43. Republic of Liberia, Truth and Reconciliation Commission, *Final Report* (Monrovia, June 29, 2009), p. 231, http://trcofliberia.org/resources/reports/final/trc -of-liberia-final-report-volume-ii.pdf.

44. U.S. ambassador to Liberia to U.S. secretary of state, August 3, 1990, U.S. Department of State, Document E39, National Security Archive, George Washington University.

45. Herman Cohen, former assistant secretary of state for African affairs, interview by author, November 11, 2011.

46. Kenneth Brown to author, November 9, 2013.

47. National Security Council, "Memorandum for ORDWAY@VAXC from WHSR@WHSR," July 3, 1990 (declassified April 22, 2013).

48. Denis Johnson, *Seek: Reports from the Edges of America and Beyond* (New York: HarperCollins, 2001), p. 10.

49. *The Execution of Former Liberian President Samuel K. Doe* (film), Monrovia, 1990, http://www.youtube.com/watch?v=W-NmMaLgrX0.

50. U.S. ambassador to Liberia to U.S. secretary of state, January 8, 1991, U.S. Department of State, Document E39, National Security Archive, George Washington University.

51. Peter da Costa, "Liberia: Peace Postponed," *Africa Special Report* 37, no. 3 (1992): 52.

52. *United States vs. Roy M. Belfast, Jr.*, U.S. District Court, Southern District of Florida, Miami Division, Trial Transcript, October 16, 2008.

53. Da Costa, "Liberia: Peace Postponed," 52.

54. Koisee Garmo, interview by author, March 7, 2010.

55. Cindor Reeves, interview by author, March 28, 2009.

56. Republic of Liberia, Truth and Reconciliation Commission, "Testimony of Joseph Kpagbor," Buchanan, Liberia, April 9, 2008.

57. Republic of Liberia, Truth and Reconciliation Commission, "Testimony of Morris Padmore," Monrovia, Liberia, January 24, 2008.

58. Samuel Nimley to author, September 11, 2010.

CHAPTER 4   Pine Hills

1. Lynn Henderson, interviews by author, January 15 and May 24, 2008; May 30, 2009; April 8, 2010; and June 2, 2011.

2. Ibid.

3. Diane Sears, "Danger's a Partner at Saturday Dances," *Orlando Sentinel*, October 4, 1992.

4. Roy Belfast Sr., conversation with author, August 2008.

5. Tia Wheeler, "Substance Abuse and Mental Health Assessment (SAMH-3), Summary of Findings and Recommendations," Human Services Associates, Inc., March 15, 1994.

6. Henderson interviews.

7. Colleen A. Ward and Michael H. Beaubrun, "The Psychodynamics of Demon Possession," *Journal for the Scientific Study of Religion* 19, no. 2 (1980): 201.

8. Ibid.

9. Adelle E. Forth and Heather C. Burke, "Psychopathy in Adolescence: Assessment, Violence, and Developmental Precursors," *Psychopathy: Theory, Research, and Implications for Society* 88 (1998): 206.

10. Lauren Ritchie, "Rise Seen in Drive-by Shootings," *Orlando Sentinel*, July 16, 1990; "2nd Suspect in Pine Hills Shooting Arrested, Jailed," *Orlando Sentinel*, March 5, 1990.

11. *State of Florida vs. Roy M. Belfast*, Circuit Court of Orange County, Florida, Information no. CR94-3078, June 9, 1994.

12. Steven L. Klimkowski, interview by author, February 25, 2007.

13. Bernice Yolanda Emmanuel, conversations with author, summer 2006, January 18, 2008, and January 9, 2009.

CHAPTER 5   Revolution

1. Chief of mission of U.S. embassy in Monrovia to U.S. ambassador in Ougadougou, Burkina Faso, June 9, 1995, U.S. Department of State, Document E1, National Security Archive, George Washington University.
2. Mark Anthony, conversation with author, July 14, 2010.
3. Stephen Ellis, *The Mask of Anarchy: The Destruction of Liberia and the Religious Dimension of an African Civil War* (New York: New York University Press, 1999), p. 68.
4. *Liberia: America's Stepchild* (film), directed by Nancee Oku Bright, PBS, 2002.
5. *Prosecutor vs. Charles Ghankay Taylor,* Special Court for Sierra Leone, Case no. SCSL-2003-01-T, Trial Chamber II, Trial Transcript, November 18, 2009.
6. Ibid., Trial Transcript, March 4, 2010.
7. Ibid.
8. Ibid.
9. Republic of Liberia, Truth and Reconciliation Commission, *Final Report* (Monrovia, June 29, 2009), p. 249, http://trcofliberia.org/resources/reports/final/trc -of-liberia-final-report-volume-ii.pdf.
10. *Prosecutor vs. Taylor,* Trial Transcript, September 8, 2009.
11. David J. Francis, *The Politics of Economic Regionalism: Sierra Leone in ECOWAS* (Burlington, Vt.: Ashgate, 2001), p. 111.
12. U.S. secretary of state to U.S. ambassador in Accra, Ghana, November 2, 1994, U.S. Department of State, Document E13, National Security Archive, George Washington University.
13. Charles McArther Emmanuel to Lynn Henderson, ca. 1994.
14. "Liberia: Demise of an Accord," Defense Intelligence Agency, June 17, 1994, U.S. Department of State, Document E054, National Security Archive, George Washington University.
15. U.S. ambassador to Liberia to U.S. secretary of state, June 14, 1994, U.S. Department of State, Document E11, National Security Archive, George Washington University.
16. "Liberia: Demise of an Accord," Defense Intelligence Agency, June 17, 1994.
17. Charles McArther Emmanuel to Lynn Henderson, ca. 1994.
18. Adekeye Adebajo and Ismail Rashid, eds., *West Africa's Security Challenges: Building Peace in a Troubled Region* (Boulder, Colo.: Lynne Rienner Publishers, 2004), p. 203.
19. Arie Marcelo Kacowicz, *Zones of Peace in the Third World: South America and West Africa in Comparative Perspective* (Albany: State University of New York Press, 1998), p. 206.

20. Chief of mission of U.S. embassy in Monrovia to U.S. ambassador in Ouga-dougou, Burkina Faso, June 9, 1995, U.S. Department of State, Document E1, National Security Archive, George Washington University.

21. Cindor Reeves, interview by author, March 28, 2009.

22. U.S. ambassador to Liberia to U.S. secretary of state, January 30, 1995, U.S. Department of State, Document E38, National Security Archive, George Washington University.

23. Lynn Henderson, interviews by author, January 15 and May 24, 2008; May 30, 2009; April 8, 2010; and June 2, 2011.

24. U.S. ambassador to Liberia to U.S. secretary of state, July 29, 1996, U.S. Department of State, Document E38, National Security Archive, George Washington University.

25. U.S. ambassador to Liberia to U.S. liaison officer in Abuja, Nigeria, September 14, 1990, U.S. Department of State, Document E6, National Security Archive, George Washington University.

26. "Liberian Stories: A Population Caught in a Cycle of Violence and Displacement," Médecins sans frontières, July 2003.

27. *Prosecutor vs. Taylor*, Trial Transcript, September 8, 2009.

28. Ibid., Trial Transcript, July 23, 2009.

29. U.S. ambassador to Liberia to U.S. secretary of state, December 3, 1996, U.S. Department of State, Document E4, National Security Archive, George Washington University.

30. College of West Africa school officials, interview by author, June 18, 2009.

31. Samuel Nimley to author, July 20, 2010.

32. Henderson interviews.

33. College of West Africa school officials interview.

34. Henderson interviews.

35. Ibid.

36. *Prosecutor vs. Taylor*, Trial Transcript, May 14, 2008.

37. Gary Craig, "Boley Ordered Killings, Witness Says," Rochester *Democrat and Chronicle*, September 29, 2010.

38. Cindor Reeves, interview by author, March 28, 2009.

39. Henderson interviews.

40. U.S. ambassador to Liberia to U.S. secretary of state, June 28, 1999, U.S. Department of State, Document E5, National Security Archive, George Washington University.

41. U.S. Institute for Peace, "Abuja Agreement to Supplement the Cotonou and Akosombo Agreements as Subsequently Clarified by the Accra Agreement," http://www.usip.org/sites/default/files/file/resources/collections/peace_agreements/liberia_08191995.pdf.

42. David Harris, "From 'Warlord' to 'Democratic' President: How Charles Taylor Won the 1997 Liberian Elections," *Journal of Modern African Studies* 37, no. 3 (1999): 438.

43. Ibid.

44. Mary H. Moran, *Liberia: The Violence of Democracy* (Philadelphia: University of Pennsylvania Press, 2006), p. 121.

45. Harris, "From 'Warlord' to 'Democratic' President," p. 451.

46. U.S. ambassador to Liberia to U.S. secretary of state, July 25, 1997, U.S. Department of State, Document E42, National Security Archive, George Washington University.

47. Henderson interviews.

48. *President Taylor's First Hundred Days in Office (2 August 1997–10 November 1997)* (Monrovia: Department of Public Affairs, Ministry of Information, Culture and Tourism), p. 9.

49. Courtenay Griffiths, interview by author, June 11, 2014.

50. Henderson interviews.

51. U.S. ambassador to Liberia to U.S. secretary of state, September 4, 1997, U.S. Department of State, Document E59, National Security Archive, George Washington University.

52. Ibid.

53. *Prosecutor vs. Taylor,* Trial Transcript, May 14, 2008.

CHAPTER 6   Gbatala

1. U.S. secretary of state to U.S. ambassador to Liberia, May 2, 1998, U.S. Department of State, Document E114, National Security Archive, George Washington University.

2. U.S. secretary of state to U.S. ambassador to Liberia, January 17, 1998, U.S. Department of State, Document E92, National Security Archive, George Washington University.

3. Ibid.

4. James G. Antal and R. John Vanden Berghe, *On Mamba Station: U.S. Marines in West Africa, 1990–2003* (Washington, D.C.: History and Museums Division, U.S. Marine Corps, 2004), p. 107.

5. U.S. ambassador to Liberia to U.S. Information Agency, April 29, 1998, U.S. Department of State, Document E113, National Security Archive, George Washington University.

6. Christopher Menephar, interviews by author, June 18–19, 2009; August 2010; December 12, 2010.

7. *Prosecutor vs. Charles Ghankay Taylor,* Special Court for Sierra Leone, Case no. SCSL-2003-01-T, Trial Chamber II, Trial Transcript, February 11, 2008.

8. U.S. ambassador to Liberia to U.S. secretary of state, March 17, 1998, U.S. Department of State, Document E108, National Security Archive, George Washington University.

9. Menephar interviews.

10. Anonymous, interview by author, June 17, 2009.

11. UN Security Council, Resolution 788 (1992), November 19, 1992, http://www.un.org/en/ga/search/view_doc.asp?symbol=S/RES/788(1992).

12. Menephar interviews.

13. Lynn Henderson, interviews by author, January 15 and May 24, 2008; May 30, 2009; April 8, 2010; and June 2, 2011.

14. UN Security Council, *Report of the Panel of Experts Pursuant to Resolution 1343 (2001), Paragraph 19, Concerning Liberia*, October 26, 2001, S/2001/1015, http://www.un.org/Docs/sc/committees/Liberia2/1015e.pdf.

15. Republic of Liberia, Truth and Reconciliation Commission, *Final Report* (Monrovia, June 29, 2009), p. 341, http://trcofliberia.org/resources/reports/final/trc-of-liberia-final-report-volume-ii.pdf.

16. Andrew Feinstein, *The Shadow World: Inside the Global Arms Trade* (New York: Farrar, Straus and Giroux, 2011), p. 103.

17. Henderson interviews.

18. Hamza Abdul Aziz (aka Chucky Taylor) to author, November 14, 2009.

19. U.S. ambassador to Liberia to U.S. secretary of state, January 16, 1998, U.S. Department of State, Document E91, National Security Archive, George Washington University.

20. U.S. ambassador to Liberia to U.S. secretary of state, July 31, 1998, U.S. Department of State, Document E136, National Security Archive, George Washington University.

21. Stephen Ellis, *The Mask of Anarchy: The Destruction of Liberia and the Religious Dimension of an African Civil War* (New York: New York University Press, 1999), p. 253.

22. U.S. ambassador to Liberia to U.S. secretary of state, December 10, 1997, U.S. Department of State, Document E82, National Security Archive, George Washington University.

23. Kenneth Noble, "The United States, Libya and the Liberian Civil War," 1997, Alicia Patterson Foundation, http://aliciapatterson.org/stories/united-states-libya-and-liberian-civil-war.

24. UN Security Council Committee Established Pursuant to Resolution 1521 (2003) Concerning Liberia, "Travel Ban List," April 3, 2014, http://www.un.org/sc/committees/1521/tblist.shtml.

25. Robert Ferguson, interviews by author, June 10–11, 2010.

26. U.S. ambassador to Liberia to U.S. secretary of state, September 12, 1997, U.S. Department of State, Document E60, National Security Archive, George Washington University.

27. U.S. ambassador to Liberia to U.S. secretary of state, December 10, 1997, U.S. Department of State, Document E82, National Security Archive, George Washington University.

28. *Prosecutor vs. Taylor*, Trial Transcript, March 14, 2008.

29. U.S. ambassador to Liberia to U.S. secretary of state, December 10, 1997, U.S. Department of State, Document E82, National Security Archive, George Washington University.

30. Menephar interviews.

31. Ibid.

32. U.S. ambassador to Liberia to U.S. secretary of state, September 5, 1998, U.S. Department of State, Document E17, National Security Archive, George Washington University.

33. Henderson interviews.

34. U.S. ambassador to Liberia to U.S. secretary of state, September 19, 1998, U.S. Department of State, Document E15, National Security Archive, George Washington University.

35. U.S. mission to United Nations to U.S. secretary of state, March 4, 1998, U.S. Department of State, Document E107, National Security Archive, George Washington University.

36. U.S. ambassador to Liberia to U.S. secretary of state, September 19, 1998, U.S. Department of State, Document E15, National Security Archive, George Washington University.

37. U.S. secretary of state to U.S. ambassador to France, September 29, 1998, U.S. Department of State, Document E140, National Security Archive, George Washington University.

38. Ibid.

39. "Liberian Aided by U.S. Is Accepted by Ghana," *New York Times*, September 27, 1998.

40. U.S. ambassador to Liberia to U.S. secretary of state, November 5, 1998, U.S. Department of State, Document E9, National Security Archive, George Washington University.

41. "U.S.S. *Firebolt* (PC 10) Command History 1998," U.S. Navy, http://www.history.navy.mil/shiphist/f/pc-10/1998.pdf.

42. U.S. ambassador to Liberia to U.S. secretary of state, November 5, 1998, U.S. Department of State, Document E9, National Security Archive, George Washington University.

43. "Grand Gedeh Association Welcomes Release of Prisoners," *Perspective*, March 15, 2002, http://www.theperspective.org/ggedehassociation.html.

44. Menephar interviews.

CHAPTER 7 Uprising

1. Jackson Mulbah, interview by author, June 6, 2007.

2. Lynn Henderson, interviews by author, January 15 and May 24, 2008; May 30, 2009; April 8, 2010; and June 2, 2011.

3. Christopher Menephar, interviews by author, June 18–19, 2009; August 2010; December 12, 2010.

4. "Biographies," Blackpool Security and Risk Management Liberia, http://www.blackpoolsecurityservices.com/#!biographies/ctzx (accessed June 21, 2014).

5. Eeben Barlow, *Executive Outcomes: Against All Odds* (Alberton, South Africa: Galago Books, 2007).

6. UN Security Council, *Report of the Panel of Experts Appointed Pursuant to U.N. Security Council Resolution 1306(2000), Paragraph 19, in Relation to Sierra Leone*, December 2000, S/2000/1306, http://www.un.org/sc/committees/1132/pdf/sclet11951e.pdf.

7. Ibid.

8. James Brabazon, *My Friend the Mercenary* (New York: Grove Press, 2011).

9. Republic of South Africa, Regulation of Foreign Military Assistance Act, *Government Gazette* (Cape Town), May 20, 1998, http://www.ohchr.org/Documents/Issues/Mercenaries/WG/Law/SouthAfrica6.pdf.

10. UN Security Council, *Report of the Panel of Experts Appointed Pursuant to U.N. Security Council Resolution 1306(2000), Paragraph 19, in Relation to Sierra Leone*, December 2000, S/2000/1306, http://www.un.org/sc/committees/1132/pdf/sclet11951e.pdf.

11. Menephar interviews.

12. Mulbah interview.

13. Ibid.

14. Anonymous, interview by author, June 17, 2009.

15. Fred Rindel to author, April 5, 2010.

16. Fred Rindel to Charles Taylor Jr., June 10, 1999.

17. Fred Rindel to Charles Taylor Jr., May 21, 1999.

18. *Prosecutor vs. Charles Ghankay Taylor,* Special Court for Sierra Leone, Case no. SCSL-2003-01-T, Trial Chamber II, Trial Transcript, February 15, 2010.

19. John Tarnue, interview by author, June 2007.

20. Ibid.

21. U.S. ambassador to Liberia to U.S. secretary of state, February 26, 1997, U.S. Department of State, Document E40. Author's collection.

22. David Harris, "From 'Warlord' to 'Democratic' President: How Charles Taylor Won the 1997 Liberian Elections," *Journal of Modern African Studies* 37, no. 3 (1999): 431–55.

23. *Prosecutor vs. Taylor,* Trial Transcript, February 18, 2010.

24. Fred Rindel to Charles Taylor Jr., May 21, 1999.

25. Fred Rindel to author, April 5, 2010.

26. Menephar interviews.

27. Ibid.

28. Anonymous interview.

29. Menephar interviews.

30. Anonymous interview.

31. *United States vs. Roy M. Belfast, Jr.,* U.S. District Court, Southern District of Florida, Miami Division, Trial Transcript, October 2, 2008.

32. Ibid.

33. Ibid.

34. Ibid., October 1, 2008.

35. Ibid., October 2, 2008.

36. UN Security Council, *Report of the Panel of Experts Pursuant to Resolution 1343 (2001), Paragraph 19, Concerning Liberia*, October 26, 2001, S/2001/1015, http://www.un.org/Docs/sc/committees/Liberia2/1015e.pdf.

37. John-Peter Pham, *Liberia: Portrait of a Failed State* (New York: Reed Press, 2004), p. 151.

38. U.S. secretary of state to U.S. ambassador in Conakry, Guinea, July 26, 2000, U.S. Department of State, Document E346, National Security Archive, George Washington University.

39. U.S. secretary of state to Economic Organization of West African States collective, August 7, 1999, U.S. Department of State, Document E219, National Security Archive, George Washington University.

40. U.K. Home Office, Immigration and Nationality Directorate, Country Information & Policy Unit, "Country Assessment—Liberia," October 2004, http://www.justice.gov/eoir/vll/country/uk_entry_assess/oct2004/liberia.pdf.

41. U.S. ambassador to Liberia to U.S. secretary of state, April 30, 1999, U.S. Department of State, Document E191, National Security Archive, George Washington University.

42. Chargé d'affaires of U.S. embassy in Monrovia to State Department headquarters, April 30, 1999, U.S. Department of State, Document E191, National Security Archive, George Washington University.

43. Administrative section of U.S. embassy in Monrovia to State Department headquarters, June 29, 1999, Cable code PTQ1236, National Security Archive, George Washington University.

44. U.S. ambassador to Liberia to U.S. secretary of state, April 30, 1999, U.S. Department of State, Document E191, National Security Archive, George Washington University.

45. U.S. secretary of state to U.S. ambassador in Pretoria, April 28, 1999, Cable code PTQ2830, National Security Archive, George Washington University.

46. *United States vs. Roy M. Belfast, Jr.*, U.S. District Court, Southern District of Florida, Miami Division, Trial Transcript, October 2, 2008.

47. Ibid., October 1, 2008.

48. Ibid., October 2, 2008.

49. Ibid., October 1, 2008.

50. Ibid., October 2, 2008.

51. Jeff Crisp, "Africa's Refugees: Patterns, Problems and Policy Challenges," Evaluation and Policy Analysis Unit, UN Human Rights Commission, August 2000, http://www.unhcr.org/3ae6a0c78.html.

52. *United States vs. Belfast*, Trial Transcript, October 2, 2008.

53. Ibid.

54. Ibid.

55. Anonymous interview.

56. Henderson interviews.

57. *Diagnostic and Statistical Manual of Mental Disorders*, 4th ed. (Washington, D.C.: American Psychiatric Association, 2000).

58. Steven Pinker, *The Better Angels of Our Nature: Why Violence Has Declined* (New York: Viking, 2011), loc.11766, online.

59. Henderson interviews.

60. Chargé d'affaires of U.S. embassy in Monrovia to U.S. secretary of state, June 11, 1999, U.S. Department of State, Document E4, National Security Archive, George Washington University.

61. Ibid.

CHAPTER 8   Danger

1. Lynn Henderson, interviews by author, January 15 and May 24, 2008; May 30, 2009; April 8, 2010; and June 2, 2011.

2. Roy Belfast (aka Chucky Taylor), interview by author, April 15, 2012.

3. Henderson interviews.

4. Ibid.

5. U.S. ambassador to Liberia to U.S. secretary of state, August 25, 1999, U.S. Department of State, Document E223, National Security Archive, George Washington University.

6. Chargé d'affaires of U.S. embassy in Monrovia to U.S. secretary of state, June 11, 1999, Cable code PTO9213, National Security Archive, George Washington University.

7. U.S. Department of State, "Bismarck Myrick," http://2001-2009.state.gov/outofdate/bios/m/8829.htm.

8. U.S. ambassador to Liberia to U.S. secretary of state, June 28, 1999, U.S. Department of State, Document E5, National Security Archive, George Washington University.

9. *United States vs. Roy M. Belfast, Jr.*, U.S. District Court, Southern District of Florida, Miami Division, Trial Transcript, October 16, 2008.

10. U.S. ambassador to Liberia to U.S. secretary of state, June 29, 1999, U.S. Department of State, Document E6, National Security Archive, George Washington University.

11. Ibid.

12. Ibid.

13. Ibid.

14. Ibid.

15. Ibid.

16. U.S. ambassador to Liberia to U.S. secretary of state, July 16, 1999, U.S. Department of State, Document E9, National Security Archive, George Washington University.

17. Henderson interviews.

18. Ibid.

19. Ibid.

20. Ibid.

21. Ibid.

22. Lynn Henderson, personal photograph, February 27, 1999.

23. Anonymous to author, November 12, 2010.

24. Henderson interviews.

25. Lynn Henderson, personal video, August 1999.

26. Ibid.

27. U.S. ambassador to Liberia to U.S. secretary of state, October 28, 1999, U.S. Department of State, Document E10, National Security Archive, George Washington University.

28. UN Security Council, *Report of the Panel of Experts Pursuant to Resolution 1343 (2001), Paragraph 19, Concerning Liberia,* October 26, 2001, S/2001/1015, http://www.un.org/Docs/sc/committees/Liberia2/1015e.pdf.

29. "Rebels Versus Rebels," *Africa Confidential* 43, no. 4 (2002).

30. Henderson interviews.

31. U.S. ambassador to Liberia to U.S. secretary of state, August 18, 1999, U.S. Department of State, Document E221, National Security Archive, George Washington University.

32. Henderson interviews.

33. Christopher Menephar, interviews by author, June 18–19, 2009; August 2010; December 12, 2010.

34. Bartuah Gbor, interview by author, June 20, 2009.

35. Ibid.

36. *United States vs. Belfast,* Trial Transcript, September 30, 2008.

37. *Rufus Kpadeh et al. vs. Charles McCarthur Emmanuel,* U.S. District Court, Southern District of Florida, Miami Division, "Complaint—Class Action," January 9, 2009.

38. Nathaniel Koah, interview by author, December 15, 2009.

39. Menephar interviews.

40. Ibid.

41. *United States vs. Belfast,* Trial Transcript, September 30, 2008.

42. *Kpadeh et al. vs. Emmanuel,* "Complaint—Class Action," January 9, 2009.

43. Menephar interviews.

44. *Kpadeh et al. vs. Emmanuel,* "Complaint—Class Action," January 9, 2009.

45. Henderson interviews.

46. Desmond Parker, UN chief of protocol, to author, October 6, 2010.

47. *Kpadeh et al. vs. Emmanuel,* "Complaint—Class Action," January 9, 2009.

48. Menephar interviews.

49. Ibid.

50. Ibid.

51. Anonymous, interview by author, June 17, 2009.

52. Menephar interviews.

53. Ian Smillie, Lansana Gberie, and Ralph Hazleton, *The Heart of the Matter: Sierra*

Leone, Diamonds and Human Security (Complete Report) (Ottawa: Partnership Africa Canada, January 2000), p. 47, http://www.pacweb.org/Documents/diamonds _KP/heart_of_the_matter-full-2000-01-eng.pdf.

54. U.S. Institute of Peace, "Peace Agreement Between the Government of Sierra Leone and the Revolutionary United Front of Sierra Leone," July 7, 1999, http:// www.usip.org/sites/default/files/file/resources/collections/peace_agreements /sierra_leone_07071999.pdf.

55. UN Security Council, *First Report on the UN Mission in Sierra Leone (UNAMSIL)*, S/1999/1223, December 6, 1999, http://daccess-dds-ny.un.org/doc/UNDOC /GEN/N99/369/66/IMG/N9936966.pdf?OpenElement.

56. Gbor interview.

57. Menephar interviews.

58. Smillie, Gberie, and Hazleton, *Heart of the Matter*, p. 34.

59. UN Security Council, *Report of the Panel of Experts Pursuant to Resolution 1343 (2001), Paragraph 19, Concerning Liberia*, October 26, 2001, S/2001/1015, http://www.un.org/Docs/sc/committees/Liberia2/1015e.pdf.

60. U.S. ambassador to Liberia to U.S. secretary of state, March 21, 2000, U.S. Department of State, Document E292, National Security Archive, George Washington University.

61. Nicole Itano, "Liberating Liberia: Charles Taylor and the Rebels Who Unseated Him," *Institute for Security Studies*, ISS paper no. 82 (November 2003).

62. Anonymous interview.

63. Author's notes, Gbarnga, June 2007.

64. Author's notes, Monrovia, June 2007.

65. Henderson interviews.

66. Government of the Republic of Liberia, *Five-Year National Reconstruction and Development Plan, 2002–2007* (Monrovia: Ministry of Planning and Economic Affairs, 2002), p. 84.

67. U.S. ambassador to Liberia to U.S. secretary of state, January 26, 2000, U.S. Department of State, Document E276, National Security Archive, George Washington University.

68. Ibid.

69. Henderson interviews.

70. Anonymous wedding attendee to author, November 4, 2010.

71. Henderson interviews.

72. Ruth 1:16.

73. Henderson interviews.

74. Ibid.

CHAPTER 9   Resources

1. Bartuah Gbor, interview by author, June 20, 2009.

2. U.S. ambassador to Liberia to U.S. secretary of state, May 28, 1999, U.S.

Department of State, Document E3, National Security Archive, George Washington University.

3. Stephen Ellis, *The Mask of Anarchy: The Destruction of Liberia and the Religious Dimension of an African Civil War* (New York: New York University Press, 1999), p. 48.

4. Gail Wannenburg, "Catching the Middlemen Fuelling African Conflicts," *South African Yearbook of International Affairs 2002/03* (Johannesburg: South African Institute of International Affairs, 2003).

5. Patrick Johnston, "Timber Booms, State Busts: The Political Economy of Liberian Timber," *Review of African Political Economy* 101 (2004): 441–56.

6. Ibid.

7. Global Witness, *Logging Off: How the Liberian Timber Industry Fuels Liberia's Humanitarian Disaster and Threatens Sierra Leone* (London: Global Witness, September 2002).

8. Johnston, "Timber Booms, State Busts."

9. Israel Akinsanya, interview by author, October 25, 2011.

10. Charles M. Taylor, Jr., to Jeff House & Associates, August 4, 2000.

11. Akinsanya interview.

12. Ibid.

13. Ibid.

14. Ian Smillie, former member of UN Panel of Experts, interview by author, December 6, 2010.

15. Ibid.

16. Fred Rindel to author, April 5, 2010.

17. "To: 09874762520989," fax, August 1, 2000.

18. Fred Rindel to author, April 5, 2010.

19. FogJohnsen@aol.com, e-mail to Israel Akinsanya, August 10, 2000.

20. Ibid.

21. Charles McArthur Taylor 2nd to Mr. House, August 10, 2000.

22. Ian Smillie, Lansana Gberie, and Ralph Hazleton, *The Heart of the Matter: Sierra Leone, Diamonds and Human Security (Complete Report)* (Ottawa, Ontario: Partnership Africa Canada, January 2000), p. 34, http://www.pacweb.org/Documents /diamonds_KP/heart_of_the_matter-full-2000-01-eng.pdf.

23. Daniel Pohle, interview by author, December 11, 2010.

24. Benjamin Houge, interview by author, December 9, 2010.

25. U.S. ambassador to Liberia to U.S. secretary of state, April 5, 2001, U.S. Department of State, Document E12, National Security Archive, George Washington University.

26. "Vic" to Akinsanya, August 26, 2000.

27. Pohle interview.

28. U.S. ambassador to Liberia to U.S. secretary of state, October 28, 1999, U.S. Department of State, Document E361, National Security Archive, George Washington University.

29. William J. Clinton, "Statement on Suspending the Immigration of Persons

Impeding the Peace Process in Sierra Leone," October 11, 2000, Public Papers of the Presidents of the United States, http://www.gpo.gov/fdsys/pkg/PPP -2000-book2/pdf/PPP-2000-book2-Doc-pg2136.pdf.

30. izzyakin@email.msn.com, e-mail to iakinsanya@yahoo.com, September 26, 2000.

31. Leslie A. Anderson to John N.J.J. Caranda, October 20, 2000.

32. Leslie A. Anderson, interview by author, July 29, 2010.

33. UN Security Council, *Report of the Panel of Experts Appointed Pursuant to U.N. Security Council Resolution 1306(2000), Paragraph 19, in Relation to Sierra Leone,* December 2000, S/2000/1306, http://www.un.org/sc/committees/1132/pdf/ scleti1951e.pdf.

34. *The Code of Federal Regulations of the United States of America, Federal Register,* vol. 78, no. 67, April 8, 2013, notices p. 210008, http://www.gpo.gov/fdsys/pkg /FR-2013-04-08/pdf/2013-08080.pdf.

35. UN Security Council, Resolution 788 (1992), November 19, 1992, http://www .un.org/en/ga/search/view_doc.asp?symbol=S/RES/788(1992).

36. UN Security Council, *Report of the Panel of Experts Appointed Pursuant to U.N. Security Council Resolution 1306(2000), Paragraph 19, in Relation to Sierra Leone,* December 2000, S/2000/1306, http://www.un.org/sc/committees/1132/pdf /scleti1951e.pdf.

37. UN Security Council, *Report of the Panel of Experts Pursuant to Resolution 1343 (2001), Paragraph 19, Concerning Liberia,* October 26, 2001, S/2001/1015, http://www.un.org/Docs/sc/committees/Liberia2/1015e.pdf.

38. Lynn Henderson, interviews by author, January 15 and May 24, 2008; May 30, 2009; April 8, 2010; and June 2, 2011.

39. Alain Lallemand, "Drugs, Diamonds and Deadly Cargoes," November 18, 2002, Center for Public Integrity, http://www.publicintegrity.org/2002/11/18/5697 /drugs-diamonds-and-deadly-cargoes.

40. Matthew Brunwasser, "Leonid Efimovich Minin: From Ukraine, A New Kind of Arms Trafficker," PBS *Frontline/World,* http://www.pbs.org/frontlineworld/ stories/sierraleone/minin.html.

41. Ibid; UN Security Council, *Report of the Panel of Experts Pursuant to Resolution 1343 (2001), Paragraph 19, Concerning Liberia,* October 26, 2001, S/2001/1015, http://www.un.org/Docs/sc/committees/Liberia2/1015e.pdf.

CHAPTER 10   War Business

1. Roy Belfast (aka Chucky Taylor), interview by author, April 15, 2012.

2. Lynn Henderson, interviews by author, January 15 and May 24, 2008; May 30, 2009; April 8, 2010; and June 2, 2011.

3. Anonymous, interview by author, May 30, 2009.

4. Israel Akinsanya, interview by author, October 25, 2011.

5. UN Security Council Committee Established Pursuant to Resolution 1521

(2003) Concerning Liberia,"Travel Ban List," April 3, 2014, http://www.un.org /sc/committees/1521/tblist.shtml.

6. Robert Ferguson to author, March 19, 2012.

7. UN Security Council, *Report of the Panel of Experts Pursuant to Resolution 1343 (2001), Paragraph 19, Concerning Liberia*, October 26, 2001, S/2001/1015, http://www.un.org/Docs/sc/committees/Liberia2/1015e.pdf.

8. Ibid.

9. Akinsanya interview.

CHAPTER 11   Satan and The Prophet

1. Robert Ferguson, interviews by author, June 10–11, 2010.

2. "U.S. Soldier Shot in Liberia," Associated Press, June 17, 2001.

3. John Tarnue, interview by author, December 12, 2010.

4. U.S. secretary of state to U.S. ambassador to Liberia, December 9, 2000, U.S. Department of State, Document E394A, National Security Archive, George Washington University.

5. William M. Bellamy, former deputy assistant secretary of state for African affairs, interview by author, September 28, 2012.

6. Ferguson interviews.

7. U.S. ambassador to Liberia to U.S. secretary of state, May 1, 2001, U.S. Department of State, Document E410, National Security Archive, George Washington University.

8. U.S. House of Representatives, Committee on International Relations, Subcommittee on Africa, Global Human Rights, and International Operations, "The Impact of Liberia's Election on West Africa," hearing, 109th Congress, 2nd session, February 8, 2006.

9. U.S. ambassador to Liberia to U.S. secretary of state, January 29, 2001, U.S. Department of Defense, Joint Staff Communications Center, Document 4a, National Security Archive, George Washington University.

10. U.S. Department of Defense, Joint Chiefs of Staff, "Joint Staff Action Processing Form: Lethal (Offensive) Training in Guinea (U)," October 3, 2001.

11. James Brabazon, *My Friend the Mercenary* (New York: Grove Press, 2011).

12. U.S. ambassador to Guinea to U.S. secretary of state, December 29, 2000, U.S. Department of State, Document ER8, National Security Archive, George Washington University.

13. U.S. secretary of state to U.S. ambassador to Liberia, September 14, 2001, U.S. Department of State, Document E424, National Security Archive, George Washington University.

14. *Back to the Brink: War Crimes by Liberian Government and Rebels*, May 2002, Human Rights Watch, http://www.hrw.org/reports/2002/liberia.

15. Samuel Nimley, interview by author, June 3, 2007; April 22 and June 17, 2009.

16. U.S. ambassador to Liberia to U.S. secretary of state, July 26, 2000, U.S.

Department of State, Document E346, National Security Archive, George Washington University.

17. U.S. ambassador to Liberia to U.S. secretary of state, June 6, 2001, U.S. Department of State, Document E416, National Security Archive, George Washington University.

18. U.S. ambassador to Liberia to U.S. secretary of state, April 2, 2002, U.S. Department of State, Document E454, National Security Archive, George Washington University.

19. "Liberia: Ill Health of Hassan Bility—Journalist and Human Rights Defender," September 10, 2002, Amnesty International, no. AFR 34/015/2002, http://www.amnesty.org/en/library/info/AFR34/015/2002/en.

20. Hamza Abdul Aziz (aka Chucky Taylor) to author, November 14, 2009.

21. Nimley interviews.

22. Ferguson interviews.

23. Ibid.

24. Nimley interviews.

25. GlobalOptions, "Proposal for Services Prepared by: GlobalOptions Prepared for the Government of Liberia," May 22, 2002.

26. Nimley interviews.

27. *OCHA Liberia Weekly Situation Report*, May 16, 2002, ReliefWeb, http://relief web.int/report/guinea/ocha-liberia-weekly-situation-report-08-16-may-2002.

28. *OCHA Liberia Weekly Situation Report*, September 14, 2002, ReliefWeb. http://reliefweb.int/report/liberia/ocha-liberia-weekly-situation-report-01-14 -sep-2002.

29. Nimley interviews.

30. U.S. ambassador to Liberia to U.S. secretary of state, September 16, 2002, U.S. Department of State, Document E474, National Security Archive, George Washington University.

31. "Liberia: JPC, Others Want Chucky Prosecuted," *News* (Monrovia), September 30, 2002, allAfrica, http://allafrica.com/stories/200209300223.html.

32. George Wortuah, interview by author, June 7, 2007.

33. Anonymous, interview by author, June 17, 2009.

34. "The Driver of Charles Taylor's Notorious Son Beaten to Death," *Perspective*, September 20, 2002, http://www.theperspective.org/gono.html.

35. U.S. ambassador to Liberia to U.S. secretary of state, October 1, 2002, U.S. Department of State, Document E40, National Security Archive, George Washington University.

36. *United States vs. Roy M. Belfast, Jr.*, U.S. District Court, Southern District of Florida, Miami Division, Trial Transcript, October 8, 2008.

37. Christopher Menephar, "General Front Line Report Bomi, Gbojay, Arthington Mont., Bomi Co. Liberia," Anti-Terrorist Unit, Monrovia, Liberia, July 22, 2002.

38. Republic of Liberia, Truth and Reconciliation Commission, "More Revelations on Mahel Massacre?" April 30, 2008, http://trcofliberia.org/press_releases/149.

CHAPTER 12   ABT

1. U.S. ambassador to Liberia to U.S. secretary of state, October 18, 2002, U.S. Department of State, Cable code PTQ5542, National Security Archive, George Washington University.

2. *Prosecutor vs. Charles Ghankay Taylor,* Special Court for Sierra Leone, Case no. SCSL-2003-01-T, Trial Chamber II, Trial Transcript, August 27, 2009.

3. U.S. ambassador to Liberia to U.S. secretary of state, October 11, 2002, U.S. Department of State, Cable code PTO8318, National Security Archive, George Washington University.

4. Ibid.

5. U.S. ambassador to Liberia to U.S. secretary of state, October 22, 2002, U.S. Department of State, Cable code PTO8836, National Security Archive, George Washington University.

6. U.S. ambassador to Liberia to U.S. secretary of state, October 4, 2002, U.S. Department of State, Cable code PTQ8446, National Security Archive, George Washington University.

7. Christopher Neyor, "Petroleum Activities in Liberia," National Oil Company of Liberia, June 15, 2011, http://www.developingmarkets.com/sites/default/files/session-2-neyor.pdf (accessed June 23, 2014).

8. UN Security Council, Resolution 1315 (2000), August 14, 2000, http://www.un.org/en/ga/search/view_doc.asp?symbol=S/RES/1315(2000).

9. U.S. ambassador to Liberia to U.S. secretary of state, January 31, 2003, U.S. Department of State, Document E509, National Security Archive, George Washington University.

10. U.S. ambassador to Guinea to U.S. secretary of state, July 27, 2003, U.S. Department of State, Cable reference 215822, National Security Archive, George Washington University.

11. Lynn Henderson, interviews by author, January 15 and May 24, 2008; May 30, 2009; April 8, 2010; and June 2, 2011.

12. Ibid.

13. *Prosecutor vs. Charles Gankhay Taylor,* Special Court for Sierra Leone, "The Taylor Trial," http://www.rscsl.org/Taylor.html.

14. Christopher Menephar, interviews by author, June 18–19, 2009; August 2010; December 12, 2010.

15. *Prosecutor vs. Charles Gankhay Taylor,* Special Court for Sierra Leone, Case no. SCSL-2003-01-T, Trial Chamber II, Trial Transcript, July 18, 2008.

16. Menephar interviews.

17. *Prosecutor vs. Taylor,* Trial Transcript, May 15, 2008.

18. Republic of Liberia, Truth and Reconciliation Commission, "Witness: Moses Blah Participated in Sam Bockarie's Killing," January 31, 2009, http://trcofliberia.org/press_releases/48.

19. Tucker Carlson, "The League of Extraordinary Gentlemen," *Esquire,* November 1, 2003.

20. Robert Ferguson, interviews by author, June 10–11, 2010.

21. "David M. Crane," Syracuse University College of Law, http://www.law.syr.edu/deans-faculty-staff/profile.aspx?fac=152.

22. U.S. House of Representatives, Committee on International Relations, Subcommittee on Africa, Global Human Rights, and International Operations, "The Impact of Liberia's Election on West Africa," hearing, 109th Congress, 2nd session, February 8, 2006.

23. Ferguson interviews.

24. Menephar interviews.

25. Henderson interviews.

26. Ibid.

27. U.S. ambassador to Liberia to U.S. ambassador to Ghana, June 10, 2003, U.S. Department of State, Document E540, National Security Archive, George Washington University.

28. Henderson interviews.

29. Ibid.

30. Ibid.

31. Roy Belfast (aka Chucky Taylor), interview by author, April 15, 2012.

32. Henderson interviews.

33. Nimley interviews.

34. Ferguson interviews.

35. Steven Pinker, *The Better Angels of Our Nature: Why Violence Has Declined* (New York: Viking, 2011), loc. 11863, online.

CHAPTER 13   Exile

1. U.S. secretary of state to all diplomatic and consular posts, July 26, 2003, U.S. Department of State, Document E60, National Security Archive, George Washington University.

2. Ibid.

3. Kirk Semple with Somini Sengupta, "Pushing Peace in Africa, Bush Tells Liberian President to Quit," *New York Times*, June 26, 2003.

4. Robert Ferguson, interviews by author, June 10–11, 2010.

5. U.S. ambassador to Liberia to U.S. secretary of state, June 27, 2003, U.S. Department of State, Document E550, National Security Archive, George Washington University.

6. Christopher Menephar, interviews by author, June 18–19, 2009; August 2010; December 12, 2010.

7. Samuel Nimley, interview by author, June 3, 2007; April 22 and June 17, 2009.

8. *Yolanda Belfast vs. Roy Belfast*, Circuit Court of the Ninth Judicial Circuit, Orange County, Florida, Case no. DR03-7541, "Request for Admissions," p. 4.

9. Craig Timberg, "Liberia's Taylor Found and Arrested," *Washington Post*, March 30, 2006.

10. "Former Liberia Leader Was Denied an Opportunity to Run the Country, Says Ex-Wife," *Trinidad Guardian*, August 15, 2003.

11. Dion Camacho and Sean Poland, interviews by author, May 8–9, 2010.

12. Lynn Henderson to author, May 3–4, 2010.

13. *United States vs. Roy M. Belfast, Jr.*, U.S. District Court, Southern District of Florida, Miami Division, Trial Transcript, October 8, 2008.

14. John Tarnue, interview by author, June 2007.

15. Chucky Taylor, statement, August 17, 2008.

16. Lynn Henderson, interviews by author, January 15 and May 24, 2008; May 30, 2009; April 8, 2010; and June 2, 2011.

17. *Lynn Henderson v. Charles McArthur Taylor Jr.*, Circuit Court of the Ninth Judicial Circuit, Orange County, Florida, Case no. DR05-13790, "Verified Petition for Dissolution of Marriage," June 15, 2005.

18. Henderson interviews.

19. Camacho and Poland interviews.

20. Ibid.

CHAPTER 14   ICE

1. Matthew Baechtle, interviews by author, May 25 and August 16, 2010.

2. Thomas J. Ridge and Lary Bloom, *The Test of Our Times: America Under Siege . . . And How We Can Be Safe Again* (New York: Thomas Dunne Books, 2009).

3. Baechtle interviews.

4. George W. Bush, "Blocking Property of Certain Persons and Prohibiting the Importation of Certain Goods from Liberia," Executive Order 13348, July 27, 2004, http://www.treasury.gov/resource-center/sanctions/Documents/13348.pdf.

5. Baechtle interviews.

6. Johnny Dwyer, "Trying Times in Little Liberia," *Village Voice*, August 19, 2003.

7. UN Security Council, *Report of the Panel of Experts Pursuant to Resolution 1343 (2001), Paragraph 19, Concerning Liberia*, October 26, 2001, S/2001/1015, http://www.un.org/Docs/sc/committees/Liberia2/1015e.pdf.

8. Baechtle interviews.

9. John Tarnue, interview by author, June 2007.

10. *Prosecutor vs. Charles Ghankay Taylor*, Special Court for Sierra Leone, Case no. SCSL-2003-01-T, Trial Chamber II, Trial Transcript, February 18, 2010.

11. Tarnue interview.

12. *Prosecutor vs. Taylor*, Trial Transcript, February 18, 2010.

13. Tarnue interview.

14. Hassan Bility, interview by author, May 2007.

15. *United States vs. Roy M. Belfast, Jr.*, U.S. District Court, Southern District of Florida, Miami Division, Trial Transcript, October 16, 2008.

16. Mona Ragheb, interview by author, May 25, 2010.

17. Ibid.

18. U.S. secretary of state to all diplomatic and consular posts, July 26, 2003, U.S. Department of State, Document E60, National Security Archive, George Washington University.

19. Chief of mission of U.S. embassy in Monrovia, Liberia, to U.S. ambassador in Ougadougou, Burkina Faso, June 9, 1995, U.S. Department of State, Document E1, National Security Archive, George Washington University.

20. U.S. secretary of state to U.S. ambassador to Liberia, March 23, 2005, U.S. Department of State, Document E82, National Security Archive, George Washington University.

21. Ibid.

22. U.S. ambassador to Trinidad to U.S. ambassador to Liberia, March 23, 2005, U.S. Department of State, Document E82, National Security Archive, George Washington University.

23. *United States vs. Belfast*, "Government Exhibit CE-5," October 1, 2008.

24. Baechtle interviews.

25. *United States vs. Belfast*, "United States' Supplemental Pleading on Defendant's Pre-Trial Motions Referred to Magistrate Judge," Case no.1:06-cr-207 58-CMA, June 18, 2007.

26. Samuel Nimley, interviews by author, June 3, 2007; April 22 and June 17, 2009.

27. Michael D. Bayer, *The Blue Planet: Informal International Police Networks and National Intelligence* (Washington, D.C.: National Defense Intelligence College, Center for Strategic Intelligence Research, NDIC Press, 2010), p. 106.

28. *United States vs. Charles McArthur Emmanuel*, U.S. District Court, Southern District of Florida, Criminal no. 06-2355-PRP, "Affidavit of Special Agent Christopher Malone in Support of an Arrest Warrant and Criminal Complaint," March 30, 2008.

29. Ellen Johnson Sirleaf, *This Child Will Be Great: Memoir of a Remarkable Life by Africa's First Woman President* (New York: Harper, 2009), p. 179.

30. "Liberia: Staying Focused," International Crisis Group, January 13, 2006, http://www.crisisgroup.org/en/regions/africa/west-africa/liberia/B036-liberia -staying-focused.aspx.

31. U.S. House of Representatives, "Address by Her Excellency Ellen Johnson Sirleaf, President of the Republic of Liberia," 109th Congress, 2nd session, March 15, 2006, http://1.usa.gov/1nXeajt.

32. Baechtle interviews.

33. Ibid.

34. 18 US Code § 2340, http://www.law.cornell.edu/uscode/text/18/2340.

35. U.S. Congress, *Foreign Relations Authorization Act, Fiscal Years 1994 and 1995*, H.R. 2333, 103rd Congress (1993–94), https://beta.congress.gov/bill/103rd -congress/house-bill/2333.

36. Jay Bybee, "Memorandum for Alberto R. Gonzales, Counsel to the President, Re: Standards of Conduct for Interrogation under 18 U.S.C. §§ 2340-2340A," U.S. Department of Justice, Office of Legal Counsel, August 1, 2002.

37. Baechtle interviews.

38. Ragheb interview.
39. Zachary Mills, "Does the World Need Knights Errant to Combat Enemies of All Mankind? Universal Jurisdiction, Connecting Links, and Civil Liability," *Washington and Lee Law Review* 66, no. 3 (2009): 1315–67.
40. Henry Kissinger, "The Pitfalls of Universal Jurisdiction," *Foreign Affairs* (July–August 2001), online.
41. Baechtle interviews.

CHAPTER 15 Flight

1. *United States vs. Roy M. Belfast, Jr.*, U.S. District Court, Southern District of Florida, Miami Division, Trial Transcript, October 16, 2008.
2. Samuel Nimley, interview by author, June 3, 2007; April 22 and June 17, 2009.
3. Courtenay Griffiths, interview by author, June 12, 2009.
4. *United States vs. Belfast*, Trial Transcript, October 16, 2008.
5. Craig Timberg, "Liberia's Taylor Found and Arrested," *Washington Post*, March 30, 2006.
6. Matthew Baechtle, interviews by author, May 25 and August 16, 2010.
7. *United States vs. Charles McArthur Emmanuel*, U.S. District Court for the Southern District of Florida, Criminal no. 06-2355-PRP, "Affidavit of Special Agent Christopher Malone in Support of an Arrest Warrant and Criminal Complaint," March 30, 2008.
8. Baechtle interviews.
9. *United States vs. Belfast*, Trial Transcript, October 16, 2008.
10. Caroline Heck Miller, "United States Supplemental Pleading on Pre-trial Motions Referred to Magistrate Judge," June 18, 2007.
11. *United States vs. Belfast*, Trial Transcript, October 16, 2008.
12. Ibid., "Government Exhibit CE-5," October 1, 2008.
13. Ibid.
14. Ibid., Trial Transcript, October 16, 2008.

CHAPTER 16 18 U.S.C. § 2340

1. Gregory Naples, interview by author, August 17, 2010.
2. *United States vs. Roy M. Belfast, Jr.*, U.S. District Court, Southern District of Florida, Miami Division, Trial Transcript, September 30, 2008.
3. John Kroger, *Convictions: A Prosecutor's Battles Against Mafia Killers, Drug Kingpins, and Enron Thieves* (New York: Farrar, Straus and Giroux, 2008).
4. Hamza Abdul Aziz (aka Chucky Taylor) to author, March 15, 2007.

5. Alexander Acosta, former U.S. attorney for the Southern District of Florida, interview by author, October 1, 2009.

6. Caroline Heck Miller, assistant U.S. attorney, interview by author, December 16, 2009.

7. Karen Rochlin, assistant U.S. attorney, interview by author, December 16, 2009.

8. Naples interview.

9. Acosta interview.

10. Matthew Baechtle, interviews by author, May 25 and August 16, 2010.

11. Lori Lightfoot to author, June 1, 2010.

12. *United States vs. Belfast*, Trial Transcript, October 14, 2008.

13. Naples interview.

14. *United States vs. Belfast*, "Second Superceding Indictment," November 7, 2007.

15. "Charles Emmanuel to Honorable Judge Graham," Document 12-2, Case no. 1:06-CR-20758-CMA, United States District Court Southern District of Florida Miami Division, December 21, 2006.

16. Boadicea Cole to author, August 12, 2007.

17. Jane Mayer, *The Dark Side: The Inside Story of How the War on Terror Turned Into a War on American Ideals* (New York: Doubleday, 2008), p. 198.

18. Carl Levin, floor speech on the nomination of Alice Fisher for assistant attorney general, September 19, 2006, http://1.usa.gov/UOruty.

19. Hamza Abdul Aziz (aka Chucky Taylor) to author, March 15, 2007.

20. *United States vs. Belfast*, Trial Transcript, October 28, 2008.

21. Ibid., October 16, 2008.

22. Rufus Kpadeh, interview by author, December 15, 2009.

23. Author's notes, Gbatala, June 2007.

24. *United States vs. Belfast*, Trial Transcript, October 16, 2008.

25. Ibid., October 28, 2008.

26. Ibid., October 16, 2008.

CHAPTER 17   Testimony

1. Hamza Abdul Aziz (aka Chucky Taylor) to author, November 14, 2009.

2. *United States vs. Roy M. Belfast, Jr.*, U.S. District Court, Southern District of Florida, Miami Division, "Second Superceding Indictment," November 7, 2007.

3. John Wylie, interviews by author, May 21 and September 30, 2010.

4. Anonymous, interview by author, June 17, 2009.

5. U.S. Immigration and Customs Enforcement, Diana Tsang, branch chief, to George Waldroup, senior special agent, September 29, 2008.

6. Johnny Dwyer, "Bush Torture Memo Slapped Down by Court," *Time*, November 3, 2008.

7. Alexander Acosta, former U.S. attorney for the Southern District of Florida, interview by author, October 1, 2009.

8. *United States vs. Belfast*, Trial Transcript, October 16, 2008.

9. Hassan Bility, interview by author, September 2008.

10. Christopher Graveline and Michael Clemens, *The Secrets of Abu Ghraib Revealed: American Soldiers on Trial* (Washington, D.C.: Potomac Books, 2010).

11. *United States vs. Belfast*, Trial Transcript, September 29, 2008.

12. Ibid.

13. Wylie interviews.

14. *United States vs. Belfast*, Trial Transcript, September 30, 2008.

15. Caroline Heck Miller, assistant U.S. attorney, interview by author, December 16, 2009.

16. *United States vs. Belfast*, Trial Transcript, October 1, 2008.

17. Ibid., Trial Transcript, October 2, 2008.

18. Baechtle interviews.

19. *United States vs. Belfast*, Trial Transcript, October 2, 2008.

20. Ibid., Trial Transcript, October 10, 2008.

21. Ibid., Trial Transcript, October 16, 2008.

22. Ibid.

23. Ibid.

24. Baechtle interviews.

25. *United States vs. Belfast*, Trial Transcript, October 28, 2008.

26. Baechtle interviews.

27. *United States vs. Belfast*, Trial Transcript, October 10, 2008.

28. Barbara Medina to author, October 30, 2008.

29. *United States vs. Belfast*, Trial Transcript, January 9, 2009.

30. Lynn Henderson to author, November 3, 2008.

31. *United States vs. Roy M. Belfast Jr.*, U.S. Court of Appeals for the Eleventh Circuit, Appeal no. 09-10461-AA, "Brief for the Appellant Roy M. Belfast," January 23, 2009.

32. *Rufus Kpadeh et al. vs. Charles McCarthur Emmanuel*, U.S. District Court, Southern District of Florida, Miami Division, "Complaint—Class Action," January 9, 2009.

33. Ibid.

34. "United Nations Mission in Liberia (UNMIL)," UN News Center, http://www.un.org/en/peacekeeping/missions/unmil/.

35. Republic of Liberia, Truth and Reconciliation Commission, *Final Report* (Monrovia, June 29, 2009), p. 341, http://trcofliberia.org/resources/reports/final/trc-of-liberia-final-report-volume-ii.pdf.

36. "Remarks by the President and CEO of National Oil Company of Liberia (NOCAL) at 1st General Staff Meeting," National Oil Company of Liberia, February 1, 2013, http://bit.ly/109PRgV (accessed June 24, 2014).

37. Author's notes, Monrovia, October 2011.

38. *Roy M. Belfast, Jr. vs. United States*, U.S. Court of Appeals for the Eleventh Circuit, no. 10-8120, February 22, 2011.

39. Roy Belfast, Jr. (aka Chucky Taylor), interview by author, July 28, 2011.

A NOTE ON SOURCES

1. Michael Biddle, interview by author, June 2007.

2. Hamza Abdul Aziz (aka Chucky Taylor) to author, November 14, 2009.

INDEX

ILLUSTRATION CREDITS

All photographs are courtesy of the author and Lynn Henderson except for the following:

President Charles Taylor meeting Reverend Jesse Jackson: Courtesy of Associated Press
Taylor in Buchanan, Liberia; Courtesy of Getty images
The Gbatala base, Bong County, Liberia: Courtesy of Christopher Herwig
Assistant United States Attorney Karen Rochlin: Courtesy of Karen Rochlin
Immigration and Customs Enforcement Speial Agent Matthew Baechtle: Courtesy of Chris Gravelin

A NOTE ABOUT THE AUTHOR

Johnny Dwyer is a reporter living in New York City. He has written for *Esquire*, *The Guardian*, *Rolling Stone*, *Time*, *Foreign Policy*, and *The New York Times*. *American Warlord* is his first book.

A NOTE ON THE TYPE

This book was set in Janson, an example of the Dutch types that date to the second half of the seventeenth century.

Composed by North Market Street Graphics,
Lancaster, Pennsylvania

Printed and bound by Berryville Graphics,
Berryville, Virginia

Designed by Soonyoung Kwon